Online Resources & Audiobook

Included with your purchase are multiple online resources. This includes the practice tests in an interactive format and this book in audiobook format. There is also a convenient study timer to help you manage your time.

Instructions for accessing these resources can be found on the last page of this book.

CAEC® Study Guide
Test Prep and Practice Exam Book for the Canadian Adult Education Credential [Includes Detailed Answer Explanations]

Lydia Morrison

Copyright © 2025 by TPB Publishing

All rights reserved. No part of this publication may be reproduced, distributed, or transmitted in any form or by any means, including photocopying, recording, or other electronic or mechanical methods, without the prior written permission of the publisher, except in the case of brief quotations embodied in critical reviews and certain other noncommercial uses permitted by copyright law.

Written and edited by TPB Publishing.

TPB Publishing is not associated with or endorsed by any official testing organization. TPB Publishing is a publisher of unofficial educational products. All test and organization names are trademarks of their respective owners. Content in this book is included for utilitarian purposes only and does not constitute an endorsement by TPB Publishing of any particular point of view.

ISBN 13: 9781637754221

Table of Contents

Welcome 1

Quick Overview 2

Test-Taking Strategies 3

Introduction 7

Study Prep Plan for the CAEC Test 9

Reading 11
  Content and Context 11
  Structure, Elements, Techniques 20
  Grammar, Syntax, and Language Conventions 27
  Text Types 43
  Reading Practice Quiz 61
  Reading Answer Explanations 63

Writing 64
  Position and Support 64
  Voice and Presentation 72
  Conventions, Mechanics, and Syntax 74
  Writing Practice Quiz 77

Math Part I: No Calculator 81
  Mixed Numbers 81
  Add, Subtract, Multiply, and Divide Decimals, Percentages, and Integers. 84
  Solve x + a + b = c Linear Equations 86
  Evaluating Expressions Using Order of Operations 89
  Math Part I Practice Quiz 99
  Math Part I Answer Explanations 101

Math Part II: Calculator 102
  Number Sense 102

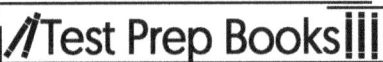

Patterns and Relations	107
Geometry and Measurement	113
Data Management and Probability	126
Math Part II Practice Quiz	139
Math Part II Answer Explanations	141

Science 142

Nature of Science	142
Scientific Inquiry Skills	145
Science, Technology, Society and Environment	162
Science Practice Quiz	167
Science Answer Explanations	169

Social Studies 170

Citizenship and Government	170
Economics and Economic Systems	176
Historical and Contemporary Canada	189
Geography and the Environment	196
Social Studies Practice Quiz	209
Social Studies Answer Explanations	213

CAEC Practice Test 214

Reading	214
Writing	230
Math Part I: No Calculator	232
Math Part II: Calculator	235
Science	240
Social Studies	252

Answer Explanations 262

Reading	262
Math Part I: No Calculator	266
Math Part II: Calculator	268

Science 273

Social Studies 279

Online Resources & Audiobook 287

Welcome

Dear Reader,

Welcome to your new Test Prep Books study guide! We are pleased that you chose us to help you prepare for your exam. There are many study options to choose from, and we appreciate you choosing us. Studying can be a daunting task, but we have designed a smart, effective study guide to help prepare you for what lies ahead.

Whether you're a parent helping your child learn and grow, a high school student working hard to get into your dream college, or a nursing student studying for a complex exam, we want to help give you the tools you need to succeed. We hope this study guide gives you the skills and the confidence to thrive, and we can't thank you enough for allowing us to be part of your journey.

In an effort to continue to improve our products, we welcome feedback from our customers. We look forward to hearing from you. Suggestions, success stories, and criticisms can all be communicated by emailing us at support@testprepbooks.com.

Sincerely,

Test Prep Books Team

Quick Overview

As you draw closer to taking your exam, effective preparation becomes more and more important. Thankfully, you have this study guide to help you get ready. Use this guide to help keep your studying on track and refer to it often.

This study guide contains several key sections that will help you be successful on your exam. The guide contains tips for what you should do the night before and the day of the test. Also included are test-taking tips. Knowing the right information is not always enough. Many well-prepared test takers struggle with exams. These tips will help equip you to accurately read, assess, and answer test questions.

A large part of the guide is devoted to showing you what content to expect on the exam and to helping you better understand that content. In this guide are practice test questions so that you can see how well you have grasped the content. Then, answer explanations are provided so that you can understand why you missed certain questions.

Don't try to cram the night before you take your exam. This is not a wise strategy for a few reasons. First, your retention of the information will be low. Your time would be better used by reviewing information you already know rather than trying to learn a lot of new information. Second, you will likely become stressed as you try to gain a large amount of knowledge in a short amount of time. Third, you will be depriving yourself of sleep. So be sure to go to bed at a reasonable time the night before. Being well-rested helps you focus and remain calm.

Be sure to eat a substantial breakfast the morning of the exam. If you are taking the exam in the afternoon, be sure to have a good lunch as well. Being hungry is distracting and can make it difficult to focus. You have hopefully spent lots of time preparing for the exam. Don't let an empty stomach get in the way of success!

When travelling to the testing center, leave earlier than needed. That way, you have a buffer in case you experience any delays. This will help you remain calm and will keep you from missing your appointment time at the testing center.

Be sure to pace yourself during the exam. Don't try to rush through the exam. There is no need to risk performing poorly on the exam just so you can leave the testing center early. Allow yourself to use all of the allotted time if needed.

Remain positive while taking the exam even if you feel like you are performing poorly. Thinking about the content you should have mastered will not help you perform better on the exam.

Once the exam is complete, take some time to relax. Even if you feel that you need to take the exam again, you will be well served by some down time before you begin studying again. It's often easier to convince yourself to study if you know that it will come with a reward!

Test-Taking Strategies

1. Predicting the Answer

When you feel confident in your preparation for a multiple-choice test, try predicting the answer before reading the answer choices. This is especially useful on questions that test objective factual knowledge. By predicting the answer before reading the available choices, you eliminate the possibility that you will be distracted or led astray by an incorrect answer choice. You will feel more confident in your selection if you read the question, predict the answer, and then find your prediction among the answer choices. After using this strategy, be sure to still read all of the answer choices carefully and completely. If you feel unprepared, you should not attempt to predict the answers. This would be a waste of time and an opportunity for your mind to wander in the wrong direction.

2. Reading the Whole Question

Too often, test takers scan a multiple-choice question, recognize a few familiar words, and immediately jump to the answer choices. Test authors are aware of this common impatience, and they will sometimes prey upon it. For instance, a test author might subtly turn the question into a negative, or he or she might redirect the focus of the question right at the end. The only way to avoid falling into these traps is to read the entirety of the question carefully before reading the answer choices.

3. Looking for Wrong Answers

Long and complicated multiple-choice questions can be intimidating. One way to simplify a difficult multiple-choice question is to eliminate all of the answer choices that are clearly wrong. In most sets of answers, there will be at least one selection that can be dismissed right away. If the test is administered on paper, the test taker could draw a line through it to indicate that it may be ignored; otherwise, the test taker will have to perform this operation mentally or on scratch paper. In either case, once the obviously incorrect answers have been eliminated, the remaining choices may be considered. Sometimes identifying the clearly wrong answers will give the test taker some information about the correct answer. For instance, if one of the remaining answer choices is a direct opposite of one of the eliminated answer choices, it may well be the correct answer. The opposite of obviously wrong is obviously right! Of course, this is not always the case. Some answers are obviously incorrect simply because they are irrelevant to the question being asked. Still, identifying and eliminating some incorrect answer choices is a good way to simplify a multiple-choice question.

4. Don't Overanalyze

Anxious test takers often overanalyze questions. When you are nervous, your brain will often run wild, causing you to make associations and discover clues that don't actually exist. If you feel that this may be a problem for you, do whatever you can to slow down during the test. Try taking a deep breath or counting to ten. As you read and consider the question, restrict yourself to the particular words used by the author. Avoid thought tangents about what the author *really* meant, or what he or she was *trying* to say. The only things that matter on a multiple-choice test are the words that are actually in the question. You must avoid reading too much into a multiple-choice question, or supposing that the writer meant something other than what he or she wrote.

5. No Need for Panic

It is wise to learn as many strategies as possible before taking a multiple-choice test, but it is likely that you will come across a few questions for which you simply don't know the answer. In this situation, avoid panicking. Because most multiple-choice tests include dozens of questions, the relative value of a single wrong answer is small. As much as possible, you should compartmentalize each question on a multiple-choice test. In other words, you should not allow your feelings about one question to affect your success on the others. When you find a question that you either don't understand or don't know how to answer, just take a deep breath and do your best. Read the entire question slowly and carefully. Try rephrasing the question a couple of different ways. Then, read all of the answer choices carefully. After eliminating obviously wrong answers, make a selection and move on to the next question.

6. Confusing Answer Choices

When working on a difficult multiple-choice question, there may be a tendency to focus on the answer choices that are the easiest to understand. Many people, whether consciously or not, gravitate to the answer choices that require the least concentration, knowledge, and memory. This is a mistake. When you come across an answer choice that is confusing, you should give it extra attention. A question might be confusing because you do not know the subject matter to which it refers. If this is the case, don't eliminate the answer before you have affirmatively settled on another. When you come across an answer choice of this type, set it aside as you look at the remaining choices. If you can confidently assert that one of the other choices is correct, you can leave the confusing answer aside. Otherwise, you will need to take a moment to try to better understand the confusing answer choice. Rephrasing is one way to tease out the sense of a confusing answer choice.

7. Your First Instinct

Many people struggle with multiple-choice tests because they overthink the questions. If you have studied sufficiently for the test, you should be prepared to trust your first instinct once you have carefully and completely read the question and all of the answer choices. There is a great deal of research suggesting that the mind can come to the correct conclusion very quickly once it has obtained all of the relevant information. At times, it may seem to you as if your intuition is working faster even than your reasoning mind. This may in fact be true. The knowledge you obtain while studying may be retrieved from your subconscious before you have a chance to work out the associations that support it. Verify your instinct by working out the reasons that it should be trusted.

8. Key Words

Many test takers struggle with multiple-choice questions because they have poor reading comprehension skills. Quickly reading and understanding a multiple-choice question requires a mixture of skill and experience. To help with this, try jotting down a few key words and phrases on a piece of scrap paper. Doing this concentrates the process of reading and forces the mind to weigh the relative importance of the question's parts. In selecting words and phrases to write down, the test taker thinks about the question more deeply and carefully. This is especially true for multiple-choice questions that are preceded by a long prompt.

Test-Taking Strategies

9. Subtle Negatives

One of the oldest tricks in the multiple-choice test writer's book is to subtly reverse the meaning of a question with a word like *not* or *except*. If you are not paying attention to each word in the question, you can easily be led astray by this trick. For instance, a common question format is, "Which of the following is...?" Obviously, if the question instead is, "Which of the following is not...?," then the answer will be quite different. Even worse, the test makers are aware of the potential for this mistake and will include one answer choice that would be correct if the question were not negated or reversed. A test taker who misses the reversal will find what he or she believes to be a correct answer and will be so confident that he or she will fail to reread the question and discover the original error. The only way to avoid this is to practice a wide variety of multiple-choice questions and to pay close attention to each and every word.

10. Reading Every Answer Choice

It may seem obvious, but you should always read every one of the answer choices! Too many test takers fall into the habit of scanning the question and assuming that they understand the question because they recognize a few key words. From there, they pick the first answer choice that answers the question they believe they have read. Test takers who read all of the answer choices might discover that one of the latter answer choices is actually *more* correct. Moreover, reading all of the answer choices can remind you of facts related to the question that can help you arrive at the correct answer. Sometimes, a misstatement or incorrect detail in one of the latter answer choices will trigger your memory of the subject and will enable you to find the right answer. Failing to read all of the answer choices is like not reading all of the items on a restaurant menu: you might miss out on the perfect choice.

11. Spot the Hedges

One of the keys to success on multiple-choice tests is paying close attention to every word. This is never truer than with words like *almost*, *most*, *some*, and *sometimes*. These words are called "hedges" because they indicate that a statement is not totally true or not true in every place and time. An absolute statement will contain no hedges, but in many subjects, the answers are not always straightforward or absolute. There are always exceptions to the rules

in these subjects. For this reason, you should favor those multiple-choice questions that contain hedging language. The presence of qualifying words indicates that the author is taking special care with his or her words, which is certainly important when composing the right answer. After all, there are many ways to be wrong, but there is only one way to be right! For this reason, it is wise to avoid answers that are absolute when taking a multiple-choice test. An absolute answer is one that says things are either all one way or all another. They often include words like *every*, *always*, *best*, and *never*. If you are taking a multiple-choice test in a subject that doesn't lend itself to absolute answers, be on your guard if you see any of these words.

12. Long Answers

In many subject areas, the answers are not simple. As already mentioned, the right answer often requires hedges. Another common feature of the answers to a complex or subjective question are qualifying clauses, which are groups of words that subtly modify the meaning of the sentence. If the question or answer choice describes a rule to which there are exceptions or the subject matter is complicated, ambiguous, or confusing, the correct answer will require many words in order to be expressed clearly and accurately. In essence, you should not be deterred by answer choices that seem excessively long. Oftentimes, the author of the text will not be able to write the correct answer without offering some qualifications and

modifications. Your job is to read the answer choices thoroughly and completely and to select the one that most accurately and precisely answers the question.

13. Restating to Understand

Sometimes, a question on a multiple-choice test is difficult not because of what it asks but because of how it is written. If this is the case, restate the question or answer choice in different words. This process serves a couple of important purposes. First, it forces you to concentrate on the core of the question. In order to rephrase the question accurately, you have to understand it well. Rephrasing the question will concentrate your mind on the key words and ideas. Second, it will present the information to your mind in a fresh way. This process may trigger your memory and render some useful scrap of information picked up while studying.

14. True Statements

Sometimes an answer choice will be true in itself, but it does not answer the question. This is one of the main reasons why it is essential to read the question carefully and completely before proceeding to the answer choices. Too often, test takers skip ahead to the answer choices and look for true statements. Having found one of these, they are content to select it without reference to the question above. The savvy test taker will always read the entire question before turning to the answer choices. Then, having settled on a correct answer choice, he or she will refer to the original question and ensure that the selected answer is relevant. The mistake of choosing a correct-but-irrelevant answer choice is especially common on questions related to specific pieces of objective knowledge.

15. No Patterns

One of the more dangerous ideas that circulates about multiple-choice tests is that the correct answers tend to fall into patterns. These erroneous ideas range from a belief that B and C are the most common right answers, to the idea that an unprepared test-taker should answer "A-B-A-C-A-D-A-B-A." It cannot be emphasized enough that pattern-seeking of this type is exactly the WRONG way to approach a multiple-choice test. To begin with, it is highly unlikely that the test maker will plot the correct answers according to some predetermined pattern. The questions are scrambled and delivered in a random order. Furthermore, even if the test maker was following a pattern in the assignation of correct answers, there is no reason why the test taker would know which pattern he or she was using. Any attempt to discern a pattern in the answer choices is a waste of time and a distraction from the real work of taking the test. A test taker would be much better served by extra preparation before the test than by reliance on a pattern in the answers.

Introduction

Function of the Test

The CAEC exam, or Canadian Adult Education Credential exam, was developed as a replacement for the GED, as of 2024. The exam is for individuals who are at least eighteen years old who did not receive a high school diploma and would like to earn certification proving they have high-school level skills. Those who pass the CAEC exam can use their credentials to become employed, gain licensing, or be eligible for promotion, among other educational and vocational opportunities.

Test Administration

The CAEC is offered throughout Canada and is designed to be taken on a computer, though a paper-based option is available. Each provincial government has its own website with additional information and instructions for taking the test. In all cases, two forms of proof of identification are necessary at the time of testing.

The CAEC is available in both English and French. Universal supports are available on computer-based tests (such as screen text highlighting, a zoom feature, and a screen color overlay), and special arrangements can be made to meet other needs if arranged with local testing centers prior to testing.

Test Format

The CAEC includes 168 questions, to be answered over a 450 minute (7 hour and 30 minute) allotted time. The test is broken down into five sections, or Subject Tests, with the Math section further divided into two sub-sections. The number of questions in each subject, along with each subject test's time allotted, is shown on the table below.

Subject Test	Number of Questions	Time Allotted
Reading	50 questions	75 minutes
Writing	1 persuasive writing task	75 minutes
Math	42 questions	120 minutes
Science	35 questions	90 minutes
Social Studies	40 questions	90 minutes
Total	168 questions	450 minutes (7 hours, 30 minutes)

The Reading, Science, and Social Studies sections consist primarily of multiple-choice questions. These questions require the test taker to read the provided question and any associated information, and then choose the best answer. Other question types include questions that ask you to select all answers that apply, to check a series of boxes, to match words together, or to fill in a blank.

The Writing section tasks test takers with writing a persuasive essay to achieve a given task. This is generally to write in support of or in opposition to a given scenario. Several pieces of evidence are provided, which the test taker must incorporate to support their position.

As mentioned above, the Math section is divided up into two parts. Part I does not allow the use of a calculator; it comprises 12 of the 42 math questions and is weighted as 25% of the total Math subject score. Part II allows the use of a calculator; it comprises 30 of the 42 math questions and is weighted to make up 75% of the total math subject score.

Scoring

Test takers must score at least 55% in each subject to officially pass the CAEC exam. Anything below this score has not met the minimum standard score needed, and the test taker will need to retake portions of the test that were not passed, and score at least 55% in each in order to receive CAEC credentials. Subject tests which were passed cannot be retaken. Each individual subject test can be retaken once per calendar month, but each subject test can only be taken up to three times in a single calendar year.

Scores for the Reading, Mathematics, Science, and Social Studies sections will be available to test takers through the online CAEC platform within about two days of taking the test. The scores received for these four sections of the test cannot be challenged. The score from the Writing section, which requires additional review, is available around 20 days after testing. The Writing section test score can be challenged, for a rescoring fee, if the test taker does not believe the received score is accurate.

Once all five subject tests have been passed, the test taker will earn the CAEC credential.

Study Prep Plan for the CAEC Test

1   **Schedule** - Use one of our study schedules below or come up with one of your own.

2   **Relax** - Test anxiety can hurt even the best students. There are many ways to reduce stress. Find the one that works best for you.

3   **Execute** - Once you have a good plan in place, be sure to stick to it.

One Week Study Schedule

Day 1	Reading
Day 2	Writing
Day 3	Math Part II: Calculator
Day 4	Science
Day 5	Social Studies
Day 6	CAEC Practice Test
Day 7	Take Your Exam!

Two Week Study Schedule

Day 1	Reading	Day 8	Data Management and Probability
Day 2	Grammar, Syntax, and Language Conventions	Day 9	Science
Day 3	Text Types	Day 10	Visualize and communicate data in...
Day 4	Writing	Day 11	Social Studies
Day 5	Math Part I: No Calculator	Day 12	Historical and contemporary Canada
Day 6	Math Part II: Calculator	Day 13	CAEC Practice Test
Day 7	Geometry and Measurement	Day 14	Take Your Exam!

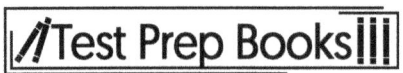

Study Prep Plan for the CAEC Test

One Month Study Schedule

Day 1	Reading	Day 11	Squares, Square Roots, Cubes, and Cube Roots	Day 21	Visualize and communicate data in...
Day 2	Structure, Elements, Techniques	Day 12	Math Part II: Calculator	Day 22	Science, technology, society and environment
Day 3	Grammar, Syntax, and Language Conventions	Day 13	Patterns and Relations	Day 23	Social Studies
Day 4	Determine and assess purpose...	Day 14	Geometry and Measurement	Day 24	Economics and economic systems
Day 5	Text Types	Day 15	Apply formulas to determine the surface...	Day 25	Evaluate and analyze economic factors...
Day 6	Informational Text	Day 16	Data Management and Probability	Day 26	Historical and contemporary Canada
Day 7	Writing	Day 17	Describing a Set of Data	Day 27	Geography and the environment
Day 8	Voice and presentation	Day 18	Science	Day 28	Examine past and present movement of peoples...
Day 9	Math Part I: No Calculator	Day 19	Scientific Inquiry Skills	Day 29	CAEC Practice Test
Day 10	Evaluating Algebraic Expressions	Day 20	Identify the appropriate techniques for storing...	Day 30	Take Your Exam!

Build your own prep plan by visiting the Online Resources page.

Instructions and a QR code can be found on the last page of this guide.

Reading

Content and Context

Locating and Retrieving Explicit Ideas or Information from Texts

Understanding Main Ideas and Details

It is very important to know the difference between the topic and the main idea of the text. Even though these two are similar because they both present the central point of a text, they have distinctive differences. A **topic** is the subject of the text; it can usually be described in a one- to two-word phrase and appears in the simplest form. On the other hand, the **main idea** is more detailed and provides the author's central point of the text. It can be expressed through a complete sentence and is often found in the beginning, middle, or end of a paragraph. In most nonfiction books, the first sentence of the passage usually (but not always) states the main idea.

Review the passage below to explore the topic versus the main idea:

> Cheetahs are one of the fastest mammals on the land, reaching up to 70 miles an hour over short distances. Even though cheetahs can run as fast as 70 miles an hour, they usually only have to run half that speed to catch up with their choice of prey. Cheetahs cannot maintain a fast pace over long periods of time because their bodies will overheat. After a chase, cheetahs need to rest for approximately 30 minutes prior to eating or returning to any other activity.

In the example above, the topic of the passage is "Cheetahs" simply because that is the subject of the text. The main idea of the text is "Cheetahs are one of the fastest mammals on the land but can only maintain a fast pace for shorter distances." While it covers the topic, it is more detailed and refers to the text in its entirety. The text continues to provide additional details called **supporting details**, which will be discussed in the next section.

How Details Develop the Main Idea

Supporting details help readers better develop and understand the main idea. Supporting details answer questions like *who, what, where, when, why,* and *how*. Different types of supporting details include examples, facts and statistics, anecdotes, and sensory details.

Persuasive and informative texts often use supporting details. In persuasive texts, authors attempt to make readers agree with their points of view, and supporting details are often used as "selling points." If authors make a statement, they need to support the statement with evidence in order to adequately persuade readers. Informative texts use supporting details such as examples and facts to inform readers. Review the previous "Cheetahs" passage to find examples of supporting details.

> Cheetahs are one of the fastest mammals on the land, reaching up to 70 miles an hour over short distances. Even though cheetahs can run as fast as 70 miles an hour, they usually only have to run half that speed to catch up with their choice of prey. Cheetahs cannot maintain a fast pace over long periods of time because their bodies will overheat. After a chase, cheetahs need to rest for approximately 30 minutes prior to eating or returning to any other activity.

In the example, supporting details include:

- Cheetahs reach up to 70 miles per hour over short distances.
- They usually only have to run half that speed to catch up with their prey.
- Cheetahs will overheat if they exert a high speed over longer distances.
- Cheetahs need to rest for 30 minutes after a chase.

Look at the diagram below (applying the cheetah example) to help determine the hierarchy of topic, main idea, and supporting details.

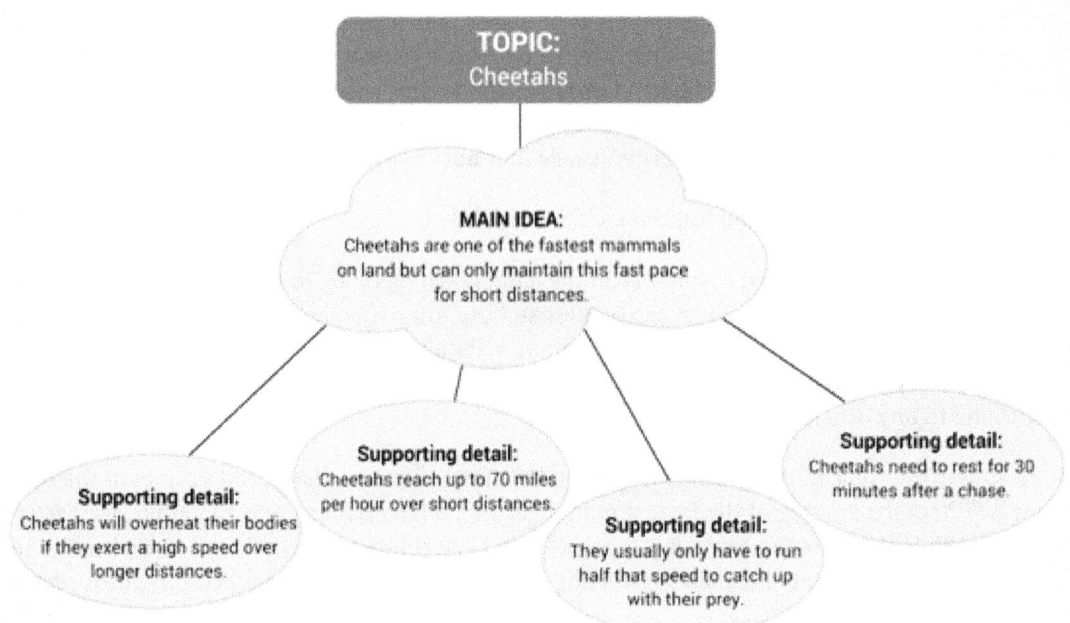

Summarizing Information from a Passage

Summarizing is an effective way to draw a conclusion from a passage. A summary is a shortened version of the original text, written by the reader in their own words. Focusing on the main points of the original text and including only the relevant details can help readers reach a conclusion. It's important to retain the original meaning of the passage.

Like summarizing, **paraphrasing** can also help a reader fully understand different parts of a text. Paraphrasing calls for the reader to take a small part of the passage and list or describe its main points. Paraphrasing is more than rewording the original passage, though. It should be written in the reader's own words, while still retaining the meaning of the original source. This will indicate an understanding of the original source, yet still help the reader expand on their interpretation.

Readers should pay attention to the **sequence**, or the order in which details are laid out in the text, as this can be important to understanding its meaning as a whole. Writers will often use transitional words to help the reader understand the order of events and to stay on track. Words like *next, then, after,* and *finally* show that the order of events is important to the author. In some cases, the author omits these transitional words, and the sequence is implied. Authors may even purposely present the information out of order to make an impact or have an effect on the reader. An example might be when a narrative writer uses **flashback** to reveal information.

Using Main Ideas to Draw Conclusions

Determining conclusions requires being an active reader, as a reader must make a prediction and analyze facts to identify a conclusion. There are a few ways to determine a logical conclusion, but careful reading is the most important. It's helpful to read a passage a few times, noting details that seem important to the text. A reader should also identify key words in a passage to determine the logical conclusion or determination that flows from the information presented.

Textual evidence helps readers draw a conclusion about a passage. **Textual evidence** refers to information—facts and examples that support the main point; it will likely come from outside sources and can be in the form of quoted or paraphrased material. In order to draw a conclusion from evidence, it's important to examine the credibility and validity of that evidence as well as how (and if) it relates to the main idea.

If an author presents a differing opinion or a **counterargument** in order to refute it, the reader should consider how and why the information is being presented. It is meant to strengthen the original argument and shouldn't be confused with the author's intended conclusion, but it should also be considered in the reader's final evaluation.

Sometimes, authors explicitly state the conclusion they want readers to understand. Alternatively, a conclusion may not be directly stated. In that case, readers must rely on the implications to form a logical conclusion:

> On the way to the bus stop, Michael realized his homework wasn't in his backpack. He ran back to the house to get it and made it back to the bus just in time.

In this example, though it's never explicitly stated, it can be inferred that Michael is a student on his way to school in the morning. When forming a conclusion from implied information, it's important to read the text carefully to find several pieces of evidence in the text to support the conclusion.

Interpreting the Literal or Figurative Meaning of Words and Phrases

Connotation and Denotation

Connotation is when an author chooses words or phrases that invoke ideas or feelings other than their literal meaning. An example of the use of connotation is the word *cheap*, which suggests something is poor in value or negatively describes a person as reluctant to spend money. When something or someone is described this way, the reader is more inclined to have a particular image or feeling about it or him/her. Thus, connotation can be a very effective language tool in creating emotion and swaying opinion. However, connotations are sometimes hard to pin down because varying emotions can be associated with a word. Generally, though, connotative meanings tend to be fairly consistent within a specific cultural group.

Denotation refers to words or phrases that mean exactly what they say. It is helpful when a writer wants to present hard facts or vocabulary terms with which readers may be unfamiliar. Some examples of denotation are the words *inexpensive* and *frugal*. *Inexpensive* refers to the cost of something, not its value, and *frugal* indicates that a person is conscientiously watching their spending. These terms do not elicit the same emotions that *cheap* does.

Authors sometimes choose to use both, but what they choose and when they use it is what critical readers need to differentiate. One method isn't inherently better than the other; however, one may create a better effect, depending upon an author's intent. If, for example, an author's purpose is to inform, to instruct, and to familiarize readers with a difficult subject, their use of connotation may be helpful. However, it may also undermine credibility and confuse readers. An author who wants to create a credible, scholarly effect in their text would most likely use denotation, which emphasizes literal, factual meaning and examples.

How Figurative Language Affects the Meaning of Words

It's important to be able to recognize and interpret **figurative,** or non-literal, language. Literal statements rely directly on the denotations of words and express exactly what's happening in reality. Figurative language uses non-literal expressions to present information in a creative way. Consider the following sentences:

   a. His pillow was very soft, and he fell asleep quickly.

   b. His pillow was a fluffy cloud and he floated away on it to the dream world.

Sentence *A* is literal, employing only the real meanings of each word. Sentence *B* is figurative. It employs a metaphor by stating that his pillow was a cloud. Of course, he isn't actually sleeping on a cloud, but the reader can draw on images of clouds as light, soft, fluffy, and relaxing to get a sense of how the character felt as he fell asleep. Also, in sentence *B*, the pillow becomes a vehicle that transports him to a magical dream world. The character isn't literally floating through the air—he's simply falling asleep! But by utilizing figurative language, the author creates a scene of peace, comfort, and relaxation that conveys stronger emotions and more creative imagery than the purely literal sentence. While there are countless types of figurative language, there are a few common ones that any reader should recognize.

Simile and **metaphor** are comparisons between two things, but their formats differ slightly. A simile says that two things are *similar* and makes a comparison using "like" or "as"—*A* is like *B*, or *A* is as [some characteristic] as *B*—whereas a metaphor states that two things are exactly the same—*A* is *B*. In both cases, simile and metaphor invite the reader to think more deeply about the characteristics of the two subjects and consider where they overlap. An example of metaphor can be found in the above sentence about the sleeper ("His pillow was a fluffy cloud"). For an example of simile, look at the first line of Robert Burns' famous poem:

   My love is like a red, red rose

This is comparison using "like," and the two things being compared are love and a rose. Some characteristics of a rose are that it's fragrant, beautiful, blossoming, colorful, vibrant—by comparing his love to a rose, Burns asks the reader to apply these qualities to his love. In this way, he implies that his love is also fresh, blossoming, and brilliant.

Similes can also compare things that appear dissimilar. Here's a song lyric from Florence and the Machine:

   Happiness hit her like a bullet in the back

"Happiness" has a very positive connotation, but getting "a bullet in the back" seems violent and aggressive, not at all related to happiness. By using an unexpected comparison, the writer forces readers to think more deeply about the comparison and ask themselves how could getting shot be similar to feeling happy. "A bullet in the back" is something that she doesn't see coming; it's sudden and forceful; and presumably, it has a strong impact on her life. So, in this way, the author seems to be saying that unexpected happiness made a sudden and powerful change in her life.

Another common form of figurative language is **personification,** when a non-human object is given human characteristics. William Blake uses personification here:

   . . . the stars threw down their spears,

   And watered heaven with their tears

He imagines the stars as combatants in a heavenly battle, giving them both action (throwing down their spears) and emotion (the sadness and disappointment of their tears). Personification helps to add emotion or develop relationships between characters and non-human objects. In fact, most people use personification in their everyday lives:

> My alarm clock betrayed me! It didn't go off this morning!
>
> The last piece of chocolate cake was staring at me from the refrigerator.

Next is **hyperbole,** a type of figurative language that uses extreme exaggeration. Sentences like, "I love you to the moon and back," or "I will love you for a million years," are examples of hyperbole. They aren't literally true—unfortunately, people cannot jump to outer space or live for a million years—but they're creative expressions that communicate the depth of feeling of the author.

Another way that writers add deeper meaning to their work is through **allusions.** An allusion is a reference to something from history, literature, or another cultural source. When the text is from a different culture or a time period, readers may not be familiar with every allusion. However, allusions tend to be well-known because the author wants the reader to make a connection between what's happening in the text and what's being referenced.

> I can't believe my best friend told our professor that I was skipping class to finish my final project! What a Judas!

This sentence contains a Biblical allusion to Judas, a friend and follower of Jesus who betrayed Jesus to the Romans. In this case, the allusion to Judas is used to give a deeper impression of betrayal and disloyalty from a trusted friend. Commonly used allusions in Western texts may come from the Bible, Greek or Roman mythology, or well-known literature such as Shakespeare. By familiarizing themselves with these touchstones of history and culture, readers can be more prepared to recognize allusions.

How Figurative Language Influences the Author's Purpose

A **rhetorical strategy**—also referred to as a **rhetorical mode**—is the structural way an author chooses to present their argument. Though the terms noted below are similar to the organizational structures noted earlier, these strategies do not imply that the entire text follows the approach. For example, a cause-and-effect organizational structure is solely that, nothing more. A persuasive text may use cause and effect as a strategy to convey a singular point. Thus, an argument may include several of the strategies as the author strives to convince their audience to take action or accept a different point of view. It is important that readers are able to identify an author's thesis and position on the topic in order to be able to identify the careful construction through which the author speaks to the reader.

The following are some of the more common rhetorical strategies:

- **Cause and effect**—establishing a logical correlation or causation between two ideas
- **Classification/division**—the grouping of similar items together or division of something into parts
- **Comparison/contrast**—the distinguishing of similarities/differences to expand on an idea
- **Definition**—used to clarify abstract ideas, unfamiliar concepts, or to distinguish one idea from another
- **Description**—use of vivid imagery, active verbs, and clear adjectives to explain ideas
- **Exemplification**—the use of examples to explain an idea
- **Narration**—anecdotes or personal experience to present or expand on a concept
- **Problem/Solution**—presentation of a problem or problems, followed by proposed solution(s)

Determining and Analyzing Supporting Ideas or Information Within Texts

Making Generalizations Based on Evidence

One way to make generalizations is to look for main topics. When doing so, pay particular attention to any titles, headlines, or opening statements made by the author. Topic sentences or repetitive ideas can be clues in gleaning inferred ideas. For example, if a passage contains the phrase *DNA testing, while some consider it infallible, is an inherently flawed technique,* the test taker can infer the rest of the passage will contain information that points to DNA testing's infallibility.

The test taker may be asked to make a generalization based on prior knowledge but may also be asked to make predictions based on new ideas. For example, the test taker may have no prior knowledge of DNA other than its genetic property to replicate. However, if the reader is given passages on the flaws of DNA testing with enough factual evidence, the test taker may arrive at the inferred conclusion or generalization that the author does not support the infallibility of DNA testing in all identification cases.

When making generalizations, it is important to remember that the critical thinking process involved must be fluid and open to change. While a reader may infer an idea from a main topic, general statement, or other clues, they must be open to receiving new information within a particular passage. New ideas presented by an author may require the test taker to alter a generalization. Similarly, when asked questions that require making an inference, it's important to read the entire test passage and all of the answer options. Often, a test taker will need to refine a generalization based on new ideas that may be presented within the text itself.

Predictions

Some texts use suspense and foreshadowing to captivate readers. For example, an intriguing aspect of murder mysteries is that the reader is never sure of the culprit until the author reveals the individual's identity. Authors often build suspense and add depth and meaning to a work by leaving clues to provide hints or predict future events in the story; this is called foreshadowing. While some instances of foreshadowing are subtle, others are quite obvious.

Inferences

Another way to read actively is to identify examples of inference within text. Making an inference requires the reader to read between the lines and look for what is implied rather than what is explicitly stated. That is, using information that is known from the text, the reader is able to make a logical assumption about information that is not explicitly stated but is probably true.

Authors employ literary devices such as tone, characterization, and theme to engage the audience by showing details of the story instead of merely telling them. For example, if an author said *Bob is selfish*, there's little left to infer. If the author said, *Bob cheated on his test, ignored his mom's calls, and parked illegally*, the reader can infer that Bob is selfish. Authors also make implications through character dialogue, thoughts, effects on others, actions, and looks. Like in life, readers must assemble all the clues to form a complete picture.

Making inferences is crucial for readers of literature, because literary texts often avoid presenting complete and direct information to readers about characters' thoughts or feelings, or they present this information in an unclear way, leaving it up to the reader to interpret clues given in the text. In order to make inferences while reading, readers should ask themselves:

- What details are being presented in the text?
- Is there any important information that seems to be missing?
- Based on the information that the author does include, what else is probably true?
- Is this inference reasonable based on what is already known?

Evaluating, Integrating, and Synthesizing Ideas or Information

Synthesizing Information from Different Sources

Synthesizing, or combining, ideas and information from different sources is a skill that helps test takers pass the GED and also thrive in the workforce. The theories and concepts offered in different passages cannot just haphazardly be tossed together. Every test taker has to come up with their own recipe for success when it comes to synthesizing separate sources.

One way for test takers to think about synthesizing sources is to imagine their written responses as empty homes that need to be decorated. They can then imagine the words, concepts, and theories in the different sources as their desired décor. At times, two different sources combine to create perfectly matched décor—the words, concepts, and theories blend ceaselessly upon the walls of the test taker's literary home, creating a balance. At other times, two different sources clash, forcing test takers to sort and separate the ideas into different rooms (for example, different paragraphs or sentences). At still other times, the two sources are incomplete, so test takers need to combine materials with their own interests and statements. If sources contradict one another, it is best to highlight these contradictions. A test taker should take note of the contradictions and use their best judgment in choosing which source is more aligned with their own theories. At times, the test taker may even disagree with information in both articles. It is perfectly acceptable to make the audience aware of all contradictions and disagreements.

Writers, like interior designers, must hone their craft through experience. The best way to begin synthesizing sources is to *practice*. There are four practical ways test takers can start practicing synthesis. Firstly, they need to learn how to properly identify and cite captivating quotations. Secondly, they need to learn how to summarize ideas succinctly in their own words. Thirdly, they need to create unique sentences that are part quotation and part summary. And, lastly, they need to ensure that all of the above is backed by sound grammar, syntax, and organization. The best way to ensure quality is to read other high-quality works and enlist a group of friends or colleagues to edit.

Drawing Conclusions

Determining conclusions requires being an active reader, as a reader must make a prediction and analyze facts to identify a conclusion. A reader should identify key words in a passage to determine the logical conclusion or determination that flows from the information presented. Consider the passage below:

> Lindsay, covered in flour, moved around the kitchen frantically. Her mom yelled from another room, "Lindsay, we're going to be late!

You can conclude that Lindsay's next steps are to finish baking, clean herself up, and head off somewhere with her baked goods. Notice that the conclusion cannot be verified factually. Many conclusions are not spelled out specifically in the text, thus they have to be identified and drawn out by the reader.

Transferring Information to New Situations

A natural extension of being able to make an inference from a given set of information is also being able to apply that information to a new context. This is especially useful in non-fiction or informative writing. Considering the facts and details presented in the text, readers should consider how the same information might be relevant in a different situation. The following is an example of applying an inferential conclusion to a different context:

> Often, individuals behave differently in large groups than they do as individuals. One example of this is the psychological phenomenon known as the bystander effect. According to the bystander effect, the more people who witness an accident or crime occur, the less likely each individual bystander is to respond or offer assistance to the victim. A classic example of this is the murder of Kitty Genovese in New York City in the 1960s. Although there were over thirty witnesses to her killing by a stabber, none of them intervened to help Kitty or contact the police.

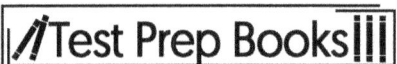

Considering the phenomenon of the bystander effect, what would probably happen if somebody tripped on the stairs in a crowded subway station?
- a. Everybody would stop to help the person who tripped
- b. Bystanders would point and laugh at the person who tripped
- c. Someone would call the police after walking away from the station
- d. Few if any bystanders would offer assistance to the person who tripped

This question asks readers to apply the information they learned from the passage, which is an informative paragraph about the bystander effect. According to the passage, this is a concept in psychology that describes the way people in groups respond to an accident—the more people are present, the less likely any one person is to intervene. While the passage illustrates this effect with the example of a woman's murder, the question asks readers to apply it to a different context—in this case, someone falling down the stairs in front of many subway passengers. Although this specific situation is not discussed in the passage, readers should be able to apply the general concepts described in the paragraph. The definition of the bystander effect includes any instance of an accident or crime in front of a large group of people. The question asks about a situation that falls within the same definition, so the general concept should still hold true: in the midst of a large crowd, few individuals are likely to actually respond to an accident. In this case, Choice *D* is the best response.

Author's Point of View and Purpose

When it comes to an author's writing, readers should always identify a **position** or **stance**. No matter how objective a text may seem, readers should assume the author has preconceived beliefs. One can reduce the likelihood of accepting an invalid argument by looking for multiple articles on the topic, including those with varying opinions. If several opinions point in the same direction and are backed by reputable peer-reviewed sources, it's more likely that the author has a valid argument. Positions that run contrary to widely held beliefs and existing data should invite scrutiny. There are exceptions to the rule, so readers should be careful consumers of information.

While themes, symbols, and motifs are buried deep within the text and can sometimes be difficult to infer, an author's **purpose** is usually obvious from the beginning. There are four purposes of writing: to inform, to persuade, to describe, and to entertain. **Informative** writing presents facts in an accessible way. **Persuasive** writing appeals to emotions and logic to inspire the reader to adopt a specific stance. Readers should be wary of this type of writing, as it can mask a lack of objectivity with powerful emotion. **Descriptive** writing is designed to paint a picture in the reader's mind, while texts that **entertain** are often narratives designed to engage and delight the reader.

The various writing styles are usually blended, with one purpose dominating the rest. A persuasive text, for example, might begin with a humorous tale to make readers more receptive to the persuasive message, or a recipe in a cookbook designed to inform might be preceded by an entertaining anecdote that makes the recipes more appealing.

Author's Position and Response to Different Viewpoints

If an author presents a differing opinion or a counterargument in order to refute it, the reader should consider how and why the information is being presented. It is meant to strengthen the original argument and shouldn't be confused with the author's intended conclusion, but it should also be considered in the reader's final evaluation.

Authors can also use bias if they ignore the opposing viewpoint or present their side in an unbalanced way. A strong argument considers the opposition and finds a way to refute it. Critical readers should look for an unfair or one-sided presentation of the argument and be skeptical, as a bias may be present. Even if this bias is unintentional, if it exists in the writing, the reader should be wary of the validity of the argument. Readers should also look for the use of stereotypes, which refer to specific groups. Stereotypes are often negative connotations about a person or place and should always be avoided. When a critical reader finds stereotypes in a piece of writing, they should be critical of the argument, and consider the validity of anything the author presents. Stereotypes reveal a flaw in the writer's thinking and may suggest a lack of knowledge or understanding about the subject.

Inferring the Author's Purpose in the Passage

In nonfiction writing, authors employ argumentative techniques to present their opinion to readers in the most convincing way. First of all, persuasive writing usually includes at least one type of appeal: an appeal to logic (**logos**), emotion (**pathos**), or credibility and trustworthiness (**ethos**). When a writer appeals to logic, they are asking readers to agree with them based on research, evidence, and an established line of reasoning. An author's argument might also appeal to readers' emotions, perhaps by including personal stories and anecdotes (a short narrative of a specific event). A final type of appeal—appeal to authority—asks the reader to agree with the author's argument on the basis of their expertise or credentials. Consider three different approaches to arguing the same opinion:

Logic (Logos)

Below is an example of an appeal to logic. The author uses evidence to disprove the logic of the school's rule (the rule was supposed to reduce discipline problems; the number of problems has not been reduced; therefore, the rule is not working) and he or she calls for its repeal.

> Our school should abolish its current ban on campus cell phone use. The ban was adopted last year as an attempt to reduce class disruptions and help students focus more on their lessons. However, since the rule was enacted, there has been no change in the number of disciplinary problems in class. Therefore, the rule is ineffective and should be done away with.

Emotion (Pathos)

An author's argument might also appeal to readers' emotions, perhaps by including personal stories and anecdotes. The next example presents an appeal to emotion. By sharing the personal anecdote of one student and speaking about emotional topics like family relationships, the author invokes the reader's empathy in asking them to reconsider the school rule.

> Our school should abolish its current ban on campus cell phone use. If students aren't able to use their phones during the school day, many of them feel isolated from their loved ones. For example, last semester, one student's grandmother had a heart attack in the morning. However, because he couldn't use his cell phone, the student didn't know about his grandmother's condition until the end of the day—when she had already passed away and it was too late to say goodbye. By preventing students from contacting their friends and family, our school is placing undue stress and anxiety on students.

Credibility (Ethos)

Finally, an appeal to authority includes a statement from a relevant expert. In this case, the author uses a doctor in the field of education to support the argument. All three examples begin from the same opinion—the school's phone ban needs to change—but rely on different argumentative styles to persuade the reader.

> Our school should abolish its current ban on campus cell phone use. According to Dr. Bartholomew Everett, a leading educational expert, "Research studies show that cell phone usage has no real impact on student attentiveness. Rather, phones provide a valuable technological resource for learning. Schools need to learn how to integrate this new technology into their curriculum." Rather than banning phones altogether, our school should follow the advice of experts and allow students to use phones as part of their learning.

Rhetorical Questions

Another commonly used argumentative technique is asking **rhetorical questions**, questions that do not actually require an answer but that push the reader to consider the topic further.

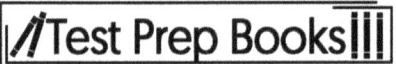

> I wholly disagree with the proposal to ban restaurants from serving foods with high sugar and sodium contents. Do we really want to live in a world where the government can control what we eat? I prefer to make my own food choices.

Here, the author's rhetorical question prompts readers to put themselves in a hypothetical situation and imagine how they would feel about it.

Structure, Elements, Techniques

Identifying and Analyzing Organizational Structures and Features

Analyzing How a Text is Organized

Depending on what the author is attempting to accomplish, certain formats or text structures work better than others. For example, a sequence structure might work for narration but not for identifying similarities and differences between concepts. Similarly, a comparison-contrast structure is not useful for narration. It's the author's job to put the right information in the correct format.

Readers should be familiar with the five main literary structures:

Sequence Structure

Sequence structure (sometimes referred to as the order structure) is when the order of events proceeds in a predictable order. In many cases, this means the text goes through the plot elements: exposition, rising action, climax, falling action, and resolution. Readers are introduced to characters, setting, and conflict in the **exposition**. In the **rising action**, there's an increase in tension and suspense. The **climax** is the height of tension and the point of no return. **Tension** decreases during the falling action. In the **resolution**, any conflicts presented in the exposition are resolved, and the story concludes. An informative text that is structured sequentially will often go in order from one step to the next.

Problem-Solution

In the **problem-solution structure**, authors identify a potential problem and suggest a solution. This form of writing is usually divided into two paragraphs and can be found in informational texts. For example, cell phone, cable, and satellite providers use this structure in manuals to help customers troubleshoot or identify problems with services or products.

Comparison-Contrast

When authors want to discuss similarities and differences between separate concepts, they arrange thoughts in a **comparison-contrast paragraph structure**. **Venn diagrams** are an effective graphic organizer for comparison-contrast structures because they feature two overlapping circles that can be used to organize similarities and differences. A comparison-contrast essay organizes one paragraph based on similarities and another based on differences. A comparison-contrast essay can also be arranged with the similarities and differences of individual traits addressed within individual paragraphs. Words such as *however*, *but*, and *nevertheless* help signal a contrast in ideas.

Descriptive

Descriptive writing is designed to appeal to your senses. Much like an artist who constructs a painting, good descriptive writing builds an image in the reader's mind by appealing to the five senses: *sight, hearing, taste, touch,* and *smell*. However, overly descriptive writing can become tedious; likewise, sparse descriptions can make settings and characters seem flat. Good authors strike a balance by applying descriptions only to facts that are integral to the passage.

Cause and Effect

Passages that use the **cause-and-effect structure** are simply asking *why* by demonstrating some type of connection between ideas. Words such as *if*, *since*, *because*, *then*, or *consequently* indicate a relationship. By switching the order of a complex sentence, the writer can rearrange the emphasis on different clauses. Saying, *If Sheryl is late, we'll miss the dance*, is different from saying *We'll miss the dance if Sheryl is late*. One emphasizes Sheryl's tardiness while the other emphasizes missing the dance. Paragraphs can also be arranged in a cause-and-effect format. Since the format—before and after—is sequential, it is useful when authors wish to discuss the impact of choices. Researchers often apply this paragraph structure to the scientific method.

Understanding the Meaning and Purpose of Transition Words

The writer should act as a guide, showing the reader how all the sentences fit together. Consider this example:

> Seat belts save more lives than any other automobile safety feature. Many studies show that airbags save lives as well. Not all cars have airbags. Many older cars don't. Air bags aren't entirely reliable. Studies show that in 15% of accidents, airbags don't deploy as designed. Seat belt malfunctions are extremely rare.

There's nothing wrong with any of these sentences individually, but together they're disjointed and difficult to follow. The best way for the writer to communicate information is through the use of transition words.

Here are examples of transition words and phrases that tie sentences together, enabling a more natural flow:

- To show causality: *as a result*, *therefore*, and *consequently*
- To compare and contrast: *however*, *but*, and *on the other hand*
- To introduce examples: *for instance*, *namely*, and *including*
- To show order of importance: *foremost*, *primarily*, *secondly*, and *lastly*

Note: This is not a complete list of transitions. There are many more that can be used; however, most fit into these or similar categories. The point is that the words should clearly show the relationship between sentences, supporting information, and the main idea.

Here is an update to the previous example using transition words. These changes make it easier to read and bring clarity to the writer's points:

> Seat belts save more lives than any other automobile safety feature. Many studies show that airbags save lives as well; however, not all cars have airbags. For instance, some older cars don't. Furthermore, air bags aren't entirely reliable. For example, studies show that in 15% of accidents, airbags don't deploy as designed; but, on the other hand, seat belt malfunctions are extremely rare.

Also, be prepared to analyze whether the writer is using the best transition word or phrase for the situation. Take this sentence for example: "As a result, seat belt malfunctions are extremely rare." This sentence doesn't make sense in the context above because the writer is trying to show the contrast between seat belts and airbags, not the causality.

How the Passage Organization Supports the Author's Ideas

Even if the writer includes plenty of information to support their point, the writing is only coherent when the information is in a logical order. **Logical sequencing** is really just common sense, but it's an important writing technique. First, the writer should introduce the main idea, whether for a paragraph, a section, or the entire piece. Second, they should present evidence to support the main idea by using transitional language. This shows the reader how the information relates to the main idea and the sentences around it. The writer should then take time to interpret the information, making sure necessary connections are obvious to the reader. Finally, the writer can summarize the information in a closing section.

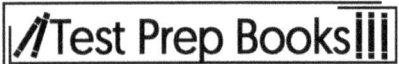

Note: Though most writing follows this pattern, it isn't a set rule. Sometimes writers change the order for effect. For example, the writer can begin with a surprising piece of supporting information to grab the reader's attention, and then transition to the main idea. Thus, if a passage doesn't follow the logical order, don't immediately assume it's wrong. However, most writing usually settles into a logical sequence after a nontraditional beginning.

Introductions and Conclusions

Examining the writer's strategies for introductions and conclusions puts the reader in the right mindset to interpret the rest of the text. Look for methods the writer might use for **introductions** such as:

- Stating the main point immediately, followed by outlining how the rest of the piece supports this claim.
- Establishing important, smaller pieces of the main idea first, and then grouping these points into a case for the main idea.
- Opening with a quotation, anecdote, question, seeming paradox, or other piece of interesting information, and then using it to lead to the main point.
- Whatever method the writer chooses, the introduction should make their intention clear, establish their voice as a credible one, and encourage a person to continue reading.

Conclusions tend to follow a similar pattern. In them, the writer restates their main idea a final time, often after summarizing the smaller pieces of that idea. If the introduction uses a quote or anecdote to grab the reader's attention, the conclusion often makes reference to it again. Whatever way the writer chooses to arrange the conclusion, the final restatement of the main idea should be clear and simple for the reader to interpret. Finally, conclusions shouldn't introduce any new information.

Putting Events in Order

One crucial is the ability to recognize the sequences of events in a text and placing the events in the correct order. Almost every text has a plot, whether it is from a short story, a manual, a newspaper article or editorial, or a historical document. Each plot has a logical order, which is also known as a sequence. Some of the most straightforward sequences can be found in technology directions, science experiments, instructional materials, and recipes. These forms of writing list actions that must occur in a proper sequence in order to get sufficient results. Other forms of writing, however, use style and ideas in ways that completely change the sequence of events. Poetry, for instance, may introduce repetitions that make the events seem cyclical. Postmodern writers are famous for experimenting with different concepts of place and time, creating "cut scenes" that distort straightforward sequences and abruptly transport the audience to different contexts or times. Even everyday newspaper articles, editorials, and historical sources may experiment with different sequential forms for stylistic effect.

Most questions that call for test takers to apply their sequential knowledge use key words such as **sequence**, **sequence of events**, or **sequential order** to cue the test taker into the task at hand. In social studies or history passages, the test questions might employ key words such as **chronology** or **chronological order** to cue the test taker. In some cases, sequence can be found through comprehension techniques. These literal passages number the sequences, or they use key words such as *firstly*, *secondly*, *finally*, *next*, or *then*. The sequences of these stories can be found by rereading the passage and charting these numbers or key words. In most cases, however, readers have to correctly order events through inferential and evaluative reading techniques; they have to place events in a logical order without explicit cues.

Analyzing Relationships within Passages

Inferences are useful in gaining a deeper understanding of how people, events, and ideas are connected in a passage. Readers can use the same strategies used with general inferences and analyzing texts—paying attention to details and using them to make reasonable guesses about the text—to read between the lines and get a more complete picture of how (and why) characters are thinking, feeling, and acting. Read the following passage from O. Henry's story "The Gift of the Magi":

> One dollar and eighty-seven cents. That was all. And sixty cents of it was in pennies. Pennies saved one and two at a time by bulldozing the grocer and the vegetable man and the butcher until one's cheeks burned with the silent imputation of parsimony that such close dealing implied. Three times Della counted it. One dollar and eighty-seven cents. And the next day would be Christmas. There was clearly nothing to do but flop down on the shabby little couch and howl. So Della did it.

This paragraph introduces the reader to the character Della. Even though the author doesn't include a direct description of Della, the reader can already form a general impression of her personality and emotions. One detail that should stick out to the reader is repetition: "one dollar and eighty-seven cents." This amount is repeated twice in the paragraph, along with other descriptions of money: "sixty cents of it was in pennies," "pennies saved one and two at a time." The story's preoccupation with money parallels how Della herself is constantly thinking about her finances: "three times Della counted" her meager savings. Already the reader can guess that Della is having money problems. Next, think about her emotions. The paragraph describes haggling over groceries "until one's cheeks burned"—another way to describe blushing. People tend to blush when they are embarrassed or ashamed, so readers can infer that Della is ashamed by her financial situation. This inference is also supported when she flops down and howls on her "shabby little couch." Clearly, she's in distress. Without saying, "Della has no money and is embarrassed to be poor," O. Henry is able to communicate the same impression to readers through his careful inclusion of details.

A character's **motive** is their reason for acting a certain way. Usually, characters are motivated by something that they want. In the passage above, why is Della upset about not having enough money? There's an important detail at the end of the paragraph: "the next day would be Christmas." Why is money especially important around Christmas? Christmas is a holiday when people exchange gifts. If Della is struggling with money, she's probably also struggling to buy gifts. A shrewd reader should be able to guess that Della's motivation is wanting to buy a gift for someone—but she's currently unable to afford it, leading to feelings of shame and frustration.

In order to understand characters in a text, readers should keep the following questions in mind:

- What words does the author use to describe the character? Are these words related to any specific emotions or personality traits (for example, characteristics like rude, friendly, unapproachable, or innocent)?
- What does the character say? Does their dialogue seem to be straightforward, or are they hiding some thoughts or emotions?
- What actions can be observed from this character? How do their actions reflect their feelings?
- What does the character want? What do they do to get it?

Determining and Evaluate the Purpose and Effect of Literary Devices in Texts

How Rhetorical Language Conveys Meaning, Emotion, or Persuades Readers

A **rhetorical device** is the phrasing and presentation of an idea that reinforces and emphasizes a point in an argument. A rhetorical device is often quite memorable. One of the more famous uses of a rhetorical device is in John F. Kennedy's 1961 inaugural address: "Ask not what your country can do for you, ask what you can do for your country." The contrast of ideas presented in the phrasing is an example of the rhetorical device of antimetabole. Some other common examples are provided below, but test takers should be aware that this is not a complete list.

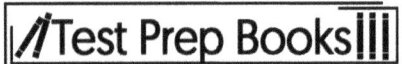

Device	Definition	Example
Alliteration	Repeating the same beginning sound or letter in a phrase for emphasis	The busy baby babbled.
Allusion	A reference to a famous person, event, or significant literary text as a form of significant comparison	"We are apt to shut our eyes against a painful truth, and listen to the song of that siren till she transforms us into beasts." Patrick Henry
Anaphora	The repetition of the same words at the beginning of successive words, phrases, or clauses, designed to emphasize an idea	"We shall not flag or fail. We shall go on to the end. We shall fight in France, we shall fight on the seas and oceans, we shall fight with growing confidence … we shall fight in the fields and in the streets, we shall fight in the hills. We shall never surrender." Winston Churchill
Antithesis	A part of speech where a contrast of ideas is expressed by a pair of words that are opposite of each other.	"That's one small step for man, one giant leap for mankind." Neil Armstrong
Foreshadowing	Giving an indication that something is going to happen later in the story	I wasn't aware at the time, but I would come to regret those words.
Hyperbole	Using exaggeration not meant to be taken literally	The girl weighed less than a feather.
Idiom	Using words with predictable meanings to create a phrase with a different meaning	The world is your oyster.
Imagery	Appealing to the senses by using descriptive language	The sky was painted with red and pink and streaked with orange.
Metaphor	Compares two things as if they are the same	He was a giant teddy bear.
Onomatopoeia	Using words that imitate sound	The tire went off with a bang and a crunch.
Parallelism	A syntactical similarity in a structure or series of structures used for impact of an idea, making it memorable	"A penny saved is a penny earned." Ben Franklin
Personification	Attributing human characteristics to an object or an animal	The house glowered menacingly with a dark smile.

24

Reading

Device	Definition	Example
Rhetorical question	A question posed that is not answered by the writer though there is a desired response, most often designed to emphasize a point	"Can anyone look at our reduced standing in the world today and say, 'Let's have four more years of this?'" Ronald Reagan
Simile	Compares two things using "like" or "as"	Her hair was like gold.
Symbolism	Using symbols to represent ideas and provide a different meaning	The ring represented the bond between us.
Understatement	A statement meant to portray a situation as less important than it actually is to create an ironic effect	"The war in the Pacific has not necessarily developed in Japan's favor." Emperor Hirohito, surrendering Japan in World War II

Sarcasm

Depending on the tone of voice or the words used, sarcasm can be expressed in many different ways. **Sarcasm** is defined as a bitter or ambiguous declaration that intends to cut or taunt. Most of the ways we use sarcasm is saying something and not really meaning it. In a way, sarcasm is a contradiction that is understood by both the speaker and the listener to convey the opposite meaning. For example, let's say Bobby is struggling to learn how to play the trumpet. His sister, Gloria, walks in and tells him: "What a great trumpet player you've become!" This is a sort of verbal irony known as sarcasm. Gloria is speaking a contradiction, but Bobby and Gloria both know the truth behind what she's saying: that Bobby is not a good trumpet player. Sarcasm can also be accompanied by nonverbal language, such as a smirk or a head tilt. Remember that sarcasm is not always clear to the listener; sometimes sarcasm can be expressed by the speaker but lost on the listener.

Irony

Irony is a device that authors use when pitting two contrasting items or ideas against each other in order to create an effect. It's frequently used when an author wants to employ humor or convey a sarcastic tone. Additionally, it's often used in fictional works to build tension between characters, or between a particular character and the reader. An author may use **verbal irony** (sarcasm), **situational irony** (where actions or events have the opposite effect than what's expected), and **dramatic irony** (where the reader knows something a character does not). Examples of irony include:

- Dramatic Irony: An author describing the presence of a hidden killer in a murder mystery, unbeknownst to the characters but known to the reader.

- Situational Irony: An author relating the tale of a fire captain who loses her home in a five-alarm conflagration.

- Verbal Irony: This is where an author or character says one thing but means another. For example, telling a police officer "Thanks a lot" after receiving a ticket.

Understatement

Making an **understatement** means making a statement that gives the illusion of something being smaller than it actually is. Understatement is used, in some instances, as a humorous rhetorical device. Let's say that there are two friends. One of the friends, Kate, meets the other friend's, Jasmine's, boyfriend. Jasmine's boyfriend, in Kate's opinion, is attractive, funny, and intelligent. After Kate meets her friend's boyfriend, Kate says to Jasmine, "You could do worse." Kate and Jasmine both know from Kate's tone that this means Kate is being ironic—Jasmine could

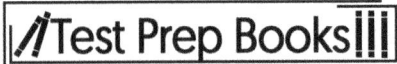

do much, much worse, because her boyfriend is considered a "good catch." The understatement was a rhetorical device used by Kate to let Jasmine know she approves.

Critical Theory

A **critical theory** can be considered a methodology for understanding art. It asks, "What is art?" and offers readers a working set of principles to understand common themes, ideas, and intent. Classifications of critical theory are often referred to as *schools of thought*. These schools are based on subdivisions in historical perspective and in philosophical thinking across analysts and critics.

Romanticism/Aestheticism

Romanticism/Aestheticism spanned the 19th century and developed in response to the idea that enlightenment and reason were the source of all truth and authority in philosophy. **Romanticism** and **Aestheticism** embraced the tenet that *aesthetics*—all that is beautiful and natural—in art and literature should be considered the highest-held principle, overriding all others. Popular authors include Oscar Wilde, Edgar Allan Poe, Mary Shelley, and John Keats.

Marxism

Marxism as a literary theory developed in the early twentieth century after the Russian October Revolution of 1917. It loosely embraced the idea that social realism was the highest form of art and that the social classes' struggle for progress was the most important concept art could emphasize. Examples of authors include Simone de Beauvoir and Bertolt Brecht.

Structuralism

Structuralism included all aspects of philosophy, linguistics, anthropology, and literary theory. Beginning in the early 1900s, this school of thought focused on ideas surrounding how human culture is understood within its larger structures and how those structures influence people's thoughts and actions. Specifically, structuralism examines how literature is interconnected through structure. It examines common elements in the stories and the myths that contribute to literature as a whole. Popular theorists and writers include Claude Levi-Strauss, Umberto Eco, and Roland Barthes.

Post-Structuralism and Deconstruction

Post-Structuralism and deconstruction developed out of structuralism in the twentieth century. It expanded on the idea of overall structure in literature, but both theories argue varying analytical concepts of how that structure should be examined and utilized. For example, while structuralism acknowledges oppositional relationships in literature—e.g., male/female, beginning/end, rational/emotional—**post-structuralism** and **deconstruction** began de-emphasizing the idea that one idea is always dominant over another. Both also assert that studying text also means studying the knowledge that produced the text. Popular theorists and writers include Roland Barthes and Michel Foucault.

New Criticism

New Criticism dominated American culture in the mid-twentieth century. It purports that close, critical reading was necessary to understanding artwork, especially poetry. Popular theory also focused on the inherent beauty of artwork itself. **New Criticism** rejected the previous critical focus of how history, use of language, and the author's experience influence art, asserting those ideas as being too loosely interpretive in examining art. As a movement, it tended to separate art from historical context and an author's intent. It embraced the idea that formal study of structure and text should not be separated. Theorists of note include Stephen Greenblatt and Jonathan Goldberg.

Grammar, Syntax, and Language Conventions

Applying and Analyzing Usage and Correctness of Grammar and Punctuation

Correct Capitalization

This is a non-exhaustive list of things that should be capitalized.

- The first word of every sentence
- The first word of every line of poetry
- The first letter of proper nouns (World War II)
- Holidays (Valentine's Day)
- The days of the week and months of the year (Tuesday, March)
- The first word, last word, and all major words in the titles of books, movies, songs, and other creative works (In the novel, *To Kill a Mockingbird*, note that *a* is lowercase since it's not a major word, but *to* is capitalized since it's the first word of the title.)
- Titles when preceding a proper noun (President Roberto Gonzales, Aunt Judy)

When simply using a word such as president or secretary, though, the word is not capitalized.

> Officers of the new business must include a *president* and *treasurer*.

Seasons—spring, fall, etc.—are not capitalized.

North, *south*, *east*, and *west* are capitalized when referring to regions but are not when being used for directions. In general, if it's preceded by *the* it should be capitalized.

> I'm from the South.

> I drove south.

Using Apostrophes with Possessive Nouns Correctly

Possessives

In grammar, **possessive nouns** show ownership, which was seen in previous examples like *mine, yours,* and *theirs*.

Singular nouns are generally made possessive with an apostrophe and an *s* (*'s*).

> My *uncle's* new car is silver.

> The *dog's* bowl is empty.

> *James's* ties are becoming outdated.

Plural nouns ending in *s* are generally made possessive by just adding an apostrophe ('):

> The pistachio nuts' saltiness is added during roasting. (The saltiness of pistachio nuts is added during roasting.)

> The students' achievement tests are difficult. (The achievement tests of the students are difficult.)

If the plural noun does not end in an *s* such as *women,* then it is made possessive by adding an **apostrophe** *s* (*'s*)—*women's*.

Indefinite possessive pronouns such as *nobody* or *someone* become possessive by adding an *apostrophe s—nobody's* or *someone's*.

Using Correct Punctuation
Ellipses

An **ellipsis** (…) consists of three handy little dots that can speak volumes on behalf of irrelevant material. Writers use them in place of words, lines, phrases, list content, or paragraphs that might just as easily have been omitted from a passage of writing. This can be done to save space or to focus only on the specifically relevant material.

> Exercise is good for some unexpected reasons. Watkins writes, "Exercise has many benefits such as…reducing cancer risk."

In the example above, the ellipsis takes the place of the other benefits of exercise that are more expected.

The ellipsis may also be used to show a pause in sentence flow.

> "I'm wondering…how this could happen," Dylan said in a soft voice.

Commas

A **comma** (,) is the punctuation mark that signifies a pause—breath—between parts of a sentence. It denotes a break of flow. As with so many aspects of writing structure, authors will benefit by reading their writing aloud or mouthing the words. This can be particularly helpful if one is uncertain about whether the comma is needed.

In a complex sentence—one that contains a **subordinate** (**dependent**) clause or clauses—the use of a comma is dictated by where the subordinate clause is located. If the subordinate clause is located before the main clause, a comma is needed between the two clauses.

> Because I don't have enough money, I will not order steak.

Generally, if the subordinate clause is placed after the main clause, no punctuation is needed.

> I did well on my exam because I studied two hours the night before.

Notice how the last clause is dependent because it requires the earlier independent clauses to make sense.

Use a comma on both sides of an interrupting phrase.

> I will pay for the ice cream, chocolate and vanilla, and then will eat it all myself.

The words forming the phrase in italics are nonessential (extra) information. To determine if a phrase is nonessential, try reading the sentence without the phrase and see if it's still coherent.

A comma is not necessary in this next sentence because no interruption—nonessential or extra information—has occurred. Read sentences aloud when uncertain.

> I will pay for the chocolate and vanilla ice cream and then eat it all myself.

If the nonessential phrase comes at the beginning of a sentence, a comma should only go at the end of the phrase. If the phrase comes at the end of a sentence, a comma should only go at the beginning of the phrase.

Other types of interruptions include the following:

- Interjections: Oh no, I am not going.
- Abbreviations: Barry Potter, M.D., specializes in heart disorders.
- Direct addresses: Yes, Claudia, I am tired and going to bed.
- Parenthetical phrases: His wife, lovely as she was, was not helpful.
- Transitional phrases: Also, it is not possible.

The second comma in the following sentence is called an Oxford comma.

> I will pay for ice cream, syrup, and pop.

It is a comma used after the second-to-last item in a series of three or more items. It comes before the word *or* or *and*. Not everyone uses the Oxford comma; it is optional, but many believe it is needed. The comma functions as a tool to reduce confusion in writing. So, if omitting the Oxford comma would cause confusion, then it's best to include it.

Commas are used in math to mark the place of thousands in numerals, breaking them up so they are easier to read. Other uses for commas are in dates (*March 19, 2016*), letter greetings (*Dear Sally,*), and in between cities and states (*Louisville, KY*).

Semicolons

The **semicolon** (;) might be described as a heavy-handed comma. Take a look at these two examples:

> I will pay for the ice cream, but I will not pay for the steak.

> I will pay for the ice cream; I will not pay for the steak.

What's the difference? The first example has a comma and a conjunction separating the two independent clauses. The second example does not have a conjunction, but there are two independent clauses in the sentence, so something more than a comma is required. In this case, a semicolon is used.

Two independent clauses can only be joined in a sentence by either a comma and conjunction or a semicolon. If one of those tools is not used, the sentence will be a run-on. Remember that while the clauses are independent, they need to be closely related in order to be contained in one sentence.

Another use for the semicolon is to separate items in a list when the items themselves require commas.

> The family lived in Phoenix, Arizona; Oklahoma City, Oklahoma; and Raleigh, North Carolina.

Colons

Colons (:) have many miscellaneous functions. Colons can be used to proceed further information or a list. In these cases, a colon should only follow an independent clause.

> Humans take in sensory information through five basic senses: sight, hearing, smell, touch, and taste.

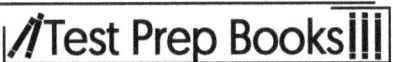

The meal includes the following components:

- Caesar salad
- Spaghetti
- Garlic bread
- Cake

The family got what they needed: a reliable vehicle.

While a comma is more common, a colon can also precede a formal quotation.

He said to the crowd: "Let's begin!"

The colon is used after the greeting in a formal letter.

Dear Sir:
To Whom It May Concern:

In the writing of time, the colon separates the minutes from the hour (*4:45 p.m.*). The colon can also be used to indicate a ratio between two numbers (*50:1*).

Hyphens

The **hyphen** (-) is a little hash mark that can be used to join words to show that they are linked.

Hyphenate two words that work together as a single adjective (a compound adjective).

honey-covered biscuits

Some words always require hyphens, even if not serving as an adjective.

merry-go-round

Hyphens always go after certain prefixes like *anti-* & *all-*.

Hyphens should also be used when the absence of the hyphen would cause a strange vowel combination (*semi-engineer*) or confusion. For example, *re-collect* should be used to describe something being gathered twice rather than being written as *recollect*, which means to remember.

Parentheses and Dashes

Parentheses are half-round brackets that look like this: ( ). They set off a word, phrase, or sentence that is an afterthought, explanation, or side note relevant to the surrounding text but not essential. A pair of commas is often used to set off this sort of information, but parentheses are generally used for information that would not fit well within a sentence or that the writer deems not important enough to be structurally part of the sentence.

The picture of the heart (see above) shows the major parts you should memorize.

Mount Everest is one of three mountains in the world that are over 28,000 feet high (K2 and Kanchenjunga are the other two).

See how the sentences above are complete without the parenthetical statements? In the first example, *see above* would not have fit well within the flow of the sentence. The second parenthetical statement could have been a separate sentence, but the writer deemed the information not pertinent to the topic.

The **dash** (—) is a mark longer than a hyphen used as a punctuation mark in sentences and to set apart a relevant thought. Even after plucking out the line separated by the dash marks, the sentence will be intact and make sense.

> Looking out the airplane window at the landmarks—Lake Clarke, Thompson Community College, and the bridge—she couldn't help but feel excited to be home.

The dashes use is similar to that of parentheses or a pair of commas. So, what's the difference? Many believe that using dashes makes the clause within them stand out while using parentheses is subtler. It's advised to not use dashes when commas could be used instead.

Quotation Marks
Here are some instances where **quotation marks** should be used:

- Dialogue for characters in narratives. When characters speak, the first word should always be capitalized, and the punctuation goes inside the quotes. For example:

    Janie said, "The tree fell on my car during the hurricane."

- Around titles of songs, short stories, essays, and chapters in books
- To emphasize a certain word
- To refer to a word as the word itself

Apostrophes
The apostrophe (') is a versatile punctuation mark. It has a few different functions:

- Quotes: Apostrophes are used when a second quote is needed within a quote.

    In my letter to my friend, I wrote, "The girl had to get a new purse, and guess what Mary did? She said, 'I'd like to go with you to the store.' I knew Mary would buy it for her."

- Contractions: Another use for an apostrophe in the quote above is a contraction. *I'd* is used for *I would*.

- Possession: An apostrophe followed by the letter *s* shows possession (*Mary's* purse). If the possessive word is plural, the apostrophe generally just follows the word.

Correcting Subject-Verb Agreement Errors
In English, verbs must agree with the subject. The form of a verb may change depending on whether the subject is singular or plural, or whether it is first, second, or third person. For example, the verb *to be* has various forms:

> I am a student.

> You are a student.

> She is a student.

> We are students.

> They are students.

Errors occur when a verb does not agree with its subject. Sometimes, the error is readily apparent:

> We is hungry.

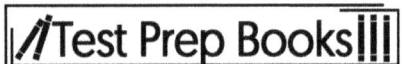

Is is not the appropriate form of *to be* when used with the third person plural *we*.

    We are hungry.

This sentence now has correct subject-verb agreement.

However, some cases are trickier, particularly when the subject consists of a lengthy noun phrase with many modifiers:

    Students who are hoping to accompany the anthropology department on its annual summer trip to Ecuador needs to sign up by March 31st.

The verb in this sentence is *needs*. However, its subject is not the noun adjacent to it—Ecuador. The subject is the noun at the beginning of the sentence—students. Because *students* is plural, *needs* is the incorrect verb form.

    Students who are hoping to accompany the anthropology department on its annual summer trip to Ecuador *need* to sign up by March 31st.

This sentence now uses correct agreement between *students* and *need*.

Another case to be aware of is a **collective noun**. A collective noun refers to a group of many things or people but can be singular in itself—e.g., *family, committee, army, pair team, council, jury*. Whether or not a collective noun uses a singular or plural verb depends on how the noun is being used. If the noun refers to the group performing a collective action as one unit, it should use a singular verb conjugation:

    The family is moving to a new neighborhood.

The whole family is moving together in unison, so the singular verb form *is* is appropriate here.

    The committee has made its decision.

The verb *has* and the possessive pronoun *its* both reflect the word *committee* as a singular noun in the sentence above; however, when a collective noun refers to the group as individuals, it can take a plural verb:

    The newlywed pair spend every moment together.

This sentence emphasizes the love between two people in a pair, so it can use the plural verb *spend*.

    The council are all newly elected members.

The sentence refers to the council in terms of its individual members and uses the plural verb *are*.

Overall, though, American English is more likely to pair a collective noun with a singular verb, while British English is more likely to pair a collective noun with a plural verb.

Which of the following sentences is correct?

    A large crowd of protesters was on hand.

    A large crowd of protesters were on hand.

Many people would say the second sentence is correct, but they'd be wrong. However, they probably wouldn't be alone. Most people just look at two words: *protesters were*. Together they make sense. They sound right. The problem is that the verb *were* doesn't refer to the word *protesters*. Here, the word *protesters* is part of a prepositional phrase that clarifies the actual subject of the sentence (*crowd*).

Take the phrase "of protesters" away and re-examine the sentences:

    A large crowd was on hand.

    A large crowd were on hand.

Without the prepositional phrase to separate the subject and verb, the answer is obvious. The first sentence is correct. On the test, look for confusing prepositional phrases when answering questions about subject-verb agreement. Take the phrase away, and then recheck the sentence.

Correcting Pronoun Errors
Pronoun Person
Pronoun person refers to the narrative voice the writer uses in a piece of writing. A great deal of nonfiction is written in third person, which uses pronouns like *he, she, it,* and *they* to convey meaning. Occasionally a writer uses first person (*I, me, we,* etc.) or second person (*you*). Any choice of pronoun person can be appropriate for a particular situation, but the writer must remain consistent and logical.

Test questions may cover examining samples that should stay in a single pronoun person, be it first, second, or third. Look out for shifts between words like *you* and *I* or *he* and *they*.

Pronoun Clarity
Pronouns always refer back to a noun. However, as the writer composes longer, more complicated sentences, the reader may be unsure which noun the pronoun should replace. For example:

    An amendment was made to the bill, but now it has been voted down.

Was the amendment voted down or the entire bill? It's impossible to tell from this sentence. To correct this error, the writer needs to restate the appropriate noun rather than using a pronoun:

    An amendment was made to the bill, but now the bill has been voted down.

Pronouns in Combination
Writers often make mistakes when choosing pronouns to use in combination with other nouns. The most common mistakes are found in sentences like this:

    Please join Senator Wilson and I at the event tomorrow.

Notice anything wrong? Though many people think the sentence sounds perfectly fine, the use of the pronoun *I* is actually incorrect. To double-check this, take the other person out of the sentence:

    Please join I at the event tomorrow.

Now the sentence is obviously incorrect, as it should read, "Please join *me* at the event tomorrow." Thus, the first sentence should replace *I* with *me*:

    Please join Senator Wilson and me at the event tomorrow.

For many people, this sounds wrong because they're used to hearing and saying it incorrectly. Take extra care when answering this kind of question and follow the double-checking procedure.

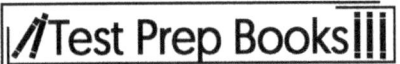

Eliminating Non-Standard English Words or Phrases

Non-standard English words and phrases, such as slang, should be eliminated, as it not only reduces the professionalism and formality of a text, but it also opens the door for confusion. Slang tends to evolve quickly, and it is less universally understood than standard English. Therefore, unless working on a narrative fiction piece that purposely includes non-standard English as part of the dialogue, writers should make every effort to eliminate this type of language from their writing.

Correcting Errors with Frequently Confused Words

There are a handful of words in the English language that writers often confuse with other words because they sound similar or identical. Errors involving these words are hard to spot because they *sound* right even when they're wrong. Also, because these mistakes are so pervasive, many people think they're correct. Here are a few examples that may be encountered on the test:

They're vs. Their vs. There

This set of words is probably the all-time winner of misuse. The word *they're* is a contraction of "they are." Remember that contractions combine two words, using an apostrophe to replace any eliminated letters. If a question asks whether the writer is using the word *they're* correctly, change the word to "they are" and reread the sentence. Look at the following example:

Legislators can be proud of they're work on this issue.

This sentence *sounds* correct, but replace the contraction *they're* with "they are" to see what happens:

Legislators can be proud of they are work on this issue.

The result doesn't make sense, which shows that it's an incorrect use of the word *they're*. Did the writer mean to use the word *their* instead? The word *their* indicates possession because it shows that something *belongs* to something else. Now put the word *their* into the sentence:

Legislators can be proud of their work on this issue.

To check the answer, find the word that comes right after the word *their* (which in this case is *work*). Pose this question: whose *work* is it? If the question can be answered in the sentence, then the word signifies possession. In the sentence above, it's the legislators' work. Therefore, the writer is using the word *their* correctly.

If the words *they're* and *their* don't make sense in the sentence, then the correct word is almost always *there*. The word *there* can be used in many different ways, so it's easy to remember to use it when *they're* and *their* don't work. Now test these methods with the following sentences:

Their going to have a hard time passing these laws.

Enforcement officials will have there hands full.

They're are many issues to consider when discussing car safety.

In the first sentence, asking the question "Whose going is it?" doesn't make sense. Thus, the word *their* is incorrect. However, when replaced with the conjunction *they're* (or *they are*), the sentence works. Thus, the correct word for the first sentence should be *they're*.

In the second sentence, ask this question: "Whose hands are full?" The answer (*enforcement officials*) is correct in the sentence. Therefore, the word *their* should replace *there* in this sentence.

In the third sentence, changing the word *they're* to "they are" ("They are are many issues") doesn't make sense. Ask this question: "Whose are is it?" This makes even less sense, since neither of the words *they're* or *their* makes sense. Therefore, the correct word must be *there*.

Who's vs. Whose
Who's is a contraction of "who is" while the word *whose* indicates possession. Look at the following sentence:

> Who's job is it to protect America's drivers?

The easiest way to check for correct usage is to replace the word *who's* with "who is" and see if the sentence makes sense:

> Who is job is it to protect America's drivers?

By changing the contraction to "Who is" the sentence no longer makes sense. Therefore, the correct word must be *whose*.

Your vs. You're
The word *your* indicates possession, while *you're* is a contraction for "you are." Look at the following example:

> Your going to have to write your congressman if you want to see action.

Again, the easiest way to check correct usage is to replace the word *Your* with "You are" and see if the sentence still makes sense.

> You are going to have to write your congressman if you want to see action.

By replacing Your with "You are," the sentence still makes sense. Thus, in this case, the writer should have used "You're."

Its vs. It's
Its is a word that indicates possession, while the word *it's* is a contraction of "it is." Once again, the easiest way to check for correct usage is to replace the word with "it is" and see if the sentence makes sense. Look at the following sentence:

> It's going to take a lot of work to pass this law.

Replacing *it's* with "it is" results in this: "It is going to take a lot of work to pass this law." This makes sense, so the contraction (*it's*) is correct. Now look at another example:

> The car company will have to redesign it's vehicles.

Replacing *it's* with "it is" results in this: "The car company will have to redesign it is vehicles." This sentence doesn't make sense, so the contraction (*it's*) is incorrect.

Than vs. Then
Than is used in sentences that involve comparisons, while *then* is used to indicate an order of events. Consider the following sentence:

> Japan has more traffic fatalities than the U.S.

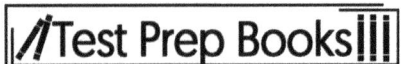

The use of the word *than* is correct because it compares Japan to the U.S. Now look at another example:

> Laws must be passed, and then we'll see a change in behavior.

Here the use of the word *then* is correct because one thing happens after the other.

Affect vs. Effect

Affect is a verb that means to change something, while *effect* is a noun that indicates such a change. Look at the following sentence:

> There are thousands of people affected by the new law.

This sentence is correct because *affected* is a verb that tells what's happening. Now look at this sentence:

> The law will have a dramatic effect.

This sentence is also correct because *effect* is a noun and the thing that happens.

Note that a noun version of *affect* is occasionally used. It means "emotion" or "desire," usually in a psychological sense.

Two vs. Too vs. To

Two is the number (2). *Too* refers to an amount of something, or it can mean *also*. *To* is used for everything else. Look at the following sentence:

> Two senators still haven't signed the bill.

This is correct because there are *two* (2) senators. Here's another example:

> There are too many questions about this issue.

In this sentence, the word *too* refers to an amount ("too many questions"). Now here's another example:

> Senator Wilson is supporting this legislation, too.

In this sentence, the word *also* can be substituted for the word *too*, so it's also correct. Finally, one last example:

> I look forward to signing this bill into law.

In this sentence, the tests for *two* and *too* don't work. Thus, the word *to* fits the bill!

Determining and Assess Purpose and Effectiveness of Syntactic Structures

Eliminating Dangling or Misplaced Modifiers

Modifiers are words or phrases (often adjectives or nouns) that add detail to, explain, or limit the meaning of other parts of a sentence. Look at the following example:

> A big pine tree is in the yard.

In the sentence, the words *big* (an adjective) and *pine* (a noun) modify *tree* (the head noun).

All related parts of a sentence must be placed together correctly. **Misplaced** and **dangling modifiers** are common writing mistakes. In fact, they're so common that many people are accustomed to seeing them and can decipher an incorrect sentence without much difficulty. On the test, expect to be asked to identify and correct this kind of error.

Misplaced Modifiers

Since modifiers refer to something else in the sentence (*big* and *pine* refer to *tree* in the example above), they need to be placed close to what they modify. If a modifier is so far away that the reader isn't sure what it's describing, it becomes a **misplaced modifier**. For example:

Seat belts almost saved 5,000 lives in 2009.

It's likely that the writer means that the total number of lives saved by seat belts in 2009 is close to 5,000. However, due to the misplaced modifier (*almost*), the sentence actually says there are 5,000 instances when seat belts *almost saved lives*. In this case, the position of the modifier is actually the difference between life and death (at least in the meaning of the sentence).

A clearer way to write the sentence is:

Seat belts saved almost 5,000 lives in 2009.

Now that the modifier is close to the 5,000 lives it references, the sentence's meaning is clearer.

Another common example of a misplaced modifier occurs when the writer uses the modifier to begin a sentence. For example:

Having saved 5,000 lives in 2009, Senator Wilson praised the seat belt legislation.

It seems unlikely that Senator Wilson saved 5,000 lives on her own, but that's what the writer is saying in this sentence. To correct this error, the writer should move the modifier closer to the intended object it modifies. Here are two possible solutions:

Having saved 5,000 lives in 2009, the seat belt legislation was praised by Senator Wilson.

Senator Wilson praised the seat belt legislation, which saved 5,000 lives in 2009.

When choosing a solution for a misplaced modifier, look for an option that places the modifier close to the object or idea it describes.

Dangling Modifiers

A modifier must have a target word or phrase that it's modifying. Without this, it's a **dangling modifier**. Dangling modifiers are usually found at the beginning of sentences:

After passing the new law, there is sure to be an improvement in highway safety.

This sentence doesn't say anything about who is passing the law. Therefore, "After passing the new law" is a dangling modifier because it doesn't modify anything in the sentence. To correct this type of error, determine what the writer intended the modifier to point to:

After passing the new law, legislators are sure to see an improvement in highway safety.

"After passing the new law" now points to *legislators*, which makes the sentence clearer and eliminates the dangling modifier.

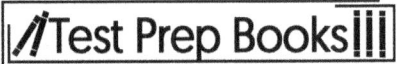

Editing Sentences for Parallel Structure and Correct Use of Conjunctions

Parallel Structure

Parallel structure occurs when phrases or clauses within a sentence contain the same structure. Parallelism increases readability and comprehensibility because it is easy to tell which sentence elements are paired with each other in meaning.

Jennifer enjoys cooking, knitting, and to spend time with her cat.

This sentence is not parallel because the items in the list appear in two different forms. Some are **gerunds**, which is the verb + ing: *cooking, knitting*. The other item uses the **infinitive** form, which is to + verb: *to spend*. To create parallelism, all items in the list may reflect the same form:

Jennifer enjoys cooking, knitting, and spending time with her cat.

All of the items in the list are now in gerund forms, so this sentence exhibits parallel structure. Here's another example:

The company is looking for employees who are responsible and with a lot of experience.

Again, the items that are listed in this sentence are not parallel. "Responsible" is an adjective, yet "with a lot of experience" is a prepositional phrase. The sentence elements do not utilize parallel parts of speech.

The company is looking for employees who are responsible and **experienced**.

"Responsible" and "experienced" are both adjectives, so this sentence now has parallel structure.

Conjunctions

Conjunctions join words, phrases, clauses, or sentences together, indicating the type of connection between these elements.

I like pizza, *and* I enjoy spaghetti.

I like to play baseball, *but* I'm allergic to mitts.

Some conjunctions are **coordinating**, meaning they give equal emphasis to two main clauses. Coordinating conjunctions are short, simple words that can be remembered using the mnemonic FANBOYS: for, and, nor, but, or, yet, so. Other conjunctions are subordinating. **Subordinating conjunctions** introduce dependent clauses and include words such as *because, since, before, after, if,* and *while*.

Conjunctions can also be classified as follows:

- **Cumulative conjunctions** add one statement to another.
    - Examples: and, both, also, as well as, not only
    - I.e., The juice is sweet *and* sour.
- **Adversative conjunctions** are used to contrast two clauses.
    - Examples: but, while, still, yet, nevertheless
    - I.e., She was tired, *but* she was happy.
- **Alternative conjunctions** express two alternatives.
    - Examples: or, either, neither, nor, else, otherwise
    - I.e., He must eat, *or* he will die.

Editing for Subject-Verb and Pronoun-Antecedent Agreement

Subject-Verb Agreement

The subject of a sentence and its verb must agree. The cornerstone rule of subject-verb agreement is that subject and verb must agree in number. Whether the subject is singular or plural, the verb must follow suit.

   Incorrect: The houses is new.

   Correct: The houses are new.

   Also Correct: The house is new.

In other words, a singular subject requires a singular verb; a plural subject requires a plural verb.

The words or phrases that come between the subject and verb do not alter this rule.

   Incorrect: The houses built of brick is new.

   Correct: The houses built of brick are new.

   Incorrect: The houses with the sturdy porches is new.

   Correct: The houses with the sturdy porches are new.

The subject will always follow the verb when a sentence begins with *here* or *there*. Identify these with care.

   Incorrect: Here *is* the *houses* with sturdy porches.

   Correct: Here *are* the *houses* with sturdy porches.

The subject in the sentences above is not *here*, it is *houses*. Remember, *here* and *there* are never subjects. Be careful that contractions such as *here's* or *there're* do not cause confusion!

Two subjects joined by *and* require a plural verb form, except when the two combine to make one thing:

   Incorrect: Garrett and Jonathan is over there.

   Correct: Garrett and Jonathan are over there.

   Incorrect: Spaghetti and meatballs are a delicious meal!

   Correct: Spaghetti and meatballs is a delicious meal!

In the example above, *spaghetti and meatballs* is a compound noun. However, *Garrett and Jonathan* is not a compound noun.

Two singular subjects joined by *or, either/or,* or *neither/nor* call for a singular verb form.

   Incorrect: Butter or syrup are acceptable.

   Correct: Butter or syrup is acceptable.

Plural subjects joined by *or, either/or,* or *neither/nor* are, indeed, plural.

The chairs or the boxes are being moved next.

If one subject is singular and the other is plural, the verb should agree with the closest noun.

> Correct: The chair or the boxes *are* being moved next.

> Correct: The chairs or the box *is* being moved next.

Some plurals of money, distance, and time call for a singular verb.

> Incorrect: Three dollars *are* enough to buy that.

> Correct: Three dollars *is* enough to buy that.

For words declaring degrees of quantity such as *many of, some of,* or *most of,* let the noun that follows *of* be the guide:

> Incorrect: Many of the books is in the shelf.

> Correct: Many of the books are in the shelf.

> Incorrect: Most of the pie *are* on the table.

> Correct: Most of the pie *is* on the table.

For indefinite pronouns like anybody or everybody, use singular verbs.

> Everybody *is* going to the store.

However, the pronouns *few, many, several, all, some,* and *both* have their own rules and use plural forms.

> Some *are* ready.

Some nouns like *crowd* and *congress* are called **collective nouns** and they require a singular verb form.

> Congress *is* in session.

> The news *is* over.

Books and movie titles, though, including plural nouns such as *Great Expectations*, also require a singular verb. Remember that only the subject affects the verb. While writing tricky subject-verb arrangements, say them aloud. Listen to them. Once the rules have been learned, one's ear will become sensitive to them, making it easier to pick out what's right and what's wrong.

Pronoun-Antecedent Agreement

An **antecedent** is the noun to which a pronoun refers; it needs to be written or spoken before the pronoun is used. For many pronouns, antecedents are imperative for clarity. In particular, a lot of the personal, possessive, and demonstrative pronouns need antecedents. Otherwise, it would be unclear who or what someone is referring to when they use a pronoun like *he* or *this*.

Pronoun reference means that the pronoun should refer clearly to one, clear, unmistakable noun (the antecedent).

Pronoun-antecedent agreement refers to the need for the antecedent and the corresponding pronoun to agree in gender, person, and number. Here are some examples:

The *kidneys* (plural antecedent) are part of the urinary system. *They* (plural pronoun) serve several roles.

The kidneys are part of the *urinary system* (singular antecedent). *It* (singular pronoun) is also known as the renal system.

Eliminating Wordiness or Awkward Sentence Structure

A great Facebook posts or Twitter story is witty, to the point, and even moving. Good writing is like a good social media post—it needs to be seamless, succinct, and sound in its organization. Alternatively, there are also social media rants so jumbled that they do not make sense or are so endless that readers lose interest. The most captivating social media entries are the ones that meet a high standard of organization. Likewise, the most captivating essays follow these same standards.

Wordiness and awkward sentence structure can happen as a result of many factors. Firstly, they can result from poor grammar or run-on sentences. In order to avoid this, test takers should try using punctuation with fidelity and breaking up independent and dependent clauses into simpler, bite-size nuggets of knowledge. Secondly, wordiness and awkward sentence structure can stem from the overuse of adjectives and adverbs. Test takers should try to limit adverbs and adjectives to ensure clarity. Lastly, wordiness and awkward sentence structure can be the product of flawed organization. Not only should sentences be succinct, but paragraphs and pages should also be succinct—they should use space efficiently and effectively. Test takers should try conveying a message using the fewest words possible.

Below are examples of ways to rectify wordiness and awkward sentences in writing.

WORDINESS:

BEFORE: Science is an important subject of study, and it is important for all students to learn because it focuses on the way the world works and it has important subfields like biology, physics, and chemistry.	AFTER: Science—which is composed of important subfields like biology, physics, and chemistry—helps students understand the way the world works.
BEFORE: History is about important people, places, events, movements, and eras in the past it is a really, really interesting field with lots of different lenses of study such as economic history, political history, and cultural history to name a few types of history.	AFTER: History can be studied through many lenses: economics, politics, and culture. However, all types of history focus on interesting people, places, events, movements, and eras in the past.

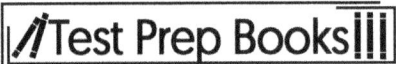

AWKWARDNESS:

BEFORE:	AFTER:
The administrative expertise of George Washington's presidential administration was known for its powerfully powerful administrators.	George Washington's presidential administration was known for its powerful leadership and expertise.
BEFORE:	AFTER:
I want to study history, working hard, and becoming a historian.	I want to study history, work hard, and become a historian.

Eliminating Run-On Sentences and Sentence Fragments

A **sentence fragment** is a failed attempt to create a complete sentence because it's missing a required noun or verb. Fragments don't function properly because there isn't enough information to understand the writer's intended meaning. For example:

> Seat belt use corresponds to a lower rate of hospital visits, reducing strain on an already overburdened healthcare system. Insurance claims as well.

Look at the last sentence: *Insurance claims as well*. What does this mean? This is a fragment because it has a noun but no verb, and it leaves the reader guessing what the writer means about insurance claims. Many readers can probably infer what the writer means, but this distracts them from the flow of the writer's argument. Choosing a suitable replacement for a sentence fragment may be one of the questions on the test. The fragment is probably related to the surrounding content, so look at the overall point the writer is trying to make and choose the answer that best fits that idea.

Remember that sometimes a fragment can *look* like a complete sentence or have all the nouns and verbs it needs to make sense. Consider the following two examples:

> Seat belt use corresponds to a lower rate of hospital visits.

> Although seat belt use corresponds to a lower rate of hospital visits.

Both examples above have nouns and verbs, but only the first sentence is correct. The second sentence is a fragment, even though it's actually longer. The key is the writer's use of the word *although*. Starting a sentence with *although* turns that part into a *subordinate clause* (more on that next). Keep in mind that one doesn't have to remember that it's called a subordinate clause on the test. Just be able to recognize that the words form an incomplete thought and identify the problem as a sentence fragment.

A **run-on sentence** is, in some ways, the opposite of a fragment. It contains two or more sentences that have been improperly forced together into one. An example of a run-on sentence looks something like this:

> Seat belt use corresponds to a lower rate of hospital visits it also leads to fewer insurance claims.

Here, there are two separate ideas in one sentence. It's difficult for the reader to follow the writer's thinking because there is no transition from one idea to the next. On the test, choose the best way to correct the run-on sentence.

Here are two possibilities for the sentence above:

> Seat belt use corresponds to a lower rate of hospital visits. It also leads to fewer insurance claims.

> Seat belt use corresponds to a lower rate of hospital visits, but it also leads to fewer insurance claims.

Both solutions are grammatically correct, so which one is the best choice? That depends on the point that the writer is trying to make. Always read the surrounding text to determine what the writer wants to demonstrate, and choose the option that best supports that thought.

Text Types

Literary Text

Poetry

The genre of **poetry** refers to literary works that focus on the expression of feelings and ideas through the use of structure and linguistic rhythm to create a desired effect.

Different poetic structures and devices are used to create the various major forms of poetry. Some of the most common forms are discussed in the following chart.

Type	Poetic Structure	Example
Ballad	A poem or song passed down orally which tells a story and in English tradition usually uses an ABAB or ABCB rhyme scheme	William Butler Yeats' "The Ballad of Father O'Hart"
Epic	A long poem from ancient oral tradition which narrates the story of a legendary or heroic protagonist	Homer's The Odyssey Virgil's The Aeneid
Haiku	A Japanese poem of three unrhymed lines with five, seven, and five syllables (in English) with nature as a common subject matter	Matsuo Bashō An old silent pond... A frog jumps into the pond, splash! Silence again.
Limerick	A five-line poem written in an AABBA rhyme scheme, with a witty focus	From Edward Lear's Book of Nonsense— "There was a Young Person of Smyrna Whose grandmother threatened to burn her..."
Ode	A formal lyric poem that addresses and praises a person, place, thing, or idea	Edna St. Vincent Millay's "Ode to Silence"
Sonnet	A fourteen-line poem written in iambic pentameter	Shakespeare's Sonnets 18 and 130

Understanding Poetic Devices and Structure
Poetic Devices
Rhyme is the poet's use of corresponding word sounds in order to create an effect. Most rhyme occurs at the ends of a poem's lines, which is how readers arrive at the **rhyme scheme**. Each line that has a corresponding rhyming sound is assigned a letter—A, B, C, and so on. When using a rhyme scheme, poets will often follow lettered patterns. Robert Frost's *"The Road Not Taken"* uses the ABAAB rhyme scheme:

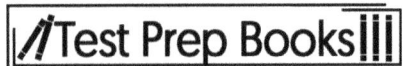

Two roads diverged in a yellow wood,	A
And sorry I could not travel both	B
And be one traveler, long I stood	A
And looked down one as far as I could	A
To where it bent in the undergrowth;	B

Another important poetic device is **rhythm**—metered patterns within poetry verses. When a poet develops rhythm through **meter**, he or she is using a combination of stressed and unstressed syllables to create a sound effect for the reader.

Rhythm is created by the use of poetic feet—individual rhythmic units made up of the combination of stressed and unstressed syllables. A line of poetry is made up of one or more poetic feet. There are five standard types in English poetry, as depicted in the chart below.

Foot Type	Rhythm	Pattern
Iamb	buh Buh	Unstressed/stressed
Trochee	Buh buh	Stressed/unstressed
Spondee	Buh Buh	Stressed/stressed
Anapest	buh buh Buh	Unstressed/unstressed/stressed
Dactyl	Buh buh buh	Stressed/unstressed/unstressed

Structure

Poetry is most easily recognized by its structure, which varies greatly. For example, a structure may be strict in the number of lines it uses. It may use rhyming patterns or may not rhyme at all. There are three main types of poetic structures:

- *Verse*—poetry with a consistent meter and rhyme scheme
- *Blank verse*—poetry with consistent meter but an inconsistent rhyme scheme
- *Free verse*—poetry with inconsistent meter or rhyme

Verse poetry is most often developed in the form of **stanzas**—groups of word lines. Stanzas can also be considered *verses*. The structure is usually formulaic and adheres to the protocols for the form. For example, the English sonnet form uses a structure of fourteen lines and a variety of different rhyming patterns. The English ode typically uses three ten-line stanzas and has a particular rhyming pattern.

Poets choose poetic structure based on the effect they want to create. Some structures—such as the ballad and haiku—developed out of cultural influences and common artistic practice in history, but in more modern poetry, authors choose their structure to best fit their intended effect.

History of Poetry's Development

Ancient Times

Poetry has been in existence for thousands of years and even predates literacy. Early poems were passed on through oral tradition and were sung or recited as a way to remember a culture's history. The ancient Greek poets were the first to write down their poetry in the seventh to fourth century BC.

Greek poetry took three forms: epic, lyric, and dramatic. It used meter, and Greeks were the first to introduce iambic pentameter. Some of the greatest poets of this time included Homer, Aeschylus, and Euripides. Homer's *The Iliad* and *The Odyssey*, which focused on Greek mythology, are two of the most famous epic poems from this time period. Lyric poets of ancient Greece included Alcaeus, Sappho, and Pindar. Sappho was a female poet from the island of Lesbos. Most of her poetry exists in fragments, though her most complete poem, "Ode to Aphrodite," is influenced by and makes references to Homer's *Iliad*. The dramatic poetry of ancient Greece was written by Aeschylus and Sophocles, among others. It was divided into the same categories seen today in modern drama of tragedy and comedy.

When Greece was conquered by the Romans, their works were borrowed and adapted and eventually became the basis for modern literature. Romans wrote in Latin, and the Greek influence is clear in their poetry. Some of the oldest Roman literature is actually a translation of Greek works. Greco-Roman poet Andronicus first translated Homer's *The Odyssey* from Greek into Latin for a Roman audience. Though this was done for educational purposes at first, it became the basis for more Roman works and helped to develop Roman literature. Ovid was one of the most famous Roman poets. He is best known for *Metamorphoses*, a narrative poem consisting of fifteen texts. It spans the history of the world in myths from creation to the time of Julius Caesar and is one of the most influential texts in poetry to date. Another of Rome's great poets, Virgil, is best known for his *Aeneid*. This epic poem, written between 29 BC and 19 BC, tells the story of mythological Trojan hero Aeneas and his journey to Italy.

Middle Ages to Seventeenth Century

Poems in the Middle Ages were influenced by the historical events of the time, including religious movements. They were often religious in nature and typically written in Latin, as this was the predominant language of the Roman Catholic Church. Geoffrey Chaucer, a famous medieval writer, experimented with using the vernacular, or common, language of the people, writing works such as *The Parliament of Birds* and *The Canterbury Tales* in English. *Beowulf*, written by an anonymous Anglo-Saxon poet, is probably the most well-known poem to come out of the medieval period. It is an epic written in Old English, the vernacular language of the time. While its origins are unknown, this is the first time *Beowulf* was taken from oral tradition to written format.

The Renaissance brought with it one of the most prolific times in poetry's history. This cultural movement saw creative advancements in literature, art, and music, lasting from the fifteenth to the seventeenth century. Some of the most famous poetry to come from this time period includes William Shakespeare's sonnets. During the Enlightenment period that followed, there was a return to the style of the ancient Greeks, with a concentration on the epic poem. Alexander Pope was the most famous poet of this time, known for his satirical works and the use of the heroic couplet. The end of the eighteenth century brought about the birth of Romanticism and such famous British poets as William Blake, Lord Byron, William Wordsworth, and John Keats. Many of these poets got their inspiration from the natural world, which was in contrast to the religious themes in the poetry that came before it.

Nineteenth Century

Romanticism carried over into the nineteenth century, when there was also a rise in American poetry. These early American poets included Walt Whitman, Robert Frost, and Henry Wadsworth Longfellow. Whitman was known as the father of free verse. Most of these poets were known as transcendentalists, focusing on themes of spirituality, nature, and utopian values. Whitman's *Leaves of Grass*, published in 1855, was his idea of an American epic. The poetry in *Leaves of Grass* does not follow any rhythmic or metric patterns. Its themes of sensual pleasures and the natural world were novel and controversial at this time, but it has become one of the most influential works of American poetry.

Poetry of the nineteenth century also saw more working-class themes and authors from working-class backgrounds. This poetry had its roots in politics, rather than religion, nature, or romantic themes. This was also an important time for women in poetry, with the works of Emily Dickinson, Emily Bronte, and Elizabeth Browning gaining popularity. Dickinson's lyric poems used short lines, unconventional spelling and punctuation, and often lacked titles. While she wrote hundreds of poems in her lifetime, because of its unconventional style, most of Dickinson's work was published after her death. Her "Because I Could Not Stop for Death," published posthumously in 1890, exemplified her unique and influential style of meter and rhyme. Modernist poetry also got its start in the late nineteenth century. This format is marked by a movement from the personal to the world around the individual. It was born in the nineteenth century but flourished in the early twentieth century.

Twentieth Century

Modernist poetry continued into the twentieth century, with poets such as T. S. Eliot, Ezra Pound, and Gertrude Stein. Modernist poetry is characterized by the use of allusion and fragmented language. Some smaller movements that grew out of modernism include free verse, Dadaism, and surrealism. The twentieth century also saw a rise in African American poets with the Harlem Renaissance spanning the 1920s and 1930s. The publishing industry sought out African American writers whose poetry focused on realistic portrayals of their lives. One of the most important writers to come out of this movement was Langston Hughes, whose poetry honestly depicted his life and struggles as a black man living in America.

Another important poetry movement of the twentieth century was the Beat movement. Beat poetry, born out of New York and San Francisco, was characterized by anti-conformist themes and influenced by ideas of sexual freedom and drug use. Some of the most famous Beat poets include Allen Ginsberg and Lawrence Ferlinghetti, whose works challenged the social norms of the time. The second half of the twentieth century saw the advent of confessional poetry with the works of Sylvia Plath. Her poetry was deeply personal and rooted in natural themes in a lyrical style. Near the end of the nineteenth century, the New Formalism movement brought back the meter and rhyme of more traditional poetry. Poets such as Charles Martin, Brad Leithauser, and Molly Peacock adopted this New Formalist style.

Twenty-First Century

Contemporary poetry takes many forms and abides by no strict rules. Poets of the twenty-first century write about anything, from technology to love to civil rights. Their poetry tends to be more realistic in nature, and liberties are taken with form and structure. Poets of the twenty-first century often inject humor into their poetry and do not take form quite as seriously as those that came before them. Sherman Alexie, for example, writes about the plight of Native Americans but does so using irony and dark humor. Rita Dove, a poet laureate to both the state of Virginia and the Library of Congress, is another important twenty-first-century poet. Her work often has historical aspects and uses themes from other art forms, such as music and dance. Dove's *Sonata Mullatica*, published in 2009, is a collection of poetry about the life of George Bridgetower, a biracial musician, and his friendship with Beethoven. Poetry in the twenty-first century has been affected by the digital age, and many poems are now exclusively written and published in electronic format. The Internet has created a new forum for poetry that has helped it to continue to develop into the modern age.

Drama

Drama is a type of fiction that is based on a script that is meant to be performed. Works of drama are called **plays**. Plays are intended to be performed on a stage by actors in front of an audience. Like other works of fiction, plays contain characters, plot, setting, theme, symbolism, and imagery. The main difference is that plays are sectioned into acts and scenes rather than chapters or stanzas. Drama is one of the oldest forms of literature, and it has evolved from the first Greek tragedies, such as *Antigone* and *Prometheus Bound*, into what is performed on modern stages today.

Like prose fiction, drama has several genres. The following are the most common ones:

- Comedy: a humorous play designed to amuse and entertain, often with an emphasis on the common person's experience, generally resolved in a positive way—e.g., Richard Sheridan's *School for Scandal*, Shakespeare's *Taming of the Shrew*, Neil Simon's *The Odd Couple*
- History: a play based on recorded history where the fate of a nation or kingdom is at the core of the conflict—e.g., Christopher Marlowe's *Edward II*, Shakespeare's *King Richard III*, Arthur Miller's *The Crucible*

Reading

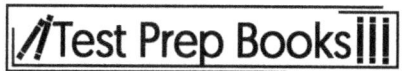

- Tragedy: a serious play that often involves the downfall of the protagonist. In modern tragedies, the protagonist is not necessarily in a position of power or authority—e.g., Jean Racine's *Phèdre*, Arthur Miller's *Death of a Salesman*, John Steinbeck's *Of Mice and Men*
- Melodrama: a play that emphasizes heightened emotion and sensationalism, generally with stereotypical characters in exaggerated or realistic situations and with moral polarization—e.g., Jean-Jacques Rousseau's *Pygmalion*
- Tragicomedy: a play that has elements of both tragedy—a character experiencing a tragic loss—and comedy—the resolution is often positive with no clear distinctive mood for either—e.g., Shakespeare's *The Merchant of Venice*, Anton Chekhov's *The Cherry Orchard*

Structural Elements

The text of the play is called a **script**, and it is made up of both stage directions and dialogue. Stage directions are sections of the play that set the scene. Set directions might include information on what the scenery should look like and where the actors should stand. Plays also contain **dialogue**, which refers to the actual words the actors should speak. The difference in a play and other literary forms is in its construction and that it is intended to be performed. Plays are typically made up of acts. A playwright might use acts to indicate a change in time, setting, or mood. Acts can also be divided into scenes. A scene change may be used to indicate a change in the action, to introduce new characters, or to indicate a change in setting at the same time. In a play, there may be a protagonist, or central character, and an antagonist, who opposes the protagonist. A play, like fictional prose, often uses the following plot structure known as dramatic structure or Freytag's pyramid: exposition, rising action, climax, falling action, and denouement.

- *Exposition*—The first part of the play that introduces background information about setting, characters, plot, backstories, etc.
- *Rising action*—A series of events that build up to the main event of the story
- *Climax*—The main event or turning point of the play, when things turn around for a protagonist in a comedy or start to go bad for the protagonist in a tragedy
- *Falling action*—The part when the plot slows down and starts moving toward a conclusion, often the logical consequence of the climax
- *Denouement*—The ending of the play when conflicts are resolved

A longer play may also contain subplots, which are secondary or in contrast to the main plot. A play can have one or more themes, depending on its length.

As an example, the following dramatic structure is used in Shakespeare's *Romeo and Juliet*:

Exposition: The setting of Verona, Italy; protagonists Romeo and Juliet are introduced; and the feud between the Capulets and the Montagues is revealed.

Rising action: Romeo and Juliet meet and fall in love but cannot be together because of the feud.

Climax: Juliet's cousin Tybalt kills Mercutio, igniting the feud. Romeo kills Tybalt and is banished. Romeo and Juliet secretly marry.

Falling action: Juliet fakes her death to avoid an arranged marriage and be with Romeo; Romeo plans his own suicide when he learns she has (seemingly) died.

Denouement: Romeo commits suicide at Juliet's tomb. She wakes to find him dead and also commits suicide. When the families learn they were secretly married, they resolve to end their long-standing feud.

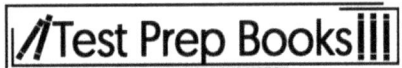

History of Drama's Development

Ancient Times

The ancient Greeks are widely accepted as the inventors of drama. The word *drama* comes from the Greek word meaning action. The earliest plays were religious in nature, focusing on the Greek gods. Greek drama included comedy, which was satirical and made light of the foils of men in power. The Greek tragedies were a bit more involved, including themes of love and loss. They typically involved the downfall of the protagonist, an otherwise good person, because of a fatal flaw. For example, in Sophocles' *Antigone*, the title character's tragic flaw is her loyalty to the gods.

Greek drama also included a chorus, masked performers who represent the voice of society. They spoke in unison and offered commentary on the dramatic action of the play. The chorus also sang, danced, and recited poetry during the play. Important playwrights of this time included Aeschylus, Sophocles, and Euripides. These early Greek playwrights greatly influenced the writers who came after them, with Aeschylus being called the father of modern drama. Aeschylus' *Oresteia* is likely the first example of a play in trilogy format. Other important works of this time included Sophocles' *Antigone* and *Oedipus Rex*, Euripides' *Medea*, and Aeschylus' *Prometheus Bound*.

Middle Ages

In the Middle Ages, drama continued to be influenced by religion. Three types of drama began to emerge in the medieval period: mystery play, miracle play, and morality play. The **mystery play** focused on biblical stories. These plays contained multiple acts and were performed by religious figures such as priests or monks. The **miracle play**, also with a religious theme, focused on the life of a saint. The **morality play** was meant to teach the audience a lesson based on the rules of the church. Two kinds of stages were invented for medieval drama: the fixed stage and the movable stage. While there were some comic elements to medieval plays, their religious nature made them mostly serious in tone. Secular plays were less popular at this time but did exist, particularly in France, where the farce was typically performed by professional actors in public forums.

Renaissance

The Renaissance was a prolific time for drama. This time period gave birth to the Elizabethan drama, popularized by playwrights such as Ben Jonson, Christopher Marlowe, and William Shakespeare. Shakespeare wrote both drama and comedy, and his plays such as *Romeo and Juliet, Hamlet, Macbeth,* and many more are some of the most recognized and acclaimed plays of all time. He also popularized a new type of drama, the romantic play, which did not fit in either of the previous categories. Elizabethan drama saw a break from the religious themes of the plays that came before it and a shift in focus from God to people. Like in the Greek tragedies before them, the tragedies of this period were marked by a protagonist with a central flaw, which ultimately brings him to his downfall.

An important development during this period was the establishment of permanent theaters. These large theaters were profitable and gave playwrights a designated place to showcase their plays. Having designated theaters allowed the creation of theater companies made up of common men, and young boys often played the roles of women. Women were not allowed to act in plays until after 1660, as it was not deemed a suitable profession for them. Queen Elizabeth I loved drama and was a patron of Shakespeare. Her interest in and support for the theater helped it to flourish during her reign.

Seventeenth and Eighteenth Centuries

The Elizabethan playwrights continued to develop plays in the seventeenth century, but the Puritanical government shut down theaters for a time. When King Charles II came into power in 1660, the theater ban was lifted. Theaters once again flourished after the English Restoration. Women were now able to perform in these dramas, bringing life to the intended female roles, with Margaret Hughes credited as the first female actress in English theater. This time period also saw the first recognized female playwright, Aphra Behn. Her two-part play, *The Rover*, was written in 1677. New types of drama that were developed at this time included heroic drama and Restoration comedy, which made use of immoral themes. The eighteenth century saw the fall of Restoration comedy and the rise of musical comedies and themes much more geared to musical entertainment than serious drama. John Gay's *The Beggar's Opera*, for example, was written to the tune of popular music of the time.

Nineteenth Century to the Present

In the nineteenth century, drama was influenced by the Victorian era. **Closet drama**, a type of dramatic play that is meant to be read rather than performed, became more popular. As for the stage, melodrama became very popular at this time. Melodrama used music to enhance the more dramatic scenes of plays. Shorter musical acts were also included in nineteenth-century productions and often interspersed between acts of plays. Toward the end of the nineteenth century, modernist plays such as Henrik Ibsen's *A Doll's House,* written in 1879, tackled such issues as the emancipation of women. Russian playwright Anton Chekhov also wrote modernist plays at this time. His works were unique in that the most meaningful parts of the play were not in the words but in the set direction for the actors. In the early twentieth century, playwrights such as T. S. Eliot and American playwrights such as Arthur Miller and Tennessee Williams saw their plays not only produced for the stage, but also the screen. The advent of television and film created a new format and a wider audience for these dramatic plays. Miller's *Death of a Salesman* and *The Crucible* were made into television and motion picture films, respectively. Williams' *A Streetcar Named Desire* was made into a major motion picture that went on to win four Academy Awards. More recent contemporary playwrights such as David Mamet often write both stage plays and screenplays for films. Mamet has won the Pulitzer Prize for his dramatic plays *Speed-the-Plow* and *Glengarry Glen Ross* and earned Oscar nominations for his screenplays.

Prose Fiction

Literary Elements of Fiction

There is no one, final definition of what literary elements are. They can be considered features or characteristics of fiction, but they are really more of a way that readers can unpack a text for the purpose of analysis and understanding the meaning. The elements contribute to a reader's literary interpretation of a passage as to how they function to convey the central message of a work. The most common literary elements used for analysis are the following:

- The **theme** is the central message of a fictional work, whether that work is structured as prose, drama, or poetry. It is the heart of what an author is trying to say to readers through the writing, and theme is largely conveyed through literary elements and techniques. Poetic elements overlap these elements and will be addressed separately.

- The **plot** is what happens in the story. Plots may be singular, containing one problem, or they may be very complex, with many sub-plots. All plots have exposition, a conflict, a climax, and a resolution. The *conflict* drives the plot and is something that the reader expects to be resolved. The plot carries those events along until there is a resolution to the conflict.

- **Characters** are the story's figures that assume primary, secondary, or minor roles. **Central** or major characters are those integral to the story—the plot cannot be resolved without them. A central character can be a **protagonist** or hero. There may be more than one protagonist, and he/she doesn't always have to possess good characteristics. A character can also be an **antagonist**—the force against a protagonist.

  Character development is when the author takes the time to create dynamic characters that add uniqueness and depth to the story. *Dynamic* characters are characters that change over the course of the plot time. **Stock** characters are those that appear across genres and embrace stereotypes—e.g., the cowboy of the Wild West or the blonde bombshell in a detective novel. A **flat** character is one that does not present a lot of complexity or depth, while a **rounded** character does. Sometimes, the **narrator** of a story or the speaker in a poem can be a character—e.g., Nick Carraway in Fitzgerald's *The Great Gatsby* or the speaker

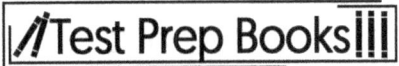

in Browning's "My Last Duchess." The narrator might also function as a character in prose, though not be part of the story—e.g., Dicken's narrator of *A Christmas Carol*.

- The **setting** is the time, place, or set of surroundings in which the story occurs. It includes time or time span, place(s), climates, geography—man-made or natural—or cultural environments. Emily Dickenson's poem "Because I could not stop for Death" has a simple setting—the narrator's symbolic ride with Death through town towards the local graveyard. Conversely, Leo Tolstoy's War and Peace encompasses numerous settings within settings in the areas affected by the Napoleonic Wars, spanning 1805 to 1812.

- The **point of view** is the position the narrator takes when telling the story in prose. If a narrator is incorporated in a drama, the point of view may vary; in poetry, point of view refers to the position the speaker in a poem takes.

    o The **first-person** point of view is when the writer uses the word "I" in the text. Poetry often uses first person, e.g., William Wordsworth's "I Wandered Lonely as a Cloud." Two examples of prose written in first person are Suzanne Collins's *The Hunger Games* and Anthony Burgess's *A Clockwork Orange*.

    o The **second person** point of view is when the writer uses the pronoun "you." It is not widely used in prose fiction, but as a technique, it has been used by writers such as William Faulkner in *Absalom, Absalom* and Albert Camus in *The Fall*. It is more common in poetry—e.g., Pablo Neruda's "If You Forget Me."

    o **Third person** point of view is when the writer utilizes pronouns such as him, her, or them. It may be the most utilized point of view in prose as it provides flexibility to an author and is the one with which readers are most familiar. There are two main types of third person used in fiction:

        ▪ *Third person omniscient*—narrator is all-knowing, relating the story by conveying and interpreting thoughts/feelings of all characters

        ▪ *Third person limited*—narrator relates the story through the perspective of one character's thoughts/feelings, usually the main character

Genres

Fiction written in prose can be further broken down into **fiction genres**—types of fiction. Some of the more common genres of fiction are as follows:

- **Classical fiction**: a work of fiction considered timeless in its message or theme, remaining noteworthy and meaningful over decades or centuries—e.g., Charlotte Brontë's *Jane Eyre*, Mark Twain's *Adventures of Huckleberry Finn*

- **Fables**: short fiction that generally features animals, fantastic creatures, or other forces within nature that assume human-like characters and has a moral lesson for the reader—e.g., *Aesop's Fables*

- **Fairy tales**: children's stories with magical characters in imaginary, enchanted lands, usually depicting a struggle between good and evil, a sub-genre of folklore—e.g., Hans Christian Anderson's *The Little Mermaid*, *Cinderella* by the Brothers Grimm

- **Fantasy**: fiction with magic or supernatural elements that cannot occur in the real world, sometimes involving medieval elements in language, usually includes some form of sorcery or witchcraft and sometimes set on a different world—e.g., J.R.R. Tolkien's *The Hobbit*, J.K. Rowling's *Harry Potter and the Sorcerer's Stone*, George R.R. Martin's *A Game of Thrones*

- **Folklore**: types of fiction passed down from oral tradition, stories indigenous to a particular region or culture, with a local flavor in tone, designed to help humans cope with their condition in life and validate cultural traditions, beliefs, and customs—e.g., William Laughead's *Paul Bunyan and The Blue Ox*, the Buddhist story of "The Banyan Deer"

- **Mythology**: closely related to folklore but more widespread, features mystical, otherworldly characters and addresses the basic question of why and how humans exist, relies heavily on allegory and features gods or heroes captured in some sort of struggle—e.g., Greek myths, Arthurian legends

- **Science fiction**: fiction that uses the principle of extrapolation—loosely defined as a form of prediction—to imagine future realities and problems of the human experience—e.g., Robert Heinlein's *Stranger in a Strange Land*, Ayn Rand's *Anthem*, Isaac Asimov's *I, Robot*, Philip K. Dick's *Do Androids Dream of Electric Sheep?*

- **Short stories**: short works of prose fiction with fully-developed themes and characters, focused on mood, generally developed with a single plot, with a short period of time for settings—e.g., Edgar Allan Poe's "Fall of the House of Usher," Shirley Jackson's "The Lottery," Isaac Bashevis Singer's "Gimpel the Fool"

Identifying Literary Contexts

Understanding that works of literature emerged either because of a particular context—or perhaps despite a context—is key to analyzing them effectively.

Historical Context

The **historical context** of a piece of literature can refer to the time period, setting, or conditions of living at the time it was written as well as the context of the work. For example, Hawthorne's *The Scarlet Letter* was published in 1850, though the setting of the story is 1642-1649. Historically, then, when Hawthorne wrote his novel, the United States found itself at odds as the beginnings of a potential Civil War were in view. Thus, the historical context is potentially significant as it pertains to the ideas of traditions and values, which Hawthorne addresses in his story of Hester Prynne in the era of Puritanism.

Cultural Context

The **cultural context** of a piece of literature refers to cultural factors, such as the beliefs, religions, and customs that surround and are in a work of literature. The Puritan's beliefs, religion, and customs in Hawthorne's novel would be significant as they are at the core of the plot—the reason Hester wears the A and why Arthur kills himself. The customs of people in the Antebellum Period, though not quite as restrictive, were still somewhat similar. This would impact how the audience of the time received the novel.

Literary Context

Literary context refers to the consideration of the genre, potentially at the time the work was written. In 1850, Realism and Romanticism were the driving forces in literature in the U.S., with depictions of life as it was at the time in which the work was written or the time it was written *about* as well as some works celebrating the beauty of nature. Thus, an audience in Hawthorne's time would have been well satisfied with the elements of both offered in the text. They would have been looking for details about everyday things and people (Realism), but they also would appreciate his approach to description of nature and the focus on the individual (American Romanticism). The contexts would be significant as they would pertain to evaluating the work against those criteria.

Here are some questions to use when considering context:

- When was the text written?
- What was society like at the time the text was written, or what was it like, given the work's identified time period?
- Who or what influenced the writer?
- What political or social influences might there have been?

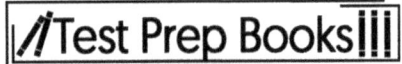

- What influences may there have been in the genre that may have affected the writer?

Additionally, test takers should familiarize themselves with literary periods such as Old and Middle English, American Colonial, American Renaissance, American Naturalistic, and British and American Modernist and Post-Modernist movements. Most students of literature will have had extensive exposure to these literary periods in history, and while it is not necessary to recognize every major literary work on sight and associate that work to its corresponding movement or cultural context, the test taker should be familiar enough with the historical and cultural significance of each test passage in order to be able to address test questions correctly.

The following brief description of some literary contexts and their associated literary examples follows. It is not an all-inclusive list. The test taker should read each description, then follow up with independent study to clarify each movement, its context, its most familiar authors, and their works.

Metaphysical Poetry

Metaphysical poetry is the descriptor applied to 17th century poets whose poetry emphasized the lyrical quality of their work. These works contain highly creative poetic conceits or metaphoric comparisons between two highly dissimilar things or ideas. **Metaphysical poetry** is characterized by highly prosaic language and complicated, often layered, metaphor.

Poems such as John Donne's "The Flea," Andrew Marvell's "To His Coy Mistress," George Herbert's "The Collar," Henry Vaughan's "The World," and Richard Crashaw's "A Song" are associated with this type of poetry.

British Romanticism

British Romanticism was a cultural and literary movement within Europe that developed at the end of the 18th century and extended into the 19th century. It occurred partly in response to aristocratic, political, and social norms and partly in response to the Industrial Revolution of the day. Characterized by intense emotion, major literary works of **British Romanticism** embrace the idea of aestheticism and the beauty of nature. Literary works exalted folk customs and historical art and encouraged spontaneity of artistic endeavor. The movement embraced the heroic ideal and the concept that heroes would raise the quality of society.

Authors who are classified as British Romantics include Samuel Taylor Coleridge, John Keats, George Byron, Mary Shelley, Percy Bysshe Shelley, and William Blake. Well-known works include Samuel Taylor Coleridge's "Kubla Khan," John Keats's "Ode on a Grecian Urn," George Byron's "Childe Harold's Pilgrimage," Mary Shelley's *Frankenstein*, Percy Bysshe Shelley's "Ode to the West Wind," and William Blake's "The Tyger."

American Romanticism

American Romanticism occurred within the American literary scene beginning early in the 19th century. While many aspects were similar to British Romanticism, it is further characterized as having gothic aspects and the idea that individualism was to be encouraged. **American Romanticism** also embraced the concept of the *noble savage*—the idea that indigenous culture uncorrupted by civilization is better than advanced society.

Well-known authors and works include Nathanial Hawthorne's *The House of the Seven Gables*, Edgar Allan Poe's "The Raven" and "The Cask of Amontillado," Emily Dickinson's "I Felt a Funeral in My Brain" and James Fenimore Cooper's *The Last of the Mohicans*.

Transcendentalism

Transcendentalism was a movement that applied to a way of thinking that developed within the United States, specifically New England, around 1836. While this way of thinking originally employed philosophical aspects, **transcendentalism** spread to all forms of art, literature, and even to the ways people chose to live. It was born out of a reaction to traditional rationalism and purported concepts such as a higher divinity, feminism, humanitarianism, and communal living. Transcendentalism valued intuition, self-reliance, and the idea that human nature was inherently good.

Well-known authors include Ralph Waldo Emerson, Henry David Thoreau, Louisa May Alcott, and Ellen Sturgis Hooper. Works include Ralph Waldo Emerson's "Self-Reliance" and "Uriel," Henry David Thoreau's *Walden* and *Civil Disobedience*, Louisa May Alcott's *Little Women*, and Ellen Sturgis Hooper's "I Slept, and Dreamed that Life was Beauty."

The Harlem Renaissance

The Harlem Renaissance is the descriptor given to the cultural, artistic, and social boom that developed in Harlem, New York, at the beginning of the 20th century, spanning the 1920s and 1930s. Originally termed *The New Negro Movement*, it emphasized African American urban cultural expression and migration across the United States. It had strong roots in African American Christianity, discourse, and intellectualism. The **Harlem Renaissance** heavily influenced the development of music and fashion as well. Its singular characteristic was to embrace Pan-American culturalisms; however, strong themes of the slavery experience and African American folk traditions also emerged. A hallmark of the Harlem Renaissance was that it laid the foundation for the future Civil Rights Movement in the United States.

Well-known authors and works include Zora Neale Hurston's *Their Eyes Were Watching God*, Richard Wright's *Native Son*, Langston Hughes' "I, Too," and James Weldon Johnson's "God's Trombones: Seven Negro Sermons in Verse" and *The Book of American Negro Poetry*.

History of the Novel's Development

Eighteenth Century

The novel as it is known today first appeared in the eighteenth century. The word **novel** comes from the Italian word *novella,* which means new, referring to a new type of writing. Before this time, prose existed, but it wasn't realistic. Religion's hold over literature started to wane at this time, and authors began to write about the world around them. The novel was popularized by the use of realistic characters, set in real geographical locations and engaged in real-life situations. The earliest novels included *Robinson Crusoe* and *Moll Flanders* by Daniel Defoe. These works used the common man and woman as characters, unlike the prose that came before them, which used plots that centered on heroes, legends, and gods. Other popular novelists of this time included Jonathan Swift, Henry Fielding, and Samuel Richardson. Swift's *Gulliver's Travels* is considered an early version of the fantasy novel. The novel also flourished at this time with the growth of the printing industry. Books were readily available, and for the first time, the middle class was able to afford them. Many of the readers of these realistic stories were women. Writers took this into account and created characters that represented a wider range of people, including women and the middle class. For example, in the late eighteenth century, Jane Austen's books were populated with female characters, and Defoe's books centered on the common man. Another development that aided the popularity of novels in the eighteenth century was the creation of libraries. The ability to borrow books made literature much more widely available to lower classes, and novels flourished in this environment.

Nineteenth Century

The trend in nineteenth-century novels was again realism. Characters and settings were realistic, and they encountered realistic situations. Some of the most important and critically acclaimed novelists come out of this era, including Jane Austen, Charles Dickens, and the Bronte sisters. Austen's novels such as *Pride and Prejudice* and *Sense and Sensibility* were extremely popular and dealt with the issue of women and their dependence on marriage in the nineteenth century for social status and economic standing. Dickens' work focused on the people of London in the Victorian age. He used realistic characters and injected humor into his works, such as *Great Expectations* and *Oliver Twist*.

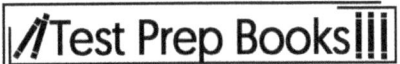

In America, writers like Nathaniel Hawthorne and Mark Twain were crafting the great American novel. Twain's *Adventures of Huckleberry Finn* and Hawthorne's *The Scarlet Letter* are revered as some of the best novels of all time, each making social commentary on the American experience. Hawthorne's work in particular featured the people of Puritan New England. His work often made social commentary on his anti-Puritan views. Hawthorne was considered part of a dark Romantic movement, focusing on themes of intense emotion such as horror, apprehension, and awe. Edgar Allan Poe was also part of the Romantic movement, and his novels included these same themes, particularly horror.

Twentieth Century

The novel continued its popularity in the twentieth century. Novelists such as George Orwell, James Joyce, F. Scott Fitzgerald, Ernest Hemingway, John Steinbeck, Edith Wharton, Toni Morrison, and Franz Kafka developed novels that are still read in high school classrooms all over the world. Varying subtypes of the novel developed at this time as well. Because of the great number of novels being written, they could be classified into categories such as romance, science fiction, mystery, fantasy, and historical fiction. The science fiction novel was even further popularized by authors such as George Orwell and H. G. Wells. Readers loved this new type of novel, and Wells' *War of the Worlds* was famously read on the radio in 1938, sparking fear in listeners that it was an actual news report of an invasion by Martians.

The first part of the century focused on modernism in literature, which centered more on the decline in civilization. Authors such as D. H. Lawrence and James Joyce wrote modernist novels, with Joyce's *Ulysses* being a prime example. Virginia Woolf, along with her husband, Leonard Woolf, established the Hogarth Press, which printed her own books as well as works by T. S. Eliot. Woolf's works, such as *Mrs. Dalloway* and *To the Lighthouse,* were experimental in form, and she is considered the foremost lyrical novelist of her time. Other authors were developing their own type of novels with writers like Agatha Christie popularizing the mystery novel in the 1930s.

The world was profoundly changed by World War I and World War II, and this can be seen in the novels of the second half of the twentieth century. Postwar novelists were from many different backgrounds as a reflection of the changes in the world after the war. They were the children of immigrants in America, and authors such as Truman Capote and Tennessee Williams are homosexual or bisexual. Many novelists wrote about World War II and its impact, such as Norman Mailer's critically acclaimed *The Naked and the Dead*, published in 1948. Mailer used journalistic style in his account of the lives of a platoon of soldiers stationed in the Pacific during World War II. Joseph Heller's *Catch 22,* written after his own experience as a bombardier in the US Air Force, took a more satirical approach to the war and is considered an example of dark surrealism. Postwar novels were also influenced by the Beat movement, with Jack Kerouac's *On the Road* being one of the prime examples of this movement.

Twenty-First Century

The twenty-first century saw a blurring of the lines of fiction. Novelists tended to cross genres, combining the elements of romance, fantasy, science fiction, and mystery into one book. The Young Adult category was created and gained much popularity with adult readers. An example of this is the Harry Potter series by J. K. Rowling. These novels cannot be confined to a category, as they contain elements of mystery, fantasy, and romance. They were also intended for young adults but were widely read by both children and adults alike. Another important development was the advancement of the graphic novel, which combines art along with the narrative. More than a comic book, the first graphic novel was published in the late twentieth century, but it became more widely published in the twenty-first century. Graphic novels are written in many genres, but supernatural themes are widely used. The so-called death of print also has an effect on the novel as e-books and e-readers become available.

The Short Story

The short story is a work of prose fiction that is typically much shorter than a novel. It is meant to be read in one sitting. Because of its length, the short story focuses on just one plot, with a single main character, central theme, and minimal secondary characters. There is no set length of a short story, though they are typically between one thousand and twenty thousand words. The idea of a short story dates back to the time of oral traditions such as fables, parables, and fairy tales. The father of the modern American short story is said to be Edgar Allan Poe. His works are widely used as an example of the short story. Other important short story writers include Ernest Hemingway, James Joyce, and Joyce Carol Oates.

The structure of the short story is similar to that of a novel, but it differs in that a novel may contain multiple themes, plots, or characters, and a short story typically contains just one of each. The short story focuses on a single main character who faces a challenge. The plot of the short story is the arrangement of the events. Many short story authors use a chronological order of events, telling the story from beginning to end in the order that it happened. Other authors break from this chronological order using devices such as flashback. Telling the events out of order can have an effect on the writing, creating suspense or allowing the reader to have knowledge of a later event throughout the story. An example of flashback would be revealing the ending at the beginning of the story. The effect might be to show that the journey is more important than the destination. Short stories usually contain a singular central theme. The theme is the overall idea that an author wants to convey. It can also be considered a lesson in some short stories. Setting is where and when a short story takes place. Setting can refer to time of day, time of year, or time in history. Other elements, such as the author's point of view, symbolism, and imagery, are important elements to the structure of a short story.

History of the Short Story's Development

Middle Ages

Like the poetry of the Middle Ages, fiction was also influenced by religion. While the short story wasn't actually called this, it did exist in some forms. At this time, it was more like a tale than the formal short story format of today. These tales were a reflection of the norms of the cultures that created them. The most notable form was written by author Geoffrey Chaucer. His *Canterbury Tales* is a collection of short narrative works about a group of Pilgrims on a journey from London to Canterbury Cathedral. This work is well loved for its vivid characters and is widely accepted as a predecessor to the modern short story. *The Canterbury Tales* is also significant because it was one of the first major works of literature written in the English language. After this time, works of short fiction saw a decline in the seventeenth and eighteenth centuries in favor of other types of literature.

Nineteenth Century

The modern short story as it's known today was created in the nineteenth century. Short story writers emerged in both Europe and America. Perhaps the most famous of these writers was Edgar Allan Poe. Poe's tales of horror such as "The Telltale Heart" and "The Cask of Amontillado" included all the elements of the modern short story, such as a single main character or narrator, a limited setting, and a singular central theme. Another subgenre that emerged at this time was southern gothic writing, which centered on the American South. The characters in these stories were deeply flawed and even disturbed. Rural communities were often the setting in the works of authors such as William Faulkner and Flannery O'Connor. O'Connor's "Good Country People" is an example of a southern gothic story, set in rural Georgia, populated by the common people of the South. O'Connor used this setting to make social commentary on the lack of vision or knowledge of these people.

Other important short story writers from this time included Nathaniel Hawthorne, Mark Twain, and Guy de Maupassant. Modernism was an important literary movement in the late nineteenth century, and the short story was influenced by it. Examples of the modernist movement can be seen in Anton Chekhov's "Gusev," the story of discharged soldiers dying of consumption. The late nineteenth century also included more women authors, and works by Charlotte Perkins Gilman and Kate Chopin were published. Kate Chopin wrote important short stories about women's issues, such as independence and their reliance on marriage for status. Chopin's most popular works include "Paul's Case," "Desiree's Baby," and "The Story of an Hour."

Twentieth Century

The short story continued to gain popularity in the twentieth century. Many writers of poems, plays, and novels also began to produce short stories. Writers such as Ernest Hemingway, William Faulkner, D. H. Lawrence, Kate Chopin, and James Joyce published short stories in addition to their other works at this time. Short story writers found a forum for their work in magazine format. This was the perfect way to deliver these short narratives to readers. Writers often found they could finance their larger projects such as novels and plays by selling short stories to magazines. Herman Melville said that he hated writing stories and only did so to make money.

The rise of the film industry took its toll on the short story and decreased the need for these short works. In turn, the short story also began to evolve into a new format. Writers in the nineteenth century were more concerned with plot and its resolution. In the second half of the twentieth century, short story authors began to experiment with form and often centered their stories on motifs rather than plot. Writers like Raymond Carver revived the short story a bit through this experimentation with form, and though the short story still exists today, it has never again reached the heights it did in the early part of the twentieth century.

Informational Text

Nonfiction Prose

Nonfiction works are best characterized by their subject matter, which must be factual and real, describing true life experiences. There are several common types of literary non-fiction.

Biography

A biography is a work written about a real person (historical or currently living). It involves factual accounts of the person's life, often in a re-telling of those events based on available, researched factual information. The re-telling and dialogue, especially if related within quotes, must be accurate and reflect reliable sources. A **biography** reflects the time and place in which the person lived, with the goal of creating an understanding of the person and their human experience. Examples of well-known biographies include *The Life of Samuel Johnson* by James Boswell and *Steve Jobs* by Walter Isaacson.

Autobiography

An autobiography is a factual account of a person's life written by that person. It may contain some or all of the same elements as a biography, but the author is the subject matter. An **autobiography** will be told in first person narrative. Examples of well-known autobiographies in literature include *Night* by Elie Wiesel and *Margaret Thatcher: The Autobiography* by Margaret Thatcher.

Memoir

A memoir is a historical account of a person's life and experiences written by one who has personal, intimate knowledge of the information. The line between memoir, autobiography, and biography is often muddled, but generally speaking, a memoir covers a specific timeline of events as opposed to the other forms of nonfiction. A **memoir** is less all-encompassing. It is also less formal in tone and tends to focus on the emotional aspect of the presented timeline of events. Some examples of memoirs in literature include *Angela's Ashes* by Frank McCourt and *All Creatures Great and Small* by James Herriot.

Journalism

Some forms of **journalism** can fall into the category of literary non-fiction—e.g., travel writing, nature writing, sports writing, the interview, and sometimes, the essay. Some examples include Elizabeth Kolbert's "The Lost World, in the Annals of Extinction series for *The New Yorker* and Gary Smith's "Ali and His Entourage" for ***Sports Illustrated.***

The Essay

An essay is a short piece of nonfiction writing. It typically uses the opinion of the author on a single subject. Essay authors can write about virtually any subject, as there are no rules for the content of an essay. It is often used to convey a point about a subject but can also be written simply for pleasure. **Essays** can make use of different writing modes, such as argument, persuasion, causal analysis, critique, or observation. They can be formal or informal, serious in tone, satirical, or even humorous. Organization is up to the author and does not follow any strict rules. Virginia Woolf wrote a series of essays, most notably about the struggle for survival in her essay "Death of a Moth." George Orwell's essay "Shooting an Elephant" includes his graphic account of shooting an elephant as social commentary on anti-colonialism.

The Speech

A speech is a formal address meant to be spoken aloud to an audience. The purpose of a speech can vary, but it is typically to persuade, argue, inform, or inspire the audience. **Speeches** can be political in nature but don't have to be. Some of the most famous speeches include Martin Luther King's "I Have a Dream" speech, Abraham Lincoln's Gettysburg Address, and John F. Kennedy's inaugural address. Some important components of a speech are the style, substance, and impact of the words. While the writing of a speech is important, the delivery is important as well.

Speeches can be delivered in four methods: **impromptu**, with little to no preparation; **extemporaneous**, which involves preparation but is not read directly from cards; **manuscript**, which is read directly from a script or teleprompter; and **memorized**, which is a written speech delivered from the speaker's memory. The speech delivery type depends on the situation and reaction a speaker wants from the audience. Extemporaneous speaking is the most common delivery method, and many great speakers have used this format because it appears more natural to the audience. It is widely known that Martin Luther King's "I Have a Dream" speech was delivered extemporaneously, as he largely improvised the second half of the speech, including the portion where he states, "I have a dream." George W. Bush's Bullhorn speech, delivered at ground zero on September 14, 2001, in the wake of the September 11 terror attacks, is an example of an impromptu speech. Though he had not planned to speak at the event and was even advised against it, Bush took a bullhorn and spoke to the crowd, aiming to lift the spirits of a broken nation, delivering a memorable impromptu speech.

Visual and Performing Arts Reviews

Visual and performing arts includes film, theater, poetry performance, photography, painting, sculpting, public speech, dance, and music. Anything performed for a live audience is in the realm of this genre. A passage in the GED may be a critical review of one of these performances. Critical reviews go deeper than simply summary; they analyze the work with thoughtfulness to each of its components and how they relate to its contribution to the artform. For example, a reviewer might raise the question of how a photographer's use of light lends to the meaning of the subject in the photo. In visual and performing arts, meaning goes beyond subject; there are usually multiple components that enhance a piece's meaning, such as a dancer's technique within a solo. In order to analyze successfully, reviewers and test takers must be aware of critical theory and historical contexts. This will aid test takers in understanding how the reviewers go beyond summary of an artwork.

Workplace and Community Documents

Following a Given Set of Directions

When you read a comic or magazine, it's not necessary to understand everything. However, other more technical readings, such as directions for setting up a coffeemaker or a new phone app, require more attention to detail. Read each step all the way through, and don't skip ahead. While you may think that you know all or some of the steps, it's important to read directions in the manner that the writer intended. This aids in comprehension and ensures that you catch all relevant information. Take your time and reread sentences and passages if necessary. Look up unfamiliar words or concepts, and jot comments, called annotations, in the margins.

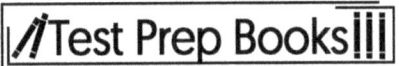

Identifying Specific Information from a Printed Communication
While expository in nature, memorandums (memos) are designed to convey basic information in a specific and concise message. Memos have a heading, which includes the information **to**, **from**, **date**, and **subject**, and a body, which is either in paragraph form or bullet points that detail what was in the subject line.

Though e-mails often replace memos in the modern workplace, printed memos still have a place. For example, if a supervisor wants to relate information, such as a company-wide policy change, to a large group, posting a memo in a staff lounge or other heavily traveled area is an efficient way to do so.

Posted announcements are useful to convey information to a large group of people. Announcements, however, take on a more informal tone than a memo. Common announcement topics include items for sale, services offered, lost pets, or business openings. Since posted announcements are found in public places, like grocery or hardware stores, they include contact information, purpose, meeting times, and prices, as well as pictures, graphics, and colors to attract the reader's eye.

Classified advertisements are another useful medium to convey information to large groups. Consider using classified advertisements when you want to buy and sell items or look for services. Classified ads are found in newspapers, or online through **Craigslist**, **eBay**, or similar websites and blogs. While newspapers rely on ads to help fund their publications and often provide only local exposure, online sites provide a statewide or even global platform, thus shipping costs are an important consideration when looking at the cost of the item.

Regardless of the medium, all advertisements offer basic information, such as the item in question, a description, picture, cost, and the seller's contact information. It may also note a willingness to negotiate on the price or offer an option to trade in lieu of a sale. As websites like **Craigslist** and **Buy/Sell/Trade** increase in popularity, more localities offer "safe zones," where purchases and trades are conducted in supervised environments.

Identifying Information from a Graphic Representation of Information
Texts may have graphic representations to help illustrate and visually support assertions made. For example, graphics can be used to express samples or segments of a population or demonstrate growth or decay. Three of the most popular graphic formats include line graphs, bar graphs, and pie charts.

Line graphs rely on a horizontal X axis and a vertical Y axis to establish baseline values. Dots are plotted where the horizontal and vertical axes intersect, and those dots are connected with lines. Compared to bar graphs or pie charts, line graphs are more useful for looking at the past and present and predicting future outcomes. For instance, a potential investor would look for stocks that demonstrated steady growth over many decades when examining the stock market. Note that severe spikes up and down indicate instability, while line graphs that display a slow but steady increase may indicate good returns.

Bar graphs are usually displayed on a vertical Y axis. The bars themselves can be two- or three-dimensional, depending on the designer's tastes. Unlike a line graph, which shows the fluctuation of only one variable, the X axis on a bar graph is excellent for making comparisons, because it shows differences between several variables. For instance, if a consumer wanted to buy a new tablet, she could narrow the selection down to a few choices by using a bar graph to plot the prices side by side. The tallest bar would be the most expensive tablet, the shortest bar would be the cheapest.

A pie chart is divided into wedges that represent a numerical piece of the whole. Pie charts are useful for demonstrating how different categories add up to 100 percent. However, pie charts are not useful in comparing dissimilar items. High schools tend to use pie charts to track where students end up after graduation. Each wedge, for instance, might be labeled **vocational school**, **two-year college**, **four-year college**, **workforce**, or **unemployed**. By calculating the size of each wedge, schools can offer classes in the same ratios as where students will end up after high school. Pie charts are also useful for tracking finances. Items such as car payments, insurance, rent, credit cards, and entertainment would each get their own wedge proportional to the amount spent in a given time period. If one wedge is inordinately bigger than the rest, or if a wedge is expendable, it might be time to create a new financial strategy.

Identifying Scale Readings

Most measuring instruments have scales to allow someone to determine precise measurement. Many of these instruments are becoming digitized, such as their screens' output measurements; for example, weighing scales and tire-pressure gauges often have digital screens. However, it's still important to know how to read scales. Many rulers have scales for inches on one side and scales for centimeters on the other side. On the inches' side, the longest black lines indicate the inch marks, and the slightly shorter lines indicate the half-inch marks. Progressively shorter black lines indicate the quarter-inch, eighth-inch, and sometimes even sixteenth-inch marks.

Using Legends and Map Keys

Legends and map keys are placed on maps to identify what the symbols on the map represent. Generally, map symbols stand for things like railroads, national or state highways, and public parks. Legends and maps keys can generally be found in the bottom right corner of a map. They are necessary to avoid the needless repetition of the same information because of the large amounts of information condensed onto a map. In addition, there may be a compass rose that shows the directions of north, south, east, and west. Most maps are oriented such that the top of the map is north.

Maps also have scales, which are a type of legend or key that show relative distances between fixed points. If you were on a highway and nearly out of gas, a map's scale would help you determine if you could make it to the next town before running out of fuel.

Evaluating Product Information to Determine the Most Economical Buy

When evaluating product information, be on the lookout for bolded and italicized words and numbers, which indicate the information is especially important. Also be on the lookout for repeated or similar information, which indicates importance. If you're trying to find the best deal, it might be useful to do a side-by-side comparison. Using software, like Microsoft Excel, can help you organize and compare costs systematically.

In addition, being a savvy shopper in today's market means not only having a decent grasp of math, but also understanding how retailers use established techniques to encourage consumers to spend more. Look for units of measurement—pounds, ounces, liters, grams, etc.—then divide the amount by the cost. By comparing this way, you may find products on sale cost more than ones that are not.

You should also take into consideration any tax or shipping costs. Obviously, the more an item costs, the more tax or shipping tends to cost too. Most brick-and-mortar establishments, like Target, Walmart, and Sears, are required to charge tax based on location, but some internet sites, like Amazon, Overstock, and eBay, will offer no tax or free shipping as an incentive. Comparisons between local stores and internet sites can aid in finding the best deal.

Reading Practice Quiz

The next five questions are based on the following passage:

As long ago as 1860 it was the proper thing to be born at home. At present, so I am told, the high gods of medicine have decreed that the first cries of the young shall be uttered upon the anesthetic air of a hospital, preferably a fashionable one. So young Mr. and Mrs. Roger Button were fifty years ahead of style when they decided, one day in the summer of 1860, that their first baby should be born in a hospital. Whether this anachronism had any bearing upon the astonishing history I am about to set down will never be known.

I shall tell you what occurred, and let you judge for yourself.

The Roger Buttons held an enviable position, both social and financial, in ante-bellum Baltimore. They were related to the This Family and the That Family, which, as every Southerner knew, entitled them to membership in that enormous peerage which largely populated the Confederacy. This was their first experience with the charming old custom of having babies—Mr. Button was naturally nervous. He hoped it would be a boy so that he could be sent to Yale College in Connecticut, at which institution Mr. Button himself had been known for four years by the somewhat obvious nickname of "Cuff."

On the September morning consecrated to the enormous event he arose nervously at six o'clock, dressed himself, adjusted an impeccable stock, and hurried forth through the streets of Baltimore to the hospital, to determine whether the darkness of the night had borne in new life upon its bosom.

When he was approximately a hundred yards from the Maryland Private Hospital for Ladies and Gentlemen, he saw Doctor Keene, the family physician, descending the front steps, rubbing his hands together with a washing movement—as all doctors are required to do by the unwritten ethics of their profession.

Mr. Roger Button, the president of Roger Button & Co., Wholesale Hardware, began to run toward Doctor Keene with much less dignity than was expected from a Southern gentleman of that picturesque period. "Doctor Keene!" he called. "Oh, Doctor Keene!"

The doctor heard him, faced around, and stood waiting, a curious expression settling on his harsh, medicinal face as Mr. Button drew near.

"What happened?" demanded Mr. Button, as he came up in a gasping rush. "What was it? How is she? A boy? Who is it? What—"

"Talk sense!" said Doctor Keene sharply. He appeared somewhat irritated.

"Is the child born?" begged Mr. Button.

Doctor Keene frowned. "Why, yes, I suppose so—after a fashion." Again he threw a curious glance at Mr. Button.

From The Curious Case of Benjamin Button by F.S. Fitzgerald, 1922.

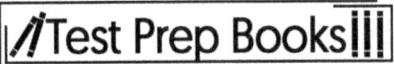

Reading

1. According to the passage, what major event is about to happen in this story?
    a. Mr. Button is about to go to a funeral.
    b. Mr. Button's wife is about to have a baby.
    c. Mr. Button is getting ready to go to the doctor's office.
    d. Mr. Button is about to go shopping for new clothes.

2. What kind of tone does the above passage have?
    a. Nervous and Excited
    b. Sad and Angry
    c. Irate and Belligerent
    d. Grateful and Joyous

3. As it is used in the fourth paragraph, the word *consecrated* most nearly means:
    a. Numbed
    b. Chained
    c. Dedicated
    d. Moved

4. What does the author mean to do by adding the following statement?
    "rubbing his hands together with a washing movement—as all doctors are required to do by the unwritten ethics of their profession."
    a. Suggesting that Mr. Button is tired of the doctor
    b. Trying to explain the detail of the doctor's profession
    c. Hinting to readers that the doctor is an unethical man
    d. Giving readers a visual picture of what the doctor is doing

5. Which of the following best describes the development of this passage?
    a. It starts in the middle of a narrative in order to transition smoothly to a conclusion
    b. It is a chronological narrative from beginning to end
    c. The sequence of events is backwards—we go from future events to past events
    d. To introduce the setting of the story and its characters

See answers on the next page.

Reading Answer Explanations

1. B: Mr. Button's wife is about to have a baby. The passage begins by giving the reader information about traditional birthing situations. Then, we are told that Mr. and Mrs. Button decide to go against tradition to have their baby in a hospital. The next few passages are dedicated to letting the reader know how Mr. Button dresses and goes to the hospital to welcome his new baby. There is a doctor in this excerpt, as Choice *C* indicates, and Mr. Button does put on clothes, as Choice *D* indicates. However, Mr. Button is not going to the doctor's office nor is he about to go shopping for new clothes.

2. A: The tone of the above passage is nervous and excited. We are told in the fourth paragraph that Mr. Button "arose nervously." We also see him running without caution to the doctor to find out about his wife and baby—this indicates his excitement. We also see him stuttering in a nervous yet excited fashion as he asks the doctor if it's a boy or girl.

3. C: Dedicated. Mr. Button is dedicated to the task before him. Choice *A*, *numbed*, Choice *B*, *chained*, and Choice *D*, *moved*, all could grammatically fit in the sentence. However, they are not synonyms with *consecrated* like Choice *C* is.

4. D: Giving readers a visual picture of what the doctor is doing. The author describes a visual image—the doctor rubbing his hands together—first and foremost. The author may be trying to make a comment about the profession; however, the author does not "explain the detail of the doctor's profession" as Choice *B* suggests.

5. D: To introduce the setting of the story and its characters. We know we are being introduced to the setting because we are given the year in the very first paragraph along with the season: "one day in the summer of 1860." This is a classic structure of an introduction of the setting. We are also getting a long explanation of Mr. Button, what his work is, who is related to him, and what his life is like in the third paragraph.

Writing

Position and Support

Addressing the Significance and Complexity of the Issue and Context

Taking a position is an essential part of an argumentative or persuasive piece of writing. These essays involve logical and relevant proof for a claim or an assertion. Regarded as a more sophisticated form of writing, argumentative or persuasive writing works to change the point of view of the readers or ignite a call-to-action response. This form of writing does not shy away from contradicting points of view but, instead, brings them to light and then works to disprove or discredit each opposing claim. Some examples of argumentative or persuasive writing include essays, reviews, and letters to the editor.

Basic Essay Writing

Brainstorming

One of the most important steps in writing an essay is prewriting. Before drafting an essay, it's helpful to think about the topic for a moment or two, in order to gain a more solid understanding of the task. Then, spending about five minutes jotting down the immediate ideas that could work for the essay is recommended. It is a way to get some words on the page and offer a reference for ideas when drafting. Scratch paper is provided for writers to use any prewriting techniques such as webbing, free writing, or listing. The goal is to get ideas out of the mind and onto the page.

Considering Opposing Viewpoints

In the planning stage, it's important to consider all aspects of the topic, including different viewpoints on the subject. There are more than two ways to look at a topic, and a strong argument considers those opposing viewpoints. Considering opposing viewpoints can help writers present a fair, balanced, and informed essay that shows consideration for all readers. This approach can also strengthen an argument by recognizing and potentially refuting opposing viewpoint(s).

Drawing from personal experience may help to support ideas. For example, if the goal for writing is a personal narrative, then the story should come from the writer's own life. Many writers find it helpful to draw from personal experience, even in an essay that is not strictly narrative. Personal anecdotes or short stories can help to illustrate a point in other types of essays as well.

Moving from Brainstorming to Planning

Once the ideas are on the page, it's time to turn them into a solid plan for the essay. The best ideas from the brainstorming results can then be developed into a more formal outline. An outline typically has one main point (the thesis) and at least three sub-points that support the main point. Here's an example:

Main Idea

- Point #1
- Point #2
- Point #3

Of course, there will be details under each point, but this approach is the best for dealing with timed writing.

Writing

Staying on Track

Basing the essay on the outline aids in both organization and coherence. The goal is to ensure that there is enough time to develop each sub-point in the essay, roughly spending an equal amount of time on each idea. Keeping an eye on the time will help. If there are fifteen minutes left to draft the essay, then it makes sense to spend about 5 minutes on each of the ideas. Staying on task is critical to success, and timing out the parts of the essay can help writers avoid feeling overwhelmed.

Parts of the Essay

The introduction has to do a few important things:

- Establish the topic of the essay in original wording (i.e., not just repeating the prompt)
- Clarify the significance/importance of the topic or purpose for writing (not too many details, a brief overview)
- Offer a thesis statement that identifies the writer's own viewpoint on the topic (typically one-two brief sentences as a clear, concise explanation of the main point on the topic)

Body paragraphs reflect the ideas developed in the outline. Three-four points is probably sufficient for a short essay, and they should include the following:

- A topic sentence that identifies the sub-point (e.g., a reason why, a way how, a cause or effect)
- A detailed explanation of the point, explaining why the writer thinks this point is valid
- Illustrative examples, such as personal examples or real-world examples, that support and validate the point (i.e., "prove" the point)
- A concluding sentence that connects the examples, reasoning, and analysis to the point being made

The conclusion, or final paragraph, should be brief and should reiterate the focus, clarifying why the discussion is significant or important. It is important to avoid adding specific details or new ideas to this paragraph. The purpose of the conclusion is to sum up what has been said to bring the discussion to a close.

Don't Panic!

Writing an essay can be overwhelming, and performance panic is a natural response. The outline serves as a basis for the writing and helps writers keep focused. Getting stuck can also happen, and it's helpful to remember that brainstorming can be done at any time during the writing process. Following the steps of the writing process is the best defense against writer's block.

Timed essays can be particularly stressful, but assessors are trained to recognize the necessary planning and thinking for these timed efforts. Using the plan above and sticking to it helps with time management. Timing each part of the process helps writers stay on track. Sometimes writers try to cover too much in their essays. If time seems to be running out, this is an opportunity to determine whether all of the ideas in the outline are necessary. Three body paragraphs are sufficient, and more than that is probably too much to cover in a short essay.

More isn't always better in writing. A strong essay will be clear and concise. It will avoid unnecessary or repetitive details. It is better to have a concise, five-paragraph essay that makes a clear point, than a ten-paragraph essay that doesn't. The goal is to write one to two pages of quality writing. Paragraphs should also reflect balance; if the introduction goes to the bottom of the first page, the writing may be going off-track or be repetitive. It's best to fall into the one-two page range, but a complete, well-developed essay is the ultimate goal.

Presenting Persuasive Arguments

The Steps of an Argument

Strong arguments tend to follow a fairly defined format. In the introduction, background information regarding the problem is shared, the implications of the issue are stated, and the author's thesis or claims are given. Supporting evidence is then presented in the body paragraphs, along with the counterargument, which then gets refuted with specific evidence. Lastly, in the conclusion, the author summarizes the points and claims again.

Evidence Used to Support a Claim or Conclusion

Premises are the evidence or facts supporting why a **conclusion** is logical and valid. Take the following argument for example:

> Julie is a Canadian track athlete. She is the star of the number one collegiate team in the country. Her times are consistently at the top of national rankings. Julie is extremely likely to represent Canada at the upcoming Olympics.

In this example, the conclusion is that she will likely be on the Canadian Olympic team. The author supports this conclusion with two premises. First, Julie is the star of an elite track team. Second, she runs some of the best times of the country. This is the *why* behind the conclusion. The following builds off this basic argument:

> Julie is a Canadian track athlete. She's the star of the number one collegiate team in the country. Her times are consistently at the top of national rankings. Julie is extremely likely to represent Canada at the upcoming Olympics. Julie will continue to develop after the Olympic trials. She will be a frontrunner for the gold. Julie is likely to become a world-famous track star.

These additions to the argument make the conclusion different. Now, the conclusion is that Julie is likely to become a world-famous track star. The previous conclusion, Julie will likely be on the Olympic team, functions as a **sub-conclusion** in this argument. Like conclusions, premises must adequately support sub-conclusions. However, sub-conclusions function like premises, since sub-conclusions also support the overall conclusion.

Determining Whether Evidence is Relevant and Sufficient

A **hasty generalization** involves an argument relying on insufficient statistical data or inaccurately generalizing. One common generalization occurs when a group of individuals under observation have some quality or attribute that is asserted to be universal or true for a much larger number of people than actually documented. Here's an example of a hasty generalization:

> A man smokes a lot of cigarettes, but so did his grandfather. The grandfather smoked nearly two packs per day since his World War II service until he died at ninety years of age. Continuing to smoke cigarettes will clearly not impact the grandson's long-term health.

This argument is a hasty generalization because it assumes that one person's addiction and lack of consequences will naturally be reflected in a different individual. There is no reasonable justification for such extrapolation. It is common knowledge that any smoking is detrimental to everyone's health. The fact that the man's grandfather smoked two packs per day and lived a long life has no logical connection with the grandson engaging in similar behavior. The hasty generalization doesn't take into account other reasons behind the grandfather's longevity. Nor does the author offer evidence that might support the idea that the man would share a similar lifetime if he smokes. It might be different if the author stated that the man's family shares some genetic trait rendering them immune to the effects of tar and chemicals on the lungs.

Determining Whether a Statement Is or Is Not Supported

The basic tenet of reading comprehension is the ability to read and understand text. One way to understand text is to look for information that supports the author's main idea, topic, or position statement. This information may be factual, or it may be based on the author's opinion.

In order to identify factual information within one or more text passages, begin by looking for statements of fact. Factual statements can be either true or false. Identifying factual statements as opposed to opinion statements is important in demonstrating full command of evidence in reading. For example, the statement *The temperature outside was unbearably hot* may seem like a fact; however, it's not. While anyone can point to a temperature gauge as factual evidence, the statement itself reflects only an opinion. Some people may find the temperature unbearably hot. Others may find it comfortably warm. Thus, the sentence, *The temperature outside was unbearably hot,* reflects the opinion of the author who found it unbearable. If the text passage followed up the sentence with atmospheric conditions indicating heat indices above 140 degrees Fahrenheit, then the reader knows there is factual information that supports the author's assertion of *unbearably hot*.

In looking for information that can be proven or disproven, it's helpful to scan for dates, numbers, timelines, equations, statistics, and other similar data within any given text passage. These types of indicators will point to proven particulars. For example, the statement, *The temperature outside was unbearably hot on that summer day, July 10, 1913,* most likely indicates factual information, even if the reader is unaware that this is the hottest day on record in the United States. Be careful when reading biased words from an author. Biased words indicate opinion, as opposed to fact. See the list of biased words below and keep in mind that it's not an inclusive list:

- Good/bad
- Great/greatest
- Better/best/worst
- Amazing
- Terrible/bad/awful
- Beautiful/handsome/ugly
- More/most
- Exciting/dull/boring
- Favorite
- Very
- Probably/should/seem/possibly

Remember, most of what is written is actually opinion or carefully worded information that seems like fact when it isn't. To say, *duplicating DNA results is not cost-effective* sounds like it could be a scientific fact, but it isn't. Factual information can be verified through independent sources.

The simplest type of test question may provide a text passage, then ask the test taker to distinguish the correct factual supporting statement that best answers the corresponding question on the test. However, be aware that most questions may ask the test taker to read more than one text passage and identify which answer best supports an author's topic. While the ability to identify factual information is critical, these types of questions require the test taker to identify chunks of details, and then relate them to one another.

Assessing Whether an Argument is Valid

Although different from conditions and if/then statements, **reasonableness** is another important foundational concept. Evaluating an argument for reasonableness and validity entails evaluating the evidence presented by the author to justify their conclusions. Everything contained in the argument should be considered, but remember to ignore outside biases, judgments, and knowledge. For the purposes of this test, the test taker is a one-person jury at a criminal trial using a standard of reasonableness under the circumstances presented by the argument.

These arguments are encountered on a daily basis through social media, entertainment, and cable news. An example is:

> Although many believe it to be a natural occurrence, some believe that the red tide that occurs in Florida each year may actually be a result of human sewage and agricultural runoff. However, it is arguable that both natural and human factors contribute to this annual phenomenon. On one hand, the red tide has been occurring every year since the time of explorers like Cabeza de Vaca in the 1500's. On the other hand, the red tide seems to be getting worse each year, and scientists from the Florida Fish & Wildlife Conservation say the bacteria found inside the tide feed off of nutrients found in fertilizer runoff.

The author's conclusion is that both natural phenomena and human activity contribute to the red tide that happens annually in Florida. The author backs this information up by historical data to prove the natural occurrence of the red tide, and then again with scientific data to back up the human contribution to the red tide. Both of these statements are examples of the premises in the argument. Evaluating the strength of the logical connection between the premises and conclusion is how reasonableness is determined. Another example is:

> The local railroad is a disaster. Tickets are exorbitantly priced, bathrooms leak, and the floor is sticky.

The author is clearly unhappy with the railroad service. They cite three examples of why they believe the railroad to be a disaster. An argument more familiar to everyday life is:

> Alexandra said the movie she just saw was amazing. We should go see it tonight.

Although not immediately apparent, this is an argument. The author is making the argument that they should go see the movie. This conclusion is based on the premise that Alexandra said the movie was amazing. There's an inferred note that Alexandra is knowledgeable on the subject, and she's credible enough to prompt her friends to go see the movie. This seems like a reasonable argument. A less reasonable argument is:

> Alexandra is a film student, and she's written the perfect romantic comedy script. We should put our life savings toward its production as an investment in our future.

The author's conclusion is that they should invest their life savings into the production of a movie, and it is justified by referencing Alexandra's credibility and current work. However, the premises are entirely too weak to support the conclusion. Alexandra is only a film *student*, and the script is seemingly her first work. This is not enough evidence to justify investing one's life savings in the film's success.

Assumptions in an Argument

Think of assumptions as unwritten premises. Although they never explicitly appear in the argument, the author is relying on it to defend the argument, just like a premise. Assumptions are the most important part of an argument that will never appear in an argument.

An argument in the abstract is: The author concludes Z based on W and X premises. But the W and X premises actually depend on the unmentioned assumption of Y. Therefore, the author is really saying that X, W, and Y make Z correct, but Y is assumed.

People assume all of the time. Assumptions and inferences allow the human mind to process the constant flow of information. Many assumptions underlie even the most basic arguments. However, in the world of Legal Reasoning arguments, assumptions must be avoided. An argument must be fully presented to be valid; relying on an

Writing

assumption is considered weak. The test requires that test takers identify these underlying assumptions. One example is:

> Peyton Manning is the most over-rated quarterback of all time. He lost more big games than anyone else. Plus, he allegedly assaulted his female trainer in college. Peyton clearly shouldn't make the Hall of Fame.

The author certainly relies on a lot of assumptions. A few assumptions are:

- Peyton Manning plays quarterback.
- He is considered to be a great quarterback by at least some people.
- He played in many big games.
- Allegations and past settlements without any admission of guilt from over a decade ago can be relied upon as evidence against Hall of Fame acceptance.
- The Hall of Fame voters factor in off-the-field incidents, even if true.
- The best players should make the Hall of Fame.
- Losing big games negates, at least in part, the achievement of making it to those big games
- Peyton Manning is retired, and people will vote on whether he makes the Hall of Fame at some point in the future.

The author is relying on all of these assumptions. Some are clearly more important to his argument than others. In fact, disproving a necessary assumption can destroy a premise and possibly an entire conclusion. For example, what if the Hall of Fame did not factor in any of the off-the-field incidents? Then the alleged assault no longer factors into the argument. Even worse, what if making the big games actually was more important than losing those games in the eyes of the Hall of Fame voters? Then the whole conclusion falls apart and is no longer justified if that premise is disproven.

Assumption questions test this exact point by asking the test taker to identify which assumption the argument relies upon. If the author is making numerous assumptions, then the most important *one* assumption must be chosen.

If the author truly relies on an assumption, then the argument will completely fall apart if the assumption isn't true. **Negating** a necessary assumption will *always* make the argument fall apart. This is a universal rule of logic and should be the first thing done in testing answer choices.

Here are some ways that underlying assumptions will appear as questions:

- Which of the following is a hidden assumption that the author makes to advance his argument?
- Which assumption, if true, would support the argument's conclusion (make it more logical)?
- The strength of the argument depends on which of the following?
- Upon which of the following assumptions does the author rely?
- Which assumption does the argument presuppose?

Imagine the following example is a question on a test:

> Frank Underwood is a terrible president. The man is a typical spend, spend, spend liberal. His employment program would exponentially increase the annual deficit and pile on the national debt. Not to mention, Underwood is also on the verge of starting a war with Russia.

Upon which of the following assumptions does the author's argument most rely?
a. Frank Underwood is a terrible president.
b. The United States cannot afford Frank Underwood's policy plans without spending more than the country raises in revenue.
c. No spend, spend, spend liberal has ever succeeded as president.

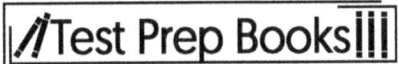

    d. Starting a war with Russia is beneficial to the United States.

Use the negation rule to find the correct answer in the choices below.

Choice *A* is not an assumption—it is the author's conclusion. This type of restatement will never be the correct answer, but test it anyway. After negating the choice, what remains is: *Frank Underwood is a fantastic president.* Does this make the argument fall apart? No, it just becomes the new conclusion. The argument is certainly worse since it does not seem reasonable for someone to praise a president for being a spend, spend, spend liberal or raising the national debt; however, the argument still makes *logical* sense. Eliminate this choice.

Choice *B* is certainly an assumption. It underlies the premises that the country cannot afford Underwood's economic plans. When reversed to: *The United States can afford Frank Underwood's policy plans without spending more than the country raises in revenue,* this destroys the argument. If the United States can afford his plans, then the annual deficit and national debt won't increase; therefore, Underwood being a terrible president would only be based on the final premise. The argument is much weaker without the two sentences involving the financials. Keep it as a benchmark while working through the remaining choices.

Choice *C* is irrelevant. The author is not necessarily claiming that all loose-pocket liberals make for bad presidents. His argument specifically pertains to Underwood. Negate it— *Some spend, spend, spend liberals have succeeded as president.* This does not destroy the argument. Some other candidate could have succeeded as president. However, the author is pointing out that those policies would be disastrous considering the rising budget and debt. The author is not making an appeal to historical precedent. Although not a terrible choice, it is certainly weaker than Choice *B*. Eliminate this choice.

Choice *D* is definitely not an assumption made by the author. The author is assuming that a war with Russia is disastrous. Negate it anyway—*Starting a war with Russia is not beneficial for the United States.* This does not destroy the argument; it makes it stronger. Eliminate this choice.

Supporting arguments through evidence

Data, Graphs, or Pictures as Evidence

Some writing in the test contains **infographics** such as charts, tables, or graphs. In these cases, interpret the information presented and determine how well it supports the claims made in the text. For example, if the writer makes a case that seat belts save more lives than other automobile safety measures, they might want to include a graph (like the one below) showing the number of lives saved by seat belts versus those saved by air bags.

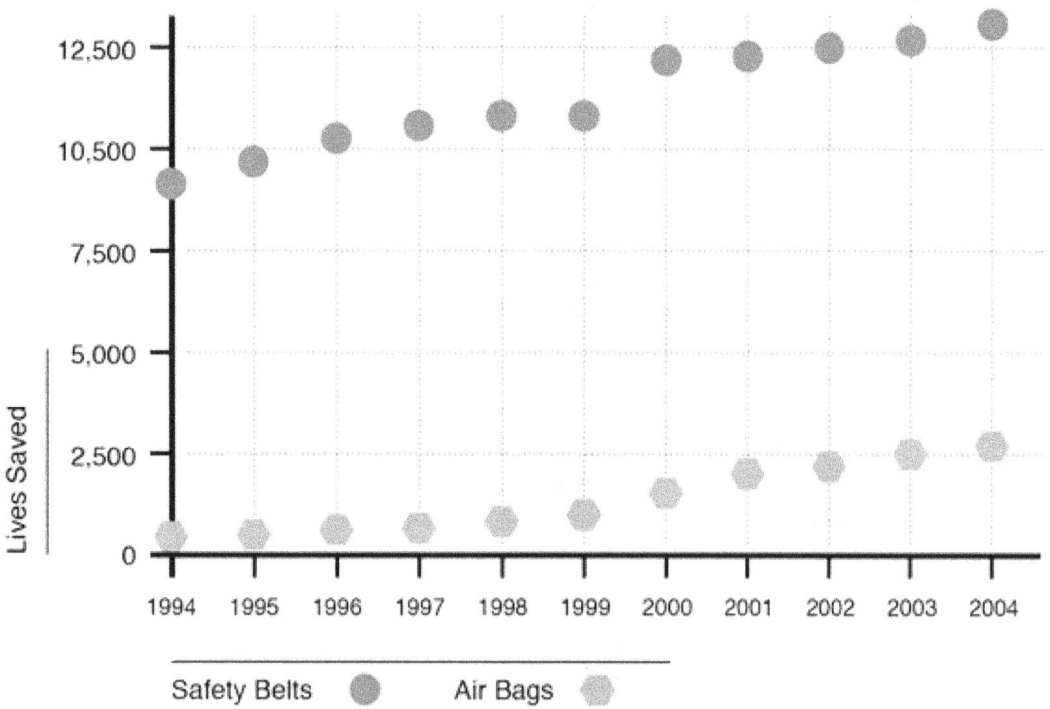

Based on data from the National Highway Traffic Safety Administration

If the graph clearly shows a higher number of lives are saved by seat belts, then it's effective. However, if the graph shows air bags save more lives than seat belts, then it doesn't support the writer's case.

Finally, graphs should be easy to understand. Their information should immediately be clear to the reader at a glance. Here are some basic things to keep in mind when interpreting infographics:

- In a **bar graph**, higher bars represent larger numbers. Lower bars represent smaller numbers.
- **Line graphs** are the same, but often show trends over time. A line that consistently ascends from left to right shows a steady increase over time. A line that consistently descends from left to right shows a steady decrease over time. If the line bounces up and down, this represents instability or inconsistency in the trend. When interpreting a line graph, determine the point the writer is trying to make, and then see if the graph supports that point.
- **Pie charts** are used to show proportions or percentages of a whole but are less effective in showing change over time.
- **Tables** present information in numerical form, not as graphics. When interpreting a table, make sure to look for patterns in the numbers.

There can also be timelines, illustrations, or maps on the test. When interpreting these, keep in mind the writer's intentions and determine whether or not the graphic supports the case.

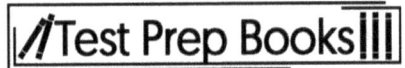

Voice and Presentation

Showing Awareness of Audience and Tone

Audience

It is important to understand your audience. Who is going to be reading what you write? What will they expect your writing to deliver? What level of knowledge do they have on the topic, and what level of interest can you assume they have coming in? Consider not only the information that your audience will need in order to understand your writing, but also the tone and style that you should use to address them. A more formal, academic tone, for instance, would be appropriate for an essay written for an audience of college professors, while a more casual tone is best for addressing the general public in something like a newspaper article. Vocabulary choices are crucial in preserving the voice that you wish to use. Overly complex technical jargon would be unwise to include in that newspaper article intended for laypeople to read.

Tone

Tone refers to the writer's attitude toward the subject matter. For example, the tone conveys how the writer feels about the topic he or she is writing about. A lot of nonfiction writing has a neutral tone, which is an important tone for the writer to take. A neutral tone demonstrates that the writer is presenting a topic impartially and letting the information speak for itself. On the other hand, nonfiction writing can be just as effective and appropriate if the tone isn't neutral. For instance, consider this example:

> Seat belts save more lives than any other automobile safety feature. Many studies show that airbags save lives as well; however, not all cars have airbags. For instance, some older cars don't. Furthermore, air bags aren't entirely reliable. For example, studies show that in 15% of accidents, airbags don't deploy as designed; but, on the other hand, seat belt malfunctions are extremely rare. The number of highway fatalities has plummeted since laws requiring seat belt usage were enacted.

In this passage, the writer mostly chooses to retain a neutral tone when presenting information. If the writer would instead include their own personal experience of losing a friend or family member in a car accident, the tone would change dramatically. The tone would no longer be neutral and would show that the writer has a personal stake in the content, allowing them to interpret the information in a different way. When analyzing tone, consider what the writer is trying to achieve in the text and how they *create* the tone using style.

An author's choice of words—also referred to as **diction**—helps to convey their meaning in a particular way. Through diction, an author can convey a particular tone—e.g., a humorous tone, a serious tone—in order to support the thesis in a meaningful way to the reader.

Using Diction and Stylistic Choices to Create Voice

Consider the impact of word choice on how your audience will receive your writing. Using more formal language can help to create a sense of authority in your work, so it should be used in situations that require conveying a tone of experience and expertise. If the goal is to give off a more approachable vibe, colloquial language is your friend. The connotations of the words that you use should not be overlooked, not only in the sense of keeping track of positive and negative connotations but also in the more nuanced emotional implications they may have. References to *home* will evoke more of an impression of warmth than referring to a person's *residence* or *domicile* will. Such choices of diction should remain consistent throughout the whole piece to refine and strengthen your overall voice.

Sentence structure should always be varied to keep readers engaged, but particular structural choices can also evoke certain feelings in readers. Short, punchy sentences can be used to build a sense of urgency or impact, while longer, more complex sentences filled with detailed explanations of concepts will give a very different feeling. The rhythm of your writing can be altered by using different mixes of sentence types, and the same is true of paragraph length as well. Short paragraphs, like short sentences, add to that sense of urgency, while deep exploration is best suited to longer ones.

Rhetorical devices like metaphor, simile, personification, etc. can also assist in creating a distinct voice in a piece. Alliteration and assonance can add a musical quality to your writing, as can strategic repetition of key phrases. Making allusions to other pieces of writing can help readers to connect your writing with both the concepts within those works as well as the feeling of reading them. In less formal writing, pop culture references can serve a similar purpose.

Focusing and Organizing Writing for Persuasion

In order to properly persuade your audience, you must know exactly what idea that you want them to accept. What should the audience believe and do after reading what you have written on this subject? Consider the call to action (a strong statement that urges your audience to act on the new stance that you have hopefully prompted them to take) that your readers will receive at the end of the piece, how their values and prior beliefs will affect how they may respond to such a message, and the potential objections they may have to the idea. Knowing your audience on this level will allow you to tailor your argument specifically to resonate with them and to address the aforementioned counterarguments. Opposing views should be acknowledged specifically and refuted with evidence that supports your claim. Providing rebuttals in this way demonstrates a more thorough understanding of the topic than would be apparent in a paper that ignores any possible objections to its claims, and this helps readers to trust that the conclusions you draw will be well thought out and reasonable.

Once you have a clear idea of what your argument will be, the next task will be to encapsulate the whole of it in one or two sentences. A clear and concise thesis presented early in the piece will prime reader expectations of where the rest of your writing will go. This thesis should be introduced with sufficient context about the subject of your writing to properly frame your argument. In an essay arguing that schools should be required to provide works from modern writers that students enjoy, for instance, important background information would include what kinds of books and other media are currently included in the curriculum of the schools being urged to change their selection. The essay would then go on to prove its points in its body paragraphs, equipped with clear topic sentences that each reinforce and add to the main idea being expressed. The evidence used to support this main idea is of crucial importance because if the evidence is clearly not credible, the quality of the writing around it will not be sufficient to convince readers that it is. Facts—statistics, expert quotes, specific examples of the concept in execution, etc.—will form the foundation to hold up the scaffolding of the opinions that the audience is being encouraged to share. The call to action mentioned earlier will only resonate with an audience that has been primed to accept it.

There are three specific kinds of appeals that can help the audience become more open to persuasion. Appeals to ethos include establishing credibility by citing reputable sources, as referenced above, as well as sharing any qualifications you, the author, have that will lend authority to your words. Referencing expert opinions will also help accomplish this end, using their authority to increase the credibility of your argument. Appeals to pathos are appeals to the audience's emotions. Vivid language and personal stories can provoke certain feelings in readers. Be sure that you are always aware of the feeling that you are aiming for so that you can use these tools effectively. Appeals to logos use the audience's logical thinking to aid in persuading them of your view. The data and facts presented should stand on their own as support for your main idea. Effective persuasion can lean specifically on only one of these techniques, but appealing to multiple of your readers' sensibilities will generally increase the effectiveness of your argument.

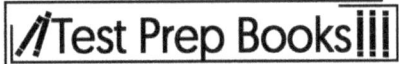

Writing

Conventions, Mechanics, and Syntax

Applying Words and Expressions Related to the Task

Take care to read the prompt carefully to identify key terms and the requirements of the task. The instructions will guide your choice of words. Look out for specific action verbs (argue, analyze, compare, etc.) that will tell you the kind of writing you are expected to deliver. Once you understand this, you can tailor your vocabulary to the subject at hand. If the topic is about environmental issues, for instance, terms like *sustainability* and *renewable resources* will be appropriate.

Be precise in your use of language, and be sure to vary your word choice to avoid accidental repetition. Deliberate repetition of key phrases can be used for specific goals like adding an emotional punch to persuasive writing; the important thing is not to stumble into it and make your writing seem like it is meandering through its points with no real sense of purpose. When working to avoid excessive repetition, take care to choose words that will still fit the context and tone of your writing, and do not make changes simply to add apparent complexity to your diction. If you want to alter the phrase *many casualties*, the word *innumerable* would not be appropriate to use in the place of *many* if you have just shared a statistic that tells the reader exactly how many casualties have been recorded because this indicates that the casualties are not, in fact, unable to be counted. If you have used the word *many* too many times in a paragraph and need to change it to avoid repetition, a word like *numerous* would work better in this case. Be sure to match the tone of your writing to your intended audience as well, and avoid using slang or overly casual expressions unless the task specifically calls for it.

Respecting Conventions and Mechanics

Maintaining an awareness of writing conventions is essential to producing good work. Grammatical errors like problems with subject-verb agreement and tense consistency will bring down the quality of your responses regardless of the content within. Be sure to leave enough time to check for problems like automatically using plural verbs for singular terms that end with an S (e.g. "linguistics are" rather than the correct "linguistics is"), and be conscious of the tense you begin writing in to avoid slipping into a different one as you go on. Also look out for errors in punctuation by staying mindful of certain things. These include making proper use of commas separating items in lists, avoiding the overuse of commas between paired descriptors that do not need them (one would be needed in the phrase "slick, sweaty skin" but not in the phrase "sweet little smile," for example), being certain that periods have been placed at the ends of sentences and not somewhere that will create a run-on sentence or fragment, etc.

Problems with spelling and word choice can also drag down the quality of your writing. Checking for spelling errors and being mindful of commonly confused homophones like *there, their,* and *they're* will go a long way in preventing readers from having to backtrack after reading a sentence. Also be sure to check for errors in capitalization, such as failing to capitalize a proper noun (*Canada, the United Nations*) or capitalizing a noun that does not require it (job roles like *plumber*, for instance).

Controlling Sentence Structures and Flow of Communication

To be better able to guide the flow of your writing, thoroughly familiarize yourself with the three main sentence types: simple, containing only one independent clause (i.e. "The dog howled loudly."); compound, combining two independent clauses using a conjunction (i.e. "The dog howled loudly, and my grandmother jumped."); and complex, combining an independent clause with one or more dependent clauses (i.e. "Although the dog howled loudly, my grandmother continued her knitting undisturbed."). Sentences should vary among these types as well as in length and level of detail so as to avoid bogging the reader down in too many repetitions of the same sentence structure. Sentence length also helps to control pacing, with short sentences quickening the flow of reading and enhancing the impact of particular statements and longer sentences providing more in-depth explanations and allowing the reader to take a moment to think about the information shared.

Pay attention also to whether your sentences are written in active or passive voice. In active voice, the subject directly performs the action ("I caught the ball."), while in passive voice, the action is being performed on the subject ("The ball was caught."). For the purposes of writing for the CAEC, favor active voice to maintain a dynamic pace and ensure clarity in your writing. Aim for conciseness, avoiding the temptation to add more words simply for the sake of increasing word count, so that the flow of your writing will not be broken by random pauses to elaborate on a point you have already explained. Be aware of what is happening to the structure of a sentence if you change your mind about what to include in it as it is being written. Otherwise, you could inadvertently create run-on sentences after adding extra clauses improperly or create sentence fragments after removing a clause that was needed for the structure of the sentence.

Sentence beginnings should be as varied as sentence length and complexity to maintain a smooth flow between ideas. Be sure to use transitional phrases or sentences where needed so as not to disrupt the flow of ideas by seeming to switch to another out of nowhere, but take care not to repeat the same transition too many times. The effect of neglecting this is like listening to a story told by a child full of repetitions of "and then...and then...and then...".

Writing Practice Quiz

Persuasive Writing

Read the situation described below and use it to complete the writing task that follows.

The Situation: A local school district is considering extending the school day by one hour to provide students with additional academic support. The plan's supporters expect this change to improve student performance and increase learning opportunities. Opponents, however, argue that student burnout could increase with longer school days.

The school district is accepting feedback from parents and members of the community about the plan. You are the parent of a student in this district who has gathered information and opinions about the plan from various sources, and you now feel prepared to share your opinion.

The Task: Write a letter or email to your local school board that clearly explains why you AGREE or DISAGREE with the district's plan to extend the school day.

In preparing your letter or email, BE SURE TO:

- Read the information in the sources.
- Clearly state whether you AGREE or DISAGREE with the proposal.
- Develop and support your arguments with appropriate details.
- Organize your arguments in a logical order.
- Consider your audience, your tone, and your voice.
- Check sentence structures, usage, grammar, words, and expressions.

To support your position, you may use:

- The information in the sources
- Your own knowledge and/or experiences
- A combination of both

The Support:

Graph showing the effect on student test scores of implementing this change in a different school district:

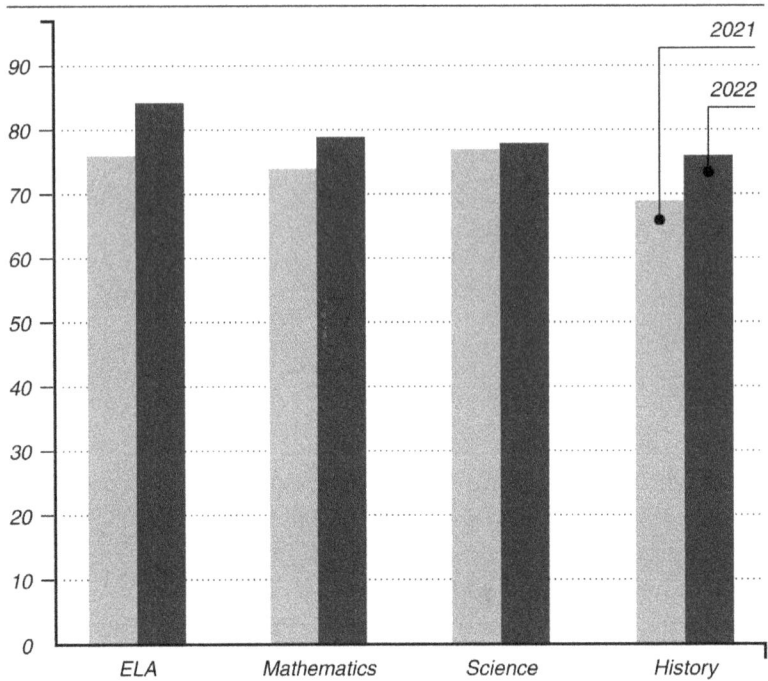

Average Standardized Test Scores in the Laird Valley School District Before and After 2022 Extended Hours

Email from a teacher:

Dear Lakeview Parents,

I hope this message finds you well. I would like to share my thoughts with you all on the proposed extension of the school day from my perspective as a teacher in our district.

In my experience, students can significantly benefit from additional instruction time. An extended day would allow us to add study hall time for struggling students, and enrichment activities could be provided for students who are already excelling so that they will benefit from the added time as well. Especially in subjects like math and reading, extra learning time can only improve academic outcomes.

Longer school days will also allow more planning time for teachers and more chances to engage students in hands-on projects to build their critical thinking skills. I feel this plan would help us better prepare our students to meet future academic challenges.

Thank you for your consideration.

Best Regards,

Eudora Malley
8th Grade Math
Lakeview Middle School

Parent survey on school day extension:

School Day Extension Survey:

Total Responses: 150

In Favor of Extended School Day: 57 (38%)

Against Extended School Day: 93 (62%)

Comments from Parents:

In favor:

"I know I'm not the only one whose kid could use some more time to catch up."

"This could let kids who have extra time accommodations on their IEPs stand out less because the whole class will have extra time, too."

Against:

"My child is already exhausted at the end of a long school day. She would absolutely end up burned out if this were to go through."

"What will happen with extracurricular activities if this plan comes to pass? There is a limit to how late kids can stay."

Excerpt from news article: "Longer School Days: Helpful or Harmful?"

Published: April 25th, 2023

As school districts across the country debate extending the school day in a bid to improve flagging test scores, educators and parents remain divided on the potential impact of the change. Proponents are saying that additional learning time enhances students' performance, citing studies that show higher test scores in districts that have implemented extended hour plans.

Opponents see it differently. Child psychologist Dr. Mel Ransome has concerns about the effects of extended hours on student well-being. "Especially among younger students, longer school days can lead to more stress and fatigue," says Ransome. "We cannot overlook outcomes on children's well-being for the hope of higher test scores."

The debate rages on as school districts weigh the potential educational benefits against the potential drawbacks for children forced to remain in school for an extra hour each day. Many have advocated for a pilot program to test effectiveness before committing to such a plan long term.

Math Part I: No Calculator

Mixed Numbers

Fractions and Decimals in Order

Rational numbers are those that can be written as a fraction or ratio. Within the set of rational numbers, several subsets exist that are referenced throughout the mathematics topics. Counting numbers are the first numbers learned as a child. Counting numbers consist of 1, 2, 3, 4, and so on. Whole numbers include all counting numbers and zero (0, 1, 2, 3, 4, …). Integers include counting numbers, their opposites, and zero (…, -3, -2, -1, 0, 1, 2 ,3 ,…). Rational numbers include integers, fractions, and decimals that terminate (1.7, 0.04213) or repeat ($0.13\bar{6}$).

Placing numbers in an order in which they are listed from smallest to largest is known as **ordering**. Ordering numbers properly can help in the comparison of different quantities of items.

When comparing two numbers to determine if they are equal or if one is greater than the other, it is best to look at the digit furthest to the left of the decimal place (or the first value of the decomposed numbers). If this first digit of each number being compared is equal in place value, then move one digit to the right to conduct a similar comparison. Continue this process until it can be determined that both numbers are equal or a difference is found, showing that one number is greater than the other. If a number is greater than the other number it is being compared to, a symbol such as > (greater than) or < (less than) can be utilized to show this comparison. It is important to remember that the "open mouth" of the symbol should be nearest the larger number.

For example:

1,023,100 compared to 1,023,000

First, compare the digit farthest to the left. Both are decomposed to 1,000,000, so this place is equal.

Next, move one place to right on both numbers being compared. This number is zero for both numbers, so move on to the next number to the right. The first number decomposes to 20,000, while the second decomposes to 20,000. These numbers are also equal, so move one more place to the right. The first number decomposes to 3,000, as does the second number, so they are equal again. Moving one place to the right, the first number decomposes to 100, while the second number is zero. Since 100 is greater than zero, the first number is greater than the second. This is expressed using the greater than symbol:

1,023,100 > 1,023,000 because 1,023,100 is greater than 1,023,000 (Note that the "open mouth" of the symbol is nearest to 1,023,100).

Notice the > symbol in the above comparison. When values are the same, the equals sign (=) is used. However, when values are unequal, or an **inequality** exists, the relationship is denoted by various inequality symbols. These symbols describe in what way the values are unequal. A value could be greater than (>); less than (<); greater than or equal to ($\geq$); or less than or equal to ($\leq$) another value. The statement "five times a number added to forty is more than sixty-five" can be expressed as $5x + 40 > 65$. Common words and phrases that express inequalities are:

Symbol	Phrase
<	is under, is below, smaller than, beneath
>	is above, is over, bigger than, exceeds
$\leq$	no more than, at most, maximum
$\geq$	no less than, at least, minimum

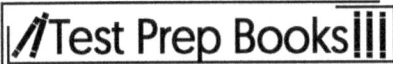

Math Part I: No Calculator

Another way to compare whole numbers with many digits is to use place value. In each number to be compared, it is necessary to find the highest place value in which the numbers differ and to compare the value within that place value. For example, 4,523,345 < 4,532,456 because of the values in the ten thousands place.

Comparing Fractions

To compare fractions with either the same **numerator** (top number) or same **denominator** (bottom number), it is easiest to visualize the fractions with a model.

For example, which is larger, $\frac{1}{3}$ or $\frac{1}{4}$? Both numbers have the same numerator, but a different denominator. In order to demonstrate the difference, shade the amounts on a pie chart split into the number of pieces represented by the denominator.

The first pie chart represents $\frac{1}{3}$, a larger shaded portion, and is therefore a larger fraction than the second pie chart representing $\frac{1}{4}$.

If two fractions have the same denominator (or are split into the same number of pieces), the fraction with the larger numerator is the larger fraction, as seen below in the comparison of $\frac{1}{3}$ and $\frac{2}{3}$:

$\frac{1}{3}$ $\frac{2}{3}$

As mentioned, a **unit fraction** is one in which the numerator is 1 ($\frac{1}{2}, \frac{1}{3}, \frac{1}{8}, \frac{1}{20}$, etc.). The denominator indicates the number of equal pieces that the whole is divided into. The greater the number of pieces, the smaller each piece will be. Therefore, the greater the denominator of a unit fraction, the smaller it is in value. Unit fractions can also be compared by converting them to decimals. For example, $\frac{1}{2} = 0.5$, $\frac{1}{3} = 0.\overline{3}$, $\frac{1}{8} = 0.125$, $\frac{1}{20} = 0.05$, etc.

Comparing two fractions with different denominators can be difficult if attempting to guess at how much each represents. Using a number line, blocks, or just finding a common denominator with which to compare the two fractions makes this task easier.

For example, compare the fractions $\frac{3}{4}$ and $\frac{5}{8}$.

The number line method of comparison involves splitting one number line evenly into 4 sections, and the second number line evenly into 8 sections total, as follows:

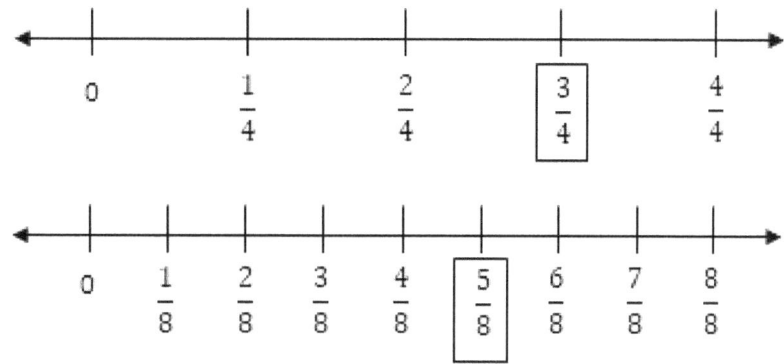

Here it can be observed that $\frac{3}{4}$ is greater than $\frac{5}{8}$, so the comparison is written as $\frac{3}{4} > \frac{5}{8}$.

This could also be shown by finding a common denominator for both fractions, so that they could be compared. First, list out factors of 4: 4, **8**, 12, 16.

Then, list out factors of 8: **8**, 16, 24.

Both share a common factor of 8, so they can be written in terms of 8 portions. In order for $\frac{3}{4}$ to be written in terms of 8, both the numerator and denominator must be multiplied by 2, thus forming the new fraction $\frac{6}{8}$. Now the two fractions can be compared.

Because both have the same denominator, the numerator will show the comparison.

$$\frac{6}{8} > \frac{5}{8}$$

Ordering Numbers

Whether the question asks to order the numbers from greatest to least or least to greatest, the crux of the question is the same—convert the numbers into a common format. Generally, it's easiest to write the numbers as whole numbers and decimals so they can be placed on a number line. Follow these examples to understand this strategy.

1) Order the following rational numbers from greatest to least:

$$\sqrt{36}, 0.65, 78\%, \frac{3}{4}, 7, 90\%, \frac{5}{2}$$

Of the seven numbers, the whole number (7) and decimal (0.65) are already in an accessible form, so concentrate on the other five.

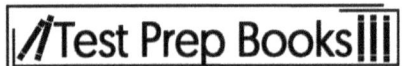

First, the square root of 36 equals 6. (If the test asks for the root of a non-perfect root, determine which two whole numbers the root lies between.) Next, convert the percentages to decimals. A percentage means "per hundred," so this conversion requires moving the decimal point two places to the left, leaving 0.78 and 0.9. Lastly, evaluate the fractions: $\frac{3}{4} = \frac{75}{100} = 0.75$; $\frac{5}{2} = 2\frac{1}{2} = 2.5$

Now, the only step left is to list the numbers in the requested order:

$$7, \sqrt{36}, \frac{5}{2}, 90\%, 78\%, \frac{3}{4}, 0.65$$

2) Order the following rational numbers from least to greatest:

$$2.5, \sqrt{9}, -10.5, 0.853, 175\%, \sqrt{4}, \frac{4}{5}$$

$$\sqrt{9} = 3$$

$$175\% = 1.75$$

$$\sqrt{4} = 2$$

$$\frac{4}{5} = 0.8$$

From least to greatest, the answer is: $-10.5, \frac{4}{5}, 0.853, 175\%, \sqrt{4}, 2.5, \sqrt{9}$

It is not possible to give similar relationships between two complex numbers $a + ib$ and $c + id$. This is because the real numbers cannot be identified with the complex numbers, and there is no form of comparison between the two. However, given any polynomial equation, its solutions can be solved in the complex field. If the zeros are real, they can be written as $a + i \times 0$; if they are complex, they can be written as $a + ib$; and if they are imaginary, they can be written as ib.

Add, Subtract, Multiply, and Divide Decimals, Percentages, and Integers.

Comparing and Ordering Decimals

To compare decimals and order them by their value, utilize a method similar to that of ordering large numbers.

The main difference is where the comparison will start. Assuming that any numbers to left of the decimal point are equal, the next numbers to be compared are those immediately to the right of the decimal point. If those are equal, then move on to compare the values in the next decimal place to the right.

For example:

Which number is greater, 12.35 or 12.38?

Check that the values to the left of the decimal point are equal:

$$12 = 12$$

Next, compare the values of the decimal place to the right of the decimal:

$$12.3 = 12.3$$

Those are also equal in value.

Finally, compare the value of the numbers in the next decimal place to the right on both numbers:

$$12.3\mathbf{5} \text{ and } 12.3\mathbf{8}$$

Here the 5 is less than the 8, so the final way to express this inequality is:

$$12.35 < 12.38$$

Comparing decimals is regularly exemplified with money because the "cents" portion of money ends in the hundredths place. When paying for gasoline or meals in restaurants, and even in bank accounts, if enough errors are made when calculating numbers to the hundredths place, they can add up to dollars and larger amounts of money over time.

Number lines can also be used to compare decimals. Tick marks can be placed within two whole numbers on the number line that represent tenths, hundredths, etc. Each number being compared can then be plotted. The value farthest to the right on the number line is the largest.

Implications for Addition and Subtraction

For addition, if all numbers are either positive or negative, they are simply added together. For example, $4 + 4 = 8$ and $-4 + -4 = -8$. However, things get tricky when some of the numbers are negative and some are positive.

For example, with $6 + (-4)$, the first step is to take the absolute values of the numbers, which are 6 and 4. Second, the smaller value is subtracted from the larger. The equation becomes $6 - 4 = 2$. Third, the sign of the original larger number is placed on the sum. Here, 6 is the larger number, and it's positive, so the sum is 2.

Here's an example where the negative number has a larger absolute value: $(-6) + 4$. The first two steps are the same as the example above. However, on the third step, the negative sign must be placed on the sum, because the absolute value of (-6) is greater than 4. Thus, $-6 + 4 = -2$.

The absolute value of numbers implies that subtraction can be thought of as flipping the sign of the number following the subtraction sign and simply adding the two numbers. This means that subtracting a negative number will, in fact, be adding the positive absolute value of the negative number.

Here are some examples:

$$-6 - 4 = -6 + -4 = -10$$
$$3 - -6 = 3 + 6 = 9$$
$$-3 - 2 = -3 + -2 = -5$$

Implications for Multiplication and Division

For multiplication and division, if both numbers are positive, then the product or quotient is always positive. If both numbers are negative, then the product or quotient is also positive. However, if the numbers have opposite signs, the product or quotient is always negative.

Simply put, the product in multiplication and quotient in division is always positive, unless the numbers have opposing signs, in which case it's negative. Here are some examples:

$$(-6) \times (-5) = 30$$

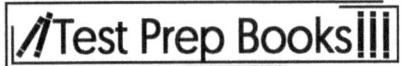

$$(-50) \div 10 = -5$$

$$8 \times |-7| = 56$$

$$(-48) \div (-6) = 8$$

If there are more than two numbers in a multiplication or division problem, then whether the product or quotient is positive or negative depends on the number of negative numbers in the problem. If there is an odd number of negatives, then the product or quotient is negative. If there is an even number of negative numbers, then the result is positive.

Here are some examples:

$$(-6) \times 5 \times (-2) \times (-4) = -240$$

$$(-6) \times 5 \times 2 \times (-4) = 240$$

Undefined Expressions

Expressions can be undefined when they involve dividing by zero or having a zero denominator. In simple fractions, the numerator and denominator can be nearly any integer. However, the denominator of a fraction can never be zero, because dividing by zero is a function which is undefined. Trying to take the square root of a negative number also yields an undefined result.

Solve x + a + b = c Linear Equations

Adding, Subtracting, Multiplying, and Factoring Linear Expressions

Algebraic expressions look similar to equations, but they do not include the equal sign. Algebraic expressions are comprised of numbers, variables, and mathematical operations. Some examples of algebraic expressions are:

$$8x + 7y - 12z, 3a^2, \text{ and } 5x^3 - 4y^4$$

Algebraic expressions consist of variables, numbers, and operations. A term of an expression is any combination of numbers and/or variables, and terms are separated by addition and subtraction. For example, the expression $5x^2 - 3xy + 4 - 2$ consists of 4 terms: $5x^2$, -3xy, 4y, and -2. Note that each term includes its given sign (+ or −). The variable part of a term is a letter that represents an unknown quantity. The coefficient of a term is the number by which the variable is multiplied. For the term 4y, the variable is y, and the coefficient is 4. Terms are identified by the power (or exponent) of its variable.

A number without a variable is referred to as a constant. If the variable is to the first power (x^1 or simply x), it is referred to as a linear term. A term with a variable to the second power (x^2) is quadratic and a term to the third power (x^3) is cubic. Consider the expression $x^3 + 3x - 1$. The constant is -1. The linear term is 3x. There is no quadratic term. The cubic term is x^3.

An algebraic expression can also be classified by how many terms exist in the expression. Any like terms should be combined before classifying. A monomial is an expression consisting of only one term. Examples of monomials are: 17, 2x, and $-5ab^2$. A binomial is an expression consisting of two terms separated by addition or subtraction. Examples include $2x - 4$ and $-3y^2 + 2y$. A trinomial consists of 3 terms. For example, $5x^2 - 2x + 1$ is a trinomial.

Algebraic expressions and equations can represent real-life situations and model the behavior of different variables. For example, $2x + 5$ could represent the cost to play games at an arcade. In this case, 5 represents the price of admission to the arcade and 2 represents the cost of each game played. To calculate the total cost, use the number of games played for x, multiply it by 2, and add 5.

Adding and Subtracting Linear Algebraic Expressions

An algebraic expression is simplified by combining like terms. A term is a number, variable, or product of a number, and variables separated by addition and subtraction. For the algebraic expression $3x^2 - 4x + 5 - 5x^2 + x - 3$, the terms are $3x^2$, -4x, 5, -5x^2, x, and -3. Like terms have the same variables raised to the same powers (exponents). The like terms for this example are $3x^2$ and -5x^2, -4x and x, 5 and -3. To combine like terms, the coefficients (numerical factors of the term including sign) are added, and the variables and their powers are kept the same. Note that if a coefficient is not written, it is an implied coefficient of 1 ($x = 1x$). In this example, the equation will simplify to $-2x^2 - 3x + 2$.

When adding or subtracting algebraic expressions, each expression is written in parenthesis. The negative sign is distributed when necessary, and like terms are combined. Consider the following:

$$\text{add } 2a + 5b - 2 \text{ to } a - 2b + 8c - 4$$

The sum is set as follows:

$$(a - 2b + 8c - 4) + (2a + 5b - 2)$$

In front of each set of parentheses is an implied positive one, which, when distributed, does not change any of the terms. Therefore, the parentheses are dropped and like terms are combined:

$$a - 2b + 8c - 4 + 2a + 5b - 2$$

$$3a + 3b + 8c - 6$$

Consider the following problem:

$$\text{Subtract } 2a + 5b - 2 \text{ from } a - 2b + 8c - 4$$

The difference is set as follows:

$$(a - 2b + 8c - 4) - (2a + 5b - 2)$$

The implied one in front of the first set of parentheses will not change those four terms. However, distributing the implied -1 in front of the second set of parentheses will change the sign of each of those three terms:

$$a - 2b + 8c - 4 - 2a - 5b + 2$$

Combining like terms yields the simplified expression: $-a - 7b + 8c - 2$.

Distributive Property

The **distributive property** states that multiplying a sum (or difference) by a number produces the same result as multiplying each value in the sum (or difference) by the number and adding (or subtracting) the products. Using mathematical symbols, the distributive property states $a(b + c) = ab + ac$. The expression $4(3 + 2)$ is simplified using the order of operations. Simplifying inside the parenthesis first produces 4×5, which equals 20. The expression $4(3 + 2)$ can also be simplified using the distributive property:

$$4(3 + 2)$$

$$4 \times 3 + 4 \times 2$$

$$12 + 8$$

$$20$$

Consider the following example: $4(3x - 2)$. The expression cannot be simplified inside the parenthesis because $3x$ and -2 are not like terms, and therefore cannot be combined. However, the expression can be simplified by using the distributive property and multiplying each term inside of the parenthesis by the term outside of the parenthesis: $12x - 8$. The resulting equivalent expression contains no like terms, so it cannot be further simplified.

Consider the expression:

$$(3x + 2y + 1) - (5x - 3) + 2(3y + 4)$$

Again, there are no like terms, but the distributive property is used to simplify the expression. Note there is an implied one in front of the first set of parentheses and an implied -1 in front of the second set of parentheses. Distributing the one, -1, and 2 produces:

$$1(3x) + 1(2y) + 1(1) - 1(5x) - 1(-3) + 2(3y) + 2(4)$$

$$3x + 2y + 1 - 5x + 3 + 6y + 8$$

This expression contains like terms that are combined to produce the simplified expression:

$$-2x + 8y + 12$$

Algebraic expressions are tested to be equivalent by choosing values for the variables and evaluating both expressions (see 2.A.4). For example, $4(3x - 2)$ and $12x - 8$ are tested by substituting 3 for the variable x and calculating to determine if equivalent values result.

Evaluating Algebraic Expressions

To evaluate the expression, the given values for the variables are substituted (or replaced) and the expression is simplified using the order of operations. Parenthesis should be used when substituting. Consider the following: Evaluate $a - 2b + ab$ for $a = 3$ and $b = -1$. To evaluate, any variable a is replaced with 3 and any variable b with -1, producing:

$$(3) - 2(-1) + (3)(-1)$$

Next, the order of operations is used to calculate the value of the expression, which is 2.

Here's another example:

$$\text{Evaluate } a - 2b + ab \text{ for } a = 3 \text{ and } b = -1$$

To evaluate an expression, the given values should be substituted for the variables and simplified using the order of operations. In this case:

$$(3) - 2(-1) + (3)(-1)$$

Parentheses are used when substituting.

Given an algebraic expression, students may be asked to simplify the expression. For example:

$$\text{Simplify } 5x^2 - 10x + 2 - 8x^2 + x - 1.$$

Math Part I: No Calculator

Simplifying algebraic expressions requires combining like terms. A term is a number, variable, or product of a number and variables separated by addition and subtraction. The terms in the above expressions are: $5x^2, -10x, 2, -8x^2, x$, and -1. Like terms have the same variables raised to the same powers (exponents). To combine like terms, the coefficients (numerical factor of the term including sign) are added, while the variables and their powers are kept the same. The example above simplifies to:

$$-3x^2 - 9x + 1$$

Let's try two more.

Evaluate $\frac{1}{2}x^2 - 3, x = 4$.

The first step is to substitute in 4 for x in the expression:

$$\frac{1}{2}(4)^2 - 3$$

Then, the order of operations is used to simplify.

The exponent comes first, $\frac{1}{2}(16) - 3$, then the multiplication $8 - 3$, and then, after subtraction, the solution is 5.

Evaluate $4|5 - x| + 2y, x = 4, y = -3$.

The first step is to substitute 4 in for x and -3 in for y in the expression:

$$4|5 - 4| + 2(-3)$$

Then, the absolute value expression is simplified, which is:

$$|5 - 4| = |1| = 1$$

The expression is $4(1) + 2(-3)$ which can be simplified using the order of operations.

First is the multiplication, $4 + (-6)$; then addition yields an answer of -2.

Evaluating Expressions Using Order of Operations

Operations

Addition combines two quantities together. With whole numbers, this is taking two sets of things and merging them into one, then counting the result. For example, $4 + 3 = 7$. When adding numbers, the order does not matter: $3 + 4 = 7$, also. Longer lists of whole numbers can also be added together. The result of adding numbers is called the **sum**.

With fractions, the number on top is the **numerator**, and the number on the bottom is the **denominator**. To add fractions, the denominator must be the same—a **common denominator**. To find a common denominator, the existing numbers on the bottom must be considered, and the lowest number they will both multiply into must be determined. Consider the following equation:

$$\frac{1}{3} + \frac{5}{6} = ?$$

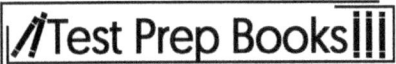

Math Part I: No Calculator

The numbers 3 and 6 both multiply into 6. Three can be multiplied by 2, and 6 can be multiplied by 1. The top and bottom of each fraction must be multiplied by the same number. Then, the numerators are added together to get a new numerator. The following equation is the result:

$$\frac{1}{3} + \frac{5}{6} = \frac{2}{6} + \frac{5}{6} = \frac{7}{6}$$

Subtraction is taking one quantity away from another, so it is the opposite of addition. The expression $4 - 3$ means taking 3 away from 4. So, $4 - 3 = 1$. In this case, the order matters, since it entails taking one quantity away from the other, rather than just putting two quantities together. The result of subtraction is also called the **difference**.

To subtract fractions, the denominator must be the same. Then, subtract the numerators together to get a new numerator. Here is an example:

$$\frac{1}{3} - \frac{5}{6} = \frac{2}{6} - \frac{5}{6} = \frac{-3}{6} = -\frac{1}{2}$$

Multiplication is a kind of repeated addition. The expression 4×5 is taking four sets, each of them having five things in them, and putting them all together. That means $4 \times 5 = 5 + 5 + 5 + 5 = 20$. As with addition, the order of the numbers does not matter. The result of a multiplication problem is called the **product**.

To multiply fractions, the numerators are multiplied to get the new numerator, and the denominators are multiplied to get the new denominator:

$$\frac{1}{3} \times \frac{5}{6} = \frac{1 \times 5}{3 \times 6} = \frac{5}{18}$$

When multiplying fractions, common factors can cancel or divide into one another, when factors appear in the numerator of one fraction and the denominator of the other fraction. Here is an example:

$$\frac{1}{3} \times \frac{9}{8} = \frac{1}{1} \times \frac{3}{8} = 1 \times \frac{3}{8} = \frac{3}{8}$$

The numbers 3 and 9 have a common factor of 3, so that factor can be divided out.

Division is the opposite of multiplication. With whole numbers, it means splitting up one number into sets of equal size. For example, $16 \div 8$ is the number of sets of eight things that can be made out of sixteen things. Thus, $16 \div 8 = 2$. As with subtraction, the order of the numbers will make a difference, here. The answer to a division problem is called the **quotient**, while the number in front of the division sign is called the **dividend** and the number behind the division sign is called the **divisor**.

To divide fractions, the first fraction must be multiplied with the reciprocal of the second fraction. The **reciprocal** of the fraction $\frac{x}{y}$ is the fraction $\frac{y}{x}$. Here is an example:

$$\frac{1}{3} \div \frac{5}{6} = \frac{1}{3} \times \frac{6}{5} = \frac{6}{15} = \frac{2}{5}$$

The value of a fraction does not change if multiplying or dividing both the numerator and the denominator by the same number (other than 0).

In other words:

$$\frac{x}{y} = \frac{a \times x}{a \times y} = \frac{x \div a}{y \div a}$$

as long as a is not 0.

This means that $\frac{2}{5} = \frac{4}{10}$, for example. If x and y are integers that have no common factors, then the fraction is said to be **simplified**. This means $\frac{2}{5}$ is simplified, but $\frac{4}{10}$ is not.

Often when working with fractions, the fractions need to be rewritten so that they all share a single denominator—this is called finding a **common denominator** for the fractions. Using two fractions, $\frac{a}{b}$ and $\frac{c}{d}$, the numerator and denominator of the left fraction can be multiplied by d, while the numerator and denominator of the right fraction can be multiplied by b. This provides the fractions $\frac{a \times d}{b \times d}$ and $\frac{c \times b}{d \times b}$ with the common denominator $b \times d$.

A fraction whose numerator is smaller than its denominator is called a **proper fraction**. A fraction whose numerator is bigger than its denominator is called an **improper fraction**. These numbers can be rewritten as a combination of integers and fractions, called a **mixed number**. For example:

$$\frac{6}{5} = \frac{5}{5} + \frac{1}{5} = 1 + \frac{1}{5}$$

and can be written as $1\frac{1}{5}$.

Estimation is finding a value that is close to a solution but is not the exact answer. For example, if there are values in the thousands to be multiplied, then each value can be estimated to the nearest thousand and the calculation performed. This value provides an approximate solution that can be determined very quickly.

Sometimes when multiplying numbers, the result can be estimated by **rounding**. For example, to estimate the value of 11.2×2.01, each number can be rounded to the nearest integer. This will yield a result of 22.

The **decimal system** is a way of writing out numbers that uses ten different numerals: 0, 1, 2, 3, 4, 5, 6, 7, 8, and 9. This is also called a "base ten" or "base 10" system. Other bases are also used. For example, computers work with a base of 2. This means they only use the numerals 0 and 1.

The decimal place denotes how far to the right of the decimal point a numeral is. The first digit to the right of the decimal point is in the tenths place. The next is the hundredths. The third is the thousandths.

So, 3.142 has a 1 in the tenths place, a 4 in the hundredths place, and a 2 in the thousandths place.

The **decimal point** is a period used to separate the **ones** place from the **tenths** place when writing out a number as a decimal.

A **decimal number** is a number written out with a decimal point instead of as a fraction, for example, 1.25 instead of $\frac{5}{4}$. Depending on the situation, it can sometimes be easier to work with fractions and sometimes easier to work with decimal numbers.

A decimal number is **terminating** if it stops at some point. It is called **repeating** if it never stops but repeats a pattern over and over. It is important to note that every rational number can be written as a terminating decimal or as a repeating decimal.

To add decimal numbers, each number in the column needs to be lined up by the decimal point. For each number being added, the zeros to the right of the last number need to be filled in so that each of the numbers has the same number of places to the right of the decimal. Then, the columns can be added together.

Here is an example of $2.45 + 1.3 + 8.891$ written in column form:

$$2.450$$
$$1.300$$
$$+\ 8.891$$

Zeros have been added in the columns so that each number has the same number of places to the right of the decimal.

Added together, the correct answer is 12.641:

$$2.450$$
$$1.300$$
$$+\ 8.891$$
$$12.641$$

When subtracting decimal numbers, the decimals are lined up in vertical columns just as they are when adding decimals. Here is $7.89 - 4.235$ written in column form:

$$7.890$$
$$-\ 4.235$$
$$3.655$$

A zero has been added in the column so that each number has the same number of places to the right of the decimal.

Decimals can be multiplied as if there were no decimal points in the problem. For example, 0.5×1.25 can be rewritten and multiplied as 5×125, which equals 625.

The final answer will have the same number of decimal places as the total number of decimal places in the problem. The first number has one decimal place, and the second number has two decimal places. Therefore, the final answer will contain three decimal places:

$$0.5 \times 1.25 = 0.625$$

Dividing a decimal by a whole number entails using long division first by ignoring the decimal point. Then, the decimal point is moved the number of places given in the problem.

For example, $6.8 \div 4$ can be rewritten as $68 \div 4$, which is 17. There is one non-zero integer to the right of the decimal point, so the final solution would have one decimal place to the right of the solution. In this case, the solution is 1.7.

Dividing a decimal by another decimal requires changing the divisor to a whole number by moving its decimal point. The decimal place of the dividend should be moved by the same number of places as the divisor. Then, the problem is the same as dividing a decimal by a whole number.

For example, 5.72 ÷ 1.1 has a divisor with one decimal place. The expression can be rewritten as 57.2 ÷ 11 by moving each decimal to the right to eliminate the decimal. The long division can be completed as 572 ÷ 11 with a result of 52. Since there is one non-zero integer to the right of the decimal point in the problem, the final solution is 5.2.

In another example, 8 ÷ 0.16 has a divisor with two decimal places. The expression can be rewritten as 800 ÷ 16 by moving each decimal point two places to the right to eliminate the decimal in the divisor. The long division can be completed with a result of 50.

Properties of Operations

Properties of operations exist to make calculations easier and solve problems for missing values. The following table summarizes commonly used properties of real numbers.

Property	Addition	Multiplication
Commutative	$a + b = b + a$	$a \times b = b \times a$
Associative	$(a + b) + c = a + (b + c)$	$(a \times b) \times c = a \times (bc)$
Identity	$a + 0 = a; 0 + a = a$	$a \times 1 = a; 1 \times a = a$
Inverse	$a + (-a) = 0$	$a \times \frac{1}{a} = 1; a \neq 0$
Distributive	$a(b + c) = ab + ac$	

The **commutative property of addition** states that the order in which numbers are added does not change the sum. Similarly, the **commutative property of multiplication** states that the order in which numbers are multiplied does not change the product. The **associative property of addition** and **multiplication** state that the grouping of numbers being added or multiplied does not change the sum or product, respectively. The commutative and associative properties are useful for performing calculations. For example, $(47 + 25) + 3$ is equivalent to $(47 + 3) + 25$, which is easier to calculate.

The **identity property of addition** states that adding zero to any number does not change its value. The **identity property of multiplication** states that multiplying a number by one does not change its value. The **inverse property of addition** states that the sum of a number and its opposite equals zero. Opposites are numbers that are the same with different signs (ex. 5 and -5; $\frac{1}{2}$ and $-\frac{1}{2}$). The **inverse property of multiplication** states that the product of a number (other than zero) and its reciprocal equals one. **Reciprocal numbers** have numerators and denominators that are inverted (ex. $\frac{2}{5}$ and $\frac{5}{2}$). Inverse properties are useful for canceling quantities to find missing values (see algebra content). For example, $a + 7 = 12$ is solved by adding the inverse of 7 (-7) to both sides in order to isolate a.

The **distributive property states** that multiplying a sum (or difference) by a number produces the same result as multiplying each value in the sum (or difference) by the number and adding (or subtracting) the products. Consider the following scenario: You are buying three tickets for a baseball game. Each ticket costs $18. You are also charged a fee of $2 per ticket for purchasing the tickets online. The cost is calculated: $3 \times 18 + 3 \times 2$. Using the distributive property, the cost can also be calculated $3(18 + 2)$.

Conversions

To convert a fraction to a decimal, the numerator is divided by the denominator. For example, $\frac{3}{8}$ can be converted to a decimal by dividing 3 by 8 ($\frac{3}{8} = 0.375$). To convert a decimal to a fraction, the decimal point is dropped, and the value is written as the numerator. The denominator is the place value farthest to the right with a digit other than zero. For example, to convert .48 to a fraction, the numerator is 48 and the denominator is 100 (the digit 8 is in the hundredths place). Therefore, .48 = $\frac{48}{100}$. Fractions should be written in the simplest form, or reduced. To reduce a fraction, the numerator and denominator are divided by the largest common factor. In the previous example, 48 and 100 are both divisible by 4. Dividing the numerator and denominator by 4 results in a reduced fraction of $\frac{12}{25}$.

To convert a decimal to a percent, the number is multiplied by 100. To convert .13 to a percent, .13 is multiplied by 100 to get 13 percent. To convert a fraction to a percent, the fraction is converted to a decimal and then multiplied by 100. For example, $\frac{1}{5}$ = .20 and .20 multiplied by 100 produces 20 percent.

To convert a percent to a decimal, the value is divided by 100. For example, 125 percent is equal to 1.25 ($\frac{125}{100}$). To convert a percent to a fraction, the percent sign is dropped, and the value is written as the numerator with a denominator of 100. For example, 80% = $\frac{80}{100}$. This fraction can be reduced ($\frac{80}{100} = \frac{4}{5}$).

Fraction Word Problems

One painter can paint a designated room in 6 hours, and a second painter can paint the same room in 5 hours. How long will it take them to paint the room if they work together?

The first painter paints $\frac{1}{6}$ of the room in an hour, and the second painter paints $\frac{1}{5}$ of the room in an hour.

Together, they can paint $\frac{1}{x}$ of the room in an hour. The equation is the sum of the painter's rate equal to the total job or $\frac{1}{6} + \frac{1}{5} = \frac{1}{x}$.

The equation can be solved by multiplying all terms by a common denominator of $30x$ with a result of $5x + 6x = 30$.

The left side can be added together to get $11x$, and then divide by 11 for a solution of $\frac{30}{11}$ or about 2.73 hours.

Squares, Square Roots, Cubes, and Cube Roots

A **root** is a different way to write an exponent when the exponent is the reciprocal of a whole number. We use the **radical** symbol to write this in the following way: $\sqrt[n]{a} = a^{\frac{1}{n}}$. This quantity is called the *n-th* **root** of *a*. The *n* is called the **index** of the radical.

Note that if the *n*-th root of *a* is multiplied by itself *n* times, the result will just be *a*. If no number *n* is written by the radical, it is assumed that *n* is 2: $\sqrt{5} = 5^{\frac{1}{2}}$. The special case of the 2nd root is called the **square root,** and the third root is called the **cube root**.

A **perfect square** is a whole number that is the square of another whole number. For example, 16 and 64 are perfect squares because 16 is the square of 4, and 64 is the square of 8.

Math Part I: No Calculator

Math Par Multiples and Factors

Multiples of a given number are found by taking that number and multiplying it by any other whole number. For example, 3 is a factor of 6, 9, and 12. Therefore, 6, 9, and 12 are multiples of 3. The multiples of any number are an infinite list. For example, the multiples of 5 are 5, 10, 15, 20, and so on. This list continues without end. A list of multiples is used in finding the **least common multiple**, or LCM, for fractions when a common denominator is needed. The denominators are written down and their multiples listed until a common number is found in both lists. This common number is the LCM.

The **factors** of a number are all integers that can be multiplied by another integer to produce the given number. For example, 2 is multiplied by 3 to produce 6. Therefore, 2 and 3 are both factors of 6. Similarly, $1 \times 6 = 6$ and $2 \times 3 = 6$, so 1, 2, 3, and 6 are all factors of 6. Another way to explain a factor is to say that a given number divides evenly by each of its factors to produce an integer. For example, 6 does not divide evenly by 5. Therefore, 5 is not a factor of 6.

Prime factorization breaks down each factor of a whole number until only prime numbers remain. All composite numbers can be factored into prime numbers. For example, the prime factors of 12 are 2, 2, and 3 ($2 \times 2 \times 3 = 12$). To produce the prime factors of a number, the number is factored, and any composite numbers are continuously factored until the result is the product of prime factors only. A **factor tree**, such as the one below, is helpful when exploring this concept.

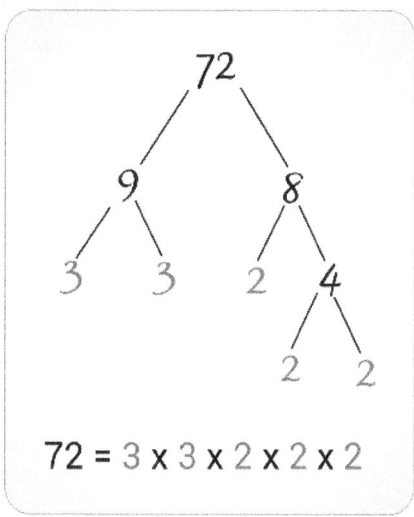

Simplifying Exponents

Exponents are used in mathematics to express a number or variable multiplied by itself a certain number of times. For example, x^3 means x is multiplied by itself three times. In this expression, x is called the **base**, and 3 is the **exponent**. Exponents can be used in more complex problems when they contain fractions and negative numbers.

Fractional exponents can be explained by looking first at the inverse of exponents, which are **roots**. Given the expression x^2, the square root can be taken, $\sqrt{x^2}$, cancelling out the 2 and leaving x by itself, if x is positive. Cancellation occurs because $\sqrt{x}$ can be written with exponents, instead of roots, as $x^{\frac{1}{2}}$. The numerator of 1 is the exponent, and the denominator of 2 is called the root (which is why it's referred to as **square root**). Taking the

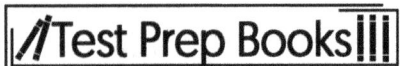

square root of x^2 is the same as raising it to the $\frac{1}{2}$ power. Written out in mathematical form, it takes the following progression:

$$\sqrt{x^2} = (x^2)^{\frac{1}{2}} = x$$

From properties of exponents, $2 \times \frac{1}{2} = 1$ is the actual exponent of x. Another example can be seen with $x^{\frac{4}{7}}$. The variable x, raised to four-sevenths, is equal to the seventh root of x to the fourth power: $\sqrt[7]{x^4}$.

In general,

$$x^{\frac{1}{n}} = \sqrt[n]{x}$$

and

$$x^{\frac{m}{n}} = \sqrt[n]{x^m}$$

Negative exponents also involve fractions. Whereas y^3 can also be rewritten as $\frac{y^3}{1}$, y^{-3} can be rewritten as $\frac{1}{y^3}$. A negative exponent means the exponential expression must be moved to the opposite spot in a fraction to make the exponent positive. If the negative appears in the numerator, it moves to the denominator. If the negative appears in the denominator, it is moved to the numerator. In general, $a^{-n} = \frac{1}{a^n}$, and a^{-n} and a^n are reciprocals.

Take, for example, the following expression:

$$\frac{a^{-4}b^2}{c^{-5}}$$

Since a is raised to the negative fourth power, it can be moved to the denominator. Since c is raised to the negative fifth power, it can be moved to the numerator. The b variable is raised to the positive second power, so it does not move.

The simplified expression is as follows:

$$\frac{b^2 c^5}{a^4}$$

In mathematical expressions containing exponents and other operations, the order of operations must be followed. **PEMDAS** states that exponents are calculated after any parenthesis and grouping symbols, but before any multiplication, division, addition, and subtraction.

There are a few rules for working with exponents. For any numbers a, b, m, n, the following hold true:

$$a^1 = a$$

$$1^a = 1$$

$$a^0, = 1$$

$$a^m \times a^n = a^{m+n}$$

$$a^m \div a^n = a^{m-n}$$

$$(a^m)^n = a^{m \times n}$$

$$(a \times b)^m = a^m \times b^m$$

$$(a \div b)^m = a^m \div b^m$$

Any number, including a fraction, can be an exponent. The same rules apply.

Math Part I Practice Quiz

1. Which of the following numbers has the greatest value?
    a. 1.43785
    b. 1.07548
    c. 1.43592
    d. 0.89409

2. The value of 6 × 12 is the same as:
    a. 2 × 4 × 4 × 2
    b. 7 × 4 × 3
    c. 6 × 6 × 3
    d. 3 × 3 × 4 × 2

3. This chart indicates how many sales of CDs, vinyl records, and MP3 downloads occurred over the last year. Approximately what percentage of the total sales was from CDs?

    a. 55%
    b. 25%
    c. 40%
    d. 5%

4. Alan currently weighs 200 pounds, but he wants to lose weight to get down to 175 pounds. What is this difference in kilograms? (1 pound is approximately equal to 0.45 kilograms.)
    a. 9 kg
    b. 11.25 kg
    c. 78.75 kg
    d. 90 kg

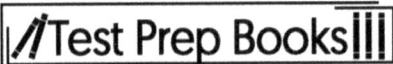

5. Which of the following is NOT a way to write 40 percent of N?
    a. $(0.4)N$
    b. $\frac{2}{5}N$
    c. $40N$
    d. $\frac{4}{10}N$

See answers on the next page.

Math Part I Answer Explanations

1. A: Compare each number after the decimal point to figure out which overall number is greatest. In Choices A (1.43785) and C (1.43592), both have the same tenths place (4) and hundredths place (3). However, the thousandths place is greater in Choice A (7), so Choice A has the greatest value overall.

2. D: By grouping the four numbers in the answer into factors of the two numbers of the question (6 and 12), it can be determined that:

$$(3 \times 2) \times (4 \times 3) = 6 \times 12$$

Alternatively, you could find the prime factorization of each answer choices and compare it to the original value. The product of 6×12 is 72 and has a prime factorization of $2^3 \times 3^2$. The answer choices respectively have values of 64, 84, 108, 72, and 360 and prime factorizations of 2^6, $2^2 \times 3 \times 7$, $2^2 \times 3^3$, $2^3 \times 3^2$, and $2^3 \times 3^2 \times 5$, so Choice D is the correct choice.

3. C: The total percentage of a pie chart equals 100%. We can see that CD sales make up less than half of the chart (50%) but more than a quarter (25%), and the only answer choice that meets these criteria is Choice C, 40%.

4. B: Using the conversion rate, multiply the projected weight loss of 25 lb by $0.45 \frac{kg}{lb}$ to get the amount in kilograms (11.25 kg).

5. C: $40N$ would be 4,000% of N. All of the other coefficients are equivalent to $\frac{40}{100}$ or 40%.

Math Part II: Calculator

Number Sense

Solving Problems in Financial or Other Contexts

Exponential growth and decay can be found in real-world situations. For example, if a piece of notebook paper is folded 25 times, the thickness of the paper can be found. To model this situation, a table can be used. The initial point is one-fold, which yields a thickness of 2 papers. For the second fold, the thickness is 4. Since the thickness doubles each time, the table below shows the thickness for the next few folds. Notice the thickness changes by the same factor each time. Since this change for a constant interval of folds is a factor of 2, the function is exponential. The equation for this is $y = 2^x$. For twenty-five folds, the thickness would be 33,554,432 papers.

x (folds)	y (paper thickness)
0	1
1	2
2	4
3	8
4	16
5	32

One exponential formula that is commonly used is the **interest formula**: $A = Pe^{rt}$. In this formula, interest is compounded continuously. A is the value of the investment after the time, t, in years. P is the initial amount of the investment, r is the interest rate, and e is the constant equal to approximately 2.718. Given an initial amount of $200 and a time of 3 years, if interest is compounded continuously at a rate of 6%, the total investment value can be found by plugging each value into the formula. The invested value at the end is $239.44. In more complex problems, the final investment may be given, and the rate may be the unknown. In this case, the formula becomes $239.44 = 200e^{r3}$.

Solving Problems in Financial and Real-World Contexts

Unit Rates

Unit rate word problems will ask you to calculate the rate or quantity of something in a different value. For example, a problem might say that a car drove a certain number of miles in a certain number of minutes and then ask how many miles per hour the car was traveling. These questions involve solving proportions. Consider the following examples:

1) Alexandra made $96 during the first 3 hours of her shift as a temporary worker at a law office. She will continue to earn money at this rate until she finishes in 5 more hours. How much does Alexandra make per hour? How much will Alexandra have made at the end of the day?

This problem can be solved in two ways. The first is to set up a proportion, as the rate of pay is constant. The second is to determine her hourly rate, multiply the 5 hours by that rate, and then add the $96.

To set up a proportion, put the money already earned over the hours already worked on one side of an equation. The other side has x over 8 hours (the total hours worked in the day). It looks like this: $\frac{96}{3} = \frac{x}{8}$. Now, cross-multiply to get $768 = 3x$. To get x, divide by 3, which leaves $x = 256$. Alternatively, as x is the numerator of one of the proportions, multiplying by its denominator will reduce the solution by one step. Thus, Alexandra will make $256 at the end of the day. To calculate her hourly rate, divide the total by 8, giving $32 per hour.

Alternatively, it is possible to figure out the hourly rate by dividing $96 by 3 hours to get $32 per hour. Now her total pay can be figured by multiplying $32 per hour by 8 hours, which comes out to $256.

2) Jonathan is reading a novel. So far, he has read 215 of the 335 total pages. It takes Jonathan 25 minutes to read 10 pages, and the rate is constant. How long does it take Jonathan to read one page? How much longer will it take him to finish the novel? Express the answer in time.

To calculate how long it takes Jonathan to read one page, divide the 25 minutes by 10 pages to determine the page per minute rate. Thus, it takes 2.5 minutes to read one page.

Jonathan must read 120 more pages to complete the novel. (This is calculated by subtracting the pages already read from the total.) Now, multiply his rate per page by the number of pages. Thus, $120 \div 2.5 = 300$. Expressed in time, 300 minutes is equal to 5 hours.

3) At a hotel, $\frac{4}{5}$ of the 120 rooms are booked for Saturday. On Sunday, $\frac{3}{4}$ of the rooms are booked. On which day are more of the rooms booked, and by how many more?

The first step is to calculate the number of rooms booked for each day. Do this by multiplying the fraction of the rooms booked by the total number of rooms.

Saturday: $\frac{4}{5} \times 120 = \frac{4}{5} \times \frac{120}{1} = \frac{480}{5} = 96$ rooms

Sunday: $\frac{3}{4} \times 120 = \frac{3}{4} \times \frac{120}{1} = \frac{360}{4} = 90$ rooms

Thus, more rooms were booked on Saturday by 6 rooms.

4) In a veterinary hospital, the veterinarian-to-pet ratio is 1:9. The ratio is always constant. If there are 45 pets in the hospital, how many veterinarians are currently in the veterinary hospital?

Set up a proportion to solve for the number of veterinarians: $\frac{1}{9} = \frac{x}{45}$

Cross-multiplying results in $9x = 45$, which works out to 5 veterinarians.

Alternatively, as there are always 9 times as many pets as veterinarians, it is possible to divide the number of pets (45) by 9. This also arrives at the correct answer of 5 veterinarians.

5) At a general practice law firm, 30% of the lawyers work solely on tort cases. If 9 lawyers work solely on tort cases, how many lawyers work at the firm?

First, solve for the total number of lawyers working at the firm, which will be represented here with x. The problem states that 9 lawyers work solely on torts cases, and they make up 30% of the total lawyers at the firm. Thus, 30% multiplied by the total, x, will equal 9. Written as equation, this is: $30\% \times x = 9$.

It's easier to deal with the equation after converting the percentage to a decimal, leaving $0.3x = 9$. Thus, $x = \frac{9}{0.3} = 30$ lawyers working at the firm.

6) Xavier was hospitalized with pneumonia. He was originally given 35mg of antibiotics. Later, after his condition continued to worsen, Xavier's dosage was increased to 60mg. What was the percent increase of the antibiotics? Round the percentage to the nearest tenth.

An increase or decrease in percentage can be calculated by dividing the difference in amounts by the original amount and multiplying by 100. Written as an equation, the formula is:

$$\frac{new\ quantity - old\ quantity}{old\ quantity} \times 100$$

Here, the question states that the dosage was increased from 35mg to 60mg, so these are plugged into the formula to find the percentage increase.

$$\frac{60 - 35}{35} \times 100 = \frac{25}{35} \times 100 = .7142 \times 100 = 71.4\%$$

Objects at Scale

Scale drawings are used in designs to model the actual measurements of a real-world object. For example, the blueprint of a house might indicate that it is drawn at a scale of 3 inches to 8 feet. Given one value and asked to determine the width of the house, a proportion should be set up to solve the problem. Given the scale of 3in:8ft and a blueprint width of 1 ft (12 in.), to find the actual width of the building, the proportion $\frac{3}{8} = \frac{12}{x}$ should be used. This results in an actual width of 32 ft.

The ratio between two similar geometric figures is called the **scale factor**. For example, a problem may depict two similar triangles, A and B. The scale factor from the smaller triangle A to the larger triangle B is given as 2 because the length of the corresponding side of the larger triangle, 16, is twice the corresponding side on the smaller triangle, 8. This scale factor can also be used to find the value of a missing side, x, in triangle A. Since the scale factor from the smaller triangle (A) to larger one (B) is 2, the larger corresponding side in triangle B (given as 25) can be divided by 2 to find the missing side in A ($x = 12.5$). The scale factor can also be represented in the equation $2A = B$ because two times the lengths of A gives the corresponding lengths of B. This is the idea behind similar triangles.

Solving Real-World Problems Involving Ratios and Rates of Change

Ratios are used to show the relationship between two quantities. The ratio of oranges to apples in the grocery store may be 3 to 2. That means that for every 3 oranges, there are 2 apples. This comparison can be expanded to represent the actual number of oranges and apples. Another example may be the number of boys to girls in a math class. If the ratio of boys to girls is given as 2 to 5, that means there are 2 boys to every 5 girls in the class. Ratios can also be compared if the units in each ratio are the same. The ratio of boys to girls in the math class can be compared to the ratio of boys to girls in a science class by stating which ratio is higher and which is lower.

Rates are used to compare two quantities with different units. **Unit rates** are the simplest form of rate. With unit rates, the denominator in the comparison of two units is one. For example, if someone can type at a rate of 1000 words in 5 minutes, then their unit rate for typing is $\frac{1000}{5} = 200$ words in one minute or 200 words per minute. Any rate can be converted into a unit rate by dividing to make the denominator one. 1000 words in 5 minutes has been converted into the unit rate of 200 words per minute.

Ratios and rates can be used together to convert rates into different units. For example, if someone is driving 50 kilometers per hour, that rate can be converted into miles per hour by using a ratio known as the **conversion factor**. Since the given value contains kilometers and the final answer needs to be in miles, the ratio relating miles to kilometers needs to be used. There are 0.62 miles in 1 kilometer. This, written as a ratio and in fraction form, is $\frac{0.62\ miles}{1\ km}$. To convert 50km/hour into miles per hour, the following conversion needs to be set up:

$$\frac{50\ km}{hour} \times \frac{0.62\ miles}{1\ km} = 31\ miles\ per\ hour$$

When dealing with word problems, there is no fixed series of steps to follow, but there are some general guidelines to use. It is important that the quantity to be found is identified. Then, it can be determined how the given values can be used and manipulated to find the final answer.

Example: Jana wants to travel to visit Alice, who lives one hundred and fifty miles away. If she can drive at fifty miles per hour, how long will her trip take?

The quantity to find is the *time* of the trip. The time of a trip is given by the distance to travel divided by the speed to be traveled. The problem determines that the distance is one hundred and fifty miles, while the speed is fifty miles per hour. Thus, 150 divided by 50 is $150 \div 50 = 3$. Because *miles* and *miles per hour* are the units being divided, the miles cancel out. The result is 3 hours.

Example: Bernard wishes to paint a wall that measures twenty feet wide by eight feet high. It costs ten cents to paint one square foot. How much money will Bernard need for paint?

The final quantity to compute is the *cost* to paint the wall. This will be ten cents ($0.10) for each square foot of area needed to paint. The area to be painted is unknown, but the dimensions of the wall are given; thus, it can be calculated.

The dimensions of the wall are 20 feet wide and 8 feet high. Since the area of a rectangle is length multiplied by width, the area of the wall is $8 \times 20 = 160 \ square \ feet$. Multiplying 0.1×160 yields $16 as the cost of the paint.

Solving Real-World Problems Involving Proportions

Much like a scale factor can be written using an equation like $2A = B$, a **relationship** is represented by the equation $Y = kX$. X and Y are proportional because as values of X increase, the values of Y also increase. A relationship that is inversely proportional can be represented by the equation $Y = \frac{k}{X}$, where the value of Y decreases as the value of x increases and vice versa.

Proportional reasoning can be used to solve problems involving ratios, percentages, and averages. Ratios can be used in setting up proportions and solving them to find unknowns. For example, if a student completes an average of 10 pages of math homework in 3 nights, how long would it take the student to complete 22 pages? Both ratios can be written as fractions. The second ratio would contain the unknown.

The following proportion represents this problem, where x is the unknown number of nights:

$$\frac{10 \ pages}{3 \ nights} = \frac{22 \ pages}{x \ nights}$$

Solving this proportion entails cross-multiplying and results in the following equation: $10x = 22 \times 3$. Simplifying and solving for x results in the exact solution: $x = 6.6 \ nights$. The result would be rounded up to 7 because the homework would actually be completed on the 7th night.

The following problem uses ratios involving percentages:

If 20% of the class is girls and 30 students are in the class, how many girls are in the class?

To set up this problem, it is helpful to use the common proportion: $\frac{\%}{100} = \frac{is}{of}$. Within the proportion, % is the percentage of girls, 100 is the total percentage of the class, *is* is the number of girls, and *of* is the total number of students in the class. Most percentage problems can be written using this language. To solve this problem, the proportion should be set up as $\frac{20}{100} = \frac{x}{30}$, and then solved for x. Cross-multiplying results in the equation $20 \times 30 = 100x$, which results in the solution $x = 6$. There are 6 girls in the class.

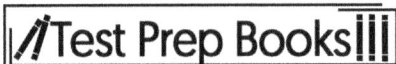

Problems involving volume, length, and other units can also be solved using ratios. For example, a problem may ask for the volume of a cone to be found that has a radius:

$$r = 7m$$

and a height:

$$h = 16m$$

Referring to the formulas provided on the test, the volume of a cone is given as: $V = \pi r^2 \frac{h}{3}$, where r is the radius, and h is the height. Plugging $r = 7$ and $h = 16$ into the formula, the following is obtained:

$$V = \pi(7^2)\frac{16}{3}$$

Therefore, the volume of the cone is found to be $821m^3$. Sometimes, answers in different units are sought. If this problem wanted the answer in liters, $821m^3$ would need to be converted. Using the equivalence statement 1m³ = 1000L, the following ratio would be used to solve for liters:

$$821 m^3 \times \frac{1000L}{1m^3}$$

Cubic meters in the numerator and denominator cancel each other out, and the answer is converted to 821,000 liters, or 8.21×10^5 L.

Other conversions can also be made between different given and final units. If the temperature in a pool is 30°C, what is the temperature of the pool in degrees Fahrenheit? To convert these units, an equation is used relating Celsius to Fahrenheit. The following equation is used:

$$T_{°F} = 1.8 T_{°C} + 32$$

Plugging in the given temperature and solving the equation for T yields the result:

$$T_{°F} = 1.8(30) + 32 = 86°F$$

Units in both the metric system and U.S. customary system are widely used.

Here are some more examples of how to solve for proportions:

1) $\frac{75\%}{90\%} = \frac{25\%}{x}$

To solve for x, the fractions must be cross multiplied: $(75\% x = 90\% \times 25\%)$. To make things easier, let's convert the percentages to decimals: $(0.9 \times 0.25 = 0.225 = 0.75x)$. To get rid of x's co-efficient, each side must be divided by that same coefficient to get the answer $x = 0.3$. The question could ask for the answer as a percentage or fraction in lowest terms, which are 30% and $\frac{3}{10}$, respectively.

2) $\frac{x}{12} = \frac{30}{96}$

Cross-multiply: $96x = 30 \times 12$

Multiply: $96x = 360$

Divide: $x = 360 \div 96$

Answer: $x = 3.75$

3) $\frac{0.5}{3} = \frac{x}{6}$

Cross-multiply: $3x = 0.5 \times 6$

Multiply: $3x = 3$

Divide: $x = 3 \div 3$

Answer: $x = 1$

You may have noticed there's a faster way to arrive at the answer. If there is an obvious operation being performed on the proportion, the same operation can be used on the other side of the proportion to solve for x. For example, in the first practice problem, 75% became 25% when divided by 3, and upon doing the same to 90%, the correct answer of 30% would have been found with much less legwork. However, these questions aren't always so intuitive, so it's a good idea to work through the steps, even if the answer seems apparent from the outset.

Solving Real-World Problems Involving Percentages

Questions dealing with percentages can be difficult when they are phrased as word problems. These word problems almost always come in three varieties. The first type will ask to find what percentage of some number will equal another number. The second asks to determine what number is some percentage of another given number. The third will ask what number another number is a given percentage of.

One of the most important parts of correctly answering percentage word problems is to identify the numerator and the denominator. This fraction can then be converted into a percentage, as described above.

The following word problem shows how to make this conversion: A department store carries several different types of footwear. The store is currently selling 8 athletic shoes, 7 dress shoes, and 5 sandals. What percentage of the store's footwear are sandals?

First, calculate what serves as the **whole**, as this will be the denominator. How many total pieces of footwear does the store sell? The store sells 20 different types (8 $athletic$ + 7 $dress$ + 5 $sandals$). Second, what footwear type is the question specifically asking about? Sandals. Thus, 5 is the numerator. Third, the resultant fraction must be expressed as a percentage. The first two steps indicate that $\frac{5}{20}$ of the footwear pieces are sandals. This fraction must now be converted into a percentage:

$$\frac{5}{20} \times \frac{5}{5} = \frac{25}{100} = 25\%$$

Patterns and Relations

Interpreting and Extending Patterns and Relationships

A **sequence** is an enumerated set of numbers, and each term or member is defined by the number it represents within the sequence. It can be **recursively defined**, which means each term is defined using prior terms. Also, it can be **explicitly defined** using only the number it represents within the sequence. The **Fibonacci numbers** are a famous recursively defined sequence where the first and second terms are equal to 1 and every other term is equal to the sum of the two previous terms. Therefore, the first six Fibonacci numbers are 1, 1, 2, 3, 5, and 8. An example of an explicitly defined sequence is one where the nth term is:

$$f_n = 2n + 1$$

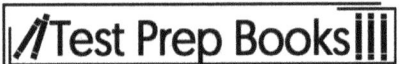

The first six terms of this sequence are 3, 5, 7, 9, 11, and 13. Both types of sequences can be used to model situations in the same way that functions are used to model real-life applications.

Number Patterns

Given a sequence of numbers, a mathematical rule can be defined that represents the numbers if a pattern exists within the set. For example, consider the sequence of numbers 1, 4, 9, 16, 25, etc. This set of numbers represents the positive integers squared, and an explicitly defined sequence that represents this set is $f_n = n^2$. An important mathematical concept is recognizing patterns in sequences and translating the patterns into an explicit formula. Once the pattern is recognized and the formula is defined, the sequence can be extended easily. For example, the next three numbers in the sequence are 36, 49, and 64.

Predicting Values

In a similar sense, patterns can be used to make conjectures, predictions, and generalizations. If a pattern is recognized in a set of numbers, values can be predicted that aren't originally provided. For example, if an experiment results in the sequence of numbers 1, 4, 9, 16, and 25, where 1 represents the first trial, 2 represents the second trial, etc., one expects the tenth trial to result in a value of 100 because that value is equal to the square of the trial number.

Writing and Solving Linear Equations

A linear expression is a statement about an unknown quantity expressed in mathematical symbols. The statement "five times a number added to forty" can be expressed as $5x + 40$. A linear equation is a statement in which two expressions (at least one containing a variable) are equal to each other. The statement "five times a number added to forty is equal to ten" can be expressed as $5x + 40 = 10$.

Real world scenarios can also be expressed mathematically. Suppose a job pays its employees $300 per week and $40 for each sale made. The weekly pay is represented by the expression $40x + 300$ where x is the number of sales made during the week.

Consider the following scenario: Bob had $20 and Tom had $4. After selling 4 ice cream cones to Bob, Tom has as much money as Bob. The cost of an ice cream cone is an unknown quantity and can be represented by a variable (x). The amount of money Bob has after his purchase is four times the cost of an ice cream cone subtracted from his original $20 → $20 - 4x$. The amount of money Tom has after his sale is four times the cost of an ice cream cone added to his original $4 → $4x + 4$. After the sale, the amounts of money that Bob and Tom have are equal → $20 - 4x = 4x + 4$.

When expressing a verbal or written statement mathematically, it is key to understand words or phrases that can be represented with symbols. The following are examples:

Symbol	Phrase
+	added to, increased by, sum of, more than
−	decreased by, difference between, less than, take away
x	multiplied by, 3 (4, 5 . . .) times as large, product of
÷	divided by, quotient of, half (third, etc.) of
=	is, the same as, results in, as much as
$x, t, n, etc.$	a number, unknown quantity, value of

Addition and subtraction are **inverse operations**. Adding a number and then subtracting the same number will cancel each other out, resulting in the original number, and vice versa. For example, $8 + 7 - 7 = 8$ and $137 - 100 + 100 = 137$. Similarly, multiplication and division are inverse operations. Therefore, multiplying by a number and then dividing by the same number results in the original number, and vice versa. For example, $8 \times 2 \div 2 = 8$ and $12 \div 4 \times 4 = 12$. Inverse operations are used to work backwards to solve problems. In the case that 7 and a number add to 18, the inverse operation of subtraction is used to find the unknown value ($18 - 7 = 11$). If a school's entire 4th grade was divided evenly into 3 classes each with 22 students, the inverse operation of multiplication is used to determine the total students in the grade ($22 \times 3 = 66$). Additional scenarios involving inverse operations are included in the tables below.

Recall that a rational expression is a fraction where the numerator and denominator are both polynomials. Some examples of rational expressions include the following: $\frac{4x^3y^5}{3z^4}$, $\frac{4x^3+3x}{x^2}$, and $\frac{x^2+7x+10}{x+2}$. Since these refer to expressions and not equations, they can be simplified but not solved. Using the rules in the previous Exponents and Roots sections, some rational expressions with monomials can be simplified. Other rational expressions such as the last example,

$$\frac{x^2 + 7x + 10}{x + 2}$$

take more steps to be simplified. First, the polynomial on top can be factored from $x^2 + 7x + 10$ into $(x + 5)(x + 2)$. Then the common factors can be canceled, and the expression can be simplified to $(x + 5)$.

Consider this problem as an example of using rational expressions. Reggie wants to lay sod in his rectangular backyard. The length of the yard is given by the expression $4x + 2$ and the width is unknown. The area of the yard is $20x + 10$. Reggie needs to find the width of the yard. Knowing that the area of a rectangle is length multiplied by width, an expression can be written to find the width: $\frac{20x+10}{4x+2}$, area divided by length. Simplifying this expression by factoring out 10 on the top and 2 on the bottom leads to this expression:

$$\frac{10(2x + 1)}{2(2x + 1)}$$

By cancelling out the $2x + 1$, that results in $\frac{10}{2} = 5$. The width of the yard is found to be 5 by simplifying a rational expression.

Creating Polynomials from Written Descriptions

Polynomials that represent mathematical or real-world problems can also be created from written descriptions, much like algebraic expressions. For example, polynomials might be created when working with formulas. Formulas are mathematical expressions that define the value of one quantity, given the value of one or more different quantities. Formulas look like equations because they contain variables, numbers, operators, and an equal sign. All formulas are equations but not all equations are formulas. A formula must have more than one variable. For example, $2x + 7 = y$ is an equation and a formula (it relates the unknown quantities x and y). However, $2x + 7 = 3$ is an equation but not a formula (it only expresses the value of the unknown quantity x).

Formulas are typically written with one variable alone (or isolated) on one side of the equal sign. This variable can be thought of as the **subject** in that the formula is stating the value of the subject in terms of the relationship between the other variables. Consider the distance formula: $distance = rate \times time$ or $d = rt$. The value of the subject variable d (distance) is the product of the variable r and t (rate and time). Given the rate and time, the distance traveled can easily be determined by substituting the values into the formula and evaluating.

The formula $P = 2l + 2w$ expresses how to calculate the perimeter of a rectangle (P) given its length (l) and width (w). To find the perimeter of a rectangle with a length of 3ft and a width of 2ft, these values are substituted into the

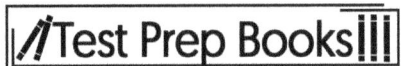

formula for *l* and *w*: $P = 2(3ft) + 2(2ft)$. Following the order of operations, the perimeter is determined to be 10ft. When working with formulas such as these, including units is an important step.

Given a formula expressed in terms of one variable, the formula can be manipulated to express the relationship in terms of any other variable. In other words, the formula can be rearranged to change which variable is the *subject*. To solve for a variable of interest by manipulating a formula, the equation may be solved as if all other variables were numbers. The same steps for solving are followed, leaving operations in terms of the variables instead of calculating numerical values. For the formula $P = 2l + 2w$, the perimeter is the subject expressed in terms of the length and width. To write a formula to calculate the width of a rectangle, given its length and perimeter, the previous formula relating the three variables is solved for the variable *w*. If *P* and *l* were numerical values, this is a two-step linear equation solved by subtraction and division. To solve the equation $P = 2l + 2w$ for *w*, 2*l* is first subtracted from both sides:

$$P - 2l = 2w$$

Then both sides are divided by 2:

$$\frac{P - 2l}{2} = w$$

Test questions may involve creating a polynomial based on a formula. For example, using the perimeter of a rectangle formula, a problem may ask for the perimeter of a rectangle with a length of $2x + 12$ and a width of $x + 1$. Using the formula $P = 2l + 2w$, the perimeter would then be:

$$P = 2(2x + 12) + 2(x + 1)$$

This equals:

$$4x + 24 + 2x + 2 = 6x + 26$$

The area of the same rectangle, which uses the formula $A = l \times w$, would be:

$$A = (2x + 12)(x + 1)$$

$$2x^2 + 2x + 12x + 12$$

$$2x^2 + 14x + 12$$

Applying and Manipulating a Given Equation or Formula

Adding, Subtracting, Multiplying, Dividing Rational Expressions

A fraction, or ratio, wherein each part is a polynomial, defines **rational expressions**. Some examples include $\frac{2x+6}{x}$, $\frac{1}{x^2-4x+8}$, and $\frac{z^2}{x+5}$. Exponents on the variables are restricted to whole numbers, which means roots and negative exponents are not included in rational expressions.

Rational expressions can be transformed by factoring. For example, the expression $\frac{x^2-5x+6}{(x-3)}$ can be rewritten by factoring the numerator to obtain:

$$\frac{(x-3)(x-2)}{(x-3)}$$

Therefore, the common binomial $(x - 3)$ can cancel so that the simplified expression is:

$$\frac{(x - 2)}{1} = (x - 2)$$

Additionally, other rational expressions can be rewritten to take on different forms. Some may be factorable in themselves, while others can be transformed through arithmetic operations. Rational expressions are closed under addition, subtraction, multiplication, and division by a nonzero expression. **Closed** means that if any one of these operations is performed on a rational expression, the result will still be a rational expression. The set of all real numbers is another example of a set closed under all four operations.

Adding and subtracting rational expressions is based on the same concepts as adding and subtracting simple fractions. For both concepts, the denominators must be the same for the operation to take place. For example, here are two rational expressions:

$$\frac{x^3 - 4}{(x - 3)} + \frac{x + 8}{(x - 3)}$$

Since the denominators are both $(x - 3)$, the numerators can be combined by collecting like terms to form:

$$\frac{x^3 + x + 4}{(x - 3)}$$

If the denominators are different, they need to be made common (the same) by using the **least common denominator (LCD)**. Each denominator needs to be factored, and the LCD contains each factor that appears in any one denominator the greatest number of times it appears in any denominator. The original expressions need to be multiplied by a form of 1 such as 5/5 or x-2/x-2, which will turn each denominator into the LCD. This process is like adding fractions with unlike denominators. It is also important when working with rational expressions to define what value of the variable makes the denominator zero. For this particular value, the expression is undefined.

Multiplication of rational expressions is performed like multiplication of fractions. The numerators are multiplied; then, the denominators are multiplied. The final fraction is then simplified. The expressions are simplified by factoring and canceling out common terms. In the following example, the numerator of the second expression can be factored first to simplify the expression before multiplying:

$$\frac{x^2}{(x - 4)} \times \frac{x^2 - x - 12}{2}$$

$$\frac{x^2}{(x - 4)} \times \frac{(x - 4)(x + 3)}{2}$$

The $(x - 4)$ on the top and bottom cancel out:

$$\frac{x^2}{1} \times \frac{(x + 3)}{2}$$

Then multiplication is performed, resulting in:

$$\frac{x^3 + 3x^2}{2}$$

Dividing rational expressions is similar to the division of fractions, where division turns into multiplying by a reciprocal. Thus, the following expression can be rewritten as a multiplication problem:

$$\frac{x^2 - 3x + 7}{x - 4} \div \frac{x^2 - 5x + 3}{x - 4}$$

$$\frac{x^2 - 3x + 7}{x - 4} \times \frac{x - 4}{x^2 - 5x + 3}$$

The $x - 4$ cancels out, leaving:

$$\frac{x^2 - 3x + 7}{x^2 - 5x + 3}$$

The final answers should always be completely simplified. If a function is composed of a rational expression, the zeros of the graph can be found from setting the polynomial in the numerator as equal to zero and solving. The values that make the denominator equal to zero will either exist on the graph as a **hole** or a **vertical asymptote**.

A **complex fraction** is a fraction in which the numerator and denominator are themselves fractions, of the form:

$$\frac{\left(\frac{a}{b}\right)}{\left(\frac{c}{d}\right)}$$

These can be simplified by following the usual rules for the order of operations, or by remembering that dividing one fraction by another is the same as multiplying by the reciprocal of the divisor. This means that any complex fraction can be rewritten using the following form:

$$\frac{\left(\frac{a}{b}\right)}{\left(\frac{c}{d}\right)} = \frac{a}{b} \times \frac{d}{c}$$

The following problem is an example of solving a complex fraction:

$$\frac{\left(\frac{5}{4}\right)}{\left(\frac{3}{8}\right)} = \frac{5}{4} \times \frac{8}{3} = \frac{40}{12} = \frac{10}{3}$$

Analyzing and Solving Problems Using Numerical and Logical Reasoning

Linear relationships describe the way two quantities change with respect to each other. The relationship is defined as linear because a line is produced if all the sets of corresponding values are graphed on a coordinate grid. When expressing the linear relationship as an equation, the equation is often written in the form $y = mx + b$ (slope-intercept form) where m and b are numerical values and x and y are variables (for example, $y = 5x + 10$). Given a linear equation and the value of either variable (x or y), the value of the other variable can be determined.

Imagine the following problem: The sum of a number and 5 is equal to -8 times the number.

To find this unknown number, a simple equation can be written to represent the problem. Key words such as difference, equal, and times are used to form the following equation with one variable: $n + 5 = -8n$. When solving for n, opposite operations are used. First, n is subtracted from $-8n$ across the equals sign, resulting in $5 = -9n$.

Then, -9 is divided on both sides, leaving $n = -\frac{5}{9}$. This solution can be graphed on the number line with a dot as shown below:

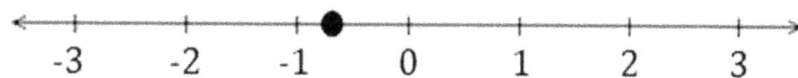

Suppose a teacher is grading a test containing 20 questions with 5 points given for each correct answer, adding a curve of 10 points to each test. This linear relationship can be expressed as the equation $y = 5x + 10$ where x represents the number of correct answers and y represents the test score. To determine the score of a test with a given number of correct answers, the number of correct answers is substituted into the equation for x and evaluated. For example, for 10 correct answers, 10 is substituted for x: $y = 5(10) + 10 \to y = 60$. Therefore, 10 correct answers will result in a score of 60. The number of correct answers needed to obtain a certain score can also be determined. To determine the number of correct answers needed to score a 90, 90 is substituted for y in the equation (y represents the test score) and solved: $90 = 5x + 10 \to 80 = 5x \to 16 = x$. Therefore, 16 correct answers are needed to score a 90.

Linear relationships may be represented by a table of 2 corresponding values. Certain tables may determine the relationship between the values and predict other corresponding sets. Consider the table below, which displays the money in a checking account that charges a monthly fee:

Month	0	1	2	3	4
Balance	$210	$195	$180	$165	$150

An examination of the values reveals that the account loses $15 every month (the month increases by one and the balance decreases by 15). This information can be used to predict future values. To determine what the value will be in month 6, the pattern can be continued, and it can be concluded that the balance will be $120. To determine which month the balance will be $0, $210 is divided by $15 (since the balance decreases $15 every month), resulting in month 14.

Geometry and Measurement

Converting Between Various Units of Measure

Unit conversions apply to many real-world scenarios, including cooking, measurement, construction, and currency. Problems on this material can be solved similarly to those involving unit rates. Given the conversion rate, it can be written as a fraction (ratio) and multiplied by a quantity in one unit to convert it to the corresponding unit. For example, someone might want to know how many minutes are in 3½ hours. The conversion rate of 60 minutes to 1 hour can be written as:

$$\frac{60 \text{ min}}{1 \text{ h}}$$

Multiplying the quantity by the conversion rate results in:

$$3\frac{1}{2}\text{h} \times \frac{60 \text{ min}}{1 \text{ h}} = 210 \text{ min}$$

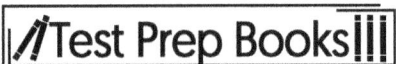

The "h" unit is canceled. To convert a quantity in minutes to hours, the fraction for the conversion rate would be flipped (to cancel the "min" unit). To convert 195 minutes to hours, the equation $195 \text{ min} \times \frac{1 \text{ h}}{60 \text{ min}}$ would be used. The result is $\frac{195 \text{ h}}{60}$, which reduces to $3\frac{1}{4}$ hours.

Converting units may require more than one multiplication. The key is to set up the conversion rates so that units cancel out each other and the desired unit is left. Suppose someone wants to convert 3.25 yards to inches, given that 1 yd = 3 ft and 12 in = 1 ft. To calculate, the equation use:

$$3.25 \text{ yd} \times \frac{3 \text{ ft}}{1 \text{ yd}} \times \frac{12 \text{ in}}{1 \text{ ft}}$$

The "yd" and "ft" units will cancel, resulting in 117 inches.

Applying Scale Factor and Properties of Similar Shapes

Sometimes, two figures are similar, meaning they have the same basic shape and the same interior angles, but they have different dimensions. If the ratio of two corresponding sides is known, then that ratio, or scale factor, holds true for all of the dimensions of the new figure.

Likewise, triangles are similar if they have the same angle measurements, and their sides are proportional to one another. Triangles are **congruent** if the angles of the triangles are equal in measurement and the sides of the triangles are equal in measurement.

There are five ways to show that triangles are congruent:

    1. SSS (Side-Side-Side Postulate) – when all three corresponding sides are equal in length, then the two triangles are congruent.

    2. SAS (Side-Angle-Side Postulate) – if a pair of corresponding sides and the angle in between those two sides are equal, then the two triangles are congruent.

    3. ASA (Angle-Side-Angle Postulate) – if a pair of corresponding angles are equal and the side lengths within those angles are equal, then the two triangles are equal.

    4. AAS (Angle-Angle-Side Postulate) – when a pair of corresponding angles for two triangles and a non-included side are equal, then the two triangles are congruent.

    5. HL (Hypotenuse-Leg Theorem) – if two right triangles have the same hypotenuse length, and one of the other sides in each triangle are of the same length, then the two triangles are congruent.

If two triangles are discovered to be similar or congruent, this information can assist in determining unknown parts of triangles, such as missing angles and sides.

The example below involves the question of congruent triangles. The first step is to examine whether the triangles are congruent. If the triangles are congruent, then the measure of a missing angle can be found.

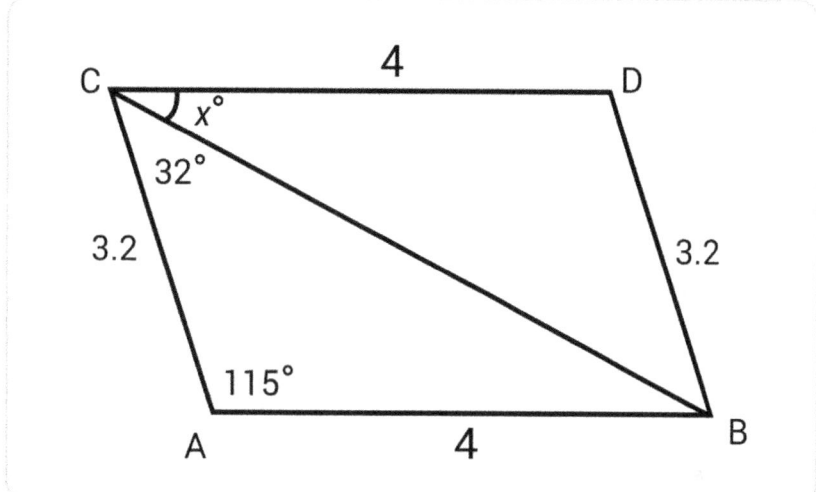

The above diagram provides values for angle measurements and side lengths in triangles CAB and CDB. Note that side CA is 3.2 and side DB is 3.2. Side CD is 4 and side AB is 4. Furthermore, line CB is congruent to itself by the reflexive property. Therefore, the two triangles are congruent by SSS (Side-Side-Side). Because the two triangles are congruent, all of the corresponding parts of the triangles are also congruent. Therefore, angle x is congruent to the inside of the angle for which a measurement is not provided in triangle CAB. Thus, $115° + 32° = 147°$. A triangle's angles sum to 180°, therefore, $180° - 147° = 33°$. Angle $x = 33°$, because the two triangles are reversed.

Applying the Pythagorean Theorem

Pythagorean Theorem

The Pythagorean theorem is an important result in geometry. It states that for right triangles, the sum of the squares of the two shorter sides will be equal to the square of the longest side (also called the **hypotenuse**). The longest side will always be the side opposite to the 90° angle. If this side is called c, and the other two sides are a and b, then the Pythagorean theorem states that $c^2 = a^2 + b^2$. Since lengths are always positive, this also can be written as:

$$c = \sqrt{a^2 + b^2}$$

A diagram to show the parts of a triangle using the Pythagorean theorem is below.

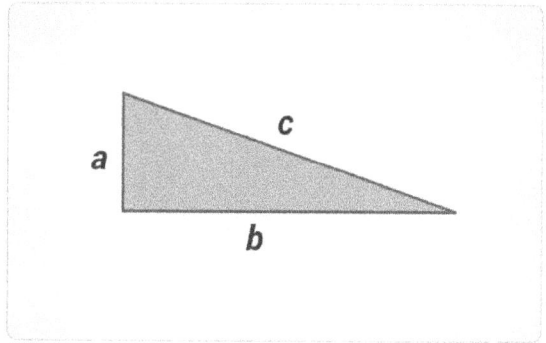

As an example of the theorem, suppose that Shirley has a rectangular field that is 5 feet wide and 12 feet long, and she wants to split it in half using a fence that goes from one corner to the opposite corner. How long will this fence need to be? To figure this out, note that this makes the field into two right triangles, whose hypotenuse will be the fence dividing it in half. Therefore, the fence length will be given by $\sqrt{5^2 + 12^2} = \sqrt{169} = 13$ feet long.

Applying Formulas to Determine the Perimeter and Area

The **perimeter** of a polygon is the distance around the outside of the two-dimensional figure. Perimeter is a one-dimensional measurement and is therefore expressed in linear units such as centimeters (*cm*), feet (*ft*), and miles (*mi*). The perimeter (*P*) of a figure can be calculated by adding together each of the sides.

Properties of certain polygons allow that the perimeter may be obtained by using formulas. A rectangle consists of two sides called the length (*l*), which have equal measures, and two sides called the width (*w*), which have equal measures. Therefore, the perimeter (*P*) of a rectangle can be expressed as:

$$P = l + l + w + w$$

This can be simplified to produce the following formula to find the perimeter of a rectangle:

$$P = 2l + 2w \text{ or } P = 2(l + w)$$

A regular polygon is one in which all sides have equal length and all interior angles have equal measures, such as a square and an equilateral triangle. To find the perimeter of a regular polygon, the length of one side is multiplied by the number of sides. For example, to find the perimeter of an equilateral triangle with a side of length of 4 feet, 4 feet is multiplied by 3 (number of sides of a triangle). The perimeter of a regular octagon (8 sides) with a side of length of $\frac{1}{2}$ cm is:

$$\frac{1}{2} cm \times 8 = 4 cm$$

The **area** of a polygon is the number of square units needed to cover the interior region of the figure. Area is a two-dimensional measurement. Therefore, area is expressed in square units, such as square centimeters (cm^2), square feet (ft^2), or square miles (mi^2). Regarding the area of a rectangle with sides of length *x* and *y*, the area is given by xy. For a triangle with a base of length *b* and a height of length *h*, the area is $\frac{1}{2}bh$. To find the area (*A*) of a parallelogram, the length of the base (*b*) is multiplied by the length of the height (*h*) → $A = b \times h$. Similar to triangles, the height of the parallelogram is measured from one base to the other at a 90° angle (or perpendicular).

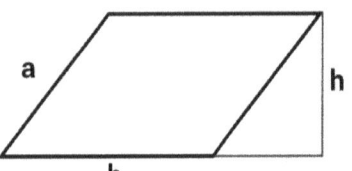

Area = bh

Perimeter = 2(a + b)

Math Part II: Calculator

The area of a trapezoid can be calculated using the formula: $A = \frac{1}{2} \times h(b_1 + b_2)$, where h is the height and b_1 and b_2 are the parallel bases of the trapezoid.

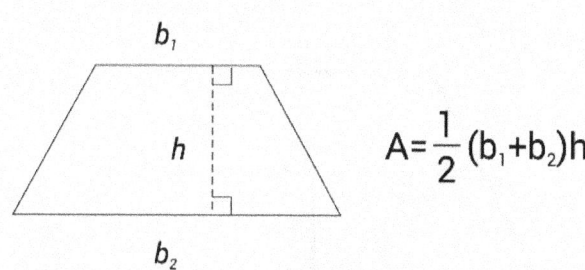

The area of a regular polygon can be determined by using its perimeter and the length of the **apothem**. The apothem is a line from the center of the regular polygon to any of its sides at a right angle. (Note that the perimeter of a regular polygon can be determined given the length of only one side.) The formula for the area (A) of a regular polygon is $A = \frac{1}{2} \times a \times P$, where a is the length of the apothem and P is the perimeter of the figure. Consider the following regular pentagon:

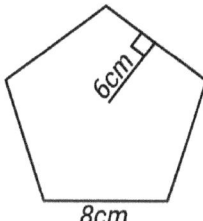

To find the area, the perimeter (P) is calculated first: $8cm \times 5 \rightarrow P = 40cm$. Then the perimeter and the apothem are used to find the area (A):

$$A = \frac{1}{2} \times a \times P$$

$$A = \frac{1}{2} \times (6cm) \times (40cm)$$

$$A = 120cm^2$$

Note that the unit is:

$$cm^2 \rightarrow cm \times cm = cm^2$$

The area of irregular polygons is found by decomposing, or breaking apart, the figure into smaller shapes. When the area of the smaller shapes is determined, the area of the smaller shapes will produce the area of the original figure when added together. Consider the example below:

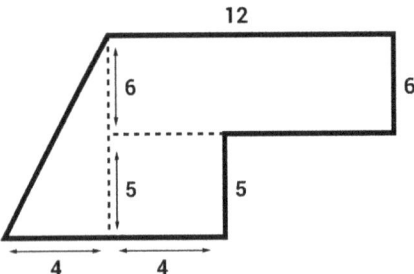

The irregular polygon is decomposed into two rectangles and a triangle. The area of the large rectangles ($A = l \times w \rightarrow A = 12 \times 6$) is 72 square units. The area of the small rectangle is 20 square units:

$$A = 4 \times 5$$

The area of the triangle:

$$A = \frac{1}{2} \times b \times h$$

$$A = \frac{1}{2} \times 4 \times 11$$

22 square units

The sum of the areas of these figures produces the total area of the original polygon:

$$A = 72 + 20 + 22$$

A = 114 square units

The perimeter (P) of the figure below is calculated by: $P = 9m + 5m + 4m + 6m + 8m \rightarrow P = 32\ m$.

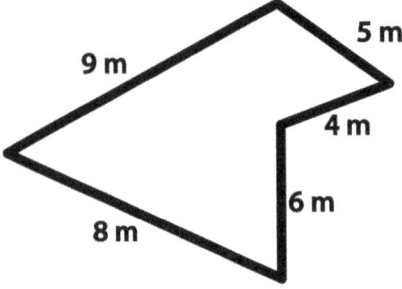

Math Part II: Calculator

Side Lengths of Shapes When Given the Area or Perimeter

The **perimeter** of a polygon is the distance around the outside of the two-dimensional figure or the sum of the lengths of all the sides. Perimeter is a one-dimensional measurement and is therefore expressed in linear units such as centimeters (*cm*), feet (*ft*), and miles (*mi*). The perimeter (*P*) of a figure can be calculated by adding together each of the sides.

Properties of certain polygons allow that the perimeter may be obtained by using formulas. A regular polygon is one in which all sides have equal length and all interior angles have equal measures, such as a square and an equilateral triangle. To find the perimeter of a regular polygon, the length of one side is multiplied by the number of sides.

A rectangle consists of two sides called the length (*l*), which have equal measures, and two sides called the width (*w*), which have equal measures. Therefore, the perimeter (*P*) of a rectangle can be expressed as $P = l + l + w + w$. This can be simplified to produce the following formula to find the perimeter of a rectangle: $P = 2l + 2w$ or $P = 2(l + w)$.

The perimeter of a square is measured by adding together all of the sides. Since a square has four equal sides, its perimeter can be calculated by multiplying the length of one side by 4. Thus, the formula is $P = 4 \times s$, where *s* equals one side. For example, the following square has side lengths of 5 meters:

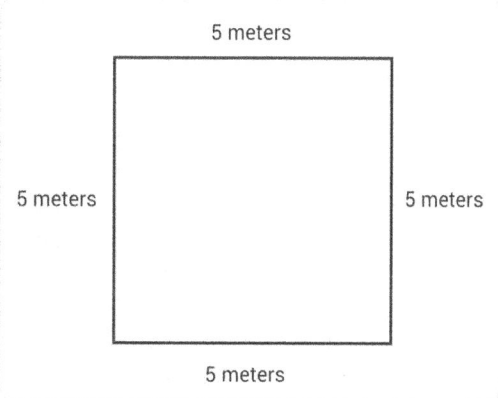

The perimeter is 20 meters because 4 times 5 is 20.

Like a square, a rectangle's perimeter is measured by adding together all of the sides. But as the sides are unequal, the formula is different. A rectangle has equal values for its lengths (long sides) and equal values for its widths (short sides), so the perimeter formula for a rectangle is:

$$P = l + l + w + w = 2l + 2w$$

l equals length
w equals width

Consider the following problem:

The total perimeter of a rectangular garden is 36m. If the length of each side is 12m, what is the width?

The formula for the perimeter of a rectangle is $P = 2L + 2W$, where *P* is the perimeter, *L* is the length, and *W* is the width. The first step is to substitute all of the data into the formula:

$$36 = 2(12) + 2W$$

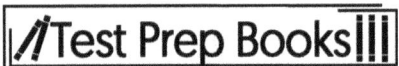

Simplify by multiplying 2×12:

$$36 = 24 + 2W$$

Simplifying this further by subtracting 24 on each side gives:

$$36 - 24 = 24 - 24 + 2W$$

$$12 = 2W$$

Divide by 2:

$$6 = W$$

The width is 6 cm. Remember to test this answer by substituting this value into the original formula:

$$36 = 2(12) + 2(6)$$

A triangle's perimeter is measured by adding together the three sides, so the formula is $P = a + b + c$, where $a, b,$ and c are the values of the three sides. The area is calculated by multiplying the length of the base times the height times ½, so the formula is:

$$A = \frac{1}{2} \times b \times h = \frac{bh}{2}$$

The base is the bottom of the triangle, and the height is the distance from the base to the peak. If a problem asks to calculate the area of a triangle, it will provide the base and height.

A circle's perimeter—also known as its circumference—is measured by multiplying the diameter (the straight line measured from one end to the direct opposite end of the circle) by π, so the formula is $\pi \times d$. This is sometimes expressed by the formula $C = 2 \times \pi \times r$, where r is the radius of the circle. These formulas are equivalent, as the radius equals half of the diameter.

Missing side lengths can be determined using subtraction. For example, if you are told that a triangle has a perimeter of 34 inches and that one side is 12 inches, another side is 16 inches, and the third side is unknown, you can calculate the length of that unknown side by setting up the following subtraction problem:

$$34 \text{ inches} = 12 \text{ inches} + 16 \text{ inches} + x$$

$$34 \text{ inches} = 28 \text{ inches} + x$$

$$6 \text{ inches} = x$$

Therefore, the missing side length is 6 inches.

Area, Circumference, Radius, and Diameter of a Circle

A **circle** can be defined as the set of all points that are the same distance (known as the **radius**, r) from a single point (known as the **center** of the circle). The center has coordinates (h, k), and any point on the circle can be labelled with coordinates (x, y).

The **circumference** of a circle is the distance traveled by following the edge of the circle for one complete revolution, and the length of the circumference is given by $2\pi r$, where r is the radius of the circle. The formula for circumference is $C = 2\pi r$.

The area of a circle is calculated through the formula $A = \pi \times r^2$. The test will indicate either to leave the answer with π attached or to calculate to the nearest decimal place, which means multiplying by 3.14 for π.

Given two points on the circumference of a circle, the path along the circle between those points is called an **arc** of the circle. For example, the arc between B and C is denoted by a thinner line:

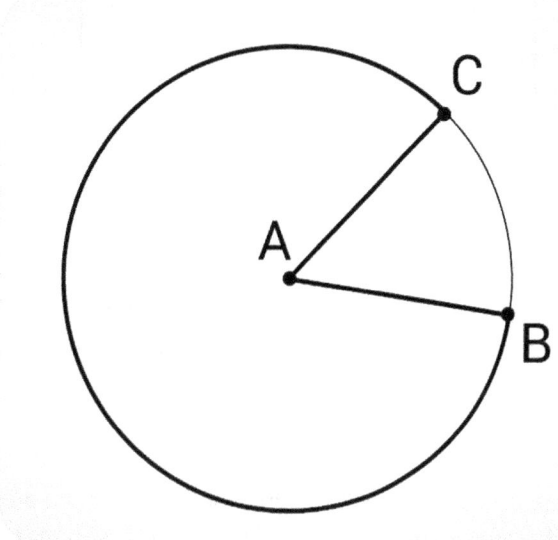

The length of the path along an arc is called the **arc length**. If the circle has radius r, then the arc length is given by multiplying the measure of the angle in radians by the radius of the circle.

Applying Formulas to Determine Surface Area and Volume

Geometry in three dimensions is similar to geometry in two dimensions. The main new feature is that three points now define a unique **plane** that passes through each of them. Three-dimensional objects can be made by putting together two-dimensional figures in different surfaces. Below, some of the possible three-dimensional figures will be provided, along with formulas for their volumes and surface areas.

Volume is the measurement of how much space an object occupies, like how much space is in the cube. Volume questions will ask how much of something is needed to completely fill the object. The most common surface area and volume questions deal with spheres, cubes, and rectangular prisms.

Surface area of a three-dimensional figure refers to the number of square units needed to cover the entire surface of the figure. This concept is similar to using wrapping paper to completely cover the outside of a box. For example, if a triangular pyramid has a surface area of 17 square inches (written $17in^2$), it will take 17 squares, each with sides one inch in length, to cover the entire surface of the pyramid. Surface area is also measured in square units.

A **rectangular prism** is a box whose sides are all rectangles meeting at 90° angles. Such a box has three dimensions: length, width, and height. If the length is x, the width is y, and the height is z, then the volume is given by $V = xyz$.

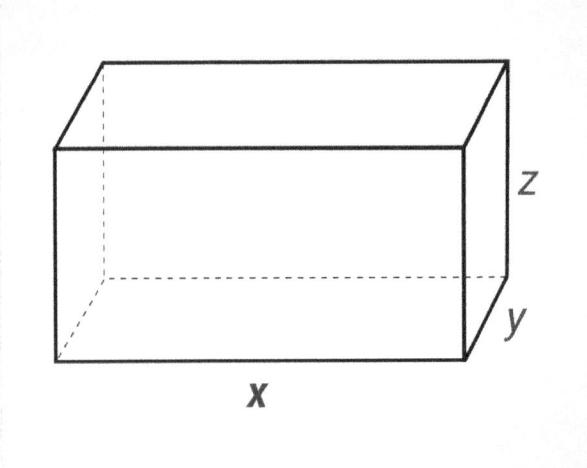

The **surface area** will be given by computing the surface area of each rectangle and adding them together. There is a total of six rectangles. Two of them have sides of length *x* and *y*, two have sides of length *y* and *z*, and two have sides of length *x* and *z*. Therefore, the total surface area will be given by:

$$SA = 2xy + 2yz + 2xz$$

A **cube** is a special type of rectangular solid in which its length, width, and height are the same. If this length is *s*, then the formula for the volume of a cube is $V = s \times s \times s$. The surface area of a cube is $SA = 6s^2$.

A **rectangular pyramid** is a figure with a rectangular base and four triangular sides that meet at a single vertex. If the rectangle has sides of length *x* and *y*, then the volume will be given by $V = \frac{1}{3}xyh$.

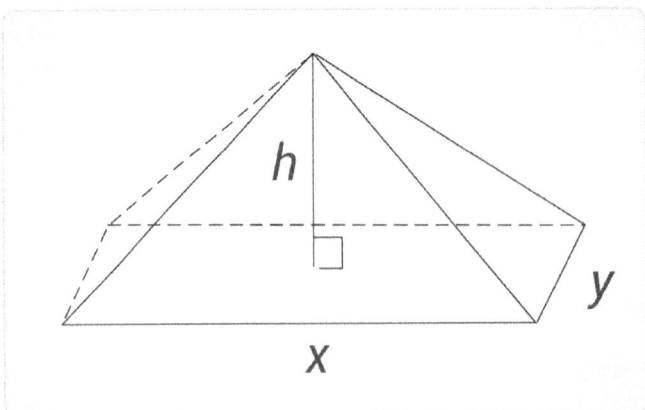

Many three-dimensional figures (solid figures) can be represented by nets consisting of rectangles and triangles. The surface area of such solids can be determined by adding the areas of each of its faces and bases. Finding the surface area using this method requires calculating the areas of rectangles and triangles. To find the area (*A*) of a rectangle, the length (*l*) is multiplied by the width (*w*) → $A = l \times w$. The area of a rectangle with a length of 8cm and a width of 4cm is calculated:

$$A = (8cm) \times (4cm) \rightarrow A = 32cm^2$$

To calculate the area (*A*) of a triangle, the product of $\frac{1}{2}$, the base (*b*), and the height (*h*) is found:

$$A = \frac{1}{2} \times b \times h$$

Note that the height of a triangle is measured from the base to the vertex opposite of it forming a right angle with the base. The area of a triangle with a base of 11cm and a height of 6cm is calculated:

$$A = \frac{1}{2} \times (11cm) \times (6cm)$$

$$A = 33cm^2$$

Consider the following triangular prism, which is represented by a net consisting of two triangles and three rectangles.

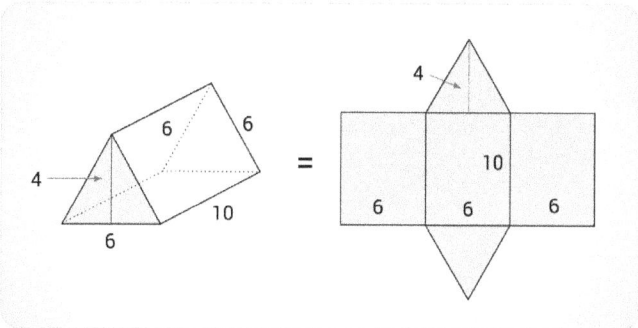

The surface area of the prism can be determined by adding the areas of each of its faces and bases. The surface area (SA) = area of triangle + area of triangle + area of rectangle + area of rectangle + area of rectangle.

$$SA = \left(\frac{1}{2} \times b \times h\right) + \left(\frac{1}{2} \times b \times h\right) + (l \times w) + (l \times w) + (l \times w)$$

$$SA = \left(\frac{1}{2} \times 6 \times 4\right) + \left(\frac{1}{2} \times 6 \times 4\right) + (6 \times 10) + (6 \times 10) + (6 \times 10)$$

$$SA = (12) + (12) + (60) + (60) + (60)$$

$SA = 204$ *square units*

A **sphere** is a set of points all of which are equidistant from some central point. It is like a circle, but in three dimensions. The volume of a sphere of radius r is given by:

$$V = \frac{4}{3}\pi r^3$$

The surface area is given by $A = 4\pi r^2$.

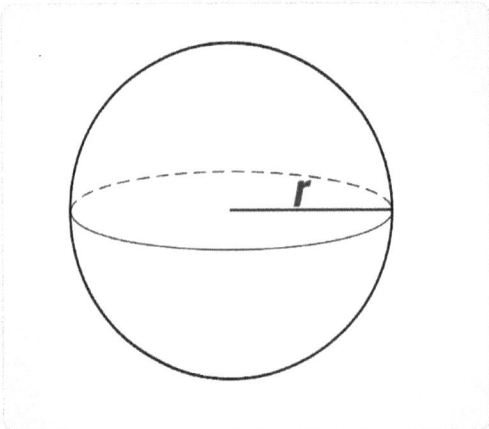

The volume of a **cylinder** is then found by adding a third dimension onto the circle. Volume of a cylinder is calculated by multiplying the area of the base (which is a circle) by the height of the cylinder. Doing so results in the equation $V = \pi r^2 h$. The volume of a **cone** is $\frac{1}{3}$ of the volume of a cylinder. Therefore, the formula for the volume of a **cone** is:

$$\frac{1}{3}\pi r^2 h$$

Solving Three-Dimensional Problems

Three-dimensional objects can be simplified into related two-dimensional shapes to solve problems. This simplification can make problem-solving a much easier experience. An isometric representation of a three-dimensional object can be completed so that important properties (e.g., shape, relationships of faces and surfaces)

Math Part II: Calculator

are noted. Edges and vertices can be translated into two-dimensional objects as well. For example, below is a three-dimensional object that's been partitioned into two-dimensional representations of its faces:

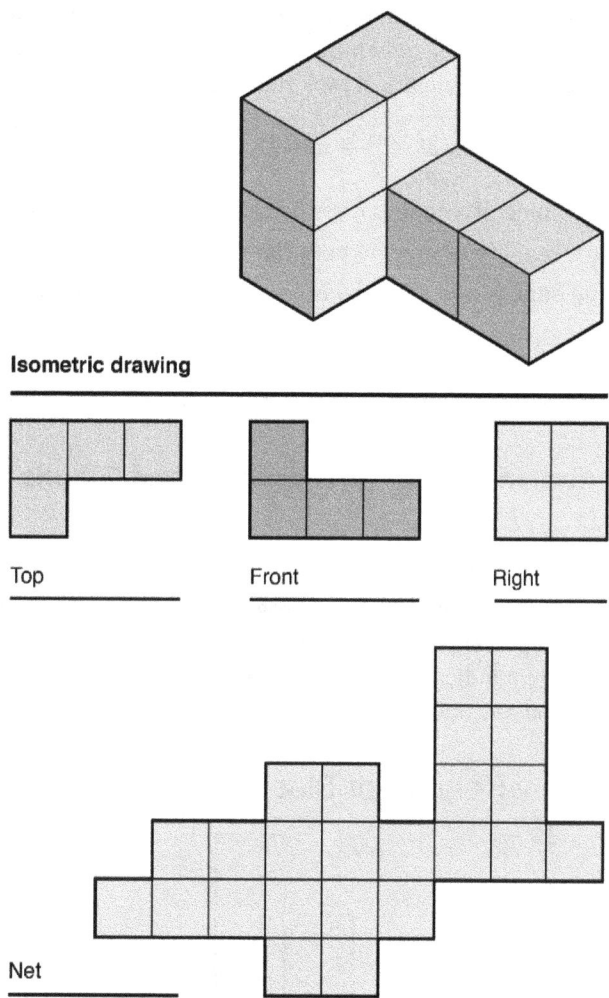

The net represents the sum of the three different faces. Depending on the problem, using a smaller portion of the given shape may be helpful, by simplifying the steps necessary to solve.

Many objects in the real world consist of three-dimensional shapes such as prisms, cylinders, and spheres. Surface area problems involve quantifying the outside area of such a three-dimensional object, and volume problems involve quantifying how much space the object takes up. Surface area of a prism is the sum of the areas, which is simplified into $SA = 2A + Bh$, where A is the area of the base, B is the perimeter of the base, and h is the height of the prism. The volume of the same prism is $V = Ah$. The surface area of a cylinder is equal to the sum of the areas of each end and the side, which is:

$$SA = 2\pi rh + 2\pi r^2$$

Its volume is:

$$V = \pi r^2 h$$

Finally, the surface area of a sphere is $SA = 4\pi r^2$, and its volume is $V = \frac{4}{3}\pi r^3$.

An example when one of these formulas should be used would be when calculating how much paint is needed for the outside of a house. In this scenario, surface area must be used. The sum of all individual areas of each side of the house must be found. Also, when calculating how much water a cylindrical tank can hold, a volume formula is used. Therefore, the amount of water that a cylindrical tank that is 8 feet tall with a radius of 3 feet is:

$$\pi \times 3^2 \times 8 = 226.1 \text{ cubic feet}$$

The formula used to calculate the volume of a cone is $\frac{1}{3}\pi r^2 h$. Essentially, the area of the base of the cone is multiplied by the cone's height. In a real-life example where the radius of a cone is 2 meters and the height of a cone is 5 meters, the volume of the cone is calculated by utilizing the formula $\frac{1}{3}\pi 2^2 \times 5$. After substituting 3.14 for π, the volume is 20.9 m^3.

Data Management and Probability

Interpreting Data Represented in Tables, Spreadsheets, and Graphs

A set of data can be visually displayed in various forms allowing for quick identification of characteristics of the set. **Histograms**, such as the one shown below, display the number of data points (vertical axis) that fall into given intervals (horizontal axis) across the range of the set. The histogram below displays the heights of black cherry trees in a certain city park. Each rectangle represents the number of trees with heights between a given five-point span. For example, the furthest bar to the right indicates that two trees are between 85 and 90 feet. Histograms can describe the center, spread, shape, and any unusual characteristics of a data set.

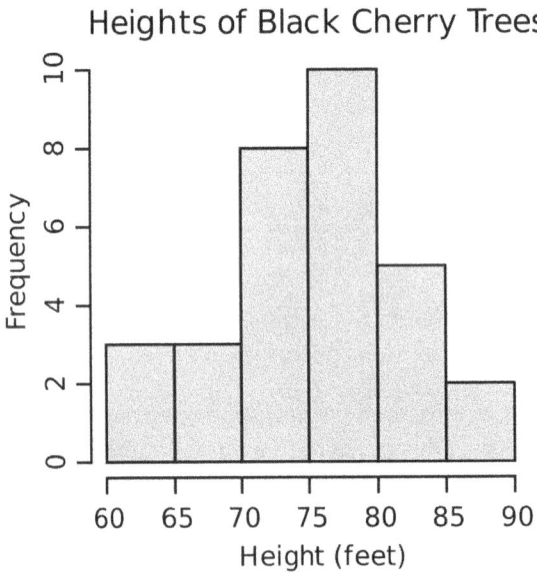

Math Part II: Calculator

A **box plot**, also called a **box-and-whisker plot**, divides the data points into four groups and displays the five-number summary for the set as well as any outliers. The five-number summary consists of:

- The lower extreme: the lowest value that is not an outlier
- The higher extreme: the highest value that is not an outlier
- The median of the set: also referred to as the second quartile or Q_2
- The first quartile or Q_1: the median of values below Q_2
- The third quartile or Q_3: the median of values above Q_2

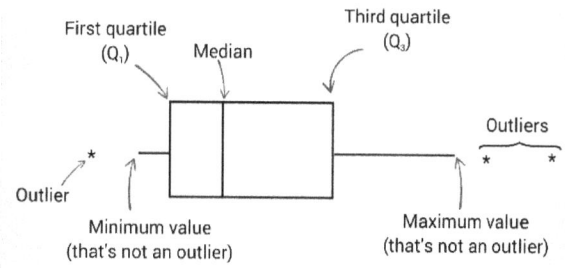

Suppose the box plot displays IQ scores for 12th grade students at a given school. The five-number summary of the data consists of: lower extreme (67); upper extreme (127); Q_2 or median (100); Q_1 (91); Q_3 (108); and outliers (135 and 140). Although all data points are not known from the plot, the points are divided into four quartiles each, including 25% of the data points. Therefore, 25% of students scored between 67 and 91, 25% scored between 91 and 100, 25% scored between 100 and 108, and 25% scored between 108 and 127. These percentages include the normal values for the set and exclude the outliers. This information is useful when comparing a given score with the rest of the scores in the set.

A **scatter plot** is a mathematical diagram that visually displays the relationship or connection between two variables. The independent variable is placed on the *x*-axis, or horizontal axis, and the dependent variable is placed on the *y*-axis, or vertical axis. When visually examining the points on the graph, if the points model a linear relationship, or a **line of best fit** can be drawn through the points with the points relatively close on either side, then a correlation exists. If the line of best fit has a positive slope (rises from left to right), then the variables have a positive correlation. If the line of best fit has a negative slope (falls from left to right), then the variables have a negative correlation. If a line of best fit cannot be drawn, then no correlation exists. A positive or negative correlation can be categorized as strong or weak, depending on how closely the points are graphed around the line of best-fit.

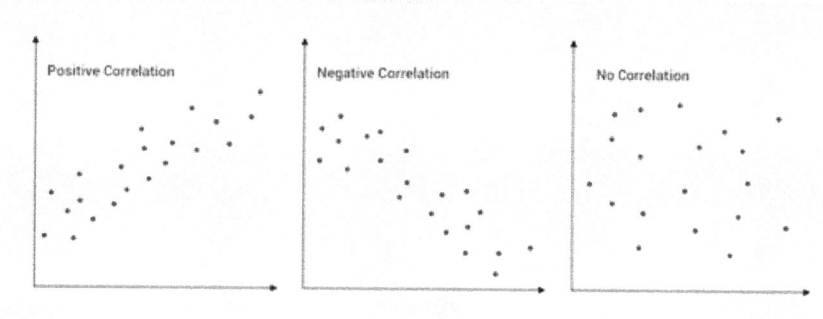

Like a scatter plot, a **line graph** compares variables that change continuously, typically over time. Paired data values (ordered pairs) are plotted on a coordinate grid with the x- and y-axis representing the variables. A line is drawn from each point to the next, going from left to right. The line graph below displays cell phone use for given years (two variables) for men, women, and both sexes (three data sets).

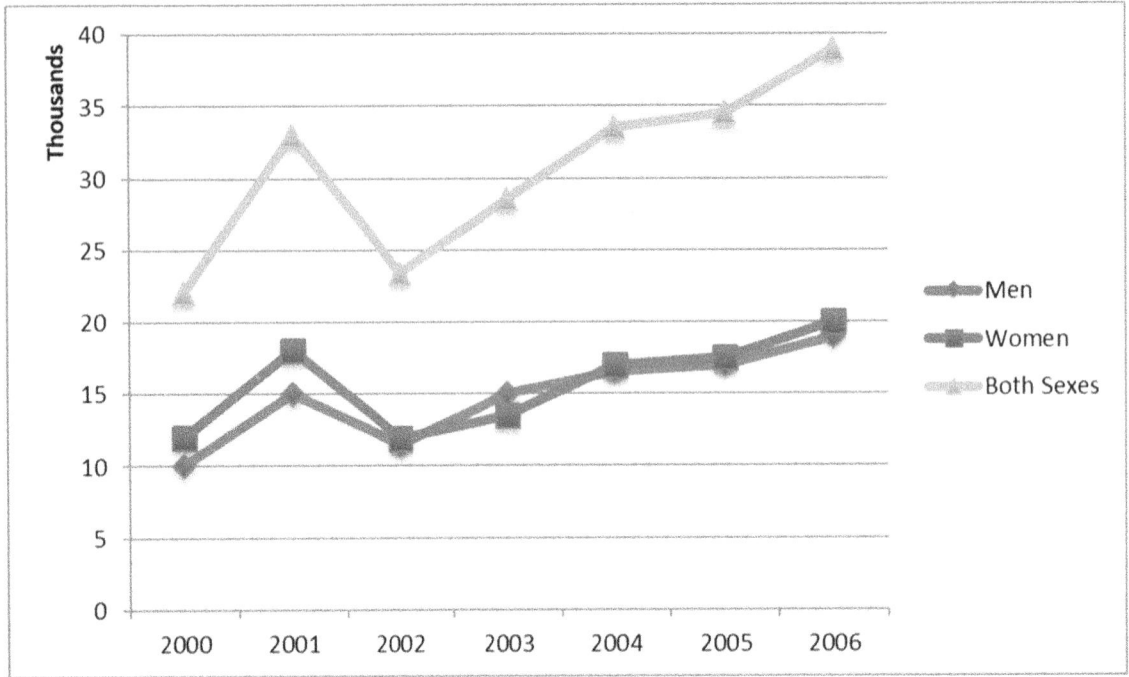

A **line plot**, also called **dot plot**, displays the frequency of data (numerical values) on a number line. To construct a line plot, a number line is used that includes all unique data values. It is marked with x's or dots above the value the number of times that the value occurs in the data set.

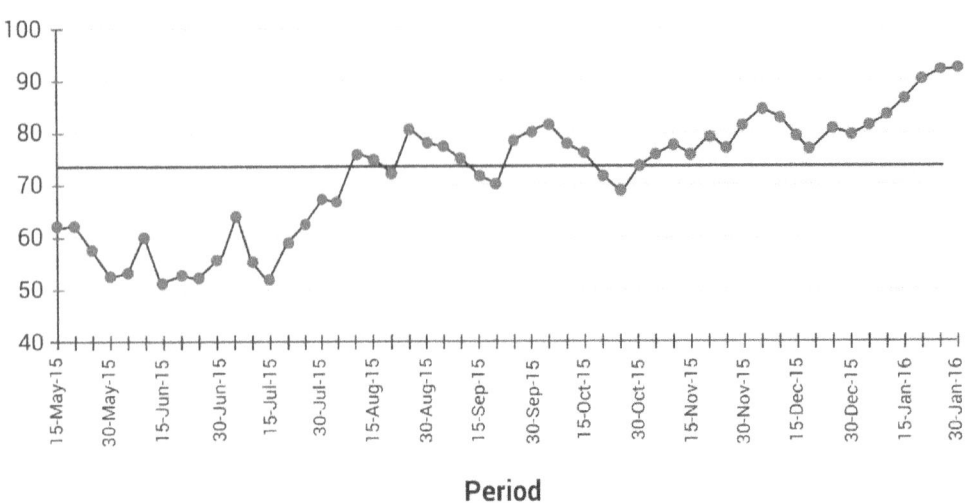

A **bar graph** is a diagram in which the quantity of items within a specific classification is represented by the height of a rectangle. Each type of classification is represented by a rectangle of equal width.

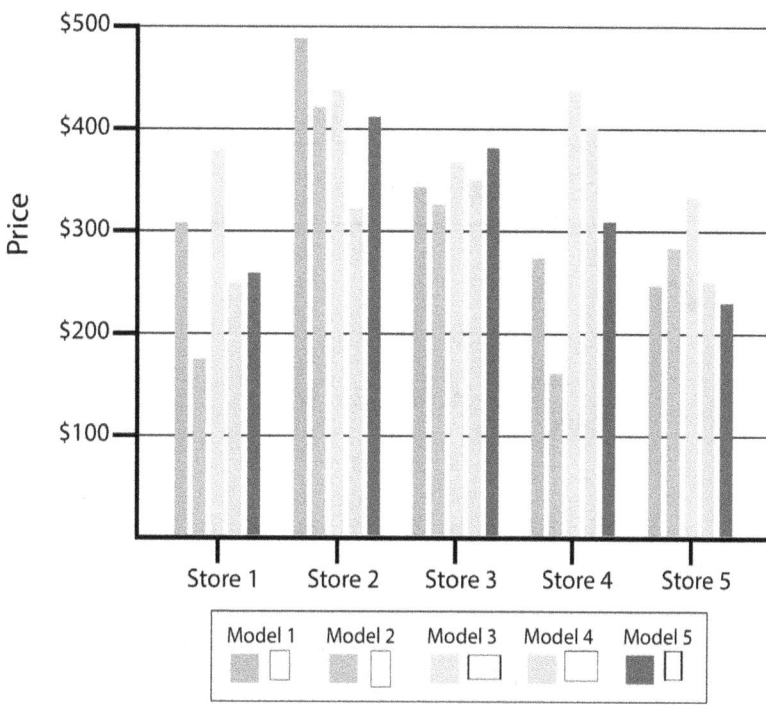

A **circle graph**, also called a **pie chart**, shows categorical data with each category representing a percentage of the whole data set. To make a circle graph, the percent of the data set for each category must be determined. To do so, the frequency of the category is divided by the total number of data points and converted to a percent. For example, if 80 people were asked what their favorite sport is and 20 responded basketball, basketball makes up 25% of the data ($\frac{20}{80}=.25=25\%$). Each category in a data set is represented by a slice of the circle proportionate to its percentage of the whole.

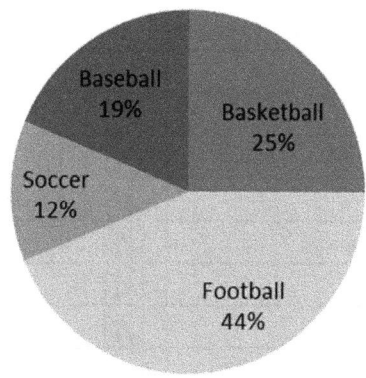

A **stem-and-leaf plot** is a method of displaying sets of data by organizing numbers by their stems (usually the tens digit) and different leaf values (usually the ones digit).

For example, to organize a number of movie critic's ratings, as listed below, a stem-and-leaf plot could be utilized to display the information in a more condensed manner.

Movie critic scores: 47, 52, 56, 59, 61, 64, 66, 68, 68, 70, 73, 75, 79, 81, 83, 85, 86, 88, 88, 89, 90, 90, 91, 93, 94, 96, 96, 99.

	Movie Ratings
4	7
5	2 6 9
6	1 4 6 8 8
7	0 3 5 9
8	1 3 5 6 8 8 9
9	0 0 1 3 4 6 6 9
Key	6 | 1 represents 61

Looking at this stem and leaf plot, it is easy to ascertain key features of the data set. For example, what is the range of the data in the stem-and-leaf plot?

Using this method, it is easier to visualize the distribution of the scores and answer the question pertaining to the range of scores, which is:

$$99 - 47 = 52$$

A **tally chart** is a diagram in which tally marks are utilized to represent data. Tally marks are a means of showing a quantity of objects within a specific classification. Here is an example of a tally chart:

Number of days with rain	Number of weeks
0	||
1	⦀⦀ |
2	⦀⦀ ||||
3	⦀⦀ ⦀⦀ ⦀⦀
4	⦀⦀
5	⦀⦀ |
6	⦀⦀
7	|

Data is often recorded using fractions, such as half a mile, and understanding fractions is critical because of their popular use in real-world applications. Also, it is extremely important to label values with their units when using data. For example, regarding length, the number 2 is meaningless unless it is attached to a unit. A measurement of 2 cm is much different than 2 miles.

Calculating and Analyzing Mean, Median, Mode and Range

Suppose that X is a set of data points $(x_1, x_2, x_3, \ldots x_n)$, and some description of the general properties of this data need to be found.

The first property that can be defined for this set of data is the **mean**. To find the mean, add up all the data points, then divide by the total number of data points. This can be expressed using **summation notation** as:

$$\bar{X} = \frac{x_1 + x_2 + x_3 + \cdots + x_n}{n} = \frac{1}{n}\sum_{i=1}^{n} x_i$$

For example, suppose that in a class of 10 students, the scores on a test were 50, 60, 65, 65, 75, 80, 85, 85, 90, 100. Therefore, the average test score will be:

$$\frac{1}{10}(50 + 60 + 65 + 65 + 75 + 80 + 85 + 85 + 90 + 100) = 75.5$$

The mean is a useful number if the distribution of data is normal (more on this later), which roughly means that the frequency of different outcomes has a single peak and is roughly equally distributed on both sides of that peak. However, it is less useful in some cases where the data might be split or where there are some outliers. **Outliers** are data points that are far from the rest of the data. For example, suppose there are 90 employees and 10 executives at a company. The executives make $1000 per hour, and the employees make $10 per hour. Therefore, the average pay rate will be:

$$\frac{1000 \times 10 + 10 \times 90}{100} = \$109 \; per \; hour$$

In this case, this average is not very descriptive.

Another useful measurement is the **median**. In a data set X consisting of data points $x_1, x_2, x_3, \ldots x_n$, the median is the point in the middle. The middle refers to the point where half the data comes before it and half comes after, when the data is recorded in numerical order. If n is odd, then the median is:

$$x_{\frac{n+1}{2}}$$

If n is even, it is defined as $\frac{1}{2}\left(x_{\frac{n}{2}} + x_{\frac{n}{2}+1}\right)$, the mean of the two data points closest to the middle of the data points. In the previous example of test scores, the two middle points are 75 and 80. Since there is no single point, the average of these two scores needs to be found. The average is:

$$\frac{75 + 80}{2} = 77.5$$

The median is generally a good value to use if there are a few outliers in the data. It prevents those outliers from affecting the "middle" value as much as when using the mean.

Since an outlier is a data point that is far from most of the other data points in a data set, this means an outlier also is any point that is far from the median of the data set. The outliers can have a substantial effect on the mean of a data set, but usually do not change the median or mode, or do not change them by a large quantity. For example, consider the data set (3, 5, 6, 6, 6, 8). This has a median of 6 and a mode of 6, with a mean of $\frac{34}{6} \approx 5.67$. Now, suppose a new data point of 1000 is added so that the data set is now (3, 5, 6, 6, 6, 8, 1000). This does not change the median or mode, which are both still 6. However, the average is now $\frac{1034}{7}$, which is approximately 147.7. In this case, the median and mode will be better descriptions for most of the data points.

The reason for outliers in a given data set is a complicated problem. It is sometimes the result of an error by the experimenter, but often they are perfectly valid data points that must be taken into consideration.

One additional measure to define for X is the **mode**. This is the data point that appears more frequently. If two or more data points all tie for the most frequent appearance, then each of them is considered a mode. In the case of the test scores, where the numbers were 50, 60, 65, 65, 75, 80, 85, 85, 90, 100, there are two modes: 65 and 85.

The **first quartile** of a set of data X refers to the largest value from the first ¼ of the data points. In practice, there are sometimes slightly different definitions that can be used, such as the median of the first half of the data points (excluding the median itself if there are an odd number of data points). The term also has a slightly different use: when it is said that a data point lies in the first quartile, it means it is less than or equal to the median of the first half of the data points. Conversely, if it lies *at* the first quartile, then it is equal to the first quartile.

When it is said that a data point lies in the **second quartile**, it means it is between the first quartile and the median.

The **third quartile** refers to data that lies between ½ and ¾ of the way through the data set. Again, there are various methods for defining this precisely, but the simplest way is to include all of the data that lie between the median and the median of the top half of the data.

Data that lies in the **fourth quartile** refers to all of the data above the third quartile.

Percentiles may be defined in a similar manner to quartiles. Generally, this is defined in the following manner:

If a data point lies *in* the n-th percentile, this means it lies in the range of the first *n*% of the data.

If a data point lies *at* the *n*-th percentile, then it means that *n*% of the data lies below this data point.

Given a data set X consisting of data points $(x_1, x_2, x_3, \ldots x_n)$, the **variance of X** is defined to be:

$$\frac{\sum_{i=1}^{n}(x_i - \bar{X})^2}{n}$$

This means that the variance of X is the average of the squares of the differences between each data point and the mean of X. In the formula, $\bar{X}$ is the mean of the values in the data set, and x_i represents each individual value in the data set. The sigma notation indicates that the sum should be found with n being the number of values to add together. $i = 1$ means that the values should begin with the first value.

Given a data set X consisting of data points $(x_1, x_2, x_3, \ldots x_n)$, the **standard deviation of X** is defined to be

$$s_x = \sqrt{\frac{\sum_{i=1}^{n}(x_i - \bar{X})^2}{n}}$$

In other words, the standard deviation is the square root of the variance.

Both the variance and the standard deviation are measures of how much the data tend to be spread out. When the standard deviation is low, the data points are mostly clustered around the mean. When the standard deviation is high, this generally indicates that the data are quite spread out, or else that there are a few substantial outliers.

As a simple example, compute the standard deviation for the data set (1, 3, 3, 5). First, compute the mean, which will be:

$$\frac{1+3+3+5}{4} = \frac{12}{4} = 3$$

Now, find the variance of X with the formula:

$$\sum_{i=1}^{4}(x_i - \bar{X})^2 = (1-3)^2 + (3-3)^2 + (3-3)^2 + (5-3)^2 = -2^2 + 0^2 + 0^2 + 2^2 = 8$$

Therefore, the variance is $\frac{8}{4} = 2$. Taking the square root, the standard deviation will be $\sqrt{2}$.

Note that the standard deviation only depends upon the mean, not upon the median or mode(s). Generally, if there are multiple modes that are far apart from one another, the standard deviation will be high. A high standard deviation does not always mean there are multiple modes, however.

Describing a Set of Data

A set of data can be described in terms of its center, spread, shape and any unusual features. The center of a data set can be measured by its mean, median, or mode. The spread of a data set refers to how far the data points are from the center (mean or median). The spread can be measured by the range or by the quartiles and interquartile range. A data set with data points clustered around the center will have a small spread. A data set covering a wide range will have a large spread.

When a data set is displayed as a **histogram** or frequency distribution plot, the shape indicates if a sample is normally distributed, symmetrical, or has measures of skewness or kurtosis. When graphed, a data set with a **normal distribution** will resemble a bell curve.

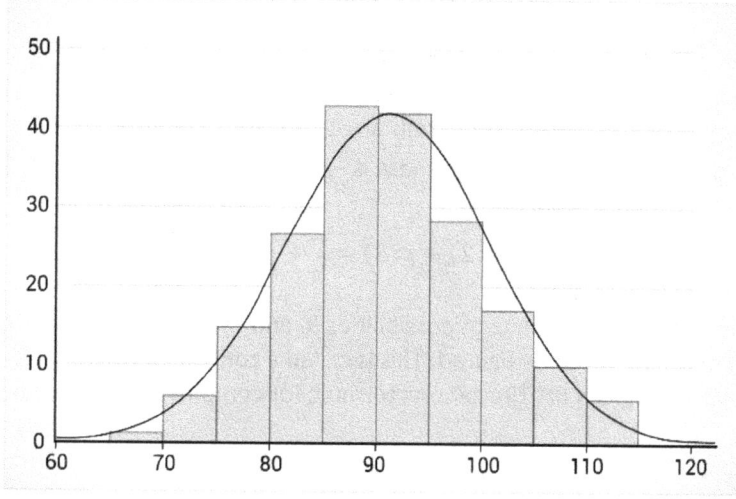

If the data set is symmetrical, each half of the graph when divided at the center is a mirror image of the other. If the graph has fewer data points to the right, the data is **skewed right**. If it has fewer data points to the left, the data is **skewed left**.

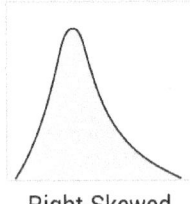 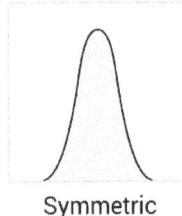 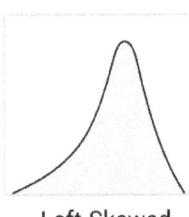

Right-Skewed   Symmetric   Left-Skewed

Kurtosis is a measure of whether the data is heavy-tailed with a high number of outliers, or light-tailed with a low number of outliers.

A description of a data set should include any unusual features such as gaps or outliers. A **gap** is a span within the range of the data set containing no data points. An **outlier** is a data point with a value either extremely large or extremely small when compared to the other values in the set.

Solving Problems That Involve Probability

Probability of an Event

Given a set of possible outcomes X, a **probability distribution** of X is a function that assigns a probability to each possible outcome. If the outcomes are $(x_1, x_2, x_3, \ldots x_n)$, and the probability distribution is p, then the following rules are applied.

- $0 \leq p(x_i) \leq 1$, for any i.
- $\sum_{i=1}^{n} p(x_i) = 1$.

In other words, the probability of a given outcome must be between zero and 1, while the total probability must be 1.

If $p(x_i)$ is constant, then this is called a **uniform probability distribution**, and $p(x_i) = \frac{1}{n}$. For example, on a six-sided die, the probability of each of the six outcomes will be $\frac{1}{6}$.

If seeking the probability of an outcome occurring in some specific range A of possible outcomes, written $P(A)$, add up the probabilities for each outcome in that range. For example, consider a six-sided die, and figure the probability of getting a 3 or lower when it is rolled. The possible rolls are 1, 2, 3, 4, 5, and 6. So, to get a 3 or lower, a roll of 1, 2, or 3 must be completed. The probabilities of each of these is $\frac{1}{6}$, so add these to get:

$$p(1) + p(2) + p(3) = \frac{1}{6} + \frac{1}{6} + \frac{1}{6} = \frac{1}{2}$$

An outcome occasionally lies within some range of possibilities B, and the probability that the outcomes also lie within some set of possibilities A needs to be figured. This is called a **conditional probability**. It is written as $P(A|B)$, which is read "the probability of A given B." The general formula for computing conditional probabilities is:

$$P(A|B) = \frac{P(A \cap B)}{P(B)}$$

However, when dealing with uniform probability distributions, simplify this a bit. Write $|A|$ to indicate the number of outcomes in A. Then, for uniform probability distributions, write:

$$P(A|B) = \frac{|A \cap B|}{|B|}$$

(recall that $A \cap B$ means "A intersect B," and consists of all of the outcomes that lie in both A and B)

This means that all possible outcomes do not need to be known. To see why this formula works, suppose that the set of outcomes X is $(x_1, x_2, x_3, \ldots x_n)$, so that $|X| = n$. Then, for a uniform probability distribution:

$$P(A) = \frac{|A|}{n}$$

However, this means:

$$(A|B) = \frac{P(A \cap B)}{P(B)} = \frac{\frac{|A \cap B|}{n}}{\frac{|B|}{n}} = \frac{|A \cap B|}{|B|}$$

Each n will be canceled out.

For example, suppose a die is rolled and it is known that it will land between 1 and 4. However, how many sides the die has is unknown. Figure the probability that the die is rolled higher than 2. To figure this, $P(3)$ or $P(4)$ does not need to be determined, or any of the other probabilities, since it is known that a fair die has a uniform probability distribution. Therefore, apply the formula $\frac{|A \cap B|}{|B|}$. So, in this case B is (1, 2, 3, 4) and $A \cap B$ is (3, 4).

Therefore:

$$\frac{|A \cap B|}{|B|} = \frac{2}{4} = \frac{1}{2}$$

Conditional probability is an important concept because, in many situations, the likelihood of one outcome can differ radically depending on how something else comes out. The probability of passing a test given that one has studied all of the material is generally much higher than the probability of passing a test given that one has not studied at all. The probability of a person having heart trouble is much lower if that person exercises regularly. The probability that a college student will graduate is higher when their SAT scores are higher, and so on. For this reason, there are many people who are interested in conditional probabilities.

Note that in some practical situations, changing the order of the conditional probabilities can make the outcome very different. For example, the probability that a person with heart trouble has exercised regularly is quite different than the probability that a person who exercises regularly will have heart trouble. The probability of a person receiving a military-only award, given that he or she is or was a soldier, is generally not very high, but the probability that a person being or having been a soldier, given that he or she received a military-only award, is 1.

However, in some cases, the outcomes do not influence one another this way. If the probability of A is the same regardless of whether B is given; that is, if $P(A|B) = P(A)$, then A and B are considered **independent**. In this case:

$$P(A|B) = \frac{P(A \cap B)}{P(B)} = P(A)$$

so $P(A \cap B) = P(A)P(B)$. In fact, if $P(A \cap B) = P(A)P(B)$, it can be determined that $P(A|B) = P(A)$ and $P(A|B) = P(B)$ by working backward. Therefore, B is also independent of A.

An example of something being independent can be seen in rolling dice. In this case, consider a red die and a green die. It is expected that when the dice are rolled, the outcome of the green die should not depend in any way on the outcome of the red die. Or, to take another example, if the same die is rolled repeatedly, then the next number rolled should not depend on which numbers have been rolled previously. Similarly, if a coin is flipped, then the next flip's outcome does not depend on the outcomes of previous flips.

This can sometimes be counter-intuitive, since when rolling a die or flipping a coin, there can be a streak of surprising results. If, however, it is known that the die or coin is fair, then these results are just the result of the fact that over long periods of time, it is very likely that some unlikely streaks of outcomes will occur. Therefore, avoid making the mistake of thinking that when considering a series of independent outcomes, a particular outcome is "due to happen" simply because a surprising series of outcomes has already been seen.

There is a second type of common mistake that people tend to make when reasoning about statistical outcomes: the idea that when something of low probability happens, this is surprising. It would be surprising that something with low probability happened after just one attempt. However, with so much happening all at once, it is easy to see at least something happen in a way that seems to have a very low probability. In fact, a lottery is a good example. The odds of winning a lottery are very small, but the odds that somebody wins the lottery each week are actually fairly high. Therefore, no one should be surprised when some low probability things happen.

A **simple event** consists of only one outcome. The most popular simple event is flipping a coin, which results in either heads or tails. A **compound event** results in more than one outcome and consists of more than one simple event. An example of a compound event is flipping a coin while tossing a die. The result is either heads or tails on the coin and a number from one to six on the die. The probability of a simple event is calculated by dividing the number of possible outcomes by the total number of outcomes. Therefore, the probability of obtaining heads on a coin is $\frac{1}{2}$, and the probability of rolling a 6 on a die is $\frac{1}{6}$. The probability of compound events is calculated using the basic idea of the probability of simple events. If the two events are independent, the probability of one outcome is equal to the product of the probabilities of each simple event. For example, the probability of obtaining heads on a coin and rolling a 6 is equal to $\frac{1}{2} \times \frac{1}{6} = \frac{1}{12}$. The probability of either A or B occurring is equal to the sum of the probabilities minus the probability that both A and B will occur. Therefore, the probability of obtaining either heads on a coin or rolling a 6 on a die is:

$$\frac{1}{2} + \frac{1}{6} - \frac{1}{12} = \frac{7}{12}$$

The two events aren't mutually exclusive because they can happen at the same time. If two events are mutually exclusive, and the probability of both events occurring at the same time is zero, the probability of event A or B occurring equals the sum of both probabilities. An example of calculating the probability of two mutually exclusive events is determining the probability of pulling a king or a queen from a deck of cards. The two events cannot occur at the same time.

Counting Techniques
The **addition rule** for probabilities states that the probability of A or B happening is:

$$P(A \cup B) = P(A) + P(B) - P(A \cap B)$$

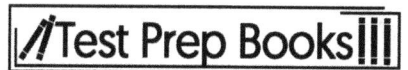

Note that the subtraction of $P(A \cap B)$ must be performed, or else it would result in double counting any outcomes that lie in both A and in B. For example, suppose that a 20-sided die is being rolled. Fred bets that the outcome will be greater than 10, while Helen bets that it will be greater than 4 but less than 15. What is the probability that at least one of them is correct?

We apply the rule:

$$P(A \cup B) = P(A) + P(B) - P(A \cap B)$$

where A is that outcome x is in the range $x > 10$, and B is that outcome x is in the range $4 < x < 15$.

$$P(A) = 10 \times \frac{1}{20} = \frac{1}{2}$$

$$P(B) = 10 \times \frac{1}{20} = \frac{1}{2}$$

$P(A \cap B)$ can be computed by noting that $A \cap B$ means the outcome x is in the range $10 < x < 15$, so

$$P(A \cap B) = 4 \times \frac{1}{20} = \frac{1}{5}$$

Therefore:

$$P(A \cup B) = P(A) + P(B) - P(A \cap B)$$

$$\frac{1}{2} + \frac{1}{2} - \frac{1}{5} = \frac{4}{5}$$

Note that in this particular example, we could also have directly reasoned about the set of possible outcomes $A \cup B$, by noting that this would mean that x must be in the range $5 \leq x$. However, this is not always the case, depending on the given information.

The **multiplication rule** for probabilities states the probability of A and B both happening is:

$$P(A \cap B) = P(A)P(B|A)$$

As an example, suppose that when Jamie wears black pants, there is a ½ probability that she wears a black shirt as well, and that she wears black pants ¾ of the time. What is the probability that she is wearing both a black shirt and black pants?

To figure this, use the above formula, where A will be "Jamie is wearing black pants," while B will be "Jamie is wearing a black shirt." It is known that $P(A)$ is ¾. It is also known that $P(B|A) = \frac{1}{2}$. Multiplying the two, the probability that she is wearing both black pants and a black shirt is:

$$P(A)P(B|A) = \frac{3}{4} \times \frac{1}{2} = \frac{3}{8}$$

Math Part II Practice Quiz

1. The table below displays the number of three-year-olds at Kids First Daycare who are potty-trained and those who still wear diapers.

	Potty-trained	Wear diapers	Sum
Boys	26	22	48
Girls	34	18	52
Total	60	40	

If a three-year-old girl is randomly selected from this school, what is the probability that she is potty-trained?
   a. 52%
   b. 34%
   c. 65%
   d. 57%

2. What is $\frac{420}{98}$ rounded to the nearest integer?

3. A traveler takes an hour to drive to a museum, spends three hours and 30 minutes there, and takes half an hour to drive home. What percentage of their time was spent driving?
   a. 15%
   b. 30%
   c. 40%
   d. 60%

4. A truck is carrying three cylindrical barrels. Each barrel has a diameter of 2 feet and a height of 3 feet. What is the total volume of the three barrels in cubic feet?
   a. 3π
   b. 9π
   c. 12π
   d. 15π

5. The perimeter of a 6-sided polygon is 56 cm. The lengths of 3 sides are 9 cm each. The lengths of 2 other sides are 8 cm each. What is the length of the missing side?

See answers on the next page.

Math Part II Answer Explanations

1. C: There are 34 girls who are potty-trained out of a total of 52 girls:

$$34 \div 52 \approx 0.65 = 65\%$$

2. 4: Dividing by 98 can be approximated by dividing by 100, which would mean shifting the decimal point of the numerator to the left two places. The result is 4.2, which rounds to 4.

3. B: The total trip time is $1 + 3.5 + 0.5 = 5$ hours. The total time driving is $1 + 0.5 = 1.5$ hours. So, the fraction of time spent driving is $\frac{1.5}{5}$ or $\frac{3}{10}$. To convert this to a percentage, multiply the top and bottom by 10 to make the denominator 100. $\frac{3}{10} \times \frac{10}{10} = \frac{30}{100}$. Since the denominator is 100, the numerator is the percentage: 30%.

4. B: The formula for the volume of a cylinder is $\pi r^2 h$, where r is the radius and h is the height. The diameter is twice the radius, so these barrels have a radius of 1 foot. That means each barrel has a volume of:

$$\pi \times (1 \text{ ft})^2 \times 3 \text{ ft} = 3\pi \text{ ft}^3$$

Since there are three of them, the total is:

$$3 \times 3\pi \text{ ft}^3 = 9\pi \text{ ft}^3$$

5. 13: The perimeter is found by calculating the sum of all sides of the polygon:

$$9 + 9 + 9 + 8 + 8 + s = 56$$

Let s be the missing side length. Therefore, $43 + s = 56$. The missing side length is 13 cm.

Science

Nature of Science

Identifying Characteristics of Science

Human beings are, by nature, very curious. Since long before the scientific method was established, people have been making observations and predicting outcomes, manipulating the physical world to create extraordinary things—from the first man-made fire in 6000 BC. to the satellite that orbited Pluto in 2016. Although the history of the scientific method is sporadic and attributed to many different people, it remains the most reliable way to obtain and utilize knowledge about the observable universe. The scientific method consists of the following steps:

- Make an observation
- Create a question
- Form a hypothesis
- Conduct an experiment
- Collect and analyze data
- Form a conclusion

Distinguishing Between Observations and Inferences

The first step is to identify a problem based on an observation—the who, what, when, where, why, and how. An **observation** is the analysis of information using basic human senses: sight, sound, touch, taste, and smell. Observations can be two different types—qualitative or quantitative. A **qualitative observation** describes what is being observed, such as the color of a house or the smell of a flower. **Quantitative observations** measure what is being observed, such as the number of windows on a house or the intensity of a flower's smell on a scale of 1-5.

Observations lead to the identification of a problem, also called an **inference.** For example, if a fire truck is barreling down a busy street, the inferences could be:

- There's a fire.
- Someone is hurt.
- Some kid pulled the fire alarm at a local school.

Inferences are logical predictions based on experience or education that lead to the formation of a hypothesis.

Distinguishing Between Questions that can be Investigated and Questions that Cannot

The nature of science is based on the collection of evidence that may change over time. Scientific inquiry is the way in which researchers or scientists study the natural world and provide explanations based on evidence collected through their work. Researchers develop scientific knowledge as they perform experiments, come to understand scientific ideas, and devise ways to study the natural world more thoroughly. Progress in science has come through trial and error, with success attributed to an attitude of inquiry and experimentation.

The scientific method can be carried out in many ways but generally involves observation, questioning, prediction, testing predictions, and drawing conclusions. A **hypothesis** is an educated guess that helps answer a scientific question. Science **facts** are agreements arrived at by observers who make a series of consistent observations in regard to a phenomenon. A hypothesis that is continually tested without the presence of a contradiction can become a **law** or principle. **Theories** are made up of a large body of information that contains all verified and well-tested hypotheses but can undergo change.

A scientific question requires a testable hypothesis. If a question remains unanswered by evidence or direct observation through experimental investigation, then the question is not testable. Scientific questions are limited and are based on the material world; they do not involve aesthetic questions, which are based on pleasantness and subjectivity. For example, "Is the building beautiful?" would be an aesthetic question, but "Is the building sturdy enough to hold people?" would be a scientific question because it's testable. Moral questions—for example, "Is cloning animals and humans moral?"—relate to ethical issues and are likewise not testable scientifically. Finally, supernatural questions— for example, "Do haunted houses really contain ghosts or spirits?"—relate to unexplainable forces outside the laws of nature and beyond scientific understanding. Science can only work with nature and not with forces beyond nature or the supernatural. While many television shows illustrate the use of cameras and digital audio recorders to study the supernatural, they generally do not employ the scientific method.

Ultimately, science is concerned with collecting and organizing knowledge. With technology, people can utilize scientific knowledge for practical applications as well as developing the instruments needed to conduct further investigations. While technology can sometimes harm the environment, overall, it's a tool that can solve many problems and improve conditions in the world.

Explaining Ways Scientific Work is Maintained

Subject to Change
The nature of science is to continuously gather knowledge in order to develop an understanding of the universe. Because of its experimental nature, there's no such thing as "absolute truth" in science. Even the oldest theories are constantly tested in order to improve our understanding or disregard those that no longer apply in light of new observations and interpretations.

Consistent with Evidence
Science is subject to change because of evidence presented in light of new findings. Science is dependent upon the inferences made from evidence obtained through observation. Introductions, expansions, and revisions of scientific theories must present evidence to ascertain that they're still true.

Based on Reproducible Evidence
Before scientific knowledge is established as true, it must be reproducible—that is, the entire experiment must be able to be duplicated by either the same scientist or a different one to ensure its validity.

Includes Unifying Concepts and Processes
Scientific knowledge must be unified, meaning there are central ideas common to all sciences from which new and improved information can grow. There are standards for unifying concepts and processes that students are required to learn in grades K-12, which include:

- Systems, Order, and Organization
  - Observing the universe in distinct parts and understanding all elements that compose these parts to form the whole—e.g., organisms, galaxies, cells, numbers, government, the entire known universe, etc.
- Evidence, Models, and Explanation
  - Scientific theories are based on collected evidence, which provides explanations and the basis for models that enhance understanding and enable scientists to make predictions.

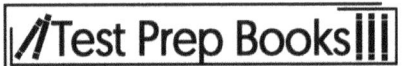

- Change, Consistency, and Measurement
    - The natural world is consistently changing, yet many patterns are repeated over time—i.e., change of seasons, tidal phases, moon phases, etc.
- Evolution and Equilibrium
    - Organisms are genetically diverse, and traits that are advantageous for survival are passed on through the generations. Natural systems all trend towards equilibrium—a state of balance between opposing processes.
- Form and Function
    - There is a relationship between an object's structure and its function—i.e., tooth shape, cell shape, leaf thickness, etc.

Identifying Factors that may Introduce Bias

Scientific studies can contain a certain degree of research bias, which can lead to incorrect conclusions. Bias can take place when collecting, analyzing, interpreting, or publishing data. Examples of scientific bias include the small study effect and publication, citation, information, interviewer, researcher, response, selection, cognitive, or interest group bias.

Information bias or measurement bias occurs during data collection. Examples include poor interviewing or cases where study variables are not measured correctly. Recall, observer, and performance bias are types of information bias. In the small study effect, smaller studies can have larger treatment effects compared to larger studies. For example, the small study effect can occur when a publication containing a small study has a strong impact or significant results; consequently, the publication is increased and the study has a disproportionately large effect. Another factor in the small study effect is the selective reporting of favorable experimental outcomes or **outcome selection bias**. Meanwhile, in selection bias, subjects in a study are selected in a way that makes a specific outcome more likely to occur compared to the entire population. An example of a selection bias may be choosing people to be part of a weight loss study program who are already interested in losing weight. The introduced self-selection bias can skew the collected data and may not represent a broader population.

In **publication bias**, the decision to publish a research study is dependent on the nature of the results. For instance, studies involving clinical trials can withhold negative results from a publication and therefore distort the literature, leading to skewed data and misguided research. Due to competition for funding, researchers are more likely to submit positive results for publication since they will be looked upon favorably by peer reviewers; once the results are published, they will be cited more. Scientific research that does not fully report findings to suppress negative or unfavorable findings is an example of **selective reporting bias**, which can lead to overestimation of treatment effects.

Citation bias involves the selection of scientific article citations based on results. Citation bias is common in the biomedical sciences and lowest in the natural sciences. Articles that are generally positive are cited twice as much compared to articles that have negative results. Consequently, literature in the sciences is not well represented in scientific publications, which can lead to false beliefs.

Another potential source of bias is the source of funding. Groundbreaking research is often funded by special interest groups and private foundations; these organizations can have a specific stance on an issue and be interested in funding a research project that will advance their goals. For instance, specific organizations in the United States have donated hundreds of thousands of dollars to universities to study hydraulic fracking in the Marcellus shale. Research funded by these organizations has produced studies suggesting that shale gas is clean, even though many researchers have suggested otherwise. When a researcher accepts grant money from an interest group, it becomes a major issue since the researcher can produce results that favor the group's cause.

Scientific Inquiry Skills

Formulating Testable Questions

Forming and Testing a Hypothesis

A **hypothesis** is a testable explanation of an observed scenario and is presented in the form of a statement. It's an attempt to answer a question based on an observation, and it allows a scientist to predict an outcome. A hypothesis makes assumptions on the relationship between two different variables, and answers the question: "If I do this, what happens to that?"

In order to form a hypothesis, there must be an independent variable and a dependent variable that can be measured. The **independent variable** is the variable that is manipulated, and the **dependent variable** is the result of the change.

For example, suppose a student wants to know how light affects plant growth. Based upon what he or she already knows, the student proposes (hypothesizes) that the more light to which a plant is exposed, the faster it will grow.

- Observation: Plants exposed to lots of light seem to grow taller.
- Question: Will plants grow faster if there's more light available?
- Hypothesis: The more light the plant has, the faster it will grow.
- Independent variable: The amount of time exposed to light (able to be manipulated)
- Dependent variable: Plant growth (the result of the manipulation)

Once a hypothesis has been formed, it must be tested to determine whether it's true or false. (How to test a hypothesis is described in a subsequent section.) After it has been tested and validated as true over and over, then a hypothesis can develop into a theory, model, or law.

Development of Theories, Models, and Laws

Theories, models, and laws have one thing in common: *they develop on the basis of scientific evidence that has been tested and verified by multiple researchers on many different occasions*. Listed below are their exact definitions:

- **Theory:** An explanation of natural patterns or occurrences—i.e., the theory of relativity, the kinetic theory of gases, etc.

- **Model:** A representation of a natural pattern or occurrence that's difficult or impossible to experience directly, usually in the form of a picture or 3-D representation—i.e., Bohr's atomic model, the double-helix model of DNA, etc.

- **Law:** A mathematical or concise description of a pattern or occurrence in the observable universe—e.g., Newton's law of gravity, the laws of thermodynamics, etc.

The terms *theory, model,* and *law* are often used interchangeably in the sciences, although there's an essential difference: theories and models are used to explain *how and why* something happens, while laws describe exactly

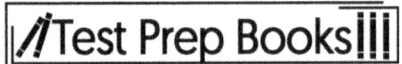

what happens. A common misconception is that theories develop into laws. But theories and models never become laws because they inherently describe different things.

Type	Function	Examples
Theory	To explain how and why something happens	Einstein's Theory of Special Relativity The Big Bang Theory
Model	To represent how and why something happens	A graphical model or drawing of an atom
Laws	To describe exactly what happens	$E = mc^2$ $F = ma$ $PV = nRT$

In order to ensure that scientific theories are consistent, scientists continually gather information and evidence on existing theories to improve their accuracy.

Formulating a Hypothesis

The skills needed to think critically, scientifically, and to follow the scientific method are referred to as **process skills**. These skills are the soil from which scientific knowledge is nurtured and grown. There are six fundamental process skills:

- **Observation**—using the senses to gather information
- **Communication**—using words, drawings, graphs, charts, or videos to effectively present observations
- **Classification**—grouping or categorizing objects or events based on certain attributes or criteria, i.e., sorting subjects into height and weight, grouping plants by species, etc.
- **Measurement**—using tools and instruments to describe dimensional variations in an object or event, such as measuring tape, graduated cylinders, clocks, etc.
- **Inference**—drawing conclusions from observations based on prior knowledge or education, i.e., "the grass is wet; it must have rained last night."
- **Prediction**—anticipating the outcome of an event based on prior knowledge or experiences, i.e., "there are many clouds in the sky; it's going to rain tonight." Prediction is the essential skill in forming a solid hypothesis.

In addition to the basic process skills, there are other skills needed in scientific experiments. One essential skill is **generalization**—a type of inference deduced by broad observations of large groups of people or objects that is used frequently in quantitative research. Because of the near-impossibility of sampling a whole population, generalizations are applied to represent a whole population as accurately as possible.

The final step of the scientific method is to make inferences from observed data, which is also known as forming a **conclusion**. Conclusions are placed at the end of scientific papers and wrap up the experimental procedure with its respective inferences. For example, if the experimental data from the plant growth experiment showed that plants with more light grew 2cm more than plants with minimal light in a given period of time, the conclusion may be that certain components of light stimulate plant growth, so the more light that a plant receives, the taller it will grow.

Determining the Design Elements of Scientific Investigations

To test a hypothesis, one must conduct a carefully designed experiment. There are four basic requirements that must be present for an experiment to be valid:

1. A control
2. Variables
3. A constant
4. Repeated and collected data

The **control** is a standard to which the resultant findings are compared. It's the baseline measurement that allows for scientists to determine whether the results are positive or negative. For the example of light affecting plant growth, the control may be a plant that receives no light at all.

The **independent variable** is manipulated (a good way to remember this is *I* manipulate the *I*ndependent variable), and the **dependent variable** is the result of changes to the independent variable. In the plant example, the independent variable is the amount of time exposed to light, and the dependent variable is the resulting growth (or lack thereof) of the plant. For this experiment, there may be three plants—one that receives a minimal amount of light, the control, and one that receives a lot of light.

Finally, there must be constants in an experiment. A **constant** is an element of the experiment that remains unchanged. Constants are extremely important in minimizing inconsistencies within the experiment that may lead to results outside the parameters of the hypothesis. For example, some constants in the above case are that all plants receive the same amount of water, all plants are potted in the same kind of soil, the species of the plant used in each condition is the same, and the plants are stored at the same temperature. If, for instance, the plants received different amounts of water as well as light, it would be impossible to tell whether the plants responded to changes in water or light.

Once the experiment begins, a disciplined scientist must always record the observations in meticulous detail, usually in a journal. A good journal includes dates, times, and exact values of both variables and constants. Upon reading this journal, a different scientist should be able to clearly understand the experiment and recreate it exactly. The journal includes all **collected data**, or any observed changes. In this case, the data is rates of plant growth, as well as any other phenomena that occurred as a result of the experiment. A well-designed experiment also includes repetition in order to get the most accurate possible readings and to account for any errors, so several trials may be conducted.

Even in the presence of diligent constants, there are an infinite number of reasons that an experiment can (and will) go wrong, known as **sources of error**. All experimental results are inherently accepted as imperfect, if ever so slightly, because experiments are conducted by human beings, and no instrument can measure anything perfectly. The goal of scientists is to minimize those errors to the best of their ability. (Determining sources of error will be discussed in a subsequent section.)

Identifying Procedures

Scientific inquiry requires that researchers design and conduct a scientific investigation, formulate logical explanations using evidence, use mathematics and technology, and defend or communicate a scientific argument. The three main stages of a scientific inquiry involve planning and initiation, performing and recording the experiment, and then analyzing and interpreting the data.

Procedures for Setting Up an Appropriate Experiment

During the initiation stage, a topic, issue, or question is identified in the community or workplace. The question that is formulated must be testable and unique and may begin with *Will*, *Does*, *What*, or *Do*. For example, does the addition of salt to a test tube containing water lower the temperature below 0°C (freezing point)? Research is then carried out to gather background information to make a hypothesis or prediction, which must be specific to the problem based on the conducted research. When collecting information and limiting bias, sources of information are collected from peer-reviewed articles and textbooks, interviews, patents, and scientific articles that include keywords for the investigation. After collecting information, an experiment must be planned to determine how the hypothesis will be tested to help answer the question. The experiment should include an objective statement that outlines what is needed to answer the question. For instance, how will different masses of salt change the freezing point of water?

During the investigation, the independent, dependent, and control variables must be identified to ensure that data collection is accurate and to allow for experimental repeatability. The **independent** or **manipulated** variable is what is changed to study the effect. Changing the mass of the salt in the freezing point experiment is an example. The **dependent** or **responding** variable is the result that is measured due to the manipulated variable. The resulting temperature, in Celsius or Fahrenheit, is the dependent variable and will depend on the amount of salt added. The control variable is a factor that is kept the same to ensure accuracy. A test tube containing only water for the freezing point test acts as the control variable. Other control variables may be the size of the test tube and the amount of water used.

When collecting materials for the experiment, a specific list of materials must be stated, which is necessary for repeatability by the researcher and other experimentalists. The type of glassware or tools used must be specified in addition to the masses or volumes of substances used. For instance, a material list might include one round-bottom test tube with a capacity of 50 mL, an outer diameter of 25 mm, and a length of 150 mm. Safety data sheets must be included when using chemicals or compounds.

The procedures must include detailed steps written in the correct order with a method for the collection, recording, and display (e.g., table) of data. Procedures and diagrams on how to use an instrument are necessary to ensure accuracy and repeatability.

Identifying Appropriate Techniques for Storing, Handling, and Disposing of Materials

A substance or material that is considered a hazardous product will be listed in the Hazardous Products Regulation. A hazardous product can be a substance, material, or mixture that is a subcategory of a hazard class found in Schedule 2. Every hazardous product in the Workplace Hazardous Materials Information System (WHMIS) that is intended for storage, handling, and use must have a Safety Data Sheet (SDS). The SDS provides information regarding the hazards of a product and how to safely handle and store the substance. Safety precautions and the correct use of protective personal equipment are generally included. In addition, consumer product symbols are included to inform the consumer of known hazards. Product symbols may include WHMIS classifications, which include different categories corresponding to potential health effects, such as acute toxicity and skin irritation. Stability and reactivity hazards are included, providing information related to incompatible materials and conditions to avoid. Release measures in the SDS sheet can include methods for containment, cleanup, and personal precautions.

Appropriate and Safe Use of Materials

The appropriate and safe use of laboratory materials not only reduces the potential harm to people and the environment, but also minimizes waste and ensures accurate data collection. The following guidelines highlight the crucial skills in safely handling chemical reagents and specimens.

Science

Identifying Hazards
The ability to identify a hazard allows one to take safety measures such as wearing the appropriate clothing and respond appropriately to spills.

Common types of laboratory hazards include:

- Chemical hazards
- Toxins
- Corrosives
- Flammables
- Reactive substances
- Biological hazards
- Animals
- Plants
- Microbes
- Genetically-modified organisms
- Physical hazards
- Extreme heat
- Extreme cold
- Noise
- Heating devices
- Projectiles
- Electrical hazards

- Fire
- Shock
- Radiation hazards
- Ionizing radiation
- Non-iodizing radiation
- Mechanical hazards
- Machinery
- Airborne hazards
- Vapor
- Fume
- Dust

Handling Chemicals and Specimens

A **specimen** is any substance or fluid taken from a plant, animal, or other object, such as urine, blood, saliva, stool, or tissue. To safely handle chemicals and specimens, one should adhere to the following guidelines:

- Always read the safety data sheet that accompanies a chemical.
- Make sure specimens and chemicals are properly stored.
- Ensure that any first-aid equipment, including eye-washing stations, are close and ready for use.
- Keep all work stations clean and sanitized.
- Use the smallest amount of chemical or specimen possible.
- Make sure all containers are properly labeled.
- Use substitutions for more harmful chemicals whenever possible.

Safe Disposal of Materials

The following are basic requirements to follow for the disposal of chemical hazardous waste:

Create a Hazardous Waste Area

- Select an area near the source of the waste, out of the way of normal lab activities, and easily accessible to all lab personnel.
- Label the area "Danger—Hazardous Waste" with the following sign:

Deposit Chemicals into the Appropriate Containers

- Make sure that containers into which the chemicals will be discarded are stable enough to hold them—chemicals must not weaken or dissolve the material of the container.
- Acids and bases cannot be stored with metal
- Hydrofluoric acid cannot be stored with glass.
- Solvents (i.e. gasoline) cannot be stored in polyethylene containers, such as a milk jug.

- Waste containers must come with lids and caps that are resistant to leakage, and containers should be closed at all times, except when opened to add more waste.
- The size of the container should be appropriate for the amount of expected waste.
- Waste containers should be placed inside a larger, empty container to catch any waste that may potentially spill or leak.

Requirements for Liquid Waste

- Don't overfill containers—be sure to leave at least 10% space between the container opening and the surface of the waste.
- Never mix liquid and solid waste.
- Double-bag small containers, such as vials, in clear plastic bags.
- Bag small containers composed of the same kind of waste.
- Attach a completed hazardous waste tag to all bags and containers.

Requirements for Solid Waste

Chemical solid waste is composed of three different categories: lab trash, dry chemicals, and sharps.

- Lab trash
- Use for waste such as Kim Wipes, disposable gloves, paper towels, and wooden stirrers
- Double-bag in clear bags
- Attach a completed hazardous waste tag to all bags
- Dry chemicals
- Return the chemical waste to the original container in which it was purchased.
- Attach a completed hazardous waste tag.
- Sharps
    - Examples include glass (broken or intact), pipettes and pipette tips, needles, X-ACTO™ knives, or anything capable of piercing, cutting, slicing, or tearing human flesh.
- Discard any used sharps into a designated sharps container with a biohazard sign.

Appropriate Storage

Proper chemical storage is imperative for laboratory operations as well as the safety of all lab personnel. The following is a list of guidelines for the appropriate storage of chemicals and other hazardous materials:

1. There must be a designated place for each type of chemical.

    - Flammables and volatile poisons (poisons that easily evaporate at room temperature) must be stored in cabinets, refrigerators, or freezers marked with a flammable label.
    - Oxidizing acids, organic and mineral acids, liquid bases, liquid oxidizers, and non-volatile liquid poisons must be stored in a safety cabinet.
    - Oxidizing acids must be double-contained.
    - Solids should be stored above liquids.
    - As a rule of thumb, different compounds should be stored separately.

2. Chemicals should not be permanently stored in any fume hood.
3. All containers should be kept sealed unless in use.
4. All chemicals must be kept away from sunlight and heat.
5. All chemicals must be labeled properly.
6. No chemical, except for bleach and cleaning agents, should be stored under the sink.

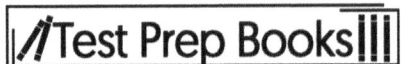

Demonstrating Effective Selection and Use of Scientific Tools

When a scientific experiment is performed, specific scientific tools are used to help gather data and accurately record observations. The conduction of an experiment requires a laboratory notebook that includes the title of the experiment, date, materials, and procedure. Many scientific tools are used to collect **quantitative data**, which are observations based on measurements with a specific unit, such as length, mass, temperature, and volume. In contrast, **qualitative data** are observations that are not necessarily measured using scientific tools but include visual observations such as appearance or color, text descriptions, and relative temperatures (hot or cold); the data that is recorded is non-numerical.

In many experiments, the physical properties of substances are measured (quantitative) and observed (qualitative) using scientific tools. Measurements of length can be carried out with a **ruler**, which is a hand-size tool for measuring lengths that have units based on the metric system. For example, a standard Rubik's cube has a length of 5.7 centimeters. A metric or meter stick has a length of 1 meter, which is equal to 100 centimeters. A protractor is a specialized tool used for measuring angles (0 to 180 degrees) and can have utility in applications from measuring the deformation of a patient's bones to measuring bond angles in hypothetical molecular models. **Mass balances** are sensitive instruments used to measure the mass of a substance or object in metric units of grams. The applications of a mass balance are numerous and can be used in the medical field to weigh the mass of drugs or to calculate the density of an object.

Scientific tools require precision and accuracy, especially when measuring physical properties and reporting data. **Precision** refers to the ability of the experimentalist to measure consistently or how close a set of measurements are to one another. In contrast, **accuracy** refers to how close a measurement is to the true value. Not all scientific tools have the same level of precision, and the ability to measure is determined by the tool. For example, an analytical balance is designed to measure small masses with a 0.1 milligram resolution. In contrast, top-loading balances are less precise and have readability ranges from 0.01 to 0.1 grams. Analytical balances are designed for small samples, while top-loading balances are better suited for large samples. When calculating the density of small objects (e.g., Rubik's cube), it is preferred to use an analytical balance.

The thermometer is another scientific tool used for finding the melting point and boiling point (physical properties) of many substances, such as water. A **thermometer** measures temperature, a measure or degree of hot and cold, or a change in temperature. The units of temperature in the metric system are Kelvin (symbol K), but the degrees Celsius (°C) and Fahrenheit (°F) are commonly reported.

Tools used for measuring the volume of pure liquids or solutions include the graduated cylinder, beaker, Erlenmeyer flask, volumetric pipet and flask, and Buret. The liter (L) is the metric unit for measuring volume; 1 liter is 1000 milliliters (mL). Graduated cylinders are cylindrical tubes with an attached flat base; they come in various sizes. Graduated cylinders are more precise for measuring volumes compared to beakers and Erlenmeyer flasks. When reading precise liquid measurements, a person's eyes must be aligned with the meniscus level.

Selecting Appropriate Units of Measurement

There are seven *base units* of measure that form the basic structure for the Système International d'unités (SI). In alphabetical order, these are *ampere* (for electric current), *candela* (for the intensity of light), *kelvin* (for temperature), *kilogram* (for mass), *metre* or *meter* (for length), *mole* (for the amount of a substance such as atoms or molecules), and *second* (for time). From these, there are additional *derived units*, which build on the system. The Système International d'unités is the modern form of the Metric System.

The Metric System was developed in France during the French Revolution in 1799, in order to distinguish itself from the British Empire and also to create a universal system of measurement. Almost every country, except three, has adopted it as their official measuring system. The physical quantities of the metric system are length, mass, volume,

Science

and time, and each has a basic unit of measurement: the meter (m), the gram (g), the liter (L), and the second (s), respectively.

Physical Quantity	Basic Unit of Measurement	Symbol
Length	meter	M
Mass	gram	G
Volume	liter	L
Time	second	S

Conversions within these measurements are easily made by multiplying or dividing by factors of ten and are indicated by the prefix attached to the unit. The most common units are listed below:

Prefix	Symbol	Factor	Power	Examples
kilo-	K	1,000	10^3	kilometer, kilogram, kiloliter, kilosecond
hecto-	H	100	10^2	hectometer, hectogram, hectoliter, hectosecond
deca-	Da	10	10^1	decameter, decagram, decaliter, decasecond
None	None	1	10^0	meter, gram, liter, second
deci-	D	0.1	10^{-1}	decimeter, decigram, deciliter, decisecond
centi-	C	0.01	10^{-2}	centimeter, centigram, centimeter, centisecond
milli-	M	0.001	10^{-3}	millimeter, milligram, milliliter, millisecond

Basic Conversions within the System

The wonderful thing about the system is it's easy to convert within the same unit of measurement by simply multiplying or dividing by ten.

Suppose a scientist wants to convert 23 meters to kilometers. The first method is to simply move the decimal point to the right or left depending on the prefix.

                LEFT   RIGHT

kilo- hecto- deca- UNIT deci- centi- milli-

3 2 1   1 2 3

A decimal point for whole numbers always follows the ones unit—in this case, after the 3. To remember where the decimal is placed, imagine the number instead as 23.0.

After the decimal has been located, move it in accordance with the prefix. As shown above, **kilo** is *three* places to the *left* of the unit (meters, in this case). Therefore, the decimal is moved three units to the left:

$$23.0m \rightarrow .0230 \rightarrow 0.023km$$

Thus, 23 meters is equivalent to 0.023 kilometers.

Another method of conversion relies on forming an equation. To demonstrate, one should follow the steps below:

1. Write down the problem.

$$23m = ?\, km$$

2. Identify the conversion.

$$1km = 1,000m$$

3. Write down the conversion as a fraction.

$$\frac{1km}{1,000m}$$

4. Write the original unit and conversion fraction as a multiplication problem.

$$23m \times \frac{1km}{1,000m}$$

5. Cancel units that appear on the top and bottom.

$$23\cancel{m} \times \frac{1km}{1,000\cancel{m}}$$

6. Solve the equation.

$$23\cancel{m} \times \frac{1km}{1,000\cancel{m}} = 0.023km$$

Again, 23 meters is equivalent to 0.023 kilometers.

Visualizing and Communicating Data in Appropriate Formats

Observations made during a scientific experiment are organized and presented as data. Data can be collected in a variety of ways, depending on the purpose of the experiment. In testing how light exposure affects plant growth, for example, the data collected would be changes in the height of the plant relative to the amount of light it received. The easiest way to organize collected data is to use a **data table.**

A data table always contains a title that relates the two variables in the experiment. Each column or row must contain the units of measurement in the heading only. See the below example (note: this is not actual data).

Plant Growth During Time Exposed to Light (130 Watts)	
Time (Hours)	Height (cm)
0	3.2
192	5.0
480	7.9
720	12.1

Data must be presented in a concise, coherent way. Most data are presented in graph form. The fundamental rule for creating a graph based on data is that the independent variable (i.e., amount of time exposed to light) is on the x-axis, and the dependent variable (i.e., height of plant) is on the y-axis.

There are many types of graphs that a person may choose to use depending on which best represents the data.

A **bar graph** is used when counting or categorizing data. For example, the number of commuters who travel via four different modes of transportation.

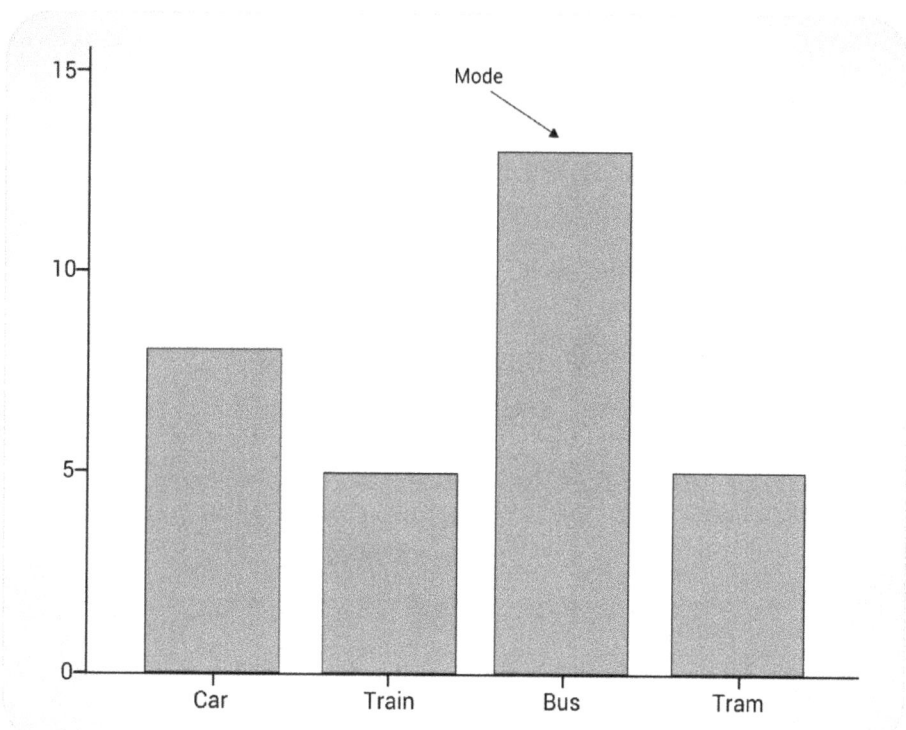

A **line graph** is used when there are changes in the dependent variable ranging from low to high, or when collecting data over a period of time. This graph would be the best to use for the plant growth experiment.

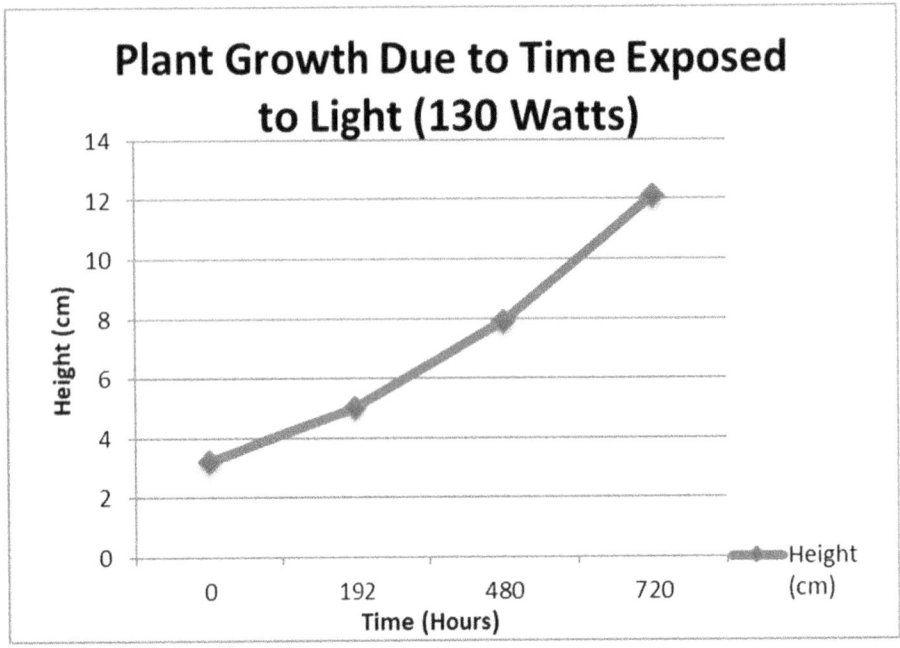

A **scatter plot** is used when more than one data point exists on the y-axis for each value of the x-axis, such as test scores dependent on the number of hours a student studied.

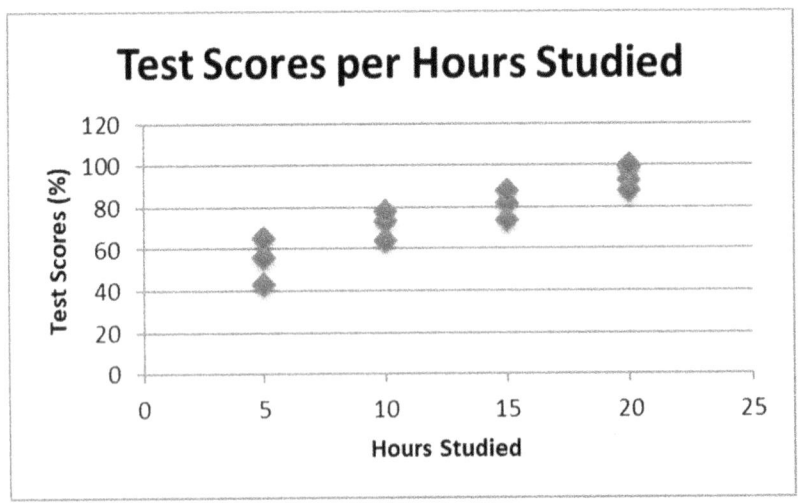

A **pie chart** or **circle graph** is used when the data sum to 100%, such as the percentage of students in each high school class interested in a trip to a local museum.

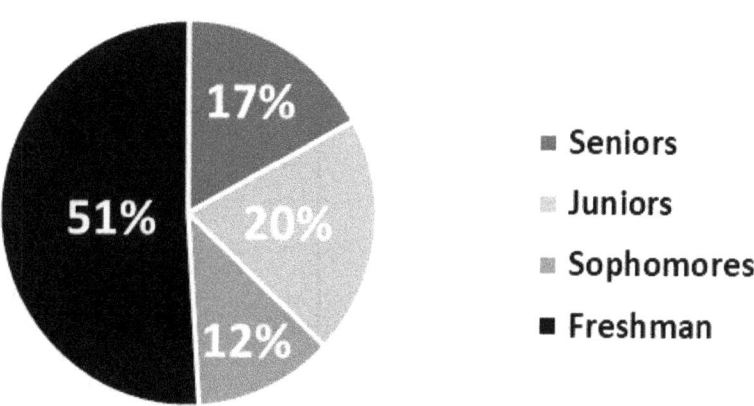

Analyzing Patterns and Trends

Trends in Data

The ability to recognize trends in data allows scientists to make predictions, not only about the present or near future (such as in a hypothesis), but also about the distant future and even the past. The practice of collecting data and spotting patterns is referred to as **trend analysis**.

Graphs, charts, and tables are helpful in interpreting quantitative data because they provide a visual representation that can be easily analyzed. Graphs are typically created from the tables and charts in which the data were collected. The line graph on plant growth, for example, was created from the data table of observations. The methods in which data are presented (graphs, charts, etc.) are simply ways for scientists to determine trends by recognizing relationships between variables.

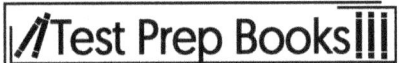

Science

Relationships Between Variables

The most common relationship examined in an experiment is between two variables (independent and dependent), most often referred to as *x* and *y*. The independent variable (*x*) is displayed on the horizontal axis of a coordinate plane, and the dependent variable (*y*) is displayed on the vertical axis.

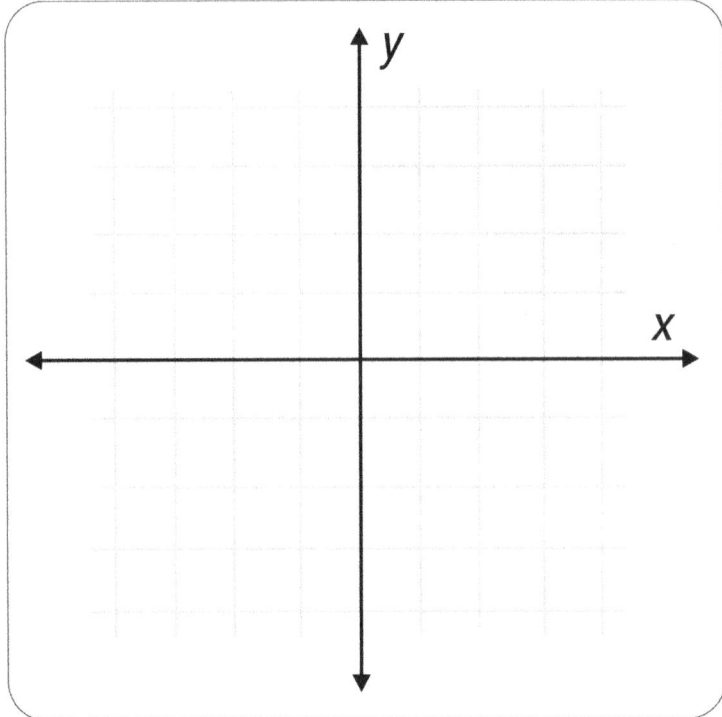

The placement of the variables in this way provides a visual representation of what happens to *y* when *x* is manipulated. In analyzing trends, *x* is used to predict *y*, and since *y* is the result of *x*, then *x* comes before *y* in time. For example, in the experiment on plant growth, the hours the plant was exposed to light had to happen before growth could occur.

When analyzing the relationship between the variables, scientists will consider the following questions:

- Does *y* increase or decrease with *x*, or does it do both?
- If it increases or decreases, how fast does it change?
- Does *y* stay steady through certain values of *x*, or does it jump dramatically from one value to the other?
- Is there a strong relationship? If given a value of *x*, can one predict what will happen to *y*?

If, in general, *y* increases as *x* increases, or *y* decreases and *x* decreases, it is known as a **positive correlation**. The data from the plant experiment show a positive correlation—as time exposed to light (*x*) increases, plant growth (*y*) increases. If the variables trend in the opposite direction of each other—that is, if *y* increases as *x* decreases, or vice versa—it is called a **negative correlation**. If there doesn't seem to be any visible pattern to the relationship, it is referred to as *no* or **zero correlation**.

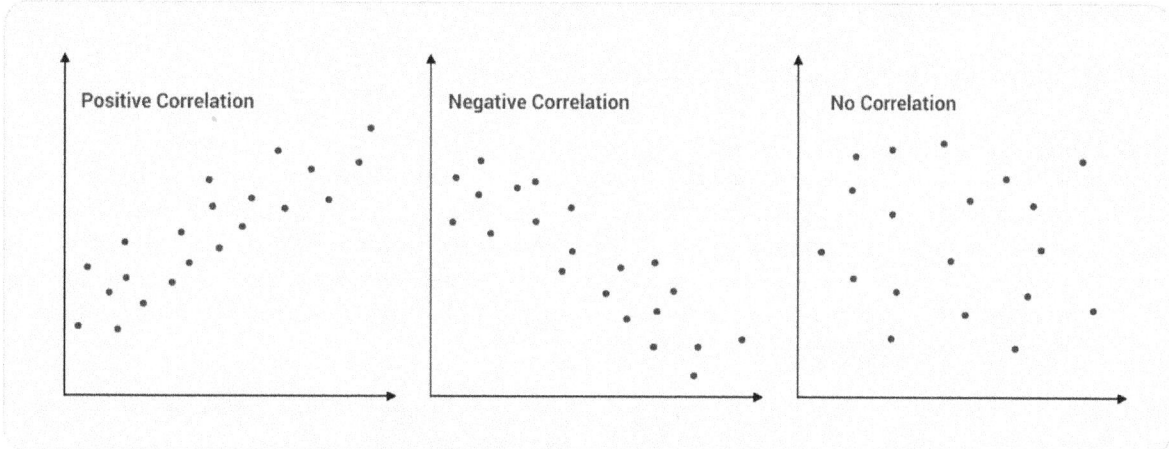

Experiments that show positive or negative correlation within their data indicate that the variables are related. This allows scientists to make predictions based on the data.

Estimating Information

Predictions Based on Data

Science is amazing in that it actually allows people to predict the future and see into the past with a certain degree of accuracy. Using numerical correlations created from quantitative data, one can see in a general way what will happen to *y* when something happens to *x*.

The best way to get a useful overview of quantitative data to facilitate predictions is to use a scatter plot, which plots each data point individually. As shown above, there may be slight fluctuations from the correlation line, so one may not be able to predict what happens with *every* change, but he or she will be able to have a general idea of what is going to happen to *y* with a change in *x*. To demonstrate, the graph with a line of best fit created from the plant growth experiment is below.

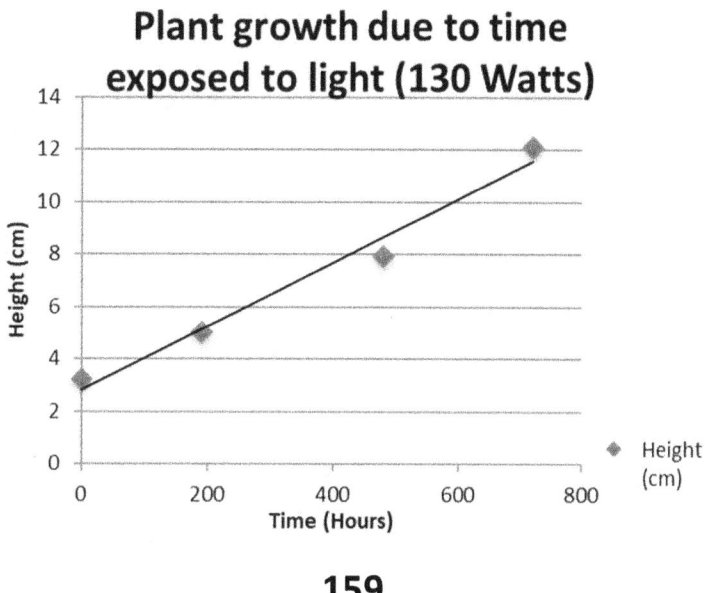

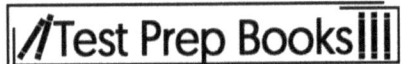

Using the trend line within the data, one can estimate what will happen to plant growth at a given length of time exposed to light. For example, it can be estimated that with 700 hours of time, the plant is expected to grow to a height of about 11 cm. The plant may not grow to exactly 11 cm, but it will likely grow to about that height based on previous data. This process allows scientists to draw conclusions based on data.

Evaluating Scientific Investigations for Sources of Error

Drawing Valid Conclusions Based on Data

Drawing conclusions is the process of analyzing patterns in data and determining whether the relationship is **causal**, meaning that one variable is the cause of the change in the other. There are many correlations that aren't casual, such as a city where alcohol sales increase as crime increases. Although there's a positive correlation between the two, crime may not be the factor that causes an increase in alcohol sales. There could be other factors, such as an increase in unemployment, which increases both alcohol sales and crime rates. Although crime and alcohol sales are positively correlated, they aren't causally correlated.

For this reason, it's important for scientists to carefully design their experiments with all the appropriate constants to ensure that the relationships are causal. If a relationship is determined to be causal by isolating the variables from all other factors, only then can conclusions be drawn based on data. In the plant growth experiment, the conclusion is that light affects plant growth because the data shows they are causally correlated since the two variables were entirely isolated.

Evaluating the Reliability, Validity, and Credibility of Scientific Investigations

For a hypothesis to be proven true or false, all experiments are subject to multiple trials in order to verify accuracy and precision. A measurement is **accurate** if the observed value is close to the "true value." For example, if someone measured the pH of water at 6.9, this measurement would be considered accurate (the pH of water is 7). On the other hand, a measurement is **precise** if the measurements are consistent—that is, if they are reproducible. If someone had a series of values for a pH of water that were 6.9, 7.0, 7.2, and 7.3, their measurements would not be precise. However, if all measured values were 6.9, or the average of these values was 6.9 with a small range, then their measurements would be precise. Measurements can fall into the following categories:

- Both accurate and precise
- Accurate but not precise
- Precise but not accurate
- Neither accurate nor precise

The accuracy and precision of observed values most frequently correspond to the amount of error present in the experiment. Aside from general carelessness, there are two primary types of error: random and systematic. **Random errors** are unpredictable variations in the experiment that occur by chance. They can be difficult to detect, but they can often be nullified using a statistical analysis and minimized by taking repeated measurements and taking an average. **Systematic errors** occur when there are imperfections in the design of the experiment itself—usually errors that affect the accuracy of the measurements. These errors can be minimized by using the most

Science

accurate equipment available and by taking proper care of instruments and measuring techniques. Common examples of errors are listed below.

Random	Systematic
Environmental factors (random changes in vibration, temperature, humidity, etc.) Differences in instrument use among scientists Errors in judgment—can be affected by state of mind Incorrectly recorded observations	Poorly maintained instruments Old or out-of-date instruments Faulty calibration of instruments Reading the instruments at an angle (parallax error) or other faulty reading errors Not accounting for lag time

The most basic method to account for the possibility of errors is to take an average (also called a **mean**) of all observed values. To do so, one must divide the number of measurements taken from the sum of all measurements.

$$\frac{Sum\ of\ Measurements}{Total\ \#\ of\ Measurements}$$

For the above example of the pH values, the average is calculated by finding the sum of the pH values ascertained and dividing by the number of values recorded.

$$\frac{6.9 + 7.0 + 7.2 + 7.3}{4} = 7.1$$

The more observations recorded, the greater the precision. It's important to first assess the accuracy of measurements before proceeding to collect multiple trials of data. If a particular trial results in measurements that are vastly different from the average, it may indicate that a random or systematic error occurred during the trial. When this happens, a scientist might decide to "throw out" the trial and run the experiment again.

Transferring Conclusions from Scientific Investigations

Conclusions are formed from the gathering and recording of experimental observations. The collection of information must be carefully processed, organized, and displayed correctly to draw the appropriate conclusions. When conducting the experiment, the data and information can be collected into a table. Mathematical calculations are then carried out and the results organized into a results table. The information from the table can then be used to plot or make a graph, which can be used to analyze and interpret data. For example, consider the following hypothesis:

The higher the level of nitrogen in fertilizer, the taller the coffee tree will grow.

As the scientist is conducting the experiment, they will need to record the mass and type of fertilizer added to the plant. The height of the plant can be recorded over a period of time to determine how mass and fertilizer type can increase plant growth. The height can be recorded daily, weekly, or monthly and must be recorded on a table or sheet. At the conclusion of the experiment, transferring the data from the table to a graph will provide better visualization of the data and will allow conclusions to be drawn more easily.

During data interpretation, two main tasks are completed. The first task requires answering the question that the scientist raised about an everyday problem. A response to the hypothesis must be given, based on the information obtained by conducting the experiment. The second component of data interpretation involves drawing conclusions or inferences based on what the scientist has learned.

A **concluding statement** provides a summary of a portion or all of the findings of the scientific investigation. For example, one conclusion from the coffee tree study may be:

Based on the graph generated from the data table for coffee tree growth, fertilizers containing high concentrations of nitrogen or ammonium nitrate increase the growth rate.

A conclusion and inference are similar but have different meanings. An **inference statement** is a logical assumption that provides a reasonable cause for the results of an investigation. For example:

Using fertilizer containing high concentrations of ammonium nitrate will make the coffee tree healthier and will allow it to grow faster.

Two tasks are involved when extending and applying knowledge to everyday life and future investigations. The first task is identifying new questions for a new investigation based on existing data. The second task is identifying information that can be applied to other scenarios. For instance, is it economical to use ammonium nitrate fertilizers to grow coffee trees whose coffee will be distributed throughout the world? Do high concentrations of nitrogen harm the coffee plant? In fact, excess nitrogen use in coffee plants can cause improved growth but lead to the poor productivity of coffee cherries.

Science, Technology, Society and Environment

Identifying Intended and Unintended Consequences

Science and technology are a cornerstone of daily living, from influencing daily consumer products to the way people communicate with others. These fields aim to improve the daily standard and quality of living for the average person.

Chemical Properties of Household Products
Common household products such as cleaners, containers, and foods may be a source of toxic chemicals, especially to younger children. As a result, many companies have focused their efforts on developing clean, green household products that limit or eliminate the presence of common chemicals such as **phthalates**, **bisphenol A (BPA)**, and food preservatives that are increasingly becoming correlated to cancers, neurological dysfunction, hormone disruption, respiratory conditions, and endocrine issues. Additionally, many of these chemicals are also harmful to the environment when washed down drains; therefore, creating less toxic household products limits soil and water pollution as well.

Communication
The presence of the Internet, wireless networks, cell phones, online applications and social media, and global positioning systems (GPS) have paved the way for instantaneous, worldwide communication. These connections allow people to work and socialize remotely, navigate without maps, access hundreds of radio and television channels, and learn from and share vast pools of information. Additionally, large-scale two-way communication has become easier. An individual can connect with a large audience through the Internet alone, which has become a place to store and share documents, photos, videos, audio files, and more. All of these items were previously separate entities that could not be easily shared.

Science Principles Applied on Commonly Used Consumer Products
Most advances to average consumer products were first used by the scientific community for a much different purpose. For example, Teflon, the non-stick coating used in most pans that the average consumer uses to cook in the home, was originally created by a chemical engineer who was researching potential refrigerants. NASA has

Water Purification

Water purification is an increasingly popular field as researchers hope to harness ocean water into potable water, purify available water in high pollution areas, and maintain increasingly stringent water purity standards. Previously, water had been primarily purified using filtration and chlorination. New water purification technologies include **membrane filtration** (which more finely filters water sources through pressurized, multiple, reverse osmosis processes), **ultraviolet radiation** (which works by sterilizing the water source), and more portable filtration systems that can be placed directly into a water source by the consumer.

Common Agricultural Practices

Agricultural practices have changed to keep up with population growth and land availability. **Genetically modified organisms (GMOs)** are those that have altered genetic coding to make them more resistant to harsh conditions and pests, or which can be grown in a lab under synthetic conditions. **Herbicides** and **insecticides** aim to eliminate common agricultural pests that destroy crops while leaving the crop intact. It is important to note that these are considered controversial practices by some consumers, who believe consumption of genetically modified food sources and the use of pesticides is linked to adverse health and environmental conditions.

DNA Evidence in Criminal Investigations

The last decade advanced the use of accurate **DNA profiling** and its ability to aid in forensic science and the judicial process. Current DNA profiling systems can match DNA samples taken from crime scenes to available DNA profiles in registered databases or from medical provisions. DNA profiling is considered to be more accurate than fingerprint testing or eyewitness testimony. It has been a fundamental tool in exonerating wrongly convicted criminals, and its present day use correlates with a reduction in overall crime rates. However, opponents argue that DNA profiling violates privacy rights and that human errors, false DNA samples, and synthetic DNA production can create inaccurate evidence.

Nanotechnology

Nanotechnology refers to new systems that result from manipulating material at the molecular level in order to create highly precise finished products. Scientists are able to use nanotechnology to change the composition of materials to make them stronger, lighter, more flexible, or able to withstand different chemical situations (such as rusting). Current nanotechnology initiatives include solar power cell manufacturing, developing medicines that can be administered at the cellular level, improving functionality of cell phones and other communication devices, removing contamination from water sources, and creating lighter yet larger memory storage (such as flash drives), space flight mechanisms, air quality improvement processes, and minute chemical detection.

Evaluate Risks and Benefits of Scientific Solutions and Technologies

Nutrition, Disease, and Medicine

Science has influenced a number of achievements in the fields of nutrition, disease, and medicine. Compounding synthetic vitamins, minerals, and other nutrients (such as collagen, amino acids, and fatty acids) provided a way for people with less access to nutrient-dense food sources or nutrition-related diseases to appropriately supplement their diets. Vaccine development has almost completely eradicated serious and crippling diseases like polio, diphtheria, tetanus, and pertussis; vaccines have also reduced the risk of contracting less fatal, but potentially critical, illnesses such as rotavirus and meningococcal viruses.

As vaccines are administered in larger and larger groups, the risk of the bacterial or viral threat is greatly reduced. Even if a select few individuals are not vaccinated, the concept of herd immunity protects them and limits the spread of the threat. Other communicable diseases are now easily managed through the development and implementation of retroviral medications. **Retroviral drugs** can help people live full, normal lives with diseases like HIV, and such drugs have provided additional protection to pregnant mothers who can prevent passing a disease they have to their fetus. Overall, these advances have contributed to a reduction in child mortality rates and an increase in human life expectancy.

Here's an illustration of how vaccines decrease the spread of disease:

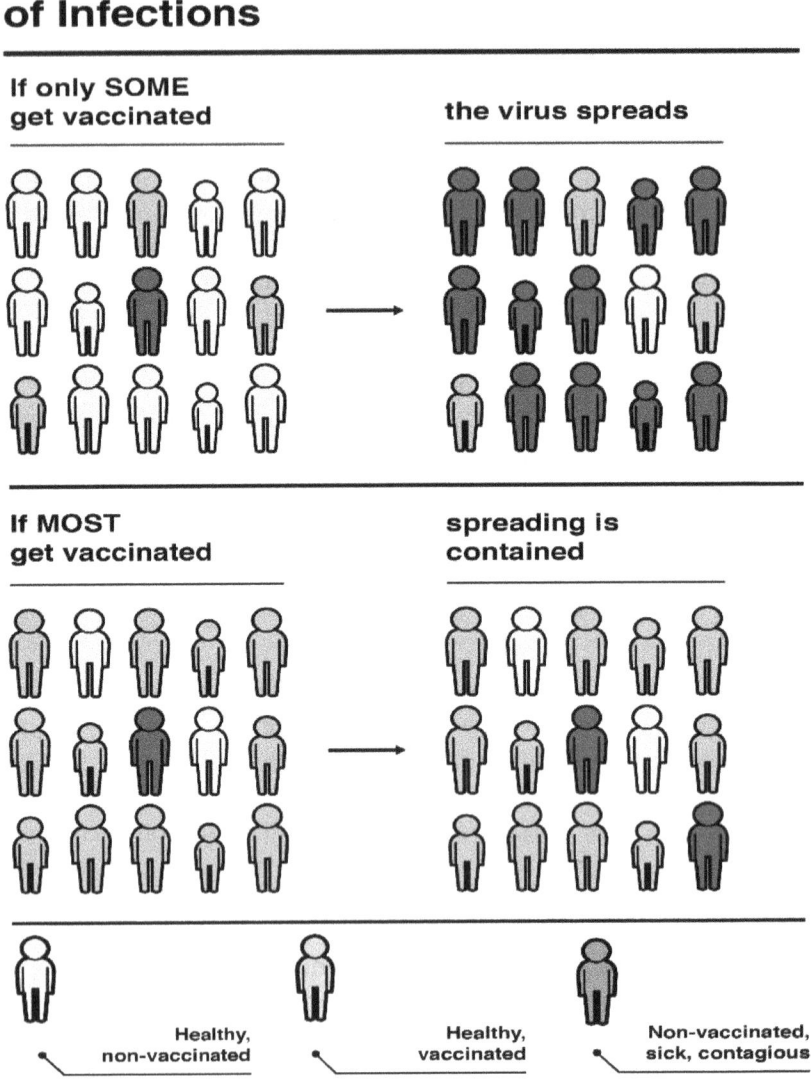

Biotechnology

The **biotechnology** field contributes to public health initiatives focused on genetic engineering, in vitro fertilization, infectious disease protection, and bioterrorist agent protection. Biotech companies contribute to the clinical development of vaccines and other pharmaceuticals and they create genetically modified crops that can withstand hazards that conventional crops may be unable to withstand. This is primarily accomplished through genome sequencing and mapping. Additionally, more biotech companies are being employed for national defense and security measures, as toxic bioterrorist agents, chemical warfare, and other risks to human biology can be used against the public. These defense measures include the development of enzymes that can neutralize threats, the development of internal barriers that protect an individual's cells from an approaching bacteria or virus, and refining DNA detection methods that show whether a population has been exposed to a biological threat. Finally, biotech companies play a role in helping victims heal from various conditions. For example, some companies focus on creating realistic yet synthetic skin grafts to help burn victims return to normalcy.

Medical Technologies

Biomedical research and device manufacturing companies play a crucial role in advancing how medical professionals can detect, manage, and eliminate disease. The last century has delivered technological advances such as x-ray machines, electrocardiograms, medical imaging, and laparoscopic devices that allow medical professionals to visually and directly examine a patient's internal state, allowing for diagnoses with a high level of accuracy, and consequently, an effective treatment plan. Medical devices such as pacemakers, stents, dialysis machines, and catheters are able to carry on life-sustaining functions for an individual who has failing organs; sometimes these devices can be used for the rest of the patient's life. Artificial joints can be placed within a patient's skeletal system to replace failing or unusable joints, such as in the case of a hip or knee replacement.

Current initiatives focus on virtual reality health delivery, augmented reality to deliver education for medical professionals, algorithm development and data analysis for data collected from popular individual fitness and wellness trackers, and the continued refinement of robotic assistance in medical centers and operating rooms. Finally, another type of technology to consider in medical contexts is the documentation process. The implementation of electronic medical records affects how healthcare is delivered, allowing for ease of communication between multiple providers and easier healthcare access for the patient. It is important to note, however, that the World Health Organization (WHO) reports that 70% of existing and emerging medical technologies cannot be used by developing nations due to reasons like lack of access, unskilled workers, and cultural fears.

Most medical technologies are developed in first-world, high income countries. Consequently, developing nations cannot access them, or do not have skilled workers to use the technologies appropriately. Additionally, some cultures do not accept foreign devices and reject them out of fear, misunderstanding, or disbelief. Consequently, many developing countries have poorer health outcomes, higher rates of disease, and lower life-expectancies because they are not benefiting from advancements in medical technology.

Evaluating Factors that Influence Scientific Research

Scientific research is influenced by a variety of social, political, and economic policy and public safety factors. Other factors, such as research funding, the peer review process, research ability, ethical factors, world health issues, and competitive pressure can also influence research. **Research funding and policymaking** from the government have a strong influence on research. The choice of a research problem is strongly dependent on the type of funding received. Problems that are considered urgent to society, e.g., coronavirus vaccines, will have greater funding since public safety is a primary responsibility held by governments. Research funding can also depend on political factors, which may raise moral/ethical standards regarding the development of weapons and materials. Government funding agencies and industrial lobbyists can also interfere with scientific autonomy for the purpose of acquiring wealth and exploiting scientists. Policymakers can become involved in scientific funding, which can cause scientists to adjust and align a specific area of research to match public policy and potentially work to hide evidence. In some cases, scientists can invent evidence to discredit others.

Studies have indicated that science has been exploited and manipulated to further political agendas. The politicization of uncertain science can be used to cast doubt on a general scientific consensus. Furthermore, due to

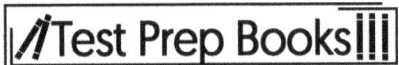

the nature of funding and its competitiveness, resources are limited. Some disciplines require equipment to perform experiments; if the equipment is not available, then the experimental results cannot be obtained.

The **academic ethos** of editors and authors can also influence scientific research. The proliferation of scientific results can depend on the **journal editor** and **reviewer's** background as well as ethical and personal values. Journal editors and reviewers have the ability to reject or accept a scientific article or proposal. Research proposals are proposed projects that may receive funding depending on the reviewers' interest and attitudes; reviewers may not favor a proposal with uncertain outcomes. Consequently, scientific progress becomes limited, especially when authors engage in academic dishonesty. **Academic competitive pressure** is another factor that can lead authors to engage in academic dishonesty due to promotion competition. Falsification is a form of academic dishonesty that can distort scientific results in a subtle manner. For example, data can be partially published to support an author's expectations or even manipulated to give an impression that the data is statistically significant.

Central dogmas in science develop when a scientific theory becomes widely accepted in a community, and any radical new idea is not taken seriously since many scientists have based their careers on the current theory. Consequently, scientific bias can occur. For instance, it took over 20 years for the discovery of viruses to be accepted by scientists.

Science Practice Quiz

1. A scientist is trying to determine the amount of poison that will kill a rat the fastest. Which of the following statements is an example of an appropriate hypothesis?
   a. Rats that are given lots of poison seem to die quickly.
   b. Does the amount of poison affect how quickly the rat dies?
   c. The more poison a rat is given, the quicker it will die.
   d. Poison is fatal to rats.

2. Which of the following correctly describes the independent and dependent variables in an experiment that tests how quickly a rat dies based on the amount of poison it eats?
   a. How quickly the rat dies is the independent variable; the amount of poison is the dependent variable.
   b. The amount of poison is the independent variable; how quickly the rat dies is the dependent variable.
   c. Whether the rat eats the poison is the independent variable; how quickly the rat dies is the dependent variable.
   d. The cage the rat is kept in is the independent variable; the amount of poison is the dependent variable.

3. Which of the following is a representation of a natural pattern or occurrence that's difficult or impossible to experience directly?
   a. A theory
   b. A model
   c. A law
   d. An observation

4. A researcher is exploring factors that contribute to the GPA of college students. While the sample is small, the researcher is trying to determine what the data shows. What can be reasoned from the table below?

Student	Maintains a Calendar?	Takes Notes?	GPA
A	sometimes	often	3.1
B	never	always	3.9
C	never	never	2.0
D	sometimes	often	2.7

   a. No college students consistently maintain a calendar of events.
   b. There is an inverse correlation between maintaining a calendar and GPA, and there is a positive correlation between taking notes and GPA.
   c. There is a positive correlation between maintaining a calendar and GPA, and there is no correlation between taking notes and GPA.
   d. There is no correlation between maintaining a calendar and GPA, and there is a positive correlation between taking notes and GPA.

5. The sun is a major external source of energy. Which of the following is the best demonstration of this?
   a. Flowers tend to bloom in the morning, after dawn.
   b. Large animals like bears do not need to eat food when hibernating.
   c. Deserts can reach scorching temperatures in daylight but subzero temperatures at night.
   d. The tides of the ocean are highly dependent on the movement of the Moon, the celestial body that is highly reflective to sunlight.

See answers on the next page.

Science Answer Explanations

1. C: A hypothesis is a statement that makes a prediction between two variables. The two variables here are the amount of poison and how quickly the rat dies. Choice C states that the more poison a rat is given, the more quickly it will die, which is a prediction. Choice A is incorrect because it's simply an observation. Choice B is incorrect because it's a question posed by the observation but makes no predictions. Choice D is incorrect because it's simply a fact.

2. B: The independent variable is the variable manipulated, and the dependent variable is the result of the changes in the independent variable. Choice B is correct because the amount of poison is the variable that is changed, and the speed of rat death is the result of the changes in the amount of poison administered. Choice A is incorrect because that answer states the opposite. Choice C is false because the scientist isn't attempting to determine whether the rat will die *if* it eats poison; the scientist is testing how quickly the rat will die depending on *how much* poison it eats. Choice D is incorrect because the cage isn't manipulated in any way and has nothing to do with the hypothesis.

3. B: Models are representations of concepts that are impossible to experience directly, such as the 3D representation of DNA, so Choice B is correct. Choice A is incorrect because theories simply explain why things happen. Choice C is incorrect because laws describe how things happen. Choice D is false because an observation analyzes situations using human senses.

4. D: Based on this table, it can be reasoned that there is not a correlation between maintaining a calendar and GPA, since Student B never maintains a calendar but has the highest GPA of the cohort. Furthermore, it can be reasoned that there is a positive correlation between taking notes and GPA since the more notes a student takes, the higher the GPA they have. Thus, Choice D is the correct answer. Choice A offers an absolute that cannot be proven based on this study; thus, it is incorrect. Choices B and C are incorrect because they have at least one incorrect correlation.

5. C: By drawing inferences from the presented information, we can deduce that deserts' temperatures are extremely hot in the day and cold at night because of the warming effects of the sun's solar rays; thus, this is the best example of the sun's energy. Although some flowers do tend to bloom after dawn, this is probably due to day/night cycles regulated by the presence of light rather than intense amounts of energy. Hibernating animals tend to use large repositories of stored nutrients as energy sources rather than relying on the sun's energy, and they may in fact be in caves or hidden underground to shelter them from the sun or weather. The tides are more dependent on the Moon due to its gravity rather than any effects its albedo moonlight may have.

Social Studies

Citizenship and Government

Identifying and Analyzing the Governments in Canada

Government is the physical manifestation of the political entity or ruling body of a state. It includes the formal institutions that manage and maintain a society. The form of government does not determine the state's economic system, though these concepts are often closely tied. Many forms of government are based on a society's economic system. However, while the form of government refers to the methods by which a society is managed, the term **economy** refers to the management of resources in a society. Many forms of government exist, often as hybrids of two or more forms of government or economic systems. Forms of government can be distinguished based on protection of civil liberties, protection of rights, distribution of power, power of government, and principles of Federalism.

Federal Government of Canada
Modeled after the British system of government, Canada is a Westminster-style parliamentary democracy and constitutional monarchy as established under the Constitution Act, 1867.

As a constitutional monarchy, the British Crown serves as the sovereign and head of state. The Crown's overriding goal is to uphold the principle of responsible government, meaning that government should reflect the will of the people. The monarch is the sole source of the Crown's authority, including the royal prerogative. In general, the royal prerogative involves powers related to the calling of elections, conducting foreign policy, and assenting to legislation. With advice from the Canadian prime minister, the British monarch appoints the Governor General of Canada, who acts as their representative.

The Parliament and Supreme Court of Canada make up the rest of the federal government. Canadian Parliament is bicameral, consisting of the Senate (upper house) and House of Commons (lower house). The governor general appoints senators on the advice of the prime minister, and members of the House of Commons are elected by the Canadian people. Following an election, the governor general appoints a prime minister to serve as the head of government. Prime ministers are typically the leader of the winning political party or governing coalition. The prime minister chairs the Cabinet of Canada and selects its ministers. Additionally, the prime minister appoints members to the Supreme Court of Canada, which is the highest level of the Canadian justice system. Supreme Court decisions are binding on all other Canadian courts unless overridden by legislation.

Analyzing and Comparing Political Systems and Models of Governance

Canada is governed using a **parliamentary system.** In this system, the public elects members to the House of Commons, while the Governor General appoints worthy persons to the nation's Senate. Elected members represent their districts in Parliament. They work together with other members of their political party to **form a coalition government** with other political parties. There are generally two types of government formed by the parliamentary system:

- A **majority government** is formed when one party possesses a majority of seats in the House of Commons when forming the government, resulting in reduced need for a coalition.
- A **minority government** is formed when the leading party *must* rely on the support of other parties to form the government in coalition.

In Canada's government, the Head of State remains the British monarch. They are represented by the Governor General, who fulfills a largely ceremonial role executing royal authority as advised by the Prime Minister.

The government formed by the coalition of political parties appoints a **Prime Minister** who then selects several other persons (usually members of the House of Commons) to be ministers on the **Privy Council.** Depending on the type of coalition formed, the ministers selected may represent the political perspectives of a single party or an array of political opinions.

The **opposition** is not typically represented on the Privy Council. Instead, political parties who are not a member of the coalition government voice their dissent in the House of Commons. While the Privy Council has wide authority to govern the nation, certain types of bills—such as budgets—must always be put before the assembly of elected representatives.

Indigenous peoples have full rights to participate in and be represented by the Canadian parliament. Each group of indigenous persons—such as the First Nations, the Inuit, and the Métis—also has the **right to self-government** under Canadian law. In particular, this includes the right of communities to choose their own leaders by the community's preferred processes. This right reflects an ongoing philosophy of change in Canadian governance, striving to depart from condescending attitudes enshrined in twentieth-century law while retaining recognition of the importance of the democratic process.

The *Indian Act of 1876* and the *First Nations Election Act of 2015* structure self-governance for a majority of Canada's First Nations. The *Indian Act* contained provisions that have become widely condemned, and has been amended many times. For example, the *Indian Act* allowed Canada's Minister of Indigenous Services to remove elected indigenous persons from office under certain circumstances, in violation of democratic principles. However, the *Indian Act* has not been wholly replaced because the *First Nations Election Act* uses an **opt-in process** for indigenous communities that wish to use the act to govern themselves. Consequently, communities that have found the amended *Indian Act* sufficient have not elected to change their mode of governance.

Under both acts, First Nations, Inuit, and Métis communities are empowered to elect their own **chief** and **councillors** to govern the community.

Canada's policies also support communities that wish to create their own methods of election and governance. Further, fully self-governing First Nations—such as the Okanagan—are not legislated by these two acts. Instead, the First Nation negotiates its own treaty with the Canadian government to establish the community's government as a member of Canada. While the process is slow, treaty negotiations are increasingly favored by Canada's indigenous peoples seeking self-governance.

Examining Democratic, Electoral, and Justice Systems in Canada

Canadian citizens are guaranteed various rights under the *Canadian Charter of Rights and Freedoms*, the first section of the *Constitution Act of 1982*. These rights include:

- The **fundamental freedoms** of all persons to think and believe as they wish, and to express themselves or associate themselves with like-minded individuals in a peaceable manner.
- All persons also have the **right of equality under the law**, without discrimination on grounds of race, ethnicity, skin color, religious belief, sex or gender, age, or disability status.
- The **democratic right** of all Canadian citizens to vote for their member of Parliament and to stand for election to that position.
- Citizens also have the **right of mobility** within Canada's provinces, or to exit and leave the country as they wish.

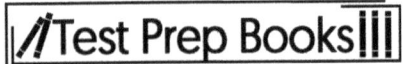

Consequently, those rights enshrined in the *Charter* can be divided into roughly two categories: **universal rights** and the **rights of citizens**. A citizen's rights are generally the right to *participate* in an element of government, while the universal rights are generally expressed as *freedoms* from control or oppression by any person or group (including the government).

The *Charter* also defines **universal legal rights** that protect all persons under Canadian law. This section of the *Charter* is more specific than the others. A person's legal rights include:

- The right to **life, liberty, and "security of person"**
- **Freedom from arbitrary detention,** including the right to **know the reason of arrest**
- **Freedom from cruel and unusual punishment**
- If accused, the **right to a prompt trial** and the right to **avoid self-incrimination**

Collectively, the legal rights define how any person accused of a crime under Canadian law must be treated by the justice system.

In exchange for the rights of citizenship, citizens also have certain responsibilities they ought to fulfill. The responsibilities of citizenship are part of the constitution's **social contract**, which is the foundation of society.

However, these responsibilities are not onerous—they simply express the principle that **citizens should participate in their government and society**. For example, the citizen has a responsibility to vote in elections for the House of Commons, serve on a jury when called, obey the laws of Canada, and respect the rights and freedoms of other persons. These responsibilities help create a peaceful and mutually supportive society.

Identifying and Comparing Local, Provincial/Territorial, and Federal Governments

Canada's government has three basic levels: federal government, provincial government, and local government.

Federal Government

The **federal government** is the level that oversees *all* aspects of Canadian governance and law. It includes the highest officials of the executive, legislative, and judicial branches (such as the Supreme Court). Major functions of the federal government include maintaining diplomatic relations with other nations (including the First Nations, which reside on traditional lands now claimed as part of Canada), establishing laws that concern the entire nation, the military defense of Canada, and resolving conflicts between the provinces.

Provincial Government

Although the *Constitution Act of 1867* initially defined the **provincial governments** as wholly subordinate to the federal government, over time the ten provinces have expanded their governmental powers. Each province is responsible for enacting and enforcing civil and criminal law, managing the creation and boundaries of cities or towns, and providing public services (such as hospitals or education).

The authority of provincial governments has expanded in particular regarding **taxation** and the **use of public land**. Each province has the authority to manage its public lands, including the rights to use natural resources in the province.

Like the federal government, provincial governments are organized using the parliamentary system. The people of each province elect members to their own House of Commons, which forms a cabinet led by the province's **premier**. A **lieutenant-governor** provides executive authority as a representative of the Governor General and the Crown.

Local Government

The local government of a city or town is often called the **municipal government**. This is the lowest level of government, and is the most directly involved in the everyday lives of its residents. For example, while the federal government's acts impact all Canadians, they remain somewhat distant and abstract. Such acts are carried out by lower levels of government until the local government resolves the concrete details.

Local governments are responsible for the maintenance and operation of their district's public services. This typically includes maintaining the roads, providing public transportation, supplying clean water, operating libraries, hiring police, and so on.

Another type of local government is the **band council**. While some First Nations are wholly self-governing, others take the role of local government within their province.

Neither municipal nor First Nations governments use the parliamentary system. Instead of a House of Commons, local governments are **led by a mayor** on a council of elected officials who govern the district directly.

Identifying and Interpreting Individual and Collective Rights in Canada

In addition to the various rights protected by the *Canadian Charter of Rights and Freedoms*, Canada also recognizes the **collective rights** of groups of people. Such rights are most easily conceived of as the rights of **indigenous communities** and of **linguistic minorities**. There is an important distinction here between the rights of *individuals* who belong to such a group, and the rights of the *group as a whole*. The term "collective rights" refers to the latter.

The collective rights of indigenous peoples are recognized for the First Nations, the Inuit, and the Métis peoples. Under Canadian law, such rights center on the principle that all members of a minority group have the **right to collective identity.** It is especially important that this right is respected and preserved due to Canada's past history of trying to weaken the sense of identity in indigenous communities. Some ways that indigenous identities have been sabotaged in the past include treaties between the Crown and the First Nations, forced relocation and re-education, and land claims made without formal agreement. New treaty negotiations between Canada and the First Nations are an ongoing process in hopes of repairing these historical injustices.

Canada recognizes two official languages: English and French. Native English-speakers are called **Anglophones,** while native French-speakers are called **Francophones.** Official linguistic minorities are recognized as groups of people whose native language is *not* the dominant language in the district or province they live in. All persons in Canada have a right to receive education in their native language if they are a member of one of these official linguistic minorities and their parents received education in that language in the same place. For example, if Francophone parents grew up in a French-speaking school in Alberta, then they have the right for their children to be educated in French as well. This collective right ensures the continuity of linguistic cultural identity for the group.

Examining how Citizenship, Leadership, and Activism can be expressed

Citizens express their political beliefs and public opinion through participation in politics. The conventional ways citizens can participate in politics in a democratic state include:

- Obeying laws
- Voting in elections
- Running for public office
- Staying interested in and informed of current events
- Learning Canadian history
- Attending public hearings to be informed and to express opinions on issues, especially on the local level
- Forming interest groups to promote common goals

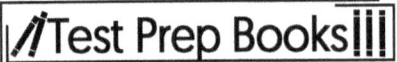

- Forming political action committees (PACs) that raise money to influence policy decisions
- Petitioning government to create awareness of issues
- Campaigning for a candidate
- Contributing to campaigns
- Using mass media to express political ideas, opinions, and grievances

Obeying Laws

Citizens living in a democracy have several rights and responsibilities to uphold. The first duty is that they uphold the established laws of the government. In a democracy, a system of nationwide laws is necessary to ensure that there is some degree of order. Therefore, citizens must obey the laws and also help enforce them because a law that is inadequately enforced is almost useless. Optimally, a democratic society's laws will be accepted and followed by the community as a whole.

However, conflict can occur when an unjust law is passed. For example, much of the civil rights movement centered around laws that supported segregation between black and whites. Yet these practices were encoded in state laws, which created a dilemma for African Americans who wanted equality but also wanted to respect the law. Fortunately, a democracy offers a system in which government leaders and policies are constantly open to change in accordance with the will of citizens. Citizens can influence the laws that are passed by voting for and electing members of the legislative and executive branches to represent them at the local, provincial, and national levels.

Voting

In a democratic state, the most common way to participate in politics is by voting for candidates in an election. Voting allows the citizens of a state to influence policy by selecting the candidates who share their views and make policy decisions that best suit their interests, or candidates who they believe are most capable of leading the country. In Canada, all citizens over 18—regardless of gender, race, or religion—are allowed to vote.

Citizens can participate by voting in the following types of elections:

- **Federal, provincial, territorial, and municipal elections:** Citizens elect their representatives in government.
- **Referendums:** Citizens can vote directly on proposed laws or constitutional amendments.
- **Recall elections:** Citizens in British Columbia have the unique opportunity to petition the government to remove an official from office before their term ends.
- **Voter initiatives:** In another process unique to British Columbia, citizens can petition their local government to propose laws that will be approved or rejected by voters.

Running for Public Office

Citizens also have the ability to run for elected office. By becoming leaders in the government, citizens can demonstrate their engagement and help determine government policy. Citizen involvement in the selection of leaders is vital in a democracy because it helps to prevent the formation of an elite group that does not answer to the public. Without the engagement of citizens who run for office, voters are limited in their ability to select candidates that appeal to them. In this case, voting options would become stagnant, inhibiting the nation's ability to grow and change over time. As long as citizens are willing to take a stand for their vision of Canada, the government will remain dynamic and diverse.

Citizen Interest

In order for a democracy to function, it is of the utmost importance that citizens care about the course of politics and be aware of current issues. Apathy among citizens is a constant problem that threatens the endurance of democracies. Citizens should have a desire to take part in the political process, lest they simply accept the status quo and fail to fulfill their civic role. Moreover, they must have acute knowledge of the political processes and the

Social Studies

issues that they can address as citizens. Without understanding the world around them, citizens may not fully grasp the significance of political actions and thereby fail to make wise decisions in that regard. Therefore, citizens must stay informed about current affairs, ranging from local to global matters, so that they can properly address them as voters or elected leaders.

Historical Knowledge

Furthermore, knowledge of the nation's history is essential for healthy citizenship. History continues to have an influence on present political decisions. It is especially critical that citizens are aware of the context in which laws were established because it helps clarify the purpose of those laws. In addition, history as a whole shapes the course of societies and the world; therefore, citizens should draw on this knowledge of the past to realize the full consequences of current actions. Issues such as climate change, conflict in the Middle East, and civil rights struggles are rooted in events and cultural developments that reach back centuries and should be addressed.

Therefore, education is a high priority in democracies because it has the potential to instill younger generations of citizens with the right mindset and knowledge required to do their part in shaping the nation. Social studies are especially important because students should understand how democracies function and understand the history of the nation and world. Historical studies should cover national and local events as well because they help provide the basis for the understanding of contemporary politics. Social studies courses should also address the histories of foreign nations because contemporary politics has global consequences. In addition, history lessons should remain open to multiple perspectives, even those that might criticize a nation's past actions, because citizens should be exposed to diverse perspectives that they can apply as voters and leaders.

Analyzing individual and collective identities and diverse perspectives

Unlike many other nations, Canada's population is comprised of an **ethnic and cultural plurality**. For example, Poland or Japan are nations in which a majority of the citizens share one identity. Because of this plurality, there is not a bullet-proof definition of what it means for a person to self-identify as a Canadian. Some collective identities are relatively easy to identify, such as Anglophones or the Inuit. This diversity of identity means that any federal legislation must be representative of as many groups of Canadians as possible if the legislation is to be truly just and democratic.

One major consequence of ethnic and cultural plurality for Canadian politics has been the gradual increase in governmental powers and authority for the provinces. Decentralization of authority is a political response to plurality that allows for a more nuanced approach to the concerns of citizens who live in different parts of the country. For example, a person from urban Toronto may well be unfamiliar with the social norms and customs of people living in a small town in Manitoba!

This decentralizing approach has been hand-in-hand with increased calls and efforts to empower indigenous self-government. Much like increasing the authority of provincial governments, placing authority in the hands of First Nations communities ensures their district's government will reflect their community's values.

However, this decentralizing impulse also carries the risk of true separation. Canada's increasingly multicultural identity threatens to separate the nation into a confederation of separate communities, whether along provincial or ethnic lines. The shared values enshrined in the *Charter* and shared participation in the House of Commons are political institutions that help preserve unity among the plural individual and collective identities of modern Canadian citizens.

Examining Factors that Contribute to Individual and Collective Identities

Canada's involvement in global affairs is strongly characterized by its involvement in the United Nations and its ongoing efforts to improve the respect and preservation of human rights globally. This intersects with the sense of

Canadian identity preserved in the *Constitution Act* particularly in efforts to extend the rights preserved in the *Canadian Charter of Rights and Freedoms* to recognition by all nations around the world. Canada's involvement in the drafting and ratification of the United Nations' *Universal Declaration of Human Rights* in 1948 is one example of this commitment.

Another way Canada interacts with the United Nations is to recognize that body's authority to evaluate and criticize the maintenance of human rights within the nation. This provides an outside perspective on Canadian law, which the government recognizes as an important corrective. In particular, this shapes Canadian identity in the international sphere by providing Canada with moral standing for its own advocacy programs.

Canada participates positively in international affairs through both knowledge-based and financial support of democratic institutions, recognition of refugee status during global crises, and advocacy for the peaceful resolution of conflicts from its position as a neutral nation. When disincentives for international misbehavior or criminality are required, Canada primarily acts through economic sanction rather than military force.

Geographically, Canadian identity is strongly defined by its location in North America and its relationship to the United States of America. Canada is allied with America, and is a member of the North Atlantic Treaty Organization (NATO) for military defense. The history shared between Canada and America often colors perceptions of Canadian identity both at home and abroad.

Economics and Economic Systems

Analyzing Canada's Economic System

Fundamental Economic Concepts

Economics is the study of human behavior in response to the production, consumption, and distribution of assets or wealth. Economics can help individuals or societies make decisions for themselves dependent upon their needs, wants, and resources. Economics is divided into two subgroups: microeconomics and macroeconomics.

Microeconomics is the study of individual or small group behaviors related to markets of goods and services. It specifically looks at single factors that could affect these behaviors and decisions. For example, the use of coupons in a grocery store could affect an individual's product choice, quantity purchased, and overall savings that could be directed to a different purchase. Microeconomics encompasses the study of many things, including scarcity, choice, opportunity costs, economics systems, factors of production, supply and demand, market efficiency, the role of government, distribution of income, and product markets.

Macroeconomics examines a much larger scale, analyzing the economy as a whole. It focuses on how aggregate factors such as demand, output, spending habits, unemployment, interest rates, price levels, and national income affect the people in a society or nation. For example, if a national company moves its production overseas to save on costs, how will production, labor, and capital be affected? Governments and corporations use macroeconomic models to help formulate economic policies and strategies.

Economy of Canada

The Canadian economy is highly developed, with a free market based on capitalist economic principles, and it regularly ranks as one of the freest marketplaces in the world. Canada's gross domestic product (GDP) was $1.6 trillion in 2020, making it the ninth largest economy in the world. Compared to other highly developed countries, Canada has relatively low income inequality due to its high taxes and generous social welfare system.

The service industry accounts for approximately 70% of Canada's GDP and 75% of its total employment. Some of the largest sectors in Canada's service industry are retail, business services, and high technology. Education and health are also amongst the largest service sectors, but they are publicly owned and operated. In sharp contrast to many other highly developed countries, Canada has maintained robust manufacturing and steel production. Canada is also one of the largest producers and exporters of agricultural products, mineral resources, natural gas, and oil. Lastly, Canada is a world leader in green energy, with 59% of electric generation coming from hydroelectricity.

Canada benefits tremendously from international trade. It is a leading member of the World Trade Organization (WTO), and it has more than a dozen active free trade agreements with its trading partners. One of its most valuable free trade agreements is the Canada–United States–Mexico Agreement, which superseded NAFTA in 2020. While free trade agreements have generally driven economic growth, they have also been heavily criticized for their harmful effects on blue-collar employment, particularly in the manufacturing sector.

Factors of Production
There are four factors of production:

- Land: both renewable and nonrenewable resources
- Labor: effort put forth by people to produce goods and services
- Capital: the tools used to create goods and services
- Entrepreneurs: persons who combine land, labor, and capital to create new goods and services

The four factors of production are used to create goods and services to make economic profit. All four factors strongly impact one another.

Product Markets
Product markets are where goods and services are bought and sold. Product markets provide a place for sellers to offer goods and services and for consumers to purchase them. The annual value of goods and services exchanged throughout the year is measured by a nation's Gross Domestic Product (GDP), a monetary measure of goods and services made either quarterly or annually. Department stores, gas stations, grocery stores, and other retail stores are all examples of product markets. However, product markets do not include any raw or unfinished materials.

Theory of the Firm
The behavior of firms is composed of several theories varying between short- and long-term goals. There are four basic firm behaviors: perfect competition, profit maximization, short run, and long run. Each firm follows a pattern, depending on its desired outcome. **Theory of the Firm** posits that firms, after conducting market research, make decisions that will maximize their profits.

- Perfect competition: several businesses are selling the same product simultaneously. There are so many businesses and consumers that none will directly impact the market. Each business and consumer is aware of the competing businesses and markets.
- Profit maximization: Firms decide the quantity of a product that needs to be produced in order to receive maximum profit gains. Profit is the total amount of revenue made after subtracting costs.
- Short run: A short amount of time where fixed prices cannot be adjusted. The quantity of the product depends on the varying amount of labor. Less labor means less product.
- Long run: An amount of time where fixed prices can be adjusted. Firms try to maximize production while minimizing labor costs.

Measures of Economic Performance
Measurements of economic performance determine if an economy is growing, stagnant, or deteriorating. To measure the growth and sustainability of an economy, several indicators can be used. Economic indicators provide data that economists can use to determine if there are faulty processes or if some form of intervention is needed.

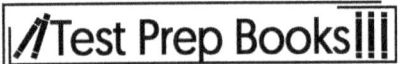

One of the main indicators of a country's economic performance is the Gross Domestic Product (GDP). GDP growth provides important information that can be used to determine fiscal or financial policies. The GDP does not measure income distribution, quality of life, or losses due to natural disasters. For example, if a community lost everything to a hurricane, it would take a long time to rebuild the community and stabilize its economy. That is why there is a need to take into account more balanced performance measures when factoring overall economic performance.

Other indicators used to measure economic performance are unemployment/employment rates, inflation, savings, investments, surpluses and deficits, debt, labor, trade terms, the HDI (Human Development Index), and the HPI (Human Poverty Index).

Analyzing and Comparing Current, Traditional and Subsistence Economic Activity

The Development and Changing Nature of Agriculture

Since the genesis of farming as a means of food production, agriculture has been essential to human existence. Humans no longer had to forage and hunt for food, and more consistent food supplies allowed societies to stabilize and grow. In modern times, farming has changed drastically in order to keep up with the increasing world population.

Until the twentieth century, the vast majority of people on Earth engaged in **subsistence farming**, the practice of growing only enough food to feed oneself and one's family. Inventions such as the steel plow, the mechanical reaper, and the seed drill allowed farmers to produce more crops on the same amount of land. As food became cheaper and easier to obtain, populations grew, but fewer people farmed. After the advent of mechanized farming in developed nations, small farms became less common, and many were either abandoned or absorbed by massive commercial farms producing staple crops and cash crops.

In recent years, agricultural practices have undergone further changes in order to keep up with the rapidly growing population. Due in part to the Green Revolution, which introduced the widespread use of fertilizers to produce massive amounts of crops, farming techniques and practices continue to evolve. For example, **genetically modified organisms**, or *GMOs*, are plants or animals whose genetic makeup has been modified using different strands of DNA in hopes of producing more resilient strains of staple crops, livestock, and other foodstuffs. This process, which is a form of biotechnology, attempts to solve the world's food production problems through the use of genetic engineering. Although these crops are abundant and resistant to pests, drought, or frost, they are also the subject of intense scrutiny. For example, the international food company, Monsanto, has faced an incredible amount of criticism regarding its use of GMOs. Many activists assert that such artificial food production processes are inherently problematic and that the resulting food products are dangerous to human health. Despite the controversy, GMOs and biotechnologies continue to change the agricultural landscape and the world's food supply.

Agribusinesses exist throughout the world and produce food for human consumption as well as farming equipment, fertilizers, agrichemicals, and breeding and slaughtering services for livestock. These companies are generally headquartered near the product they produce, like the cereal manufacturer General Mills in the Midwestern United States located near its supply of wheat and corn—the primary ingredients in its cereals.

Contemporary Patterns and Impacts of Development, Industrialization, and Globalization

As mentioned previously, **developing nations** are those that are struggling to modernize their economy, infrastructure, and government systems. Many of these nations may have difficulty providing basic services to their citizens like clean water, adequate roads, or even police protection. Furthermore, government corruption makes life even more difficult for these countries' citizens.

In contrast, **developed nations** are those that have relatively high **Gross Domestic Products** *(GDP)*, or the total value of all goods and services produced in the nation in a given year. The United States, one of the wealthiest nations on

Social Studies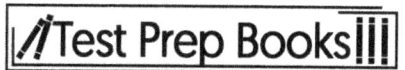

Earth, has a GDP of over twenty-one trillion dollars, while Haiti, one of the poorest nations in the Western Hemisphere, has a GDP of over fourteen billion dollars. This comparison is not intended to disparage Haiti or other developing nations, but rather to show that extreme inequities exist in very close proximity to one another, and it may be difficult for developing nations to meet the needs of their citizens and move their economic infrastructure forward toward modernization.

In the modern world, industrialization is the initial key to modernization and development. For developed nations, the process of industrialization took place centuries ago. England, where the Industrial Revolution began, actually began to utilize factories in the early 1700s. Later, the United States and some Western European nations followed suit, using raw materials brought in from their colonies abroad to make finished products. For example, elaborate weaving machines spun cotton into fabric, allowing for the mass production of textiles. As a result, nations that perfected the textile process were able to sell their products around the world, which produced enormous profits. Over time, those nations were able to accumulate wealth, improve their nation's infrastructure, and provide more services for their citizens.

Nations throughout the world are undergoing a similar process in modern times. China exemplifies this concept. While agriculture is still a dominant sector of the Chinese economy, millions of citizens are flocking to major cities like Beijing, Shanghai, and Hangzhou due to the availability of factory jobs that allow workers a certain element of social mobility, or the ability to rise up to a better socioeconomic situation.

Due to improvements in transportation and communication, the world has become figuratively smaller. For example, university students now compete directly with others all over the world to obtain the skills that employers desire. Additionally, many corporations in developed nations have begun to outsource labor to nations with high levels of educational achievement but lower wage expectations. **Globalization**, the process of opening the marketplace to all nations throughout the world, has only just started to take hold in the modern economy. As industrial sites shift to the developing world, more opportunities become available for those nation's citizens as well.

However, due to the massive amounts of pollution produced by factories, the process of globalization also has had significant ecological impacts. The most widely known impact, climate change, which most climatologists assert is caused by an increase of carbon dioxide in the atmosphere, remains a serious problem that has posed challenges for developing nations, who need industries in order to raise their standard of living, and developed nations, whose citizens use a tremendous amount of fossil fuels to run their cars, heat their homes, and maintain their ways of life.

Analyzing and Evaluating Supply, Demand, and Price

Scarcity

When a product is scarce, there is a short supply of it. Limited resources and high demand create **scarcity**. For example, when the newest version of a cellphone is released, people line up to buy the phone or put their name on a wait list if the phone is not immediately available. The new cellphone may become a scarce commodity. In turn, the phone company may raise their prices, knowing that people may be willing to pay more for an item in such high demand.

Supply and Demand

Supply and demand are the most important concepts of economics in a market economy. **Supply** is the amount of a product that a market can offer. **Demand** is the quantity of a product needed or desired by buyers. The price of a product is directly related to supply and demand. The price of a product and the demand for that product go hand in hand in a market economy. For example, when there are a variety of treats at a bakery, certain treats are in higher demand than others. The bakery can raise the cost of the more demanded items as supplies get limited.

Conversely, the bakery can sell the less desirable treats by lowering the cost of those items as an incentive for buyers to purchase them.

Applying and Analyzing Factors that Contribute to Economic Conditions

Unemployment

Unemployment occurs when an individual does not have a job, is actively trying to find employment, and is not getting paid. *Official* unemployment rates do not factor in the number of people who have stopped looking for work, but *true* unemployment rates do.

There are three types of unemployment: cyclical, frictional, and structural.

Cyclical
Comes as a result of the regular economic cycle and variations in supply and demand. This usually occurs during a recession.
Frictional
When workers voluntarily leave their jobs. An example would be a person changing careers.
Structural
When companies' needs change and a person no longer possesses the skills needed.

Given the nature of a market economy and the fluctuations of the labor market, a 100 percent employment rate is impossible to reach.

Inflation

Inflation is when the value of money decreases and the cost of goods and services increases over time. Supply, demand, and money reserves all affect inflation. Generally, inflation is measured by the Consumer Price Index (CPI), a tool that tracks price changes of goods and services. When the cost of goods and services increase, manufacturers may reduce the quantity they produce due to lower demand. This decreases the purchasing power of the consumer. Basically, as more money is printed, it holds less and less value in purchasing power. When inflation occurs, consumers spend and save less because their currency is worth less. However, if inflation occurs steadily over time, the people can better plan and prepare for future necessities.

Inflation can vary from year to year, usually never fluctuating more than 2 percent. Central banks try to prevent drastic increases or decreases of inflation to prohibit prices from rising or falling too far. Although rare, any country's economy may experience **hyperinflation** (when inflation rates increase to over 50 percent), while other economies may experience **deflation** (when the cost of goods and services decrease over time). Deflation occurs when the inflation rate drops below zero percent.

Business Cycle

A **business cycle** is when the Gross Domestic Product (GDP) moves downward and upward over a long-term growth trend. These cycles help determine where the economy currently stands, as well as where it could be heading.

Social Studies

Business cycles usually occur almost every six years and have four phases: expansion, peak, contraction, and trough. Here are some characteristics of each phase:

- Expansion: increased employment rates, production, sales, and economic growth
- Peak: employment rates are at or above full employment and the economy is at maximum productivity
- Contraction: when growth starts slowing and unemployment rises
- Trough: the cycle has hit bottom and is waiting for the next cycle to start again.

When the economy is expanding or "booming," the business cycle is going from a trough to a peak. When the economy is headed down and toward a recession, the business cycle is going from a peak to a trough.

Four phases of a business cycle:

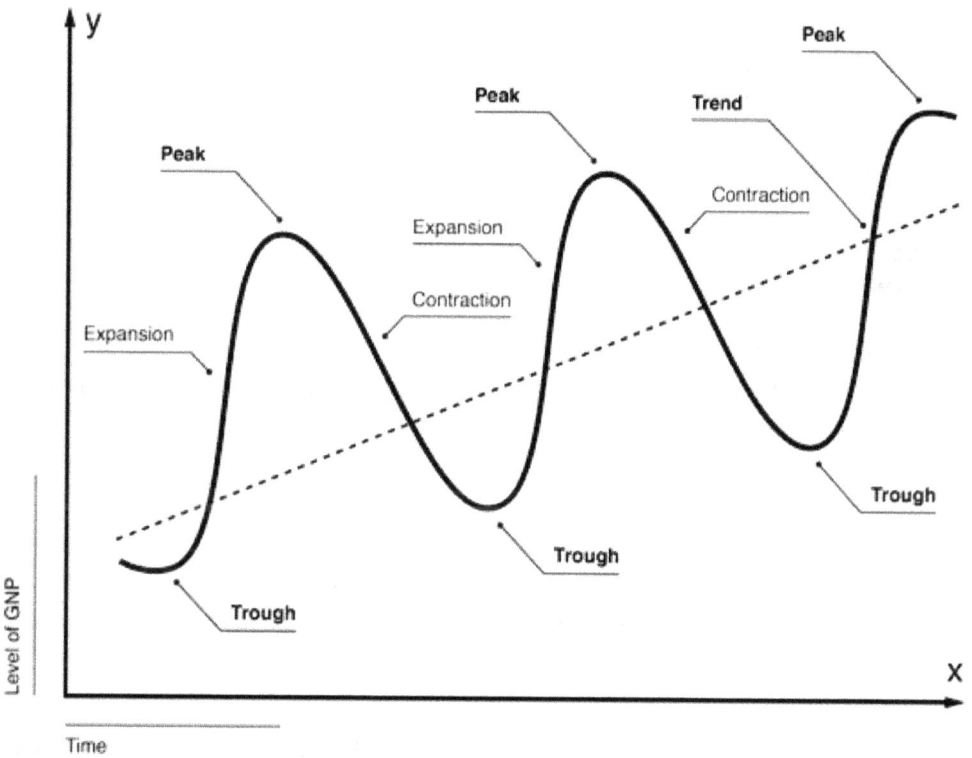

Economic Growth

The most common tool for measuring economic growth is the Gross Domestic Product (GDP). The increase of goods and services over time indicates positive movement in economic growth. The quantity of goods and services produced is not always an indicator of economic growth, however; the value matters more than the quantity.

There are many causes of economic growth, which can be short- or long-term. In the short term, if aggregate demand (the total demand for goods and services produced at a given time) increases, then the overall GDP increases as well. As the GDP increases, interest rates may decrease, which may encourage greater spending and investing. Real estate prices may also rise, and there may be lower income taxes. All of these short-term factors can stimulate economic growth.

In the long term, if aggregate supply (the total supply of goods or services in a given time period) increases, then there is potential for an increase in capital as well. With more working capital, more infrastructure and jobs can be

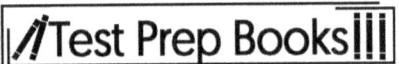

created. New technologies will be developed, and new raw materials may be discovered. All of these long-term factors can also stimulate economic growth.

Other causes of economic growth include low inflation and stability. Lower inflation rates encourage more investing as opposed to higher inflation rates that cause market instability. Stability encourages businesses to continue investing. If the market is unstable, investors may question the volatility of the market.

Potential Costs of Economic Growth:

- Inflation: When economic growth occurs, inflation tends to be high. If supply cannot keep up with demand, then the inflation rate may be unmanageable.
- Economic booms and recessions: The economy goes through cycles of booms and recessions. This causes inflation to fluctuate over time, which puts the economy into a continuous cycle of rising and falling.
- Environmental costs: When the economy is growing, there is an abundance of output, which may result in more pollutants and a reduction in quality of life.
- Inequalities: Growth occurs differently among members of society. While the wealthy may be getting richer, those living in poverty may just be getting on their feet. So, while economic growth is happening, it may happen at very different rates.

While these potential costs could affect economic growth, if the growth is consistent and stable, then it can occur without severe inflation swings. As technology improves, new ways of production can reduce negative environmental factors as well.

Renewable and Nonrenewable Resources

Renewable resources are self-replenishing, such as solar, wind, water, and geothermal energy. **Nonrenewable resources**, also known as *fossil fuels*, such as oil, natural gas, and coal, take much longer to replenish but are generally abundant and cheaper to use.

While solar energy is everywhere, the actual means to convert the sun's rays into energy is not. Conversely, coal-fired power plants and gasoline-powered engines, older technologies used during the industrial revolution, remain quite common throughout the world. Reliance on nonrenewable resources continues to grow due to availability and existing infrastructure, but use of renewable energy is also increasing as it becomes more economically competitive with nonrenewable resources.

In addition to sources of energy, nonrenewable resources also include any materials that can be exhausted, such as precious metals, precious stones, and freshwater underground aquifers. Although abundant, most nonrenewable sources of energy are not sustainable because their replenishment takes so long. While renewable resources are sustainable, their use must be properly overseen so that they remain renewable. For example, the beautiful African island of Madagascar is home to some of the most amazing rainforest trees in the world. Logging companies cut, milled, and sold thousands of them in order to make quick profits without planning how to ensure the continued health of the forests. In this way, renewable resources were mismanaged and thus essentially became nonrenewable due to the length of time it takes for replacement trees to grow.

In contrast, many United States paper companies that harvest pine trees must utilize planning techniques to ensure that mature pine trees will always be available. In this manner, these resources remain renewable for human use in a sustainable fashion.

Renewable sources of energy are relatively new in the modern economy. Even though electric cars, wind turbines, and solar panels are becoming more common, they still do not provide enough energy to power the world's economy. As a result, reliance on older forms of energy continues, which can have a devastating effect on the environment. Beijing, China, which has seen a massive boom in industrial jobs, is also one of the most polluted

Social Studies

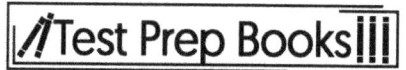

places on Earth. Furthermore, developing nations with very little modern infrastructure also rely heavily on fossil fuels due to the ease in which they are converted into usable energy. Even the United States, which has one of the most developed infrastructures in the world, still relies almost exclusively on fossil fuels, with only ten percent of the required energy coming from renewable sources.

Evaluating and Analyzing Economic Factors and Decision-making

Consumer Economics

Economics is closely linked with the flow of resources, technology, and population in societies. The use of natural resources, such as water and fossil fuels, has always depended in part on the pressures of the economy. A supply of a specific good may be limited in the market, but with sufficient demand, sellers are incentivized to increase the available quantity. Unfortunately, the demand for certain objects can often be unlimited, and a high price or limited supply may prevent consumers from obtaining the product or service. If the sellers succumb to the consumers' demand and continue to exploit a scarce resource, supply could potentially be exhausted.

The resources for most products, both renewable and nonrenewable, are finite. This is a particularly difficult issue with nonrenewable resources, but even renewable resources often have limits: organic products such as trees and animals require stable populations and sufficient habitats to support those populations. Furthermore, the costs of certain decisions can have detrimental effects on other resources. For example, industrialization provides economic benefits in many countries but also has had the negative effect of polluting surrounding environments; the pollution, in turn, often eliminates or harms fish, plants, and other potential resources.

The control of resources within an economy is particularly important in determining how resources are used. While demand may change with the consumers' choices and preferences, supply depends on the objectives of the producers. They determine how much of their supply they allot for sale, and in the case of monopolies, they might have sole access to the resource. They might limit their use of resources or gather more to meet the demand. Consumers can choose which sellers they rely on for their supply, except in the case of a monopoly because there is no alternative supplier. Therefore, the function of supply within an economy can drastically influence how resources are exploited.

The availability of resources, in turn, affects the human population. Humans require basic resources such as food and water for survival, as well as additional resources for healthy lifestyles. Therefore, access to these resources helps determine the survival rate of humans. For much of human existence, economies have had limited ability to extract resources from the natural world, which restricted the growth rate of populations. However, the development of new technologies, combined with increasing demand for certain products, has pushed resource use to a new level. On one hand, this led to higher living standards and lower death rates. On the other hand, the increasing exploitation of resources has increased the world's population as a whole to unsustainable levels. The rising population leads to higher demand for resources that cannot be met. This creates poverty, reduced living conditions, and higher death rates. As a result, economics can significantly influence local and world population levels.

Technology is also intricately related to population, resources, and economics. The role of demand within economies has incentivized people to innovate new technologies that enable societies to have a higher quality of life and greater access to resources. Entrepreneurs expand technologies by finding ways to create new products for the market. The Industrial Revolution, in particular, illustrates the relationship between economics and technology because the ambitions of businessmen led to new infrastructure that enabled more efficient and sophisticated use of resources. Many of these inventions reduced the amount of work necessary for individuals and allowed the development of leisure activities, which in turn created new economic markets. However, economic systems can also limit the growth of technology. In the case of monopolies, the lack of alternative suppliers reduces the incentive to meet and exceed consumer expectations. Moreover, as demonstrated by the effects of economics on resources,

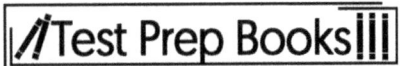

technology's increasing ability to extract resources can lead to their depletion and create significant issues that need to be addressed.

Distribution of Income

Distribution of income refers to how wages are spread across a society or segments of a society. If everyone made the same amount of money, the distribution of income would be equal. That is not the case in most societies. Wealth varies among people and companies. Income inequality gaps are present in Canada and many other nations. Taxes provide an option to redistribute income or wealth because they provide revenue to build new infrastructure and provide cash benefits to some of the poorest members in society.

Choice and Opportunity Costs

When an individual decides between possibilities, that individual is making a choice. Choices allow people to compare opportunity costs. Opportunity costs are benefits that a person could have received, but gave up, in choosing another course of action. What is an individual willing to trade or give up for a different choice? For example, if an individual pays someone to mow the lawn because he or she would rather spend that time doing something else, then the opportunity cost of paying someone to mow the lawn is worth the time gained from not doing the job himself or herself.

On a larger scale, governments have to assess different opportunity costs when it comes to using taxpayer money. Should the government build a new school, repair roads, or allocate funds to local hospitals? Each choice has a tradeoff, and decision makers must choose which option they think is best.

Identifying and Analyzing Roles and Relationships

Government Involvement in the Economy

Governments have considerable influence over the flow of economies. When a government has full control over the economic decisions of a nation, it is called a command system. This was the case in many absolute monarchies such as eighteenth-century France; King Louis XIV built his economy on the concept of mercantilism, which believed that the state should manage all resources, particularly by accumulating gold and silver. This system of economics discouraged exports and thereby limited trade.

In contrast, the market system is guided by the concept of capitalism, in which individuals and businesses have the freedom to manage their own economic decisions. This allows for private property and increases the opportunities for entrepreneurship and trade. Early proponents of capitalism emphasized *laissez-faire* policies, which means "let it be," and argued that the government should not be involved with the economy at all. They believed that the market is guided by self-interest and that individuals will optimally work for their personal success. However, individuals' interests do not necessarily correlate with the needs of the overall economy. For example, during a financial recession, consumers may decide to save up their money rather than make purchases; doing so helps them in the short run but further reduces demand in a slumping economy. Therefore, most capitalist governments still assert a degree of control over their economies while still allowing for private business.

Likewise, many command system economies have relied heavily on private businesses. Communism has been the primary form of command system economies in the modern era. Communism is a form of socialism that emphasizes communal ownership of property and government control over production. The high degree of government control gives more stability to the economy, but it also creates considerable flaws. The monopolization of the economy by the government limits its ability to respond to local economic conditions because certain regions often have unique resources and needs. With the collapse of the Soviet Union and other communist states, command systems have been largely replaced with market systems.

The Canadian government helps to manage the nation's economy through a market system in several ways. First and foremost, the Bank of Canada, the central bank, is responsible for the production of money for use within the economy; depending on how the government manages the monetary flow, it may lead to a stable economy, deflation, or inflation. Second, provincial and federal governments impose taxes on individuals, corporations, and goods. Third, the government can pass laws that require additional regulation or inspections. In addition, the government has passed competition laws to inhibit the growth of private monopolies, which could limit free growth in the market system. Debates continue over whether the government should take further action to manage private industries or reduce its control over the private sector.

Just as governments can affect the direction of the economy, so can the economy have significant implications on government policies. Financial stability is critical in maintaining a prosperous state. A healthy economy will allow for new developments that contribute to the nation's growth and create jobs. On the other hand, an economic crisis, such as a recession or depression, can gravely damage a government's stability. Without a stable economy, business opportunities plummet, and people begin to lose income and employment. This, in turn, leads to frustration and discontent in the population, which can lead to criticism of the government. This could very well lead to demands for new leadership to resolve the economic crisis.

Economic Systems

Economic systems determine what is being produced, who is producing it, who receives the product, and the money generated by the sale of the product. There are two basic types of economic systems: market economies (including free and competitive markets) and planned or command economies.

Market economies are characterized by:

- Privately owned businesses, groups, or individuals providing goods or services based on demand
- Demand determines the types of goods and services produced (supply)
- Two types: competitive market and free market.

Competitive Market	Free Market
Due to the large number of both buyers and sellers, there is no way any one seller or buyer can control the market or price.	Voluntary private trades between buyers and sellers determine markets and prices without government intervention or monopolies.

- Planned or command economies are characterized by:
- Government or central authority determines market prices of goods and services
- Government or central authority determines what is being produced and the quantity of production
- Advantage: large number of shared goods such as public services (transportation, schools, or hospitals)
- Disadvantage: wastefulness of resources

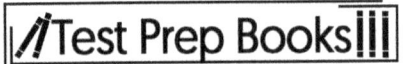

Market Efficiency and the Role of Government (Taxes, Subsidies, and Price Controls)

Market efficiency is directly affected by supply and demand. The government can help the market stay efficient by either stepping in when the market is inefficient and/or providing the means necessary for markets to run properly. The government may impose taxes, subsidies, and price controls to increase revenue, lower prices of goods and services, ensure product availability for the government, and maintain fair prices for goods and services.

The Purpose of Taxes, Subsidies, and Price Controls

Taxes	Subsidies	Price Controls
-Generate government revenue -Discourage purchase or use of "bad" products such as alcohol or cigarettes	-Lower the price of goods and services -Reassure the supply of goods and services -Allow opportunities to compete with overseas vendors	-Act as emergency measures when government intervention is necessary -Set a minimum or maximum price for goods and services

Money and Banking

Money is a means of exchange that provides a convenient way for sellers and consumers to understand the value of their goods and services. As opposed to bartering (when sellers and consumers exchange goods or services as equal trades), money is convenient for both buyers and sellers.

There are three main forms of money: commodity, fiat, and bank. Here are characteristics of each form:

- Commodity money: a valuable good, such as precious metals or tobacco, used as money
- Fiat money: currency that has no intrinsic value but is recognized by the government as valuable for trade, such as paper money
- Bank money: money that is credited by a bank to those who deposit it into bank accounts, such as checking and savings accounts or credit

While price levels within the economy set the demand for money, most countries have central banks that supply the actual money. Essentially, banks buy and sell money. Borrowers can take loans and pay back the bank, with interest, providing the bank with extra capital.

A central bank has control over the printing and distribution of money. Central banks serve three main purposes: manage monetary growth to help steer the direction of the economy, be a backup to commercial banks that are suffering, and provide options and alternatives to government taxation.

The Bank of Canada is the Canada's central bank. The Bank of Canada controls banking systems and determines the value of money in Canada. Basically, it is the bank for banks.

All Western economies have to keep a minimum amount of protected cash called *required reserve*. Once banks meet those minimums, they can then lend or loan the excess to consumers. The required reserves are used within a fractional reserve banking system (fractional because a small portion is kept separate and safe). Not only do banks reserve, manage, and loan money, but they also help form monetary policies.

Monetary Policy

The central bank and other government committees control the amount of money that is made and distributed. The money supply determines monetary policy. Three main features sustain monetary policy.

- Assuring the minimum amount held within banks (bank reserves): when banks are required to hold more money in reserve funds, they are less willing to lend money to help control inflation.

Social Studies

- Adjusting interest rates: raising interest rates makes borrowing more costly, which can slow down unsustainable growth and lower inflation. Lowering interest rates encourages borrowing and can stimulate struggling economies.
- Purchasing and selling bonds (open market operations): Controlling the money supply by buying bonds to increase it and selling bonds to reduce it.

There are two main types of monetary policy: expansionary and contractionary.

Expansionary	Contractionary
☐ Increases the money supply ☐ Lowers unemployment ☐ Increases consumer spending ☐ Increases private sector borrowing ☐ Possibly decreases interest rates to very low levels, even near zero ☐ Decreases reserve requirements and federal funds	☐ Decreases the money supply ☐ Helps control inflation ☐ Possibly increases unemployment due to slowdowns in economic growth ☐ Decreases consumer spending ☐ Decreases loans and/or borrowing

The Bank of Canada uses monetary policy to try to achieve maximum employment and secure inflation rates. Because it is the "bank of banks," it truly strives to be the last-resort option for distressed banks. This is because once these kinds of institutions begin to rely on the central bank for help, all parts of the banking industry—including those dealing with loans, bonds, interest rates, and mortgages—are affected.

International Trade and Exchange Rates

International trade is when countries import and export goods and services. Countries often want to deal in terms of their own currency. Therefore, when importing or exporting goods or services, consumers and businesses need to enter the market using the same form of currency. For example, if Canada would like to trade with China, then Canada may have to trade in China's form of currency, the *Yuan*, versus the dollar, depending on the business.

The exchange rate is what one country's currency will exchange for another. There are two forms of exchange rates: fixed and floating. Fixed exchange rates involve government interventions (like central banks) to help keep the exchange rates stable. Floating, or "flexible," exchange rates constantly change because they rely on supply and demand needs. While each type of exchange rate has advantages and disadvantages, the rate truly depends on the current state of each country's economy. Therefore, each exchange rate may differ from country to country.

Fixed Versus Floating Exchange Rates			
Fixed Exchange Rate: government intervenes to keep exchange rates stable		Floating or "Flexible" Exchange Rate: Supply and demand determines the exchange rate	
Advantages -Stable prices -Exports are more competitive and in turn more profitable -Helps keep inflation low	*Disadvantages* -Requires a large amount of reserve funds -Possible mispricing of currency values	*Advantages* -Central bank involvement is unnecessary -Facilitates free trade	*Disadvantages* -Currency speculation -Exchange rate risks -Inflation increases

Countries may have differing economic statuses and exchange rates, but they rely on one another for goods and services. Prices of imports and exports are affected by the strength of another country's currency. For example, if the Canadian dollar is at a higher value than another country's currency, imports will be less expensive because the dollar will have more value than that of the country selling its good or service. On the other hand, if the dollar is at a low value compared to the currency of another country, Canadian importers will tend to avoid buying international items from that country. However, exporters to that country could benefit from the low value of the dollar.

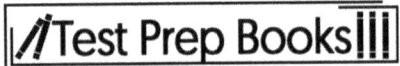

Fiscal Policy

Fiscal policy refers to how the government adjusts spending and tax rates to influence the functions of the economy. Fiscal policies can either increase or decrease tax rates and spending. These policies represent a tricky balancing act, because if the government increases taxes too much, consumer spending and monetary value will decrease. Conversely, if the government lowers taxes, consumers will have more money in their pockets to buy more goods and services, which increases demand and the need for companies to supply those goods and services. Due to the higher demand, suppliers can add jobs to fulfill that demand. While increases in supply, demand, and jobs are positive for the overall economy, they may result in a devaluation of the dollar and less purchasing power.

Estimating and Evaluating Factors that Contribute to Economic Disparity

Some households are wealthy, while others are impoverished—this simple fact is an example of **income inequality** among individuals and families. Canadians experiencing poverty are at increased risk of homelessness, food insecurity, and reduced access to education. Poverty reduces a person's **quality of life** by hindering their access to basic material needs. Such needs include:

- Food
- Clothing
- Housing
- Heating
- Healthcare

The government implements social and economic policies intended to improve the quality of life for those experiencing economic disparity. However, equality of income is *not* an objective of most social programs. These policies seek to hinder or reverse the "downward spiral" that worsens economic disparity in Canada.

Economic disparity is influenced by local, national, and international factors. These include personal choices or intergenerational discrimination on local and national levels, as well as globalized trade and immigration on the international level.

The **local** and **national** impacts on economic disparity derive from governmental policy, historical heritage, and individual (or family) economic decisions. For example, the choice of whether or not to attend university (or which degree to pursue). Heritage perpetuates income inequality through the continuing impact of discrimination against the First Nations and other minority populations in Canada. Lack of land, resources, and higher education presents a higher barrier to such peoples when seeking to participate in Canada's increasingly skill-focused and globalized economy.

The **globalization** process has both a positive and a negative impact on Canada's economic disparity. As Canada's economy has integrated through trade and the movement of people with the economy of other nations, incomes increased for those with higher education or specialized skills. Meanwhile, this process has also seen traditionally well-paying jobs that do not require secondary education or specialized skills—such as manufacturing—transition overseas. While globalization benefits Canada's economy in other ways, it has generally intensified income inequality based on education.

In the last decades, the increased need for high-skill or high-education labor has also increased due to the **implementation of new technologies**. For example, improvements in automation further reduce the availability and the wages for unspecialized labor. New technologies also contribute to economic inequality through the creation of new jobs. These new jobs in the tech industry—especially information technologies (IT) or computer engineering—often require specialized skills and education. Thus, the growth of these well-paying jobs often does little to improve prospects for the impoverished.

Social Studies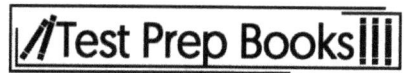

Historical and Contemporary Canada

Analyzing and Interpreting Authentic and Designed Primary and Secondary Sources

Two types of sources are used when trying to understand history: **primary** and **secondary sources**.

Primary sources **describe events firsthand** during the time period being studied. They often contain information about what was happening and opinions about current events in their time. In Canadian history, some primary sources include the documents of colonial legislation and eyewitness testimony from indigenous persons.

On a news website, a primary source would be an article describing what the author or what a person being interviewed directly experienced.

Secondary sources provide information that was not directly experienced by the author. These sources are instead **based on research and analysis** of primary sources. Other sources of historical information—such as archaeological excavation—may also be used in secondary sources. A secondary source often summarizes, evaluates, or examines the period being studied through a critical lens. For example, a secondary source about the War of 1812 might construct an *argument* about why the American invasion was unsuccessful that uses the experiences recorded in primary sources.

On a news website, a secondary source would be an article summarizing a major event that happened the previous day. Modern primary sources informing such an article might include social media posts, interviews with participants, and on-the-ground video footage from news teams.

The most common mode of recording a source is writing it down. However, a "source" is not always written. Some non-literary historical sources include:

- Photographs
- Maps
- Newspaper cartoons
- Cultural references

Visual primary sources are a robust source of information about the past because the type of information provided is often not transmitted through writing. For example, the Hudson Bay Company's territorial maps are a visual document providing evidence of the Company's unjust land claims during the European settlement of Canada. Further, the spread of photography during the mid-nineteenth century allows for direct evidence of past events. As primary sources, photographs and video are particularly valuable because there's a reduced risk of error. An eyewitness's memory might fade before recording their experiences, but information visible in a photograph does not.

However, not all visual sources are primary sources. One example of a non-literary secondary source is a work of art. Artwork can be used as a source about the values, beliefs, and opinions of the creator and their culture. Since art does not present a *direct* experience of the past, it is not a primary source. This type of secondary source—one that provides historical opinion about then-current events—is valuable for verifying accounts and attitudes recorded in the primary sources.

In history and in the present day, political cartoons in newspapers and on news websites exemplify this type of informative artwork. Authors of these cartoons often have a particular agenda or make a specific argument about the satirized events. Usually humorous and targeting a general audience, political cartoons allow historians to *infer* common attitudes and beliefs even when they are not stated directly in a primary source. For example, a racist cartoon about an indigenous person in a nineteenth-century newspaper reasonably supports inferring that the paper's readers shared those prejudices.

Cultural references are a type of oral secondary source that historians may also use to infer historical information. For example, from the modern celebration of Remembrance Day on November 11, a future historian could infer that Canadians of the twenty-first century still felt that Canada's role in World War I substantially impacted the nation's history and culture.

Interpreting and Analyzing Experiences, Perspectives, and Contributions

Prior to World War II, Canada identified itself strongly by the English and French heritages of its early settlers. The nation's stance was one of assimilating other communities (including non-English, non-French immigrants from Europe, such as Jews fleeing the Holocaust). The most impactful policy was the disruption of cultural identity and continuity among Canada's indigenous peoples. Historical experiences of oppression and discrimination shape the nation's modern cultural and social fabric.

This fabric is now recognized and celebrated as a **multicultural** society in which the perspectives of these communities ought to be cherished. Recognizing the contributions of Canada's varied heritages and communities is *not* restricted to the nation's understanding of historical injustices. First Nations, Métis, and Inuit communities also contribute to the subjective sense of what it means to be Canadian. They do so through practicing ancestral traditions as part of a multicultural nation. Indigenous languages, festivals, and beliefs help create the lived experience of *all* Canadians.

Another significant element in Canada's multicultural fabric are immigrant communities. Increased immigration following World War II caused change in the nation's cultural make-up and consequently in its identity. The twentieth century's economic need for immigrant labor diversified the cultures that constitute Canada's society. Elements of Caribbean, Asian, and African cultures have grown increasingly prominent in the nation's cultural identity.

Canadian multiculturalism is also enshrined in law. In addition to the universal claims endorsed by the *Charter of Rights and Freedoms*, the *Multiculturalism Act of 1988* instituted additional protections from discrimination for Canadians seeking to use their rights to language, religion, and other aspects of cultural identity.

Recognizing and Considering First Nations, Métis, and Inuit.

Aboriginal people lived in Canada for many centuries before the arrival of Europeans. Archaeologists believe that the first Aboriginal peoples traveled from Siberia to present-day Alaska across the Bering land bridge between 20,000 and 12,000 years ago. Small nomadic groups lived in Alaska until the glaciers melted; then, Aboriginal peoples migrated to and settled in present-day Canada. These early migrants relied on hunting big game, such as giant beaver and wooly mammoths, to survive the frigid conditions. After the climate warmed approximately 10,0000 years ago, Aboriginal peoples developed diverse cultural traditions and formed groups that would eventually develop into the First Nations.

Precolonial First Nations shared many similarities. Perhaps most importantly, the First Nations domesticated plants and animals, which paved the way for stable agricultural production. In turn, agriculture facilitated the creation of permanent settlements because Aboriginal societies were no longer completely dependent on tracking big game for survival. Furthermore, agriculture-based settlements led to a more specialized division of labor and supported the development of advanced trading networks. Aboriginal traders regularly exchanged surplus crops, tools, and natural resources over substantial distances. In addition to providing economic benefits, trade networks also enabled the diffusion of technology and culture over vast territory.

As permanent settlements stabilized and trade networks expanded, Aboriginal cultures grew increasingly complex. Aboriginal societies typically emphasized the importance of multi-generational family units and granted elder members much influence. Languages similarly became more nuanced and connected to the local culture. Likewise, Aboriginal societies adopted more elaborate religious traditions and ceremonies, incorporating both anthropomorphic and animist beliefs. Anthropomorphic religious beliefs involve attributing human characteristics to a divine entity, while animistic religious beliefs see divinity in all earthly beings.

Despite economic and cultural similarities, various precolonial First Nations still differed widely based on region. First Nations in the Pacific Northwest, such as the Squamish and Haida, hunted in the temperate rainforest of British Columbia, fished for salmon in the Pacific Ocean, and built relatively large-scale settlements featuring multi-generational homes. The Great Plains of Alberta and Saskatchewan provided First Nations with plentiful bison, so these groups tended to be more nomadic. The Blackfeet, named after the moccasins they wore, dominated the Great Plains for centuries due to a complex alliance system consisting of kinship networks called bands. Similarly, the Iroquois consolidated power in present-day Ontario and Quebec by cultivating the Three Sisters—maize, beans, and squash—to support large-scale settlement and facilitate far-ranging military campaigns.

The Aboriginal peoples living in the Arctic were distinct from the First Nations and are referred to as Inuit. The harsh Arctic climate couldn't support agriculture, so, unlike the First Nations, the Inuit consumed minimal plant-based food and established relatively small-scale settlements. The Inuit relied almost exclusively on hunting, fishing, and whaling. In order to navigate the unforgiving land and sea, the Inuit trained teams of huskies to serve as pack animals and invented highly buoyant vessels called kayaks.

The Métis are a group of people with shared heritage from both indigenous peoples and from European settlers who arrived on the plains in the 1800s. Their name comes from the French *métis*, meaning "mixed." This demographic still primarily lives in the present-day provinces of Manitoba and Alberta. Indeed, Manitoba is Canada's only province to have been founded by a person with indigenous ancestry. In 1869 Louis Riel, a man of French, Cree, and Ojibwe ancestry, led the Red River Rebellion. This conflict ultimately resulted in the founding of Manitoba and the province's entry into the Canadian confederation. It also was an important event in creating the Métis identity as a people distinct from both Europeans and peoples of the First Nations.

The definition of this identity remains somewhat in dispute in the present day. Some people advocate that all persons of shared European and indigenous ancestry have the right to self-identify as Métis. However, the federal government recognizes the Métis National Council's definition that a person is Métis if they:

- Self-identify as Métis
- Are descended from the historical Métis Nation
- Are accepted as a member by the Métis Nation

Recognizing and Considering Diverse Francophone Perspectives

The colonization of present-day Canada began as an unintended consequence of French interest in finding a northwest passage to Asia. Jacques Cartier did not find the trade route, but he did lay claim to the Gaspé Peninsula on behalf of King Francis I in 1534, and the land mass was christened "Canada." Cartier failed to establish a permanent colony, but in 1604, new French settlers tried again more successfully. A geographer named Samuel de Champlain established Quebec City in 1608, which quickly became France's most stable and successful permanent settlement in North America.

As French settlements, fishing operations, and fur trapping expeditions advanced under Champlain's leadership, the region was renamed New France, with Quebec City as its capital. During the 1630s, the Roman Catholic Church and Jesuit missionaries assumed control over New France and began converting the Aboriginal peoples. When those efforts failed, the French government intervened to stabilize the settlements, attract immigrants, and generate

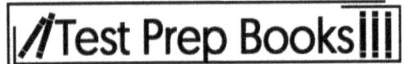

consistent economic growth. While fishing and fur trapping remained lucrative enterprises, New France struggled to attract immigrants due to the harsh conditions, lack of infrastructure, and hostile relations with the Iroquois. In contrast, Britain enjoyed tremendous success in populating the New England colonies and settlements in Nova Scotia and Newfoundland.

During the late 17th century, the rivalry between France and Britain sparked numerous conflicts in North America as the colonists competed for resources. Between 1688 and 1763, French and British colonists fought six different conflicts with the help of their respective Aboriginal allies. Britain formed a powerful alliance with the Iroquois, while the French allied with a variety of tribes, including the Wabanaki Confederacy, Algonquin, Ottawa, and Shawnee. The Seven Years' War (1754–1763) triggered the final showdown between the imperial rivals, and Britain soundly defeated France. As a result, Britain acquired all of New France, which they renamed Canada.

Britain initially struggled to exercise control over French Canadians, especially in Quebec. To soothe the hostile relations, Britain passed the Quebec Act (1774) to guarantee colonists' rights to speak French, practice Catholicism, and enforce the French Civil Code. This proved critical because the Americans attempted to exploit societal divisions in Quebec during the American Revolutionary War (1776–1783) and the War of 1812. Britain ultimately repelled both American invasions, but the peace was relatively fleeting.

Combined with the rivalry between Francophone and Anglophone colonists, undemocratic governance sparked the Rebellions of 1837–1838. Britain put down the insurrection, and Governor General Lord Durham issued a report that a political union would be necessary to assimilate French Canadians. Soon thereafter, the British Parliament enacted the Act of Union (1840) to divide the colony into Upper Canada and Lower Canada, with equal representation in the Legislative Assembly. This attempt at reconciliation satisfied neither party, and calls for a more cohesive and autonomous union mounted.

Analyzing Cause and Consequences of Significant Events and Developments

In 1864, representatives from the British colonies met to come up with a unification agreement. After the Quebec and Charlottetown conferences, the gathered politicians set forth Seventy-Two Resolutions, which outlined the creation of a unified federal system of government. Francophone Canadians hoped this framework would create a more autonomous Quebec, while Anglophone Canadians favored the creation of a united Canada to end the disproportionate representation of Francophones in the Legislative Assembly. After the London Conference of 1866, the British Parliament enacted the British North America Act, otherwise called Constitution Act, 1867. This act united the previously distinct colonies of New Brunswick, Nova Scotia, and Canada, with the latter being split into the provinces of Ontario and Quebec.

Unlike other British colonies, the Dominion of Canada was a self-governing confederation, and it mirrored the American model in its federalized power-sharing arrangement. As such, provinces enjoyed considerable authority and powers protected from federal overreach, such as exclusive control over public lands and the right to establish a legal system. The federal government was modeled after the British government, and it consisted of a bicameral legislature, a justice system, and a taxation system. Despite the unprecedented degree of autonomy granted to the dominion, it was still legally subject to the British Empire's authority.

Canada's reorganization into a united confederation triggered rapid territorial expansion. British Columbia joined the confederation in 1871 after the Canadian Parliament promised to build the Canadian Pacific Railway, a transcontinental railroad. Two years later, Prince Edward Island joined the confederation, largely because it wanted access to Canada's expanding markets. The Canadian Pacific Railway was completed in 1885, and it connected Eastern Canada and British Columbia for the first time. The CPR played a critical role in driving the development of the Canadian frontier because it functioned as the primary means of transporting passengers, goods, and materials into Western Canada. As a result, the Western provinces experienced rapid population growth as Eastern Canadians and immigrants streamed into the region in search of land, gold, and economic opportunities.

Since the confederation consisted of both pre-existing colonies and new provinces, the federal government sought to unify its patchwork legal system. The Parliament of Canada passed the Criminal Code, 1892 to standardize and simplify the criminal justice system. For example, it removed all British criminal laws unless a law was expressly intended to apply to British colonies, dominions, or possessions. The Indian Act of 1876 attempted to clarify the relationship between Aboriginal peoples and the federal government. In general, the Indian Act outlined the laws for reservations and forced some Aboriginal peoples to enfranchise for a variety of reasons, which meant that they lost their Indian Status. First Nations mostly condemned this broad statute for its attempt to coercively assimilate Aboriginal peoples into Canadian society, which led to widespread persecution and cultural suppression.

Analyzing Canada's Regional, National, and International Contributions

World Wars

The World Wars radically transformed Canada from an imperial outpost to an independent world power. At the outset of World War I (1914–1918), Canada was a British Dominion, and the British Parliament held significant control over Canadian policymaking, especially in terms of foreign policy. Thus, once the United Kingdom declared war on Germany on August 4, 1914, Canada was legally obligated to support the war effort, though the Canadian Parliament enjoyed some autonomy over its wartime commitments and deployments.

Canada successfully created a new army called the Canadian Expeditionary Force that mobilized 630,000 soldiers during World War I. The Expeditionary Force's assault teams gained international recognition for their bravery and ferocity on the Western Front, especially in the crucial Allied victories at the Battles of the Somme and Vimy Ridge. Additionally, the Canadian Royal Navy supported various British blockades and naval campaigns against German U-boats. At the tail end of the war, the Expeditionary Force defeated nearly 25% of Germany's heavy divisions on the Western Front during a series of battles referred to as "Canada's Hundred Days." Canada's commitment came at a heavy price with more than 61,000 deaths.

Unlike in World War I, Canada was not legally obligated to fight on behalf of the United Kingdom in World War II because the Statute of Westminster (1931) had granted Canada near-total autonomy. However, Canada still retained significant links to Britain and followed with its own declaration of war on Germany in 1939 after waiting one week to symbolically emphasize its independence.

Given the nation's staggering sacrifice in World War I, the Canadian Parliament initially restricted its role to supplying the Allied Powers with food and weapons. However, as the conflict escalated, Canada radically increased its commitment of troops. Overall, 1.1 million Canadians served in the military during World War II. Canadian forces fought extensively in both the Atlantic and Pacific theaters, and more than 45,000 Canadians lost their lives with another 55,000 wounded in combat. By the end of the war, Canada had established itself as one of the largest and most formidable militaries in the world, particularly in terms of its air force and navy.

The Canadian economy also advanced rapidly as a result of wartime production. Prior to World War I, the Canadian economy was primarily agrarian, but the wartime manufacturing boom led to the development of robust automobile and mining industries. Likewise, the wars would forever alter Canadian society. Women capitalized on the newly available economic opportunities and contributed indispensable labor to the wartime mobilization. As a result, white and black women gained full suffrage in 1922 everywhere except for Quebec, which followed suit in 1940. The World Wars also exacerbated divisions between Canada's Anglophone and Francophone citizens. English-speaking Canadians vocally supported both war efforts, largely out of loyalty to Britain. In contrast, French Canadians widely condemned the wars as imperialistic, and several anti-conscription riots occurred in Quebec in 1917, 1918, and 1944.

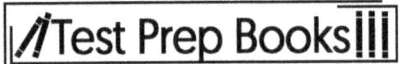

Postwar Era

Canada emerged from the Second World War as a major world power. Although Canada continued to maintain close ties to the United Kingdom, Canada's relationship to the United States most influenced its trajectory in the postwar era. Along with the Soviet Union, the United States attained global superpower status during this era. Given its geopolitical status as America's northern neighbor, Canada sought to maximize the benefit of having such proximity to the world's most productive economy and advanced military. As a result, Canada adopted capitalist policies domestically, supported the American-led international order, and provided material assistance to American and European interventions against communist threats during the Cold War (1947–1991). Additionally, Canada was a founding member of the North Atlantic Treaty Organization (NATO), an American-led military alliance formed for the explicit purpose of containing the Soviet Union.

Canada enjoyed significant economic growth for much of the postwar era, and the government invested some of its revenue into the creation of a robust, European-style social welfare system. Specifically, the Canadian Parliament passed legislation to guarantee universal healthcare, expand unemployment benefits, and provide pensions to specific groups like retirees and veterans. Canada also expanded its territory during this period. In 1949, Newfoundland held a contentious referendum and ultimately voted to become a Canadian province. Several years later, Canada enforced its territorial claims in the Arctic by relocating Inuit families under false pretenses to desolate areas further north. The Canadian government paid the survivors $10 million CAD in 1993 and officially apologized in 2010.

Two regional movements threatened Canadian national unity during the 1970s and 1980s. First, Francophone separatists advocated for the secession of Quebec, but 59% of Quebecois voters rejected secession in a 1980 referendum. Prime Minister Pierre Trudeau attempted to cool regional tensions by overseeing the passage of constitutional protections for bilingualism and multiculturalism. Second, tensions between the Western provinces and the federal government sparked a phenomenon known as "Western alienation." During the late 1970s, Alberta, British Columbia, Saskatchewan, and Manitoba alleged that they were excluded from federal policymaking, and this caused a strained relationship between the western provinces and the federal government. Alberta has historically been an especially harsh critic of the federal government's taxation policies and regulations of the province's highly lucrative oil and gas industries.

The Constitution Act, 1982 was another major development in the postwar era. Under the Statute of Westminster, 1931, the British Parliament still held the power to amend Canada's constitution. The Constitution Act, 1982 removed this power and completed the patriation of Canadian constitutional law. The Act also explicitly protected rights of Canadian Aboriginals, established procedures for constitutional amendments, and enacted a bill of rights known as the Canadian Charter of Rights and Freedoms, which is binding on all levels of Canadian government. Quebec never ratified the Constitution Act, 1982, but the Supreme Court ruled that Quebec's consent was unnecessary for enactment.

Recognizing the Significance Historical and Ongoing Legacies and Injustices

Recent History

Canadian politics has seen several unprecedented events and shifts in recent years. In 1993, Kim Campbell became the first (and so far only) female prime minister as well as the first to be born in British Columbia. In 2005, Canadian Parliament enacted the Civil Marriage Act to legalize same-sex marriage in every province. In 2003, the rise of a conservative movement challenged historic liberal dominance. Following a prolonged period of division, the Canadian Alliance and Progressive Conservative Party of Canada united to form the Conservative Party of Canada. Under the leadership of Prime Minister Stephen Harper, the Conservative Party elected a minority government in 2006 and 2008 and a majority government in 2011. Pierre Trudeau's son, Justin, led the Liberals back into power in 2015 and has remained in leadership as of 2020.

Social Studies

Recent Canadian history has been marked by increased alignment with the United States. Canada signed the North American Free Trade Agreement (NAFTA) with the United States and Mexico in 1993. In general, NAFTA slashed tariffs and other trade barriers to boost economic productivity and increase investments. Although Canadian consumers have benefited from cheaper consumer goods and more white-collar jobs, NAFTA has been highly controversial due to its negative impact on Canadian manufacturing, labor rights, and the environment. Following the September 11th terrorist attacks, Canada joined the NATO mission to support the American invasion and occupation of Afghanistan. Furthermore, Canada has been a prominent purchaser of American weaponry and has invested heavily in the F-35 fighter jet program.

Canada has continued to struggle with national unity in recent history. Quebecois separatism regained steam in the late 1980s and early 1990s, culminating in a second referendum in 1995. By the extremely narrow margin of 50.6% to 49.4%, Quebecois voters rejected the proposal to secede from Canada and declare independence. Three years later, the Canadian Supreme Court barred provinces from attempting to secede unilaterally, and Canadian Parliament enacted the Clarity Act to establish procedures for provinces seeking independence. The disproportionate attention garnered by Quebec further fueled the anger of Western provinces, especially since Quebec has historically received the greatest share of equalization payments and transfer payments from the federal government. During the late 2010s, secession gained unprecedented momentum in some Western provinces, though it has never reached levels seen in Quebec.

Issues related to Canada's treatment of Aboriginal peoples have also challenged the present-day Canadian identity. Most government actions have centered on apologizing for historic abuses. Most notably, the Truth and Reconciliation Commission of Canada (2008–2015) held extensive hearings to publicize the devastating impact of Canada's Indian residential school system, which was an acculturation program coercively imposed on Aboriginal children for more than a century. High-level Canadian officials have repeatedly discussed the repatriation of Aboriginal land, total autonomy for First Nations, and/or ambitious poverty alleviation programs, though these proposals have been mostly stalled or thwarted.

The purpose of Canada's commemorative programs and institutions is to provide redress for injustices during the nation's history with the First Nations, the Métis, and the Inuit. This redress is provided through **acknowledging the past**, supporting the **ancestral identity** of indigenous communities, and **offering restitution** through financial compensation and social programs. The final goal is to reconcile settler and indigenous communities into a mutually supportive society.

The residential "Indian schools," forced relocation, and other injustices committed in Canada's past are commemorated through holidays such as **National Indigenous Peoples Day** on June 21 and the **National Day for Truth and Reconciliation** on September 30. In 2022, the House of Commons unanimously voted that these previous injustices constituted a genocide of Canada's indigenous peoples. These efforts ensure Canada's discriminatory past shall not be forgotten.

Canada continues to negotiate new treaties with the First Nations that recognize them as communities with a **right to self-government** and a **right to identify** as their own culture. Law and policy enforce remembrance as legal statute, and self-government initiatives help to redress the impact of paternalistic colonial institutions.

One part of these negotiations is striving to recompense indigenous communities for Canada's **land claims** that deprived them of their ancestral privileges. While no amount of money can recompense for a genocide, these efforts ameliorate its impact on modern indigenous communities through reducing poverty and enabling opportunities in a reconciled future.

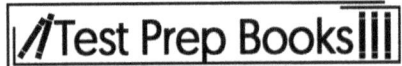

Social Studies

Geography and the Environment

Distinguishing Between Various Features of Canada

Geography of Canada

Canada is one of the largest countries in the world, trailing only Russia in terms of total area under territorial control. To the south, Canada borders the contiguous United States, and it shares another land border with the United States (Alaska) in the northwest. Canada borders the Atlantic and Pacific Oceans and shares maritime borders with Greenland to the northeast and Saint Pierre and Miquelon to the southeast.

The physical geography of Canada is immense and incredibly diverse. The Appalachian Mountains and Rocky Mountains extend from the United States northward into Canada, and the Columbia and Coast mountain ranges lie to the west of the Canadian Rockies. In Northern Canada, a series of hills and mountains known as the Canadian Shield has incredibly rich mineral reserves. Other notable geographic features include prairies in central Canada, volcanoes in British Columbia, and Arctic tundra in Nunavut.

Canada also has an abundance of water resources. The Canadian maritime coastline is the longest in the world, and every Canadian province has a maritime border except for Alberta and Saskatchewan. Canada also has more than two million freshwater lakes, which cover approximately 9% of Canadian land. Canada borders four of the five Great Lakes (Erie, Huron, Ontario, and Superior), which form the largest interconnected group of freshwater lakes in the world by total area. In addition, Canada has several enormous drainage basins and numerous rivers, with the two largest being the Mackenzie and St. Lawrence Rivers.

Types of Maps

Geographers utilize a variety of maps in their study of the spatial world. Projections are maps that represent the spherical globe on a flat surface. **Conformal projections** attempt to preserve shape but distort size and area. For example, the most well-known projection, the **Mercator projection**, drastically distorts the size of land areas at the poles. In this particular map, Antarctica, one of the smallest continents, appears massive, while the areas closer to the equator are depicted more accurately. Other projections attempt to lessen the amount of distortion; the **equal-area projection**, for example, attempts to accurately represent the size of landforms. However, equal-area projections alter the shapes and angles of landforms regardless of their positioning on the map. Other projections are hybrids of the two primary models. For example, the **Robinson projection** tries to balance form and area in order to create a more visually accurate representation of the spatial world. Despite the efforts to maintain consistency with shapes, projections cannot provide accurate representations of the Earth's surface due to their flat, two-dimensional nature. In this sense, projections are useful symbols of space, but they do not always provide the most accurate portrayal of reality. The following page displays images of these well-known conformal projections.

Social Studies

Conformal projections

Mercator projection

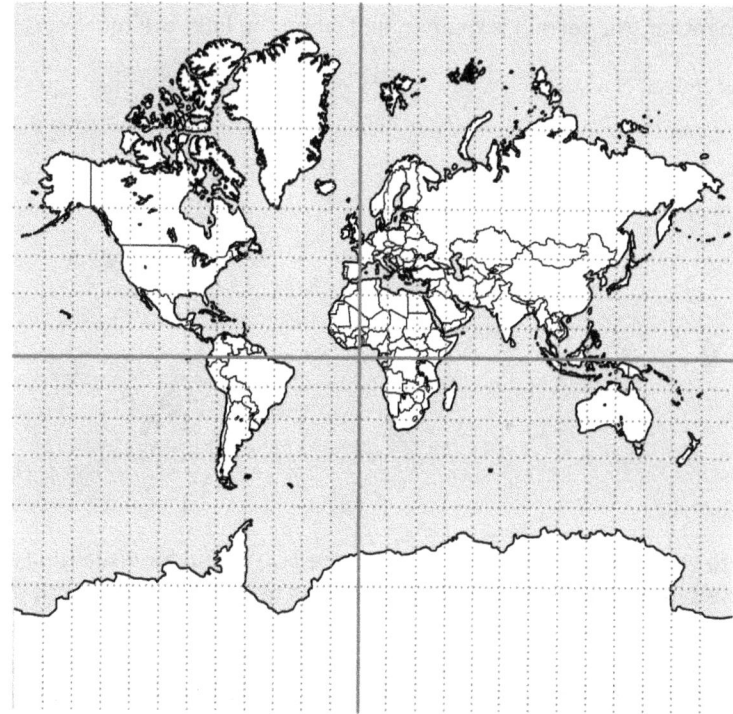

Equal area projection

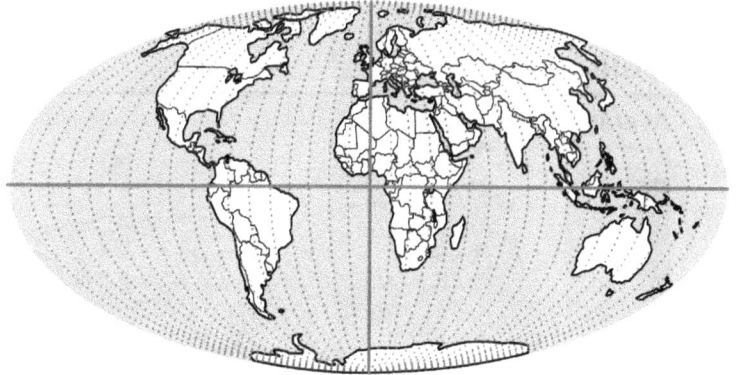

Robinson projection

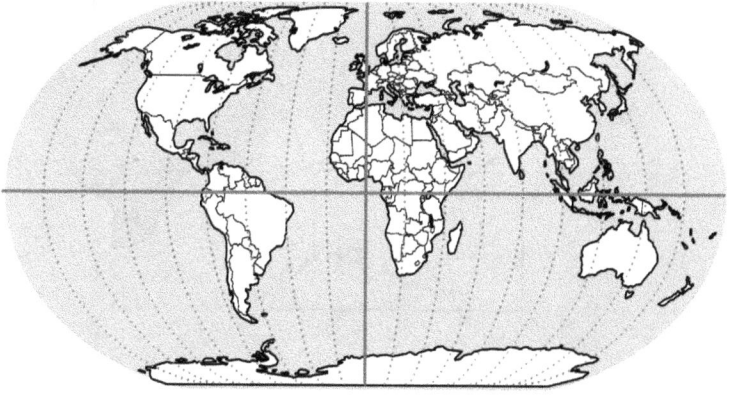

Unlike projections, **topographic maps** display contour lines, which represent the relative elevation of a particular place and are very useful for surveyors, engineers, and/or travelers. For example, hikers may refer to topographic maps to calculate their daily climbs. A section of a topographical map can be viewed below. Where the lines are closer together, the terrain is steeper, and when the lines are more spread out, the terrain is flatter.

Similar to topographic maps, **isoline maps** are also useful for visualizing and differentiating between data. These maps use symbols to represent values and lines to connect points with the same value. For example, an isoline map could display average temperatures of a given area. The sections which share the same average temperature would be grouped together by lines. Additionally, isoline maps can help geographers study the world by generating questions. For example, is elevation the only reason for differences in temperature? If not, what other factors could cause the disparity between the values?

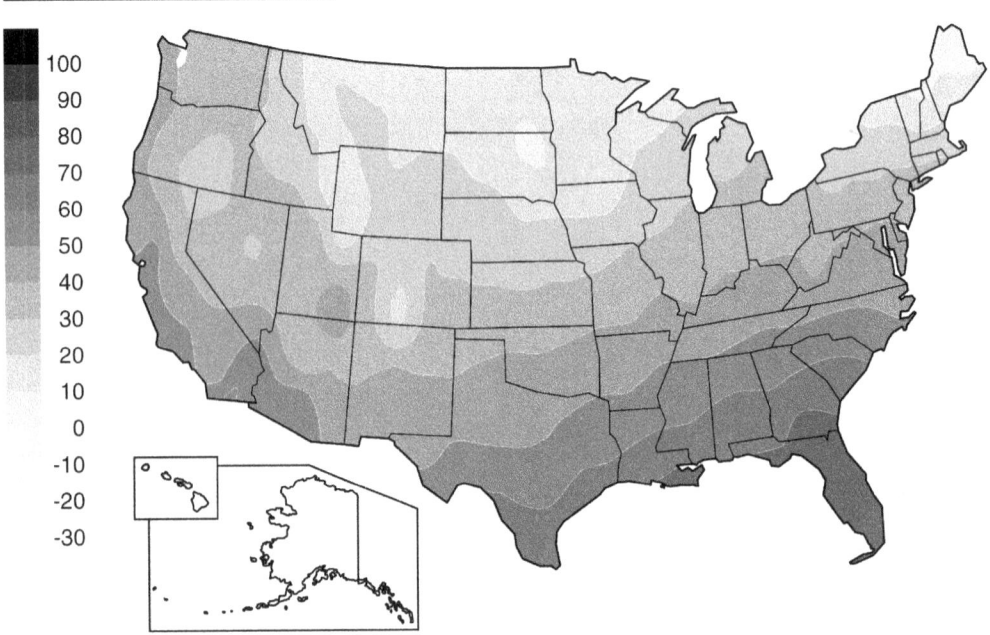

Social Studies

Thematic maps are also quite useful because they display the geographical distribution of complex political, physical, social, cultural, economic, or historical themes. For example, a thematic map could indicate an area's election results using a different color for each candidate. There are several different kinds of thematic maps, including *dot-density maps* and *flow-line maps*. A dot-density map uses dots to illustrate volume and density; these dots could represent a certain population, or the number of specific events that have taken place in an area. Flow-line maps utilize lines of varying thicknesses to illustrate the movement of goods, people, or even animals between two places. Thicker lines represent a greater number of moving elements, and thinner lines represent a smaller number. Below is a dot-density map depicting population density in an urban area.

Interpreting Maps

Geographical concepts are visually conveyed through maps. The map below illustrates some key points about geography.

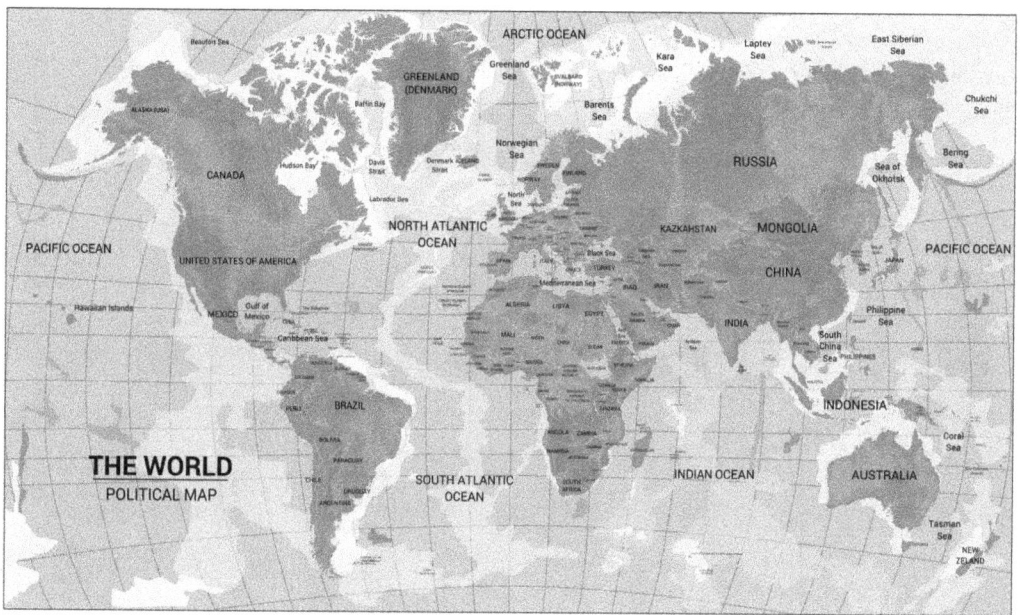

On some colored maps, the oceans, represented in blue between the continents, vary in coloration depending on depth. The differences demonstrate **bathymetry**, which is the study of the ocean floor's depth. Paler areas represent less depth, while darker spots reflect greater depth.

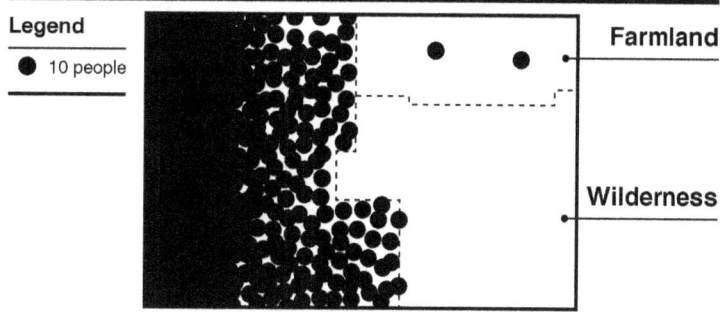

Maps may also display horizonal and vertical lines representing latitude and longitude. The horizontal lines, known as parallels, mark the calculated latitude of those locations and reveal how far north or south these areas are from the equator, which bisects the map horizontally. The vertical lines signify longitude, which determines how far east or west different regions are from each other. The lines of longitude, known as meridians, are also the basis for time zones, which determine the time for different regions. As one travels west between time zones, the given time moves backward accordingly. Conversely, if one travels east, the time moves forward.

There are two particularly significant longitudinal lines. First, the Prime [Greenwich] Meridian marks zero degrees in longitude, and thus determines the other lines. The line circles the globe and divides it into the Eastern and Western hemispheres. Second, the International Date Line represents the change between calendar days. By traveling westward across the International Date Line, a traveler would essentially leap forward a day. For example, a person departing from the United States on Sunday would arrive in Japan on Monday. By traveling eastward across the line, a traveler would go backward a day. For example, a person departing from China on Monday would arrive in Canada on Sunday.

The map below identifies the different time zones.

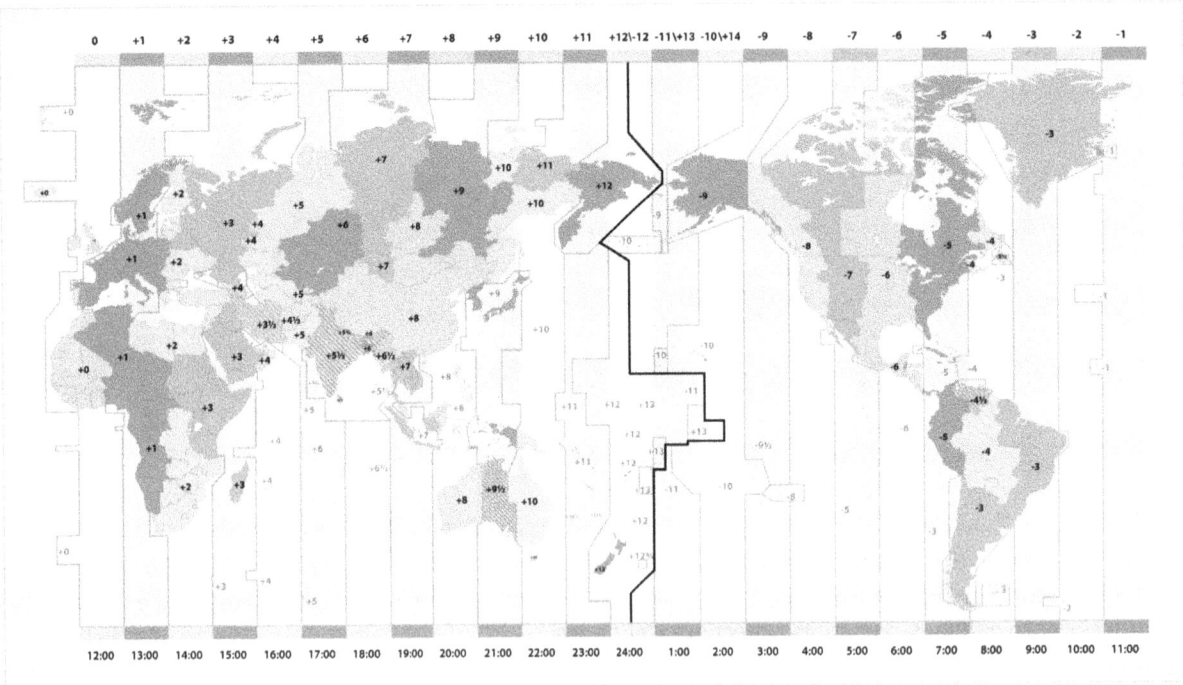

Although world maps are useful in showing the overall arrangement of continents and nations, it is also important at times to look more closely at individual countries because they have unique features that are only visible on more detailed maps.

Social Studies

For example, take the following map of Canada. The country is split into multiple provinces that have their own cultures and localized governments. Other countries are often split into various divisions, such as states, and while these features are ignored for the sake of clarity on larger maps, they are important when studying specific nations. Individual provinces can be further subdivided into counties and municipalities, which may have their own maps that can be examined for closer analysis.

Map of Present-Day Canada

Finally, one of the first steps in examining any map should be to locate its key or legend, which will explain what different symbols represent on the map. As these symbols can be arbitrary depending on the maker, a key will help to clarify the different meanings.

Legend

═══	Highway	✈	Airport
━━━	Main Road	🚢	Port
───	Secondary Road	⌒	Lake
┼┼┼	Railroad	⌇	River
─ ─ ─	State Boundary	⋈	Bridge
─ · ─ · ─	International Boundary	∧∧	Mountains
★	State Capital	▲	Peak
●	City	⚒	Mine
○	Notable City		
·	Village		

Spatial Patterns of Cultural and Economic Activities

Spatial patterns refer to where things are in the world. Elements of both physical and human geography have spatial patterns regarding where they appear on Earth.

Ethnicity

An ethnic group, or ethnicity, is essentially a group of people with a common language, society, culture, or ancestral heritage. Different ethnicities developed over centuries through historical forces, the impact of religious traditions, and other factors. Thousands of years ago, it was more common for ethnic groups to remain in one area with only occasional interaction with outside groups.

In the modern world, different ethnicities interact on a regular basis due to better transportation resources and the processes of globalization. For example, in countries like the United States and Canada, it is not uncommon for schools, workplaces, or communities to have people of Asian, African, Caucasian, European, Indian, or Native descent.

In less developed parts of the world, travel is limited due to the lack of infrastructure. Consequently, ethnic groups develop in small areas that can differ greatly from other people just a few miles away. For example, on the Balkan Peninsula in southeastern Europe, a variety of different ethnic groups live in close proximity to one another. Croats, Albanians, Serbs, Bosnians, and others all share the same land but have very different worldviews, traditions, and religious influences. Unfortunately, this diversity has not always been a positive characteristic, such as when Bosnia was the scene of a horrible genocide against Albanians in an "ethnic cleansing" effort that continued throughout the late 20th century.

Linguistics

Linguistics, or the study of language, groups certain languages together according to their commonalities. For example, the Romance languages—French, Spanish, Italian, Romanian, and Portuguese—all share language traits from Latin. As people spoke Latin in different regions of Europe, it eventually evolved into different *vernaculars*, or

Social Studies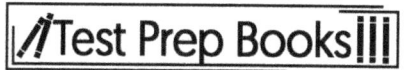

dialects, that became their own languages over time. Similarly, the Bantu people of Africa travelled extensively and spread their language, now called Swahili, which became the first Pan-African language.

Since thousands of languages exist, it is important to have a widespread means of communication that can interconnect people from different parts of the world. One way to do this is through a *lingua franca*, or a common language used for business, diplomacy, and other cross-national relationships. English is a primary lingua franca around the world, but there are many others in use as well.

Religion

Religion has played a tremendous role in creating the world's cultures. Devout Christians crossed the Atlantic in hopes of finding religious freedom in New England, Muslim missionaries and traders travelled to the Spice Islands of the East Indies to teach about the Koran, and Buddhist monks traversed the Himalayan Mountains into Tibet to spread their faith.

In some countries, religion helps to shape legal systems. These nations, termed *theocracies*, have no separation of church and state and are more common in Islamic nations such as Saudi Arabia, Iran, and Qatar. In contrast, even though religion has played a tremendous role in the history of the United States, its government remains secular, or nonreligious, due to the influence of European Enlightenment philosophy at the time of its inception.

Like ethnicity and language, religion is a primary way that individuals and people groups self-identify. As a result, religious influences can shape a region's laws, architecture, literature, and music. For example, when the Ottoman Turks, who are Muslim, conquered Constantinople, which was once the home of the Eastern Orthodox Christian Church, they replaced Christian places of worship with mosques. Additionally, they replaced different forms of Roman architecture with those influenced by Arabic traditions.

Economics

Economic activity also has a spatial component. Nations with few natural resources generally tend to import what they need from nations willing to export raw materials to them. Furthermore, areas that are home to certain raw materials generally tend to alter their environment in order to maintain production of those materials. In the San Joaquin Valley of California, an area known for extreme heat and desert-like conditions, local residents have engineered elaborate drip irrigation systems to adequately water lemon, lime, olive, and orange trees, utilizing the warm temperatures to constantly produce citrus fruits. Additionally, other nations with abundant petroleum reserves build elaborate infrastructures in order to pump, house, refine, and transport their materials to nations who require gasoline, diesel, or natural gas.

Essentially, inhabitants of different spatial regions on Earth create jobs, infrastructure, and transportation systems to ensure the continued flow of goods, raw materials, and resources out of their location so long as financial resources keep flowing into the area.

Making Connections Between People, the Land, and the Environments in Canada

Factors Affecting Human Geography

Two primary realms exist within the study of geography. The first, **physical geography**, essentially correlates with the land, water, and foliage of the Earth. The second, **human geography**, is the study of the Earth's people and how they interact with their environment. Several geographical factors impact the human condition, such as access to natural resources. For example, human populations tend to be higher around more reliable sources of fresh water. The metropolitan area of New York City, which has abundant freshwater resources, is home to over 18 million people. Australia, on the other hand, an entire country and continent, has much less accessibility to fresh water and houses only 7 million more people. Although water is not the only factor in this disparity, it certainly plays a role in **population density**—the total number of people in a particular place divided by the total land area, usually in square miles or square kilometers. Australia's population density is about 7 people per square mile, while the most densely populated nation on Earth, Bangladesh, is home to 2,889 people per square mile.

Population density can have a devastating impact on both a physical environment and the humans who live within that environment. For example, Delhi, one of India's most populated cities, is home to nearly five million gasoline-powered vehicles. Each day, those vehicles emit an enormous amount of carbon monoxide into the atmosphere, which directly affects the Delhi citizens' quality of life. In fact, the smog and pollution problems have gotten so severe that many drivers cannot see fifty feet in front of them. Additionally, densely populated areas within third-world nations, or developing nations, struggle significantly in their quest to balance the demands of the modern economy with their nation's lack of infrastructure. For example, nearly as many automobiles operate every day in major American cities like New York and Los Angeles as they do in Delhi, but they create significantly less pollution due to cleaner burning engines, better fuels, and governmental emission regulations.

Although it is a significant factor, population density is not the only source of strain on a place's resources. Historical forces such as civil war, religious conflict, genocide, and government corruption can also profoundly alter the lives of a nation's citizens. For example, the war-torn nation of Somalia has not had a functioning government for nearly three decades. As a result, the nation's citizens have virtually no access to hospital care, vaccinations, or proper facilities for childbirth. Due to these and other factors, the nation's **infant mortality rate**, or the total number of child deaths per 1,000 live births, stands at 74/1000. When compared to Iceland's 2/1000, it's quite evident that Somalia struggles to provide basic services in the realm of childbirth and there is a dire need for humanitarian assistance.

Literacy rates, like infant mortality rates, are also excellent indicators of the relative level of development in a particular place. Many developing nations have both economic and social factors that hinder their ability to educate their own citizens. Due to radical religious factions within some nations like Afghanistan and Pakistan, girls are often denied the ability to attend school, which further reduces the nation's overall literacy rate. For example, girls in Afghanistan have a 24.2 percent literacy rate, one of the lowest rates of any record-keeping nation on Earth.

Although literacy rates are useful in determining a nation's development level, high literacy rates do exist within developing nations. For example, Suriname, which has a significantly lower GDP than Afghanistan, enjoys a 94 percent literacy rate among both sexes. Utilizing this and other data, geographers can form questions and conduct further research about such phenomena. Demographic data, such as population density, the infant mortality rate, and the literacy rate all provide insight into the characteristics of a particular place and help geographers better understand the spatial world.

Physical Processes
The Earth's surface, like many other things in the broader universe, does not remain the same for long; in fact, it changes daily. The Earth's surface is subject to a variety of physical processes that continue to shape its appearance. Water, wind, temperature, or sunlight play a role in continually altering the Earth's surface.

Erosion involves the movement of soil from one place to another and can be caused by a variety of stimuli including ice, snow, water, wind, and ocean waves. Wind erosion occurs in generally flat, dry areas with loose topsoil. Over time, the persistent winds can dislodge significant amounts of soil into the air, reshaping the land and wreaking havoc on those who depend on agriculture for their livelihoods. Water can also cause erosion. For example, erosion caused by the Colorado River helped to form the Grand Canyon. Over time, the river moved millions of tons of soil, cutting a huge gorge in the Earth along the way.

In water erosion, material carried by the water is referred to as *sediment*. With time, some sediment can collect at the mouths of rivers, forming *deltas*, which become small islands of fertile soil. This process of detaching loose soils and transporting them to a different location where they remain for an extended period of time is referred to as *deposition*, which is the end result of the erosion process.

In contrast to erosion, **weathering** does not involve the movement of any outside stimuli. Instead, the surface of the Earth is broken down physically or chemically. *Physical weathering* involves the effects of atmospheric conditions such as water, ice, heat, or pressure. For example, when ice forms in the cracks of large rocks or pavement, it can break down or split open the material. *Chemical weathering* generally occurs in warmer climates and involves organic material that breaks down rocks, minerals, or soil. Scientists believe this process led to the creation of fossil fuels such as oil, coal, and natural gas.

Climate Patterns

Weather is the condition of the Earth's atmosphere at a particular time. **Climate** is different; instead of focusing on one particular day, climate is the relative pattern of weather in a place for an extended period of time. Climates are influenced by a variety of factors, including elevation, latitude, proximity to mountains, ocean currents, and wind patterns. For example, the city of Atlanta, Georgia generally has a humid subtropical climate; however, it also occasionally experiences snowstorms in the winter months. Over time, geographers, meteorologists, and other Earth scientists have determined these patterns that are indicative to north Georgia. Almost all parts of the world have predictable climate patterns, which are influenced by the surrounding geography.

The Central Coast of California is an example of a place with a predictable climate pattern. Santa Barbara, California, one of the region's larger cities, has almost the same temperature for most of the year, with only minimal fluctuation during the winter months. The temperatures there, which average between 65 and 75 degrees Fahrenheit regardless of the time of year, are influenced by a variety of different climatological factors including elevation, location relative to the mountains and ocean, and ocean currents. Similarly, Western Europe, which is at the nearly the same latitude as most of Canada, is influenced by the warm waters of the Gulf Stream, an ocean current that acts as a conveyor belt, moving warm tropical waters to the icy north. In fact, the Gulf Stream's influence is so profound that it even keeps Iceland—an island nation in the far North Atlantic—relatively warm.

Natural Hazards

Natural hazards also affect human societies. In tropical and subtropical climates, hurricanes and typhoons that form over warm water can have devastating effects. Additionally, tornadoes, which are powerful cyclonic windstorms, are responsible for widespread destruction in many parts of the world. Earthquakes, caused by shifting plates along faults deep below the Earth's surface, also bring widespread devastation, particularly in nations with poor infrastructure. For example, San Francisco, which experiences earthquakes regularly due to its position near the San Andreas Fault, saw relatively little destruction and death as a result of a major earthquake in 1989. However, in 2010, an earthquake of similar magnitude reportedly killed over 200,000 people in the Western Hemisphere's poorest nation, Haiti. Although a variety of factors may be responsible for the disparity, modern engineering methods and better building materials most likely helped to minimize destruction in San Francisco. Other natural hazards, such as tsunamis, mudslides, avalanches, forest fires, dust storms, flooding, volcanic eruptions, and blizzards, also affect human societies throughout the world.

Examining Past and Present Movement of Peoples

Patterns of Migration and Settlement

Migration is governed by two primary causes: **push factors** that cause someone to leave an area and **pull factors** that lure someone to a particular place. These two factors often work in concert with one another. For example, the United States of America has experienced significant internal migration from the industrial states in the Northeast (such as New York, New Jersey, Connecticut) to the Southern and Western states. Some push factors influencing this migration are high rents in the northeast, dreadfully cold winters, and lack of adequate retirement housing. On the other hand, lower cost of living and warmer climates are pull factors.

International migration also takes place between countries, continents, and other regions. The United States has long been the world's leading nation in regard to **immigration**, the process by which people permanently relocate to a new nation. Conversely, developing nations that suffer from high levels of poverty, pollution, warfare, and other violence all have significant push factors, which cause people to leave and move elsewhere. This process, known as **emigration**, is when people leave a particular area to seek a better life in a different location.

Demographic Patterns and Demographic Change

Demography, the study of human populations, investigates a variety of factors related to the human experience. For instance, several variables impact the geographical movement of people, such as economics, climate, natural disasters, or internal unrest. A recent example of this phenomenon is found in the millions of Syrian immigrants who have moved as far away as possible from the danger in their war-torn homeland.

As previously mentioned, people tend to live near reliable sources of food and water and away from extreme temperatures. Furthermore, the vast majority of people live in the Northern Hemisphere because more land lies in that part of the Earth. In keeping with these factors, human populations tend to be greater where human necessities are easily accessible, or at least more readily available. In other words, such areas have a greater chance of having a higher population density than places without such characteristics.

As push and pull factors fluctuate over time, demographic patterns on Earth will also change. While thousands of Europeans fled their homelands in the 1940s due to the impact of the Second World War, the opposite is true today as thousands of migrants arrive on European shores each month due to conflicts in the Levant and difficult economic conditions in Northern Africa. Furthermore, people tend to migrate to places with a greater economic potential for themselves and their families. As a result, developed nations such as the United States, Germany, Canada, and Australia have a net gain of migrants, while developing nations such as Somalia, Zambia, and Cambodia generally tend to see thousands of their citizens seek better lives elsewhere.

Religion and religious conflict also play a role in determining the composition and location of human populations. For example, the Nation of Israel won its independence in 1948 and has since attracted thousands of Jewish people from all over the world. Additionally, the United States has long been a popular destination due to its promise of religious freedom inherent within its own Constitution. In contrast, nations like Saudi Arabia and Iran do not typically tolerate different religions, resulting in a decidedly uniform religious—and oftentimes ethnic—composition. Other factors such as economic opportunity, social unrest, and cost of living also play a vital role in demographic composition.

Identifying and Analyzing Factors that Contribute to the Sense of Place and Identity

Interrelationships Between Humans and Their Environment

Humans both adapt themselves to their environment and adapt their environment to suit their needs. Humans create social systems with the goal of providing people with access to what they need to live more productive, fulfilling, and meaningful lives. Sometimes, humans create destructive systems, but generally speaking, humans tend to leverage their environments to make their lives easier. For example, in warmer climates, people tend to wear lighter clothing such as shorts, linen shirts, and hats. In the excessively sun-drenched nations of the Middle East, both men and women wear flowing white clothing complete with both a head and neck covering in order to prevent the blistering effects of exposure to the sun. Likewise, the native Inuit peoples of northern Canada and Alaska use the thick furs from the animals they kill to insulate their bodies against the bitter cold.

Humans must also manipulate their environments to ensure that they have sufficient access to food and water. In locations where water is not readily available, humans have had to invent ways to redirect water for drinking or agriculture. For example, the city of Los Angeles, America's second most populous city, did not have adequate freshwater resources to sustain its population. However, city and state officials realized that abundant water resources existed approximately three hundred miles to the east. Rather than relocating some of its population to areas with more abundant water resources, the State of California undertook one of the largest construction projects in the history of the world, the Los Angeles Aqueduct, which is a massive water transportation system that connects water-rich areas with the thirsty citizens of Los Angeles.

Farming is another way in which humans use the environment for their advantage. The very first permanent British Colony in North America, Jamestown, VA, was characterized by a hot and humid climate with fertile soil. Consequently, its inhabitants engaged in agriculture for both food and profit. Twelve years after Jamestown's founding in 1607, it was producing millions of dollars of tobacco each year. In order to sustain this booming industry, millions of African slaves and indentured servants from Europe were imported to provide labor.

Conversely, poor soil in the New England colonies did not allow for widespread cash crop production, and the settlers there generally only grew enough food for themselves on small subsistence farms. Due in part to this environmental difference, slavery failed to take a strong foothold in these states, thus creating distinct cultures within the same country.

Identifying and Evaluating Factors to Environmental Stewardship and Sustainability

As global climate change continues to impact the environment, Canada has committed to better stewardship of its natural resources. The central principle to good environmental stewardship is the use of **renewable** resources in a **sustainable** way. Sustainability is best imagined as maintaining a balance between the resources humans use and the resources required for nature to renew them.

Given the nation's size, Canada possesses a wealth of renewable and non-renewable resources. Non-renewable resources like oil may be economically valuable, but their continued use runs counter to improving stewardship of the environment. Renewable resources are typically those that are grown or replenished as part of a natural cycle, like rain or plants. However, responsible stewardship of these resources is still required for sustainability. Irresponsible cultivation of a single crop or overuse of a single resource has a domino effect on other parts of the environment. For example, if a forest is cleared to plant a field of corn, animals that also used that forest's resources no longer have a habitat. Their behavior must change, which may cause additional pressures in nearby areas.

Indigenous communities are at the forefront of Canada's environmental movement. This is typically due to the traditional values and religious beliefs of the First Nations. Indigenous respect for the environment influences Canadian culture as a whole in its attitude toward the environment. One demonstration of this is the preference for the phrase *environmental stewardship* instead of *environmental management*. In this case, the word *stewardship* lacks the connotation of human power and control implicit in *management*.

On a global scale, Canada maintains international advocacy for environmental regulation and legislation to reduce the impact of climate change. However, Canada's direct commitments and involvement have reduced over the last decade due to withdrawing from the *Kyoto Accord of 1997*. This international agreement set mutually agreed-upon emission goals in hopes of reducing environmental impacts. Under this agreement, signatories were subject to financial penalties if they failed to achieve the specified goals. Since Canada was slated to fail this goal, the nation withdrew from the *Kyoto Accord* in 2012 to avoid economic damage caused by the financial penalties.

In the years since, however, Canada's domestic environmental policy remains committed to the principles of the international environmental movement. This is demonstrated by the *Greenhouse Gas Pollution Pricing Act of 2018* and the *Canadian Energy Regulator Act of 2019*.

Social Studies Practice Quiz

Canadian Propaganda Poster (1914–1918)

1. The propaganda poster was published during which of the following conflicts?
    a. Cold War
    b. War of 1812
    c. World War I
    d. World War II

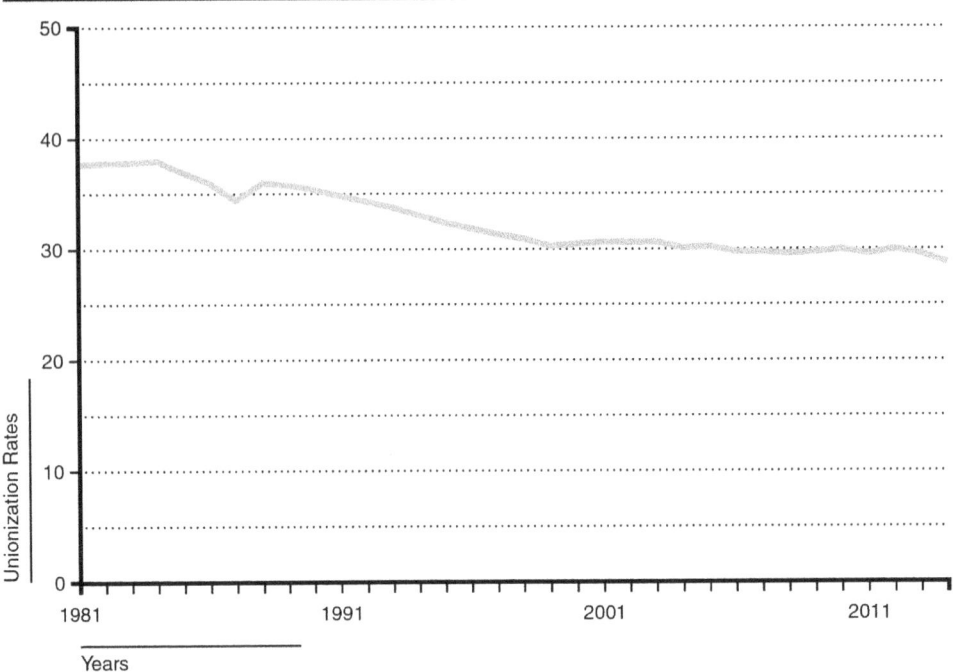

2. Which statement best explains what happened to unionization rates after 1989?
   a. The collapse of the Soviet Union triggered a worldwide recession.
   b. The United States reneged on its commitments to buy Canadian goods.
   c. Free trade weakened labor rights due to increased competition.
   d. Labor productivity steeply declined as automation decreased.

The next two questions are based on the following table.

Canadian Trade Balance with the United States from 2014 to 2019 (in billions USD)			
Years	Canadian Exports to U.S.	U.S. Imports to Canada	Canadian Trade Balance
2014	$349.3	$312.8	+ $36.5
2015	$296.3	$280.9	+ $15.5
2016	$277.7	$266.7	+ $11
2017	$299.1	$282.8	+ $16.3
2018	$318.5	$299.7	+ $18.8
2019	$319.4	$292.6	+ $26.8

United States Census Bureau, 2020, https://www.census.gov/foreign-trade/balance/c1220.html

3. Which of the following had the greatest direct effect on the data provided in the table?
   a. General Agreement on Tariffs and Trade
   b. North American Free Trade Agreement
   c. North Atlantic Treaty Organization
   d. Western Hemisphere Travel Initiative

Social Studies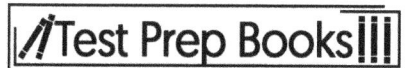

4. In which of the following years did greatest trade imbalance occur?
    a. 2016
    b. 2017
    c. 2018
    d. 2019

5. What was the most significant consequence of the Canadian Pacific Railway?
    a. It enriched the merchant class.
    b. It led to Canada becoming a confederation.
    c. It attracted immigrants to Eastern Canada.
    d. It facilitated territorial expansion.

See answers on the next page.

Social Studies Answer Explanations

1. C: Based on the context provided in the title, it can be inferred that Britain is the old lion and Canada is the young lion in the propaganda poster. Additionally, the title states that it was disseminated between 1914 and 1918. During World War I (1914–1918), Canadians fought alongside British forces because Canada was a dominion within the British Empire. Thus, Choice *C* is the correct answer. The War of 1812 (1812–1815) predated the propaganda poster by a century, so Choice *B* is incorrect. Canada was an independent country during World War II (1939–1945) and the Cold War (1947–1991), so Britain wouldn't have sought to enlist Canadian soldiers. Therefore, Choice *A* and Choice *D* are both incorrect.

2. C: The graph illustrates a consistent decline in unionization rates after 1989. The United States and Canada entered into the Canada–United States Free Trade Agreement in 1988, and the North American Free Trade Agreement (NAFTA) superseded it in 1994. Free trade generated tremendous economic growth, but it also severely undermined Canadian labor rights since NAFTA effectively created a North American labor market. Thus, Choice *C* is the correct answer. The Soviet Union collapsed in the late 1980s, but its dissolution didn't have a direct impact on Canadian labor rights. Therefore, Choice *A* is incorrect. The United States committed itself to buying far more Canadian goods when it entered into NAFTA, so Choice *B* is incorrect. Automation has very arguably contributed to a decline in unionization rates, but Choice *D* is incorrect because automation has increased and boosted labor productivity since 1989.

3. B: The table provides statistics related to trade between the United States and Canada, and both countries were signatories of the North American Free Trade Agreement (NAFTA). From 1994 until 2020, NAFTA lowered trade barriers between the United States, Canada, and Mexico. Thus, Choice *B* is the correct answer. The General Agreement on Tariffs and Trade (GATT) played a major role in promoting international free trade in the postwar era, but NAFTA had a far more direct impact on Canadian exports to the United States and American imports to Canada. Therefore, Choice *A* is incorrect. The United States and Canada are both founding members of the North Atlantic Treaty Organization (NATO); however, NATO is a military alliance, so Choice *C* is incorrect. The Western Hemisphere Travel Initiative is an American framework for border security; therefore, Choice *D* is incorrect.

4. D: A trade balance is the difference between a country's exports and imports. According to the table, Canada had a positive trade balance with the United States in all six years, meaning it exported more Canadian goods than it imported American goods. The relevant trade balances for this question were: $11 billion in 2016, Choice *A*, $16.3 billion in 2017, Choice *B*, $18.8 billion in 2018, Choice *C*, and $26.8 billion in 2019, Choice *D*. Thus, Choice *D* is the correct answer.

5. D: The Canadian Pacific Railway convinced British Columbia and Prince Edward Island to join the confederation, and the transportation of immigrants and critical supplies spurred rapid population growth in Western Canada. Thus, Choice *D* is the correct answer. The Canadian Pacific Railway indisputably enriched Canadian merchants by creating a larger and more unified marketplace; however, territorial expansion represents a broader and more significant effect, so Choice *A* is incorrect. While support for a transcontinental railroad helped build support for the confederation, it wasn't the most important factor. Additionally, construction didn't begin until after the confederation's establishment. Therefore, Choice *B* is incorrect. Choice *C* is incorrect because the railway had a much greater impact on attracting immigrants to Western Canada from Eastern Canada as well as foreign countries.

CAEC Practice Test

Reading

The next four questions are based on the following passage.

A potential post to seek figure skating sponsorships, with editing comments

@Coraline

To every member of my community who are interested in uplifting one of there own; this post is for you. If you would like a chance to help support a dedicated student athlete in pursuing a competitive career, please read on.

I am extremely dedicated to my skating training, coming to the rink every morning before school and a second time after school to keep my skills up. I am well on my way to qualifying for Regionals and beyond this year.

Though I am fully prepared athletically to compete, participation comes with costs such as travel expenses, costumes, and more ice time for extra practice leading up to competitions. I was hoping to find local businesses or individuals who would be interested in sponsoring my journey as an athlete.

I cannot go to Regionals if I cannot afford a plane ticket. Please look inside of your heart and think about what you would do if a friend or family member were in my position.

I would be immensely grateful for this opportunity to represent my community by showcasing my growth as an athlete.

#FigureSkating #SponsorshipOpportunities #SupportStudentAthletes

@Jordan

Comment 1: Check your grammar in the first sentence.

Comment 2: Be more specific about your sport and the specific regional competition you are talking about.

Comment 3: Check for inconsistency in verb tense.

Comment 4: Is this the tone you want to take with potential sponsors?

Comment 5: Revise your closing statement to make a more compelling appeal.

1. Appeals to logos use facts and statistic to serve a logical argument; appeals to ethos use the notion of a writer's authority or credibility to strengthen an argument; and appeals to pathos appeal to the emotions of the audience. Match the type of appeal with the corresponding sentence from the passage.

1. Appeal to ethos
2. Appeal to pathos
3. Appeal to logos

a. "Please look inside of your heart and think about what you would do if a friend or family member were in my position."

b. "Though I am fully prepared athletically to compete, participation comes with costs such as travel expenses, costumes, and more ice time for extra practice leading up to competitions."

c. "I am extremely dedicated to my skating training, coming to the rink every morning before school and a second time after school to keep my skills up."

2. Which of these reasons could be why Jordan made Comment 4, "Is this the tone you want to take with potential sponsors?" Select all that apply.
   a. Bringing up sponsors' friends and family may rub them the wrong way and not provoke the kind of emotional response that Coraline is looking for.
   b. Coraline seems angry with her potential sponsors here.
   c. This seems more like begging than presenting a valuable opportunity to sponsor a young athlete.
   d. Her tone is too formal in this paragraph to reach potential sponsors emotionally.
   e. This is the place for making statements, not asking questions.

3. According to Comment 3, which of the following sentences should be paired to preserve agreement in verb tense within Paragraph 3 as well as between Paragraph 3 and the rest of the passage?
First sentence:

   I. Though I am fully prepared athletically to compete, participation comes with costs such as travel expenses, costumes, and more ice time for extra practice leading up to competitions.
   II. Though I was fully prepared athletically to compete, participation comes with costs such as travel expenses, costumes, and more ice time for extra practice leading up to competitions.

Second sentence:

   III. I was hoping to find local businesses or individuals who would be interested in sponsoring my journey as an athlete.
   IV. I am looking for local businesses or individuals who would be interested in sponsoring my journey as an athlete.

   a. II and IV
   b. I and III
   c. I and IV
   d. II and III

4. The opening sentence of Coraline's post contains which of these kinds of grammatical errors? Select all that apply.
   a. Verb tense agreement

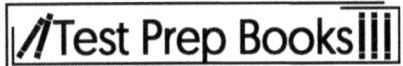

b. Subject-verb agreement
c. Misuse of homophones
d. Misused punctuation
e. Misuse of possessive signifiers

The next four questions are based on the following passage.

A piece on the superiority of having a full-yard garden to having a traditional lawn

In today's world of ever-more-strained natural resources, many have begun to rethink the traditional lawn, which guzzles water and offers little in return. I am proud to say that I made the switch two years ago to a much more practical garden, planting my entire yard with vegetables and herbs that look beautiful and keep my family fed. My journey from basic lawn-haver to accomplished gardener was highly rewarding and full of lessons about self-sufficiency and the value of hard work.

My standard lawn required constant mowing and watering as well as chemical treatments to keep it looking green and pristine. As I made the mind-numbing walk back and forth in rows that was pushing my lawnmower around, I couldn't shake the feeling that I was wasting my precious time and putting all this work into preserving something that did not help to preserve me. A quick bit of research confirmed that lawns do nothing for biodiversity and can even do harm to local ecosystems. I decided that it was time for a change.

The transformation was not without its challenges. My first big hurdle was pest control. My beloved tomatoes are also beloved by aphids, which came close to ruining my first harvest. Instead of simply falling back to the use of pesticides as I would have on my lawn, I opted to use neem oil to repel them. This approach required more effort up front than simply walking around and squeezing the trigger of a spray bottle, but it worked and kept my tomatoes free of chemicals that I would rather not have my children eat.

Watering was my next challenge. Different plants have different needs, and I needed to adapt my watering schedule accordingly. I had started with a mix of vegetables and flowers native to my area, but I quickly figured out that these plants did not thrive under the same conditions. I also realized that my garden was taking up substantially more of my time than my lawn had, and I did not want to sacrifice quite that much time to watering and otherwise tending to my plants. The solution was choosing low-maintenance plants; herbs like chives and thyme, for example, thrive with minimal attention because they grow as weeds in the wild.

Now, instead of dragging my feet every time I have to trudge out and mow the lawn again, I am happy to stroll out into my garden each day for a quick water and check of which plants have grown enough to be trimmed for use in my dinner. Gardening has taught me patience and creativity, and instead of simply being a blank expanse of green grass, it is an explosion of life that helps to sustain the person who tends it.

5. Which of the following would the author say are reasons to do away with traditional lawns? Select all that apply.
    a. Lawns require regular maintenance that gardens do not.
    b. Mowing a lawn does not result in material benefit to a household.
    c. Herbs like chives and thyme grow as weeds in the wild.
    d. Lawns do not contribute to biodiversity.
    e. Lawns consume a lot of water.

6. According to the author of this passage, what are the **two** main reasons that they personally decided to switch from a lawn to a garden?

Reasons	Select the two that apply:
A. Mowing the lawn felt like a pointless endeavor.	☐
B. Herbs like chives require little maintenance.	☐
C. Lawns do nothing for biodiversity.	☐
D. Lawns are ugly.	☐

7. Select **three** features of gardens that required the author to learn and adapt.
    a. Different plants have different watering needs.
    b. Successful gardens require knowledge of which seeds will result in strong plants.
    c. Not all plants will respond well to the same watering schedule.
    d. Grass requires regular mowing.
    e. Some plants are more labor intensive to grow.

8. Match the stated issue with lawns to the feature of gardens that the author presents as a solution.

1. Lack of tangible benefit   a. Planting a variety of vegetables and herbs

2. Lack of biodiversity   b. Attention to the varying needs of different plants

3. Chemical treatments for weeds   c. Growing food for the family

4. Boredom from monotonous mowing   d. Natural approaches like neem oil to prevent aphids

The next four questions are based on the following passage.

Home buying and home buyers in California

What is causing the California housing market to stagnate?

- Artificially limited inventory due to single family homes being purchased by investors
- Skyrocketing prices pushing out first-time buyers
- Difficulty finding buyers who can afford current market prices causing current homeowners to be unable to sell their current homes and buy new homes

Why today's home buyers have it harder:

1. Stricter lending practices: Current lending standards are far more stringent than those of days gone by, with loan applications requiring higher credit scores and extensive credit histories.
2. Economic uncertainty: Ongoing job market instability and the mismatch between the rise in minimum wage and inflation has left many who would have been able to afford a home in the past woefully unable to do so now.
3. High student debt: The rise in the cost of education has also far outpaced inflation, leaving many unable to save for a home for far longer than before.

Age of Home Buyers in California in 1960

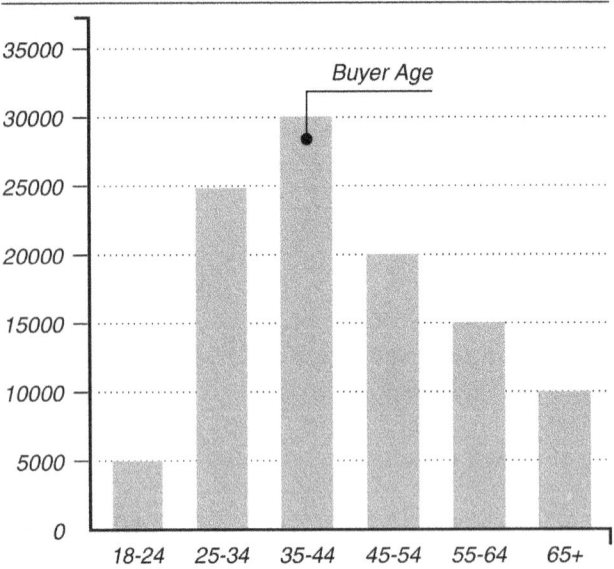

Age of Home Buyers in California in 2020

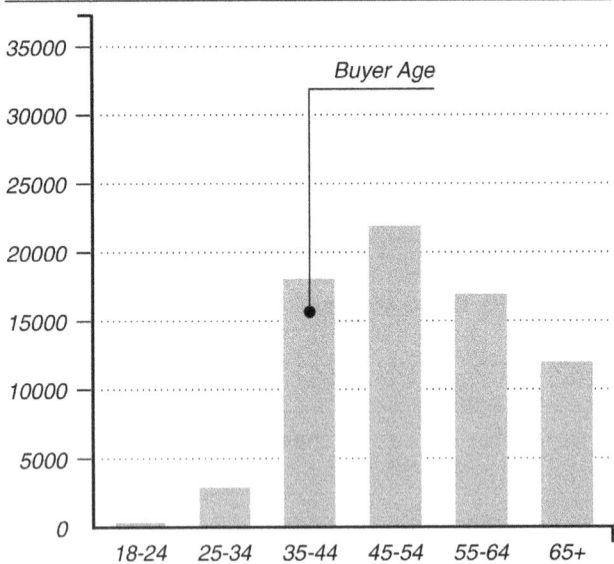

Today's housing market does not allow young professionals the chance at home ownership that those of similar ages had in the past. The combination of stagnant wage growth, rising interest rates, and soaring home prices has made the dream of homeownership more and more far-fetched for young potential buyers. The young professionals of the past were not burdened with significant student debt that limited their ability to save for a down payment. Those down payments were also not nearly as high as compared to the wages of the average person; the rise in home prices has well outstripped inflation, and those prices have now risen to a truly ludicrous level. People who may have been able to purchase a starter home in their twenties in the past may now have to wait until their forties or beyond, with many despairing of ever owning a home.

9. Which of these are factors in young people no longer being able to afford homes? (Check all that apply.)

CAEC Practice Test

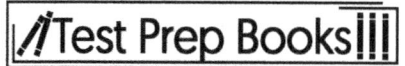

Factor	Contributes to Older Age Requirement for Home Ownership?	
Soaring home prices	☐ Yes	☐ No
Stagnant wage growth	☐ Yes	☐ No
Wages increasing faster than inflation	☐ Yes	☐ No
Significant student debt	☐ Yes	☐ No

10. Which of the following could be indicated by the two bar graphs about age of home buyers in 1960 versus 2020? Select all that apply.
    a. The number of young buyers has decreased due to homes becoming financially out of reach.
    b. Older buyers who have homes to sell are better able to meet the demands of purchasing a new home.
    c. More young people are seeking home ownership than ever before.
    d. Old people are dying before they can buy new homes.
    e. People now need to save for far longer to afford a down payment.

11. The following are issues that a new home buyer may face. Which of these is increasingly likely to happen to young buyers today?
    I. Being unable to save for a down payment
    II. Having difficulty selling a former home

Which of these is the most likely culprit for the issue mentioned above?
    III. Student debt
    IV. Stricter lending practices

    a. I and IV
    b. I and III
    c. II and III
    d. II and IV

12. Match the age group with its corresponding bar graph data:

A. 18-24	1. Has decreased by nearly half, from 30,000 to 18,000
B. 25-34	2. Has nearly vanished from the graph due to the numbers being so low
C. 35-44	3. Has plummeted from 25,000 to under 3,000
D. 45-54	4. Used to show smaller numbers than the previous age group but has overtaken it now

Text 4: Family Reunion

Pie chart made as a homework assignment by one of the children:

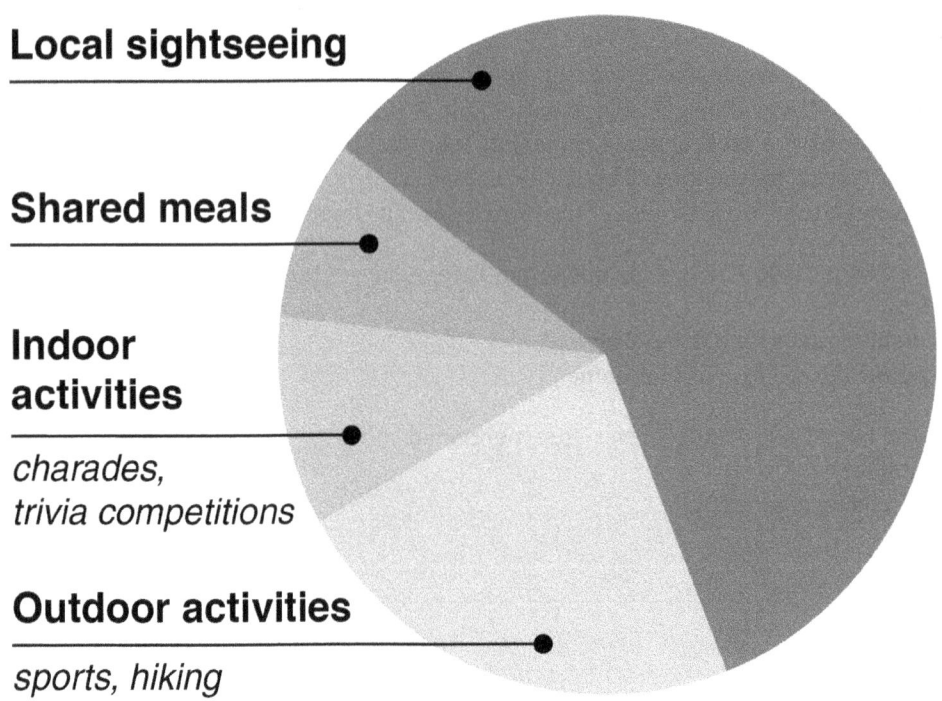

Mrs. Forrest,

This is my pie chart about my family reunions. My cousins and uncles and aunts and all the rest of the family said what we always do at reunions and I broke it down by categories.

Thanks for reading it,

Payton West

Email about family reunion activity options:

Hiya, family!

I hope you're all as excited as we are about our upcoming reunion in Spring City! I know we've all had a great time hiking in the Badlands and visiting art museums at reunions past, and we'll certainly have more adventures like those, but I've been brainstorming some fun activities that could really give us some quality time as a family.

Here are a few options to consider:

1. Private picnic and games: We can stake our claim on a part of a local park, bring all of our favorite potluck dishes and some frisbees for the kids, and really make a day of it.

CAEC Practice Test

2. Family talent show: There is a local pub that has a small stage setup that we could use, and it wouldn't be too expensive to book for a night. That way, nobody but family will see us doing our magic tricks or belting Whitney Houston songs at the top of our lungs. Laughs guaranteed!

3. Movies under the stars: Greg has a projector and screen that he can bring with enough notice. Imagine been all set up with snacks, blankets, and a good movie (appropriate for all ages, of course) under the stars. Sammys really rooting for this one. 🙂

Let me know what you think!

Sharon

13. Which of the following are grammatical errors in suggestion #3 from Sharon's email? Select all that apply.
    a. Incomplete sentence before the colon
    b. Failure to use an apostrophe in a contraction in the last sentence
    c. Use of *been* instead of *being* in the second full sentence ("Imagine...")
    d. Interrupting the sentence with a parenthetical phrase
    e. Misspelling of *routing*

14. Which of these makes the most sense as a reason that Sharon would use a numbered list in her email?
    I. To formally present herself as a credible source of information
    II. To make it easier to see her main ideas at a glance

What is her most likely reason for wanting to do this?
    III. To make sure that her ideas are viewed as important
    IV. To increase the likelihood of people reading and responding

   a. I and III
   b. I and IV
   c. II and III
   d. II and IV

15. Match the family member with their current contribution to the discussion of family reunion activities:

   1. Greg   a. A pie chart breaking down family activities by category
   2. Sammy   b. The offer of a projector and screen for movie night
   3. Sharon   c. An email laying out options for activities
   4. Payton   d. A vote in favor of movie night

16. Consider this sentence in Payton's message to his teacher:

    My cousins and uncles and aunts and all the rest of the family said what we always do at reunions and I broke it down by categories.

Select **three** ways that this sentence could be improved.
   a. "My cousins and uncles and aunts and all the rest of the family" could be shortened to "The members of my family" or "Family members at the reunion."
   b. "Said" could be changed to "answered questions about."
   c. "Broke" could be changed to "broken."
   d. "Reunions" could be changed to "reunion."

221

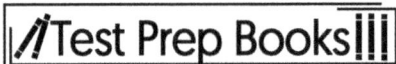

e. "I broke it down by categories" could be changed to "I broke it down by category."

The next four questions are based on the following passage.

> I sit and sew—a useless task it seems,
> My hands grown tired, my head weighed down with dreams—
> The panoply of war, the martial tred of men,
> Grim-faced, stern-eyed, gazing beyond the ken
> Of lesser souls, whose eyes have not seen Death,   5
> Nor learned to hold their lives but as a breath—
> But—I must sit and sew.
> I sit and sew—my heart aches with desire—
> That pageant terrible, that fiercely pouring fire
> On wasted fields, and writhing grotesque things   10
> Once men. My soul in pity flings
> Appealing cries, yearning only to go
> There in that holocaust of hell, those fields of woe—
> But—I must sit and sew.
> The little useless seam, the idle patch;   15
> Why dream I here beneath my homely thatch,
> When there they lie in sodden mud and rain,
> Pitifully calling me, the quick ones and the slain?
> You need me, Christ! It is no roseate dream
> That beckons me—this pretty futile seam,   20
> It stifles me—God, must I sit and sew?
>
> Poem "I Sit and Sew" by Alice Moore Dunbar-Nelson, 1918

17. In line 9, the speaker mentions a "pageant." What is she referring to?
    a. A beauty pageant
    b. The current war
    c. A popular play
    d. A wedding celebration

18. In the first stanza, who are the "martial tred of men, / Grim-faced, stern-eyed" that the speaker mentions in lines 3 and 4?
    a. Children
    b. Enemies
    c. Soldiers
    d. Neighbors

19. What idea does the speaker effectively contrast in this poem?
    a. The idea between the usefulness of sewing and the uselessness of war, namely that men's bodies are literally being wasted on the battlefield while sewing gives the opportunity of creating clothes for those same bodies.
    b. The idea between right and wrong, specifically that the war and everything relating to it is immoral, and the domestic side of life, including sewing, can be seen as doing good.
    c. The idea between sacrifice and selfishness; the speaker is admitting that she is being selfish for wanting to pursue her passion of sewing rather than helping out with the war.
    d. The idea between activeness and passiveness in the sense that the speaker views sewing as passiveness and longs to do something active in order to help out in the war.

20. What type of poetic lines are included in this poem?
    a. English sonnets
    b. Alternating tercets
    c. Rhyming couplets
    d. Syllabic haikus

The next five questions are based on the following passage.

Learning how to write a ten-minute play may seem like a monumental task at first; but, if you follow a simple creative writing strategy, similar to writing a narrative story, you will be able to write a successful drama. The first step is to open your story as if it is a puzzle to be solved. This will allow the reader a moment to engage with the story and to mentally solve the story with you, the author. Immediately provide descriptive details that steer the main idea, the tone, and the mood according to the overarching theme you have in mind. For example, if the play is about something ominous, you may open Scene One with a thunderclap. Next, use dialogue to reveal the attitudes and personalities of each of the characters who have a key part in the unfolding story. Keep the characters off balance in some way to create interest and dramatic effect. Maybe what the characters say does not match what they do. Show images on stage to speed up the narrative; remember, one picture speaks a thousand words. As the play progresses, the protagonist must cross the point of no return in some way; this is the climax of the story. Then, as in a written story, you create a resolution to the life-changing event of the protagonist. Let the characters experience some kind of self-discovery that can be understood and appreciated by the patient audience. Finally, make sure all things come together in the end so that every detail in the play makes sense right before the curtain falls.

21. Based on the passage above, which of the following statements is false?
    a. Writing a ten-minute play may seem like an insurmountable task.
    b. Providing descriptive details is not necessary until after the climax of the story line.
    c. Engaging the audience by jumping into the story line immediately helps them solve the story's developing ideas with you, the writer.
    d. Descriptive details give clues to the play's intended mood and tone.

22. Based on the passage above, which of the following is true?
    a. The class of eighth graders quickly learned that it is not that difficult to write a ten-minute play.
    b. The playwrights of the twenty-first century all use the narrative writing basic feature guide to outline their initial scripts.
    c. In order to follow a simple structure, a person can write a ten-minute play based on some narrative writing features.
    d. Women find playwriting easier than men because they are used to communicating in writing.

23. Based on your understanding of the passage, it can be assumed that which of the following statements are true?
    a. One way to reveal the identities and nuances of the characters in a play is to use dialogue.
    b. Characters should follow predictable routes in the challenge presented in the unfolding narrative, so the audience may easily follow the sequence of events.
    c. Using images in the stage design is a detrimental element of creating atmosphere and meaning for the drama.
    d. There is no need for the protagonist to come to terms with a self-discovery; he or she simply needs to follow the prescription for life lived as usual.

24. In the passage, why does the writer suggest that writing a ten-minute play is accessible for a novice playwright?
   a. It took the author of the passage only one week to write his first play.
   b. The format follows similar strategies of writing a narrative story.
   c. There are no particular themes or points to unravel; a playwright can use a stream of consciousness style to write a play.
   d. Dialogue that reveals the characters' particularities is uncommonly simple to write.

25. Based on the passage, which basic feature of narrative writing is NOT mentioned with respect to writing a ten-minute play?
   a. Style
   b. Descriptive details
   c. Dialogue
   d. Mood and tone

The next five questions are based on the following passage.

Dana Gioia argues in his article that poetry is dying, now little more than a limited art form confined to academic and college settings. Of course poetry remains healthy in the academic setting, but the idea of poetry being limited to this academic subculture is a stretch. New technology and social networking alone have contributed to poets and other writers' work being shared across the world. YouTube has emerged to be a major asset to poets, allowing live performances to be streamed to billions of users. Even now, poetry continues to grow and voice topics that are relevant to the culture of our time. Poetry is not in the spotlight as it may have been in earlier times, but it's still a relevant art form that continues to expand in scope and appeal.

Furthermore, Gioia's argument does not account for live performances of poetry. Not everyone has taken a poetry class or enrolled in university—but most everyone is online. The Internet is a perfect launching point to get all creative work out there. An example of this was the performance of Buddy Wakefield's *Hurling Crowbirds at Mockingbars*. Wakefield is a well-known poet who has published several collections of contemporary poetry. One of my favorite works by Wakefield is *Crowbirds*, specifically his performance at New York University in 2009. Although his reading was a campus event, views of his performance online number in the thousands. His poetry attracted people outside of the university setting.

Naturally, the poem's popularity can be attributed both to Wakefield's performance and the quality of his writing. *Crowbirds* touches on themes of core human concepts such as faith, personal loss, and growth. These are not ideas that only poets or students of literature understand, but all human beings: "You acted like I was hurling crowbirds at mockingbars / and abandoned me for not making sense. / Evidently, I don't experience things as rationally as you do" (Wakefield 15-17). Wakefield weaves together a complex description of the perplexed and hurt emotions of the speaker undergoing a separation from a romantic interest. The line "You acted like I was hurling crowbirds at mockingbars" conjures up an image of someone confused, seemingly out of their mind . . . or in the case of the speaker, passionately trying to grasp at a relationship that is fading. The speaker is looking back and finding the words that described how he wasn't making sense. This poem is particularly human and gripping in its message, but the entire effect of the poem is enhanced through the physical performance.

At its core, poetry is about addressing issues/ideas in the world. Part of this is also addressing the perspectives that are exiguously considered. Although the platform may look different, poetry continues to have a steady audience due to the emotional connection the poet shares with the audience.

26. Which one of the following best explains how the passage is organized?
    a. The author begins with a long definition of the main topic, and then proceeds to prove how that definition has changed over the course of modernity.
    b. The author presents a puzzling phenomenon and uses the rest of the passage to showcase personal experiences in order to explain it.
    c. The author contrasts two different viewpoints, then builds a case showing preference for one over the other.
    d. The passage is an analysis of another theory that the author has no stake in.

27. The author of the passage would likely agree most with which of the following?
    a. Buddy Wakefield is a genius and is considered at the forefront of modern poetry.
    b. Poetry is not irrelevant; it is an art form that adapts to the changing time while containing its core elements.
    c. Spoken word is the zenith of poetic forms and the premier style of poetry in this decade.
    d. Poetry is on the verge of vanishing from our cultural consciousness.

28. Which one of the following words, if substituted for the word *exiguously* in the last paragraph, would LEAST change the meaning of the sentence?
    a. Indolently
    b. Inaudibly
    c. Interminably
    d. Infrequently

29. Which of the following is most closely analogous to the author's opinion of Buddy Wakefield's performance in relation to modern poetry?
    a. Someone's refusal to accept that the Higgs Boson will validate the Standard Model.
    b. An individual's belief that soccer will lose popularity within the next fifty years.
    c. A professor's opinion that poetry contains the language of the heart, while fiction contains the language of the mind.
    d. A student's insistence that psychoanalysis is a subset of modern psychology.

30. What is the primary purpose of the passage?
    a. To educate readers on the development of poetry and describe the historical implications of poetry in media.
    b. To disprove Dana Gioia's stance that poetry is becoming irrelevant and is only appreciated in academia.
    c. To inform readers of the brilliance of Buddy Wakefield and to introduce them to other poets that have influenced contemporary poetry.
    d. To prove that Gioia's article does have some truth to it and to shed light on its relevance to modern poetry.

The next five questions are based on the following passage:

Becoming a successful leader in today's industry, government, and nonprofit sectors requires more than a high intelligence quotient (IQ). Emotional Intelligence (EI) includes developing the ability to know one's own emotions, to regulate impulses and emotions, and to use interpersonal communication skills with ease while dealing with other people. A combination of knowledge, skills, abilities, and mature emotional intelligence (EI) reflects the most effective leadership recipe. Successful leaders sharpen more than their talents and IQ levels; they practice the basic features of emotional intelligence. Some of the hallmark traits of a competent, emotionally intelligent leader include self-efficacy, drive, determination, collaboration, vision, humility, and openness to change. An unsuccessful leader exhibits opposite leadership traits: unclear directives, inconsistent vision and planning strategies, disrespect for followers, incompetence, and an uncompromising transactional leadership style. There are ways to develop emotional intelligence for the

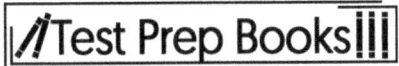

person who wants to improve their leadership style. For example, an emotionally intelligent leader creates an affirmative environment by incorporating collaborative activities, using professional development training for employee self-awareness, communicating clearly about the organization's vision, and developing a variety of resources for working with emotions. Building relationships outside the institution with leadership coaches and with professional development trainers can also help leaders who want to grow their leadership success. Leaders in today's work environment need to strive for a combination of skill, knowledge, and mature emotional intelligence to lead followers to success and to promote the vision and mission of their respective institutions.

31. The passage suggests that the term *emotional intelligence (EI)* can be defined as which of the following?
    a. A combination of knowledge, skills, abilities, and mature emotional intelligence reflects the most effective EI leadership recipe.
    b. An emotionally intelligent leader creates an affirmative environment by incorporating collaborative activities, using professional development training for employee self-awareness, communicating clearly about the organization's vision, and developing a variety of resources for working with emotions.
    c. EI includes developing the ability to know one's own emotions, to regulate impulses and emotions, and to use interpersonal communication skills with ease while dealing with other people.
    d. Becoming a successful leader in today's industry, government, and nonprofit sectors requires more than a high IQ.

32. Based on the information in the passage, a successful leader must have a high EI quotient.
    a. The above statement can be supported by the fact that Daniel Goldman conducted a scientific study.
    b. The above statement can be supported by the example that emotionally intelligent people are highly successful leaders.
    c. The above statement is not supported by the passage.
    d. The above statement is supported by the illustration that claims, "Leaders in today's work environment need to strive for a combination of skill, knowledge, and mature emotional intelligence to lead followers to success and to promote the vision and mission of their respective institutions."

33. According to the passage, some of the characteristics of an unsuccessful leader include which of the following?
    a. Talent, IQ level, and abilities
    b. Humility, knowledge, and skills
    c. Loud, demeaning actions toward female employees
    d. Transactional leadership style

34. According to the passage, which of the following must be true?
    a. The leader exhibits a healthy work/life balance lifestyle.
    b. The leader is uncompromising in transactional directives for all employees, regardless of status.
    c. The leader learns to strategize using future trends analysis to create a five-year plan.
    d. The leader uses a combination of skill, knowledge, and mature reasoning to make decisions.

35. According to the passage, which one of the following choices are true?
    a. If a leader does not have the level of emotional intelligence required for a certain job, they are capable of increasing emotional intelligence.
    b. It is not necessary for military leaders to develop emotional intelligence because they prefer a transactional leadership style.
    c. Leadership coaches cannot add value to someone who is developing their emotional intelligence.
    d. Humility is a valued character value; however, it is not necessarily a trademark of an emotionally intelligent leader.

CAEC Practice Test

The next nine questions are based on the following passage:

While all dogs (36) <u>descend through gray wolves</u>, it's easy to notice that dog breeds come in a variety of shapes and sizes. With such a (37) <u>drastic range of traits, appearances and body types</u> dogs are one of the most variable and adaptable species on the planet. (38) <u>But why so many differences.</u> The answer is that humans have actually played a major role in altering the biology of dogs. (39) <u>This was done through a process called selective breeding.</u>

(40) <u>Selective breeding which is also called artificial selection is the processes</u> in which animals with desired traits are bred in order to produce offspring that share the same traits. In natural selection, (41) <u>animals must adapt to their environments increase their chance of survival.</u> Over time, certain traits develop in animals that enable them to thrive in these environments. Those animals with more of these traits, or better versions of these traits, gain an (42) <u>advantage over others of their species.</u> Therefore, the animal's chances to mate are increased and these useful (43) <u>genes are passed into their offspring.</u> With dog breeding, humans select traits that are desired and encourage more of these desired traits in other dogs by breeding dogs that already have them.

The reason for different breeds of dogs is that there were specific needs that humans wanted to fill with their animals. For example, scent hounds are known for their extraordinary ability to track game through scent. These breeds are also known for their endurance in seeking deer and other prey. Therefore, early hunters took dogs that displayed these abilities and bred them to encourage these traits. Later, these generations took on characteristics that aided these desired traits. (44) <u>For example, Bloodhounds</u> have broad snouts and droopy ears that fall to the ground when they smell. These physical qualities not only define the look of the Bloodhound, but also contribute to their amazing tracking ability. The broad snout is able to define and hold onto scents longer than many other breeds. The long floppy hears serve to collect and hold the scents the earth holds so that the smells are clearer and able to be distinguished.

36. Which of the following would be the best choice for this sentence (reproduced below)?
   While all dogs (36) <u>descend through gray wolves</u>, it's easy to notice that dog breeds come in a variety of shapes and sizes.

   a. descend through gray wolves
   b. descend by gray wolves
   c. descend from gray wolves
   d. descended through gray wolves

37. Which of the following would be the best choice for this sentence (reproduced below)?
   With such a (37) <u>drastic range of traits, appearances and body types</u>, dogs are one of the most variable and adaptable species on the planet.

   a. NO CHANGE
   b. drastic range of traits, appearances, and body types,
   c. drastic range of traits and appearances and body types,
   d. drastic range of traits, appearances, as well as body types,

38. Which of the following would be the best choice for this sentence (reproduced below)?
   (38) <u>But why so many differences.</u>

   a. NO CHANGE
   b. But are there so many differences?
   c. But why so many differences are there.
   d. But why so many differences?

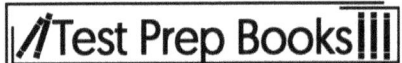

CAEC Practice Test

39. Which of the following would be the best choice for this sentence (reproduced below)?
   (39) This was done through a process called selective breeding.

   a. NO CHANGE
   b. This was done, through a process called selective breeding.
   c. This was done, through a process, called selective breeding.
   d. This was done through selective breeding, a process.

40. Which of the following would be the best choice for this sentence (reproduced below)?
   (40) Selective breeding which is also called artificial selection is the processes in which animals with desired traits are bred in order to produce offspring that share the same traits.

   a. NO CHANGE
   b. Selective breeding, which is also called artificial selection is the processes
   c. Selective breeding which is also called, artificial selection, is the processes
   d. Selective breeding, which is also called artificial selection, is the processes

41. Which of the following would be the best choice for this sentence (reproduced below)?
   In natural selection, (41) animals must adapt to their environments increase their chance of survival.

   a. NO CHANGE
   b. animals must adapt to their environments to increase their chance of survival.
   c. animals must adapt to their environments, increase their chance of survival.
   d. animals must adapt to their environments, increasing their chance of survival.

42. Which of the following would be the best choice for this sentence (reproduced below)?
   Those animals with more of these traits, or better versions of these traits, gain an (42) advantage over others of their species.

   a. NO CHANGE
   b. advantage over others, of their species.
   c. advantages over others of their species.
   d. advantage over others.

43. Which of the following would be the best choice for this sentence (reproduced below)?
   Therefore, the animal's chances to mate are increased and these useful (43) genes are passed into their offspring.

   a. NO CHANGE
   b. genes are passed onto their offspring.
   c. genes are passed on to their offspring.
   d. genes are passed within their offspring.

44 Which of the following would be the best choice for this sentence (reproduced below)?
   (44) For example, Bloodhounds have broad snouts and droopy ears that fall to the ground when they smell.

   a. NO CHANGE
   b. For example, Bloodhounds,
   c. For example Bloodhounds
   d. For example, bloodhounds

CAEC Practice Test

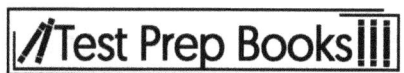

The next six questions are based on the following passage:

Since the first discovery of dinosaur bones, (45) scientists has made strides in technological development and methodologies used to investigate these extinct animals. We know more about dinosaurs than ever before and are still learning fascinating new things about how they looked and lived. However, one has to ask, whether earlier perceptions of dinosaurs continue to influence people's understanding of these creatures? Can these perceptions inhibit progress towards further understanding of dinosaurs?

(46) The biggest problem with studying dinosaurs is simply that there are no living dinosaurs to observe. All discoveries associated with these animals are based on physical remains. To gauge behavioral characteristics, scientists cross-examine these (47) finds with living animals that seem similar in order to gain understanding. While this method is effective, these are still deductions. Some ideas about dinosaurs can't be tested and confirmed simply because humans can't replicate a living dinosaur. For example, a Spinosaurus has a large sail, or a finlike structure that grows from its back. Paleontologists know this sail exists and have ideas for the function of the sail; however, they are uncertain of which idea is the true function. Some scientists believe (48) the sail serves to regulate the Spinosaurus' body temperature and yet others believe its used to attract mates. Still, other scientists think the sail is used to intimidate other predatory dinosaurs for self-defense. These are all viable explanations, but they are also influenced by what scientists know about modern animals. (49) Yet, it's quite possible that the sail could hold a completely unique function.

While it's (50) plausible, even likely that dinosaurs share many traits with modern animals, there is the danger of overattributing these qualities to a unique, extinct species. For much of the early nineteenth century, when people first started studying dinosaur bones, the assumption was that they were simply giant lizards. For the longest time this was the prevailing image of dinosaurs until evidence indicated that they were more likely warm blooded. Scientists have also discovered that many dinosaurs had feathers and actually share many traits with modern birds.

45. Which of the following would be the best choice for this sentence (reproduced below)?
Since the first discovery of dinosaur bones, (45) scientists has made strides in technological development and methodologies used to investigate these extinct animals.

   a. NO CHANGE
   b. scientists has made strides in technological development, and methodologies, used to investigate
   c. scientists have made strides in technological development and methodologies used to investigate
   d. scientists, have made strides in technological development and methodologies used, to investigate

46. Which of the following would be the best choice for this sentence (reproduced below)?
(46) The biggest problem with studying dinosaurs is simply that there are no living dinosaurs to observe.

   a. NO CHANGE
   b. The biggest problem with studying dinosaurs is simple, that there are no living dinosaurs to observe.
   c. The biggest problem with studying dinosaurs is simple. There are no living dinosaurs to observe.
   d. The biggest problem with studying dinosaurs, is simply that there are no living dinosaurs to observe.

47. Which of the following would be the best choice for this sentence (reproduced below)?
To gauge behavioral characteristics, scientists cross-examine these (47) finds with living animals that seem similar in order to gain understanding.

   a. NO CHANGE
   b. finds with living animals to explore potential similarities.
   c. finds with living animals to gain understanding of similarities.
   d. finds with living animals that seem similar, in order, to gain understanding.

229

48. Which of the following would be the best choice for this sentence (reproduced below)?
    Some scientists believe (48) <u>the sail serves to regulate the Spinosaurus' body temperature and yet others believe its used to attract mates.</u>

    a. NO CHANGE
    b. the sail serves to regulate the Spinosaurus' body temperature, yet others believe it's used to attract mates.
    c. the sail serves to regulate the Spinosaurus' body temperature and yet others believe it's used to attract mates.
    d. the sail serves to regulate the Spinosaurus' body temperature however others believe it's used to attract mates.

49. Which of the following would be the best choice for this sentence (reproduced below)?
    (49) <u>Yet, it's quite possible</u> that the sail could hold a completely unique function.

    a. NO CHANGE
    b. Yet, it's quite possible,
    c. It's quite possible,
    d. Its quite possible

50. Which of the following would be the best choice for this sentence (reproduced below)?
    While it's (50) <u>plausible, even likely that dinosaurs share many</u> traits with modern animals, there is the danger of over attributing these qualities to a unique, extinct species.

    a. NO CHANGE
    b. plausible, even likely that, dinosaurs share many
    c. plausible, even likely, that dinosaurs share many
    d. plausible even likely that dinosaurs share many

Writing

Persuasive Writing

Read the situation described below and use it to complete the writing task that follows.

The Situation: A municipal government is considering a proposal for a new bike-sharing program to reduce traffic congestion and promote sustainable transportation. Supporters believe the program will encourage more people to use a bicycle, improving public health and decreasing pollution from cars on the road. However, opponents are concerned about the safety of cyclists on busy roads as well as the cost of purchasing and maintaining the bicycles.

The Task: Write a letter or email to your city council that clearly explains why you AGREE or DISAGREE with the proposal for the bike-sharing program.

In preparing your letter or email, BE SURE TO:

- Read the information in the sources.
- Clearly state whether you AGREE or DISAGREE with the proposal.
- Develop and support your arguments with appropriate details.
- Organize your arguments in a logical order.
- Consider your audience, your tone, and your voice.
- Check sentence structures, usage, grammar, words, and expressions.

To support your position, you may use:

- The information in the sources
- Your own knowledge and/or experiences
- A combination of both

The Support:

Email from a local health organization:

Dear City Council Members,

As representatives of the Pine Valley Public Health Collective, we would like to express our support for the proposed bike-sharing program.

Research has consistently shown that cycling leads to significant health benefits. Regular bike riding has been shown to reduce the risk of chronic diseases including obesity, diabetes, and heart disease. By encouraging sedentary individuals to engage in physical activity, this bike-sharing program would promote a healthier lifestyle for all Pine Valley residents. We urge the council to vote with these potential benefits in mind.

Thank you for your time,

Rachel Kinnison

Pine Valley Public Health Collective President

Community Feedback on Bike-Sharing Program Proposal

Total Responses: 198

In Favor: 121 (61%)

Against: 42 (21%)

Undecided: 35 (18%)

Feedback Highlights

In Favor:
> "Less pollution from car exhaust fumes is always a win in my book."
> "This could really raise overall quality of life for a lot of our residents who wouldn't have gotten this kind of physical activity without a program like this."

Against:
> "How are we going to be keeping all these new cyclists safe? Will there be classes to make sure people even know how to ride?"
> "Who is going to maintain all these bikes? How much will the public be asked to pay for that?"

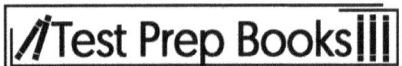

Community chat:

Bike-Sharing Proposal Discussion

@JaneDoe87: I'm all for the new bike-sharing plan! Healthier lifestyles and less traffic? It's a win-win.

@LocalMom443: I agree, Jane, but I have concerns about how safe this will be. Our streets are pretty busy, and a lot of them don't have dedicated bike lanes. Are there plans to add them?

@Concerned_Resident: I haven't seen enough planning on this, period. What are the costs? How will this be funded? I want to see the actual plans.

@DadofThree#1: I want to know about the locations of the bike-sharing stations more than the costs, personally. As long as the bikes are kept in safe, accessible places and bike lanes get added where we need them, I think this could really work.

Cost-Benefit Analysis of Proposed Bike-Sharing Program:

Item	Estimated Costs	Estimated Benefits
Initial Setup Costs	$200,000	
Maintenance and Operations (Annual)	$65,000	Est. $200,000 in reduced healthcare costs
Marketing and Community Outreach (Initial Push) Marketing and Community Outreach (Continued)	$10,000 $2,000	Environmental benefits (lower emissions)
Total	$277,000 starting costs $67,000 annually	Overall economic impact est. at least $200,000 annually

Analysis Conclusion: The anticipated benefits of the improvements to public health and reductions in traffic congestion and air pollution outweigh the concerns regarding the initial and ongoing costs of the bike-sharing program.

Math Part I: No Calculator

1. At the beginning of the day, Xavier has 20 apples. At lunch, he meets his sister Emma and gives her half of his apples. After lunch, he stops by his neighbor Jim's house and gives him 6 of his apples. He then uses $\frac{3}{4}$ of his remaining apples to make an apple pie for dessert at dinner. At the end of the day, how many apples does Xavier have left?
   a. 4
   b. 6
   c. 2
   d. 1

2. What is the product of two irrational numbers?
   a. Irrational
   b. Rational
   c. Irrational or rational
   d. Complex and imaginary

3. The graph shows the position of a car over a 10-second time interval. Which of the following is the correct interpretation of the graph for the interval 1 to 3 seconds?

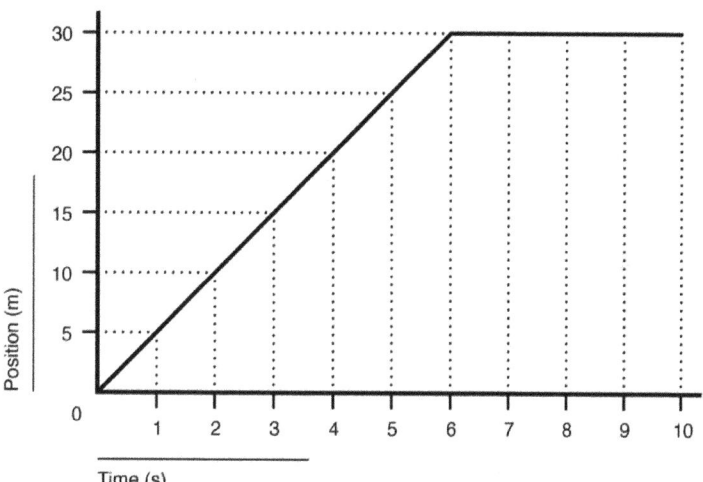

   a. The car remains in the same position.
   b. The car is traveling at a speed of 5 m/s.
   c. The car is traveling up a hill.
   d. The car is traveling at 5 mph.

4. Being as specific as possible, how is the number -4 classified?
   a. Real, rational, integer, whole, natural
   b. Real, rational, integer, natural
   c. Real, rational, integer
   d. Real, irrational, complex

5. Gary is driving home to see his parents for Christmas. He travels at a constant speed of 60 miles per hour for a total of 350 miles. How many minutes will it take him to travel home if he takes a break for 10 minutes every 100 miles?

6. What are all the factors of 12?
   a. 12, 24, 36
   b. 1, 2, 4, 6, 12
   c. 12, 24, 36, 48
   d. 1, 2, 3, 4, 6, 12

7. Solve $V = lwh$ for h.
   a. $lwV = h$
   b. $h = \frac{V}{lw}$
   c. $h = \frac{Vl}{w}$
   d. $h = \frac{Vw}{l}$

8. Twenty is 40% of what number?
   a. 60
   b. 8
   c. 200
   d. 50

9. What is the simplified form of the expression $1.2 * 10^{12} \div 3.0 * 10^8$?
   a. $0.4 * 10^4$
   b. $4.0 * 10^4$
   c. $4.0 * 10^3$
   d. $3.6 * 10^{20}$

10. Sam is twice as old as his sister, Lisa. Their oldest brother, Ray, will be 25 in three years. If Lisa is 13 years younger than Ray, how old is Sam?

11. Four people split a bill. The first person pays for $\frac{1}{5}$, the second person pays for $\frac{1}{4}$, and the third person pays for $\frac{1}{3}$. What fraction of the bill does the fourth person pay?
    a. $\frac{13}{60}$
    b. $\frac{47}{60}$
    c. $\frac{1}{4}$
    d. $\frac{4}{15}$

12. Which of the following fractions is equal to 9.3?
    a. $9\frac{3}{7}$
    b. $\frac{903}{1,000}$
    c. $\frac{9.03}{100}$
    d. $9\frac{3}{10}$

Math Part II: Calculator

1. After a 20% discount, Frank purchased a new refrigerator for $850. How much did he save from the original price?
    a. $170
    b. $212.50
    c. $105.75
    d. $200

2. A student gets an 85% on a test with 20 questions. How many questions did the student solve correctly?

3. Store brand coffee beans cost $1.23 per pound. A local coffee bean roaster charges $1.98 per 1 ½ pounds. How much more would 5 pounds from the local roaster cost than 5 pounds of the store brand?
    a. $0.55
    b. $1.55
    c. $1.45
    d. $0.45

4. What is the solution to the following problem in decimal form?
$$\frac{3}{5} \times \frac{7}{10} \div \frac{1}{2}$$
    a. 0.042
    b. 84%
    c. 0.84
    d. 0.42

5. Dwayne has received the following scores on his math tests: 78, 92, 83, and 97. What score must Dwayne get on his next math test to have an overall average of 90?
    a. 100
    b. 98
    c. 95
    d. 94

6. What is the solution to the following system of equations?
$$x^2 - 2x + y = 8$$
$$x - y = -2$$

   a. $(-2, 3)$
   b. There is no solution.
   c. $(-2, 0) (1, 3)$
   d. $(-2, 0) (3, 5)$

7. Kelly is selling cookies to raise money for the chorus. She has 500 cookies to sell. She sells 45% of the cookies to the sixth graders. At the second lunch, she sells 40% of what's left to the seventh graders. If she sells 60% of the remaining cookies to the eighth graders, how many cookies does Kelly have left at the end of all lunches?

8. Find the value of x.

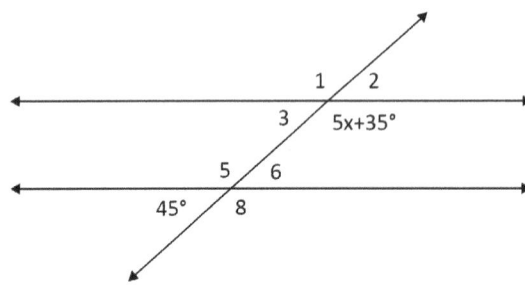

9. Which of the following is the result after simplifying the expression:
$$(7n + 3n^3 + 3) + (8n + 5n^3 + 2n^4)?$$
   a. $9n^4 + 15n - 2$
   b. $2n^4 + 5n^3 + 15n - 2$
   c. $9n^4 + 8n^3 + 15n$
   d. $2n^4 + 8n^3 + 15n + 3$

10. What is the product of the following expression?
$$(4x - 8)(5x^2 + x + 6)$$
   a. $20x^3 - 36x^2 + 16x - 48$
   b. $6x^3 - 41x^2 + 12x + 15$
   c. $20x^4 + 11x^2 - 37x - 12$
   d. $2x^3 - 11x^2 - 32x + 20$

11. The hospital has a nurse-to-patient ratio of 1:25. If there is a maximum of 325 patients admitted at a time, how many nurses are there?
   a. 13 nurses
   b. 25 nurses
   c. 325 nurses
   d. 12 nurses

CAEC Practice Test

12. Which of the following is the solution for the given equation?
$$\frac{x^2 + x - 30}{x - 5} = 11$$
   a. $x = -6$
   b. All real numbers.
   c. There is no solution.
   d. $x = 5$

13. Mom's car drove 72 miles in 90 minutes. How fast did she drive in feet per second?
   a. 0.8 feet per second
   b. 48.9 feet per second
   c. 0.009 feet per second
   d. 70.4 feet per second

14. What is the value of the following expression?
$$\sqrt{8^2 + 6^2}$$

15. If Sarah reads at an average rate of 21 pages in four nights, how long will it take her to read 140 pages?
   a. 6 nights
   b. 26 nights
   c. 8 nights
   d. 27 nights

16. The phone bill is calculated each month using the equation $c = 50g + 75$. The cost of the phone bill per month is represented by c, and g represents the gigabytes of data used that month. Identify and interpret the slope of this equation.
   a. 50 dollars per day
   b. 50 dollars per gigabyte
   c. 75 dollars per day
   d. 75 gigabytes per day

17. What is the perimeter of the following figure rounded to the nearest tenth?

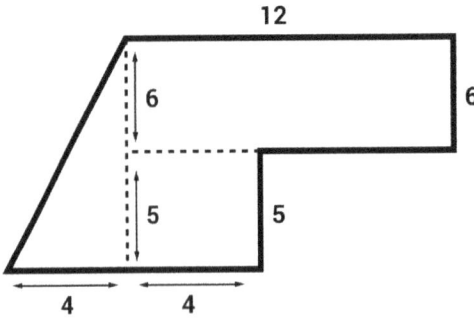

18. Solve the following:

$$(\sqrt{36} \times \sqrt{16}) - 3^2$$

19. What is the function that forms an equivalent graph to $y = \cos(x)$?
   a. $y = \tan(x)$
   b. $y = \csc(x)$
   c. $y = \sin\left(x + \frac{\pi}{2}\right)$
   d. $y = \sin\left(x - \frac{\pi}{2}\right)$

20. If $\sqrt{1 + x} = 4$, what is x?
   a. 10
   b. 15
   c. 20
   d. 25

21. A six-sided die is rolled. What is the probability that the roll is 1 or 2?
   a. $\frac{1}{6}$
   b. $\frac{1}{4}$
   c. $\frac{1}{3}$
   d. $\frac{1}{2}$

CAEC Practice Test

22. What is the overall median of Dwayne's current scores: 78, 92, 83, 97?

23. The total perimeter of a rectangle is 36 cm. If the length is 12 cm, what is the width?

24. A line passes through the origin and through the point (-3, 4). What is the slope of the line?
    a. $-\frac{4}{3}$
    b. $-\frac{3}{4}$
    c. $\frac{4}{3}$
    d. $\frac{3}{4}$

25. An investment of $2,000 is made into an account with an annual interest rate of 5%, compounded continuously. What is the total value of the investment after eight years?
    a. $2,954.91
    b. $3,000
    c. $2,983.65
    d. $2,800

26. A ball is drawn at random from a ball pit containing 8 red balls, 7 yellow balls, 6 green balls, and 5 purple balls. What's the probability that the ball drawn is yellow?
    a. $\frac{1}{26}$
    b. $\frac{19}{26}$
    c. $\frac{14}{26}$
    d. $\frac{7}{26}$

27. Two cards are drawn from a shuffled deck of 52 cards. What's the probability that both cards are kings if the first card isn't replaced after it's drawn?
    a. $\frac{1}{169}$
    b. $\frac{1}{221}$
    c. $\frac{1}{13}$
    d. $\frac{4}{13}$

28. Marty wishes to save $150 over a 4-day period. How much must Marty save each day on average?
    a. $37.50
    b. $35.00
    c. $45.50
    d. $41.00

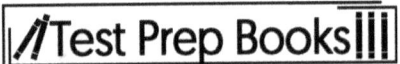

29. Bernard can make $80 per day. If he needs to make $300 and only works full days, how many days will this take?

30. What is the solution to $3\frac{2}{3} - 1\frac{4}{5}$?
    a. $1\frac{13}{15}$
    b. $\frac{14}{15}$
    c. $2\frac{2}{3}$
    d. $\frac{4}{5}$

Science

1. The scientific method generally includes which of the following features? Select all that apply.
    a. Relies on a person's subjective feelings
    b. Requires a hypothesis
    c. Involves testing observations above nature
    d. Applies technology to address moral dilemmas
    e. Depends on a collection of observations
    f. Avoids the use of technology
    g. Involves the testing of predictions
    h. Draws a conclusion

2. Which of the following is a question that is NOT scientifically testable?
    a. Will drinking tea improve stress levels?
    b. Do teas have natural sugars?
    c. Does drinking sweetened iced tea alter blood glucose levels?
    d. Does unsweetened ice tea taste more delicious compared to sweetened ice tea?

3. In one experiment studying the relationship between gas pressure and temperature, an empty flask connected to a pressure gauge was submerged in a water bath and heated until the water boiled. After the water boiled, a student recorded the pressure and temperature of the apparatus over time. The information indicated that the temperature and pressure both decreased simultaneously. The student reasoned that the decrease in pressure was due to fewer gas collisions against the container wall, which can occur if the temperature is decreased. According to this passage, the student's explanation of the decreased pressure is an example of a(n):
    a. Prediction
    b. Observation
    c. Inference
    d. Hypothesis

4. In one vaccine study, several physicians were required to give a vaccine and measure the patient outcomes. The physicians were given several vaccines, some of which were placebos, while others contained the actual vaccine. However, the physicians were not told which vaccines were placebos. The study described above is called a(n):
    a. Random study
    b. Double-blind study
    c. Bias study
    d. Observer bias

5. Which THREE of the following choices can introduce bias into a research study?
    a. In a study, data is gathered from different subgroups that make up a specific population.

b. An experiment shows that 25 percent of the results support the claim of the researcher, and a study is published so that 25 percent of the results support the claim.
c. When recording a blood pressure measurement, the blood pressure is rounded up.
d. In one study, a population is divided into specific subgroups to ensure the diversity of a sample.
e. A survey regarding the building of a commercial plaza is sent to locals via registered email addresses.
f. A survey with a sample size of n = 1000 is conducted in a school containing 2000 students.

6. In one experiment, researchers attempted to determine how much the mass of a coffee bean changed after roasting it for a specific time and under specific temperature conditions. Three different single-origin beans were used in the study, and a drum roaster was used to roast each coffee bean type for 15 minutes. The results of the study are shown below.

Coffee type	Mass of green coffee bean	Mass of coffee bean after roasting
Ethiopian	113.0 mg	96.0 mg
Indonesia	121.0 mg	93.2 mg
Brazil	115.0 mg	102.1 mg

One method that the researcher could have used to make the experiment more reliable is:
a. Decreasing the amount of heat during roasting
b. Using different roasters for each experiment
c. Repeating roasting of the coffee with the same mass
d. Roasting the coffee until the masses are the same for each bean type

7. The density of an unknown liquid substance was found to have a true value of 1.35 g/cm^3 at room temperature. The liquid was analyzed in another laboratory, and the density was calculated three different times using the same analytical balance and graduated cylinder. The density values were 1.21 g/cm^3, 1.22 g/cm^3, and 1.19 g/cm^3. The three measurements are best described as:
a. Precise and inaccurate
b. Precise and accurate
c. Imprecise and accurate
d. Imprecise and inaccurate

8. Carbon fiber is a high-strength and low-weight material that is commonly incorporated into race cars, bicycles, and airplanes. In one study, researchers wanted to test and report the mechanical strength of different carbon fiber materials produced by three different companies.

   I. Company A produces a carbon fiber material using a water-soluble precursor called polyvinyl alcohol. The method is low-cost and requires unique chemical treatments to create high-strength carbon fibers.
   II. Company B produces a carbon fiber material using polyvinyl butyral, which provides good structural integrity for carbon fiber. However, the method requires the use of a special solvent that is slightly toxic and requires moderately high temperatures.
   III. Company C produces carbon fiber from polyacrylonitrile, which creates a high mechanical strength carbon fiber. The method requires the use of toxic organic solvents and high temperatures for the production of carbon fiber.

For each of the following actions, please check the appropriate box to indicate whether the action can increase or decrease the bias in determining the mechanical strength of the carbon fiber that is produced.

Researchers' approach	Increases bias	Reduces bias

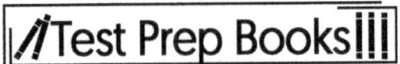

Company A provided several instruments to the researchers to perform their mechanical testing experiments.	☐	☐
The researchers were given carbon fiber samples but were not told which company produced the sample.	☐	☐
The researchers tested twenty samples from Company A, two samples from Company B, and five samples from Company C.	☐	☐
The researchers reported mechanical testing results from companies that had high mechanical strengths.	☐	☐

9. Publication bias refers to when:

   I. An article is published in a journal based on the positive significance of its results.
   II. Nonsignificant data are published to ensure proper representation of collected data.

Selective reporting bias occurs when:

   III. Negative outcomes are included in a peer-reviewed study to ensure representation.
   IV. Only positive data or outcomes are highlighted.

   a. I and III
   b. I and IV
   c. II and III
   d. II and IV

10. Researchers carried out a series of acid-base titrations to determine the amount of hard water found in a local spring, residential homes, and public schools in a local town. The local spring is found 10 miles from the small town and was determined to come from a single aquifer. The residential homes have water sources from a local water tower managed by the city's water department, which collects water from a nearby river. The public schools in the city, however, have water sourced from one large aquifer within the city.
The researchers collected five samples from each of the different locations and then used a method to extract any metals or salts in the solution.
Based on the investigation, which of the following choices would be a hypothesis when analyzing the amount of metals in the collected water samples?
   a. School officials should use the results of the investigation to determine if additional water filters should be installed in water fountains.
   b. Water found in residential areas will generally taste better since the water is suited for daily drinking and lacks metals.
   c. The city should make the city's water aquifer accessible to residential homes to help reduce the cost of drinking water.
   d. Spring water found outside the town contains less metals than town water.

11. Match each of the four different experimental descriptions with the appropriate scientific tools.

Scientific tools

Beaker	Graduated cylinder	Ruler	Thermometer

Research descriptions corresponding to required scientific tools

In a calorimeter experiment using a coffee cup, a specific tool was required to measure the thickness and length of the cup in order to study how heat transfer occurs.	
An ice bath was prepared inside this glassware in order to cool down and crystallize a mixture inside a test tube.	
In one experiment, a quantitative instrument was used to determine when a salt mixture began to freeze.	
When determining the density of an unknown liquid, a precise measurement device was needed to measure the volume correctly.	

12. The stress-strain measurement was carried out between two fiber strands, each measuring 5 millimeters in length and 0.2 millimeters in diameter. Before the tests, the carbon fiber sample was heat treated to a temperature of 800°C and then cooled to room temperature. The chemically treated fiber consisted of a polymer that was treated in an acid.

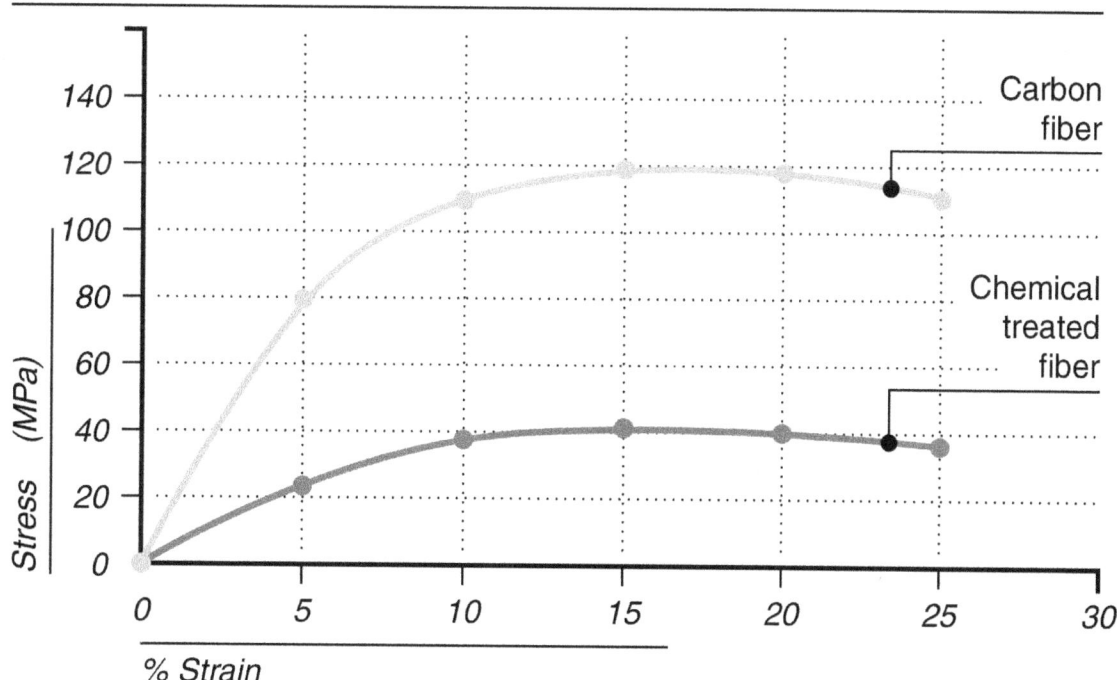

During the mechanical tests, the fibers were elongated at each terminal end until failure. The amount of strain at which both fibers reached maximum stress was _____ percent.

13. The production of carbon fiber initially requires chemical treatment of polyvinyl alcohol using a concentrated solution of sulfuric acid. The safety label on the bottle of the acid contains a label that indicates skin corrosion, eye irritation, and toxicity from inhalation.

Which TWO of the following WHMIS 2015 pictograms should be placed on the sulfuric acid container?

 a.    b.    c.    d.

14. An acid-base titration requires the use of a diprotic acid called sulfuric acid. The safety label on the container of sulfuric acid indicates acute toxicity and corrosion.
Identify the correct method of storing the bottle of sulfuric acid.
    I. Store with other materials in bulk and with incompatible materials if necessary.
    II. Store in a cool place away from sunlight.

When the experimentalist is handling sulfuric acid, determine the precaution needed below.
    III. Wear safety goggles and a face shield.
    IV. Work inside a fume hood.

  a. I and IV
  b. I and III
  c. II and IV
  d. II and III

15. An automotive performance company developed super water coolant A and claimed it could improve heat transfer out of a car's radiator and reduce the temperature of the car motor. A race car driver wanted to determine the cooling efficiency of water coolant A compared to well-established coolant B. The race car driver carried out the following tests.

- Before the addition of each of the two coolants, the driver added pure water to the car's radiator and then drove the car for 20 minutes before measuring the temperature of the coolant in the car motor.
- For the second test, the driver completely emptied pure water from the car's radiator and then filled it with super water coolant A. They drove the car for 20 minutes again before measuring the coolant temperature.
- In the last test, the driver removed coolant A from the car's radiator and replaced it with coolant B. They again drove the car for 20 minutes and then recorded the temperature.

Determine the independent and dependent variables in the water coolant tests.
Independent variable:
    I. Temperature of the motor
    II. Type of coolant added

Dependent variable:
    III. Temperature of the coolant in the motor
    IV. Pure water

  a. I and IV
  b. II and III
  c. II and IV
  d. I and III

16. In a chemical experiment involving the reaction of aluminum, a specific volume of a base called potassium hydroxide was needed to ensure the formation of a metal hydroxide. During the experiment, the base was added to a graduated cylinder, as shown in the picture below as graduated cylinder A. The experimentalist then transferred some of the base into a separate beaker containing aluminum pieces. The remaining amount of base was left inside the graduated cylinder, as shown in graduated cylinder B.

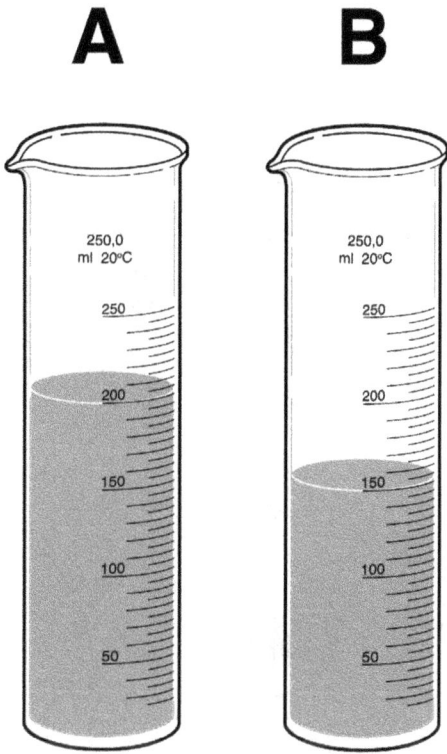

Based on the described procedure regarding the volumetric measurement of the base, the total amount of base transferred to the beaker is:
- a. 200 milliliters
- b. 350 milliliters
- c. 50 milliliters
- d. 150 milliliters

17. Which element has the fewest number of protons?
- a. Radon (Rn)
- b. Boron (B)
- c. Nitrogen (N)
- d. Hydrogen (H)

18. When calculating the density of a liquid, the mass of a substance is measured on an analytical balance, and the volume of the liquid is measured using a graduated cylinder. The formula to calculate the density is:

$$\text{Density} = \frac{\text{mass of substance in grams (g)}}{\text{volume of liquid in millliters (mL)}}$$

A 50.0 mL sample of ethanol was reported to have a mass of 0.03945 kilograms. If the sample of ethanol was placed on an analytical balance that reported the mass in grams, then the balance would show:
   a. 3.945 grams
   b. 39.45 grams
   c. 394.5 grams
   d. 3945 grams

19. Molecular modelers are generally tasked with predicting the shapes and sizes of molecules using unique programs that can display a molecule, such as water (H_2O or H-O-H), as shown below. The results of a modeling simulation will create a variety of different shapes and orientations that the water molecule will exhibit. The results of a water simulation are shown below and indicate four different angles. The molecule that shows an angle of 109 degrees is Molecule:

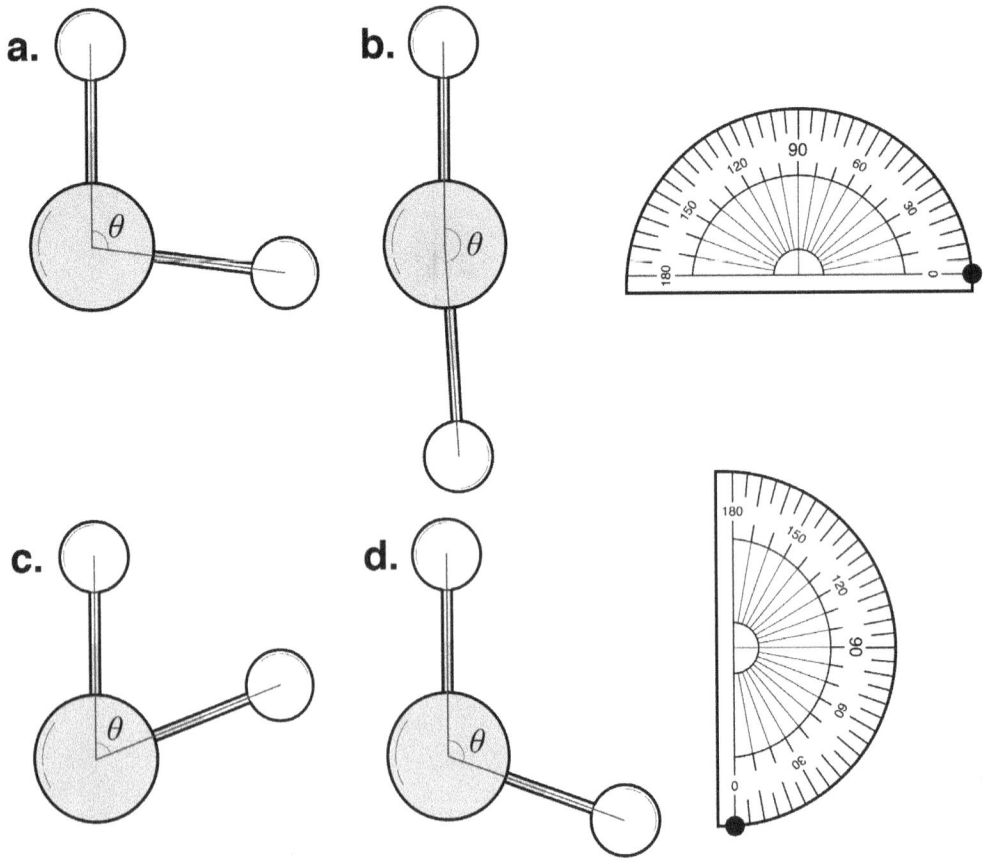

20. The coffee cherry is a red fruit grown on coffee trees that contains a green coffee bean. The cherry contains several layers that consist of the skin, pulp, parenchyma, endocarp, and silver skin. *Coffea arabica*, a species of coffee cherries, accounts for a majority of global coffee production and is generally less acidic. One coffee cherry generally contains 5–10 milligrams of caffeine and about 0.03–0.1 gram of sugar.

The masses of caffeine and sugar were analyzed for four different cherry trees of the same species on a local farm. Ten cherries were picked from each tree (samples I, II, III, IV), and the mass of caffeine and sugar was calculated and averaged. The results are shown in the table below.

Coffee tree	Mass of caffeine (milligrams)	Mass of sugar (grams)
I	5.5	0.12
II	6.7	0.09
III	27.2	0.05
IV	8.8	0.027

Which of the following statements provides a reasonable explanation of the results of the study?
a. Coffee tree I will be the least expensive since less caffeine is present.
b. The amount of caffeine in coffee tree III does not follow a consistent trend with other coffee trees.
c. Coffee tree IV is likely a light roast coffee since there is a relatively higher amount of caffeine.
d. The mass of caffeine is generally greater than the mass of sugar.

21. Polyacrylonitrile is a synthetic polymer that has been found to have many uses in clothing, such as sweaters and socks. When the polymer is blended with other polymers, it creates a stable synthetic fiber that does not break down and release toxic byproducts. However, specific oxidizing agents such as copper, a common clothing ingredient used to fight odor, have been known to accelerate the breakdown of the polymer when added in large amounts. Specifically, the release of cyanide can occur more quickly when the material containing copper is near heat sources, which causes acute toxicity in people. A manufacturer recently put out an advisory regarding the production of a small batch of clothing that contained a synthetic polymer with an excess amount of copper. For the statements shown below, determine which of the following choices are suitable.

Based on the provided information in the passage, the manufacturer should have:
   I. Added a label on the clothing that indicated copper was added
   II. Added a label that the product should not be near heat sources

The manufacturer of the fiber-infused copper clothing should conduct research and development projects to:
   III. Study how adding less copper to the material is safer
   IV. Look for an alternative odor-fighting agent that will not react with the polymer

a. II and III
b. I and IV
c. II and IV
d. I and III

22. Coffee roasting is a complex process that involves many heating stages whereby a green coffee bean is converted into a brown bean. The end result is a coffee bean that can have fruit- and chocolate-like flavors. Coffee roasters will often roast to "first crack," a state the beans reach at temperatures between 200°C and 210°C, to achieve complex and rich flavors. For home roasting, a drum or air roaster can be utilized to heat the coffee to a specified temperature, but the two methods have different heating methods. When the temperature falls between the first crack range, a "popping" sound follows, which signifies a physical transformation of the bean that results in the release of carbon dioxide.

A single batch of single-origin Ethiopian coffee was roasted four times, each with the same starting mass of 115 grams, until the first crack became audible.

Roast number	Mass of coffee (grams)	Time in minutes at which first crack was detected	Chemical analysis of sugar content (%)
Roast 1	115.0	8 minutes and 15 seconds	7%
Roast 2	115.0	8 minutes and 45 seconds	6%
Roast 3	115.0	7 minutes and 29 seconds	0.1%
Roast 4	115.0	7 minutes and 58 seconds	6.2%

One way the roaster could have increased the consistency and reliability of the roasting process would have been to:
   a. Taste the coffee.
   b. Use a different coffee roast for each trial.
   c. Use a different roaster for each roast.
   d. Use a temperature probe.

23. A clothing company developed odor-fighting material X and claimed it could reduce odors by eliminating the amount of bacteria that can grow on clothing. A researcher wanted to compare material X to another antibacterial material Y. The researcher carried out the following tests.

- The researcher gathered three people who were free from sweat. Each person was asked to remain in a clean, sterilized room for 30 minutes.
- Person A received material X, Person B used material Y, and Person C received regular clothing material Z, which was not antibacterial.
- Each person was then asked to exercise and run outside for a total of 30 minutes.
- The shirts were removed from each subject and analyzed to determine the amount of bacteria.

Which of the following choices can NOT be accurately tested by scientific inquiry? Select all that apply.
   a. Remaining sweat-free before the study does not alter the outcome of the experiment.
   b. Material Z is more antibacterial than X and Y.
   c. Material Y is more antibacterial than Z.
   d. The production of material Y is more ethical than that of material Z.
   e. Person A smells better than Person B.
   f. Increasing the amount of antibacterial agent decreases the odor.

24. A researcher is testing a herbicide or weed killer that removes a variety of weeds, such as clovers and docks. The researcher made the following hypothesis:

   The addition of herbicide to a lawn containing weeds and grass will cause grass to grow taller.

The researcher's reasoning was attributed to a competition for resources. If weeds are removed, then the grass will have more nutrients. A growth spurt will consequently occur. However, if herbicide is added to an area containing only grass, then a growth spurt will not be seen since nutrients will still be distributed the same way. Which of the following choices would represent an experimental design that can test the researcher's hypothesis?
   a. Add herbicide to an area containing grass and weeds. Then add water to an area containing only grass.

b. Add herbicide to an area containing grass and weeds. Then add the herbicide to an area containing only grass.
c. Add water to an area containing grass and weeds. Then add the herbicide to an area containing only grass.
d. Add herbicide to an area containing weeds. Then add the herbicide to an area containing only grass.

25. A person normally brews coffee using a pour-over technique and wants to determine which method produces coffee the fastest.

The person purchased different types of coffee funnels, which are used to hold the coffee filter and ground coffee. Each coffee funnel was tested one at a time, and the funnel was placed over a coffee cup. First, 20 grams of ground coffee was placed in each funnel, then 200 grams of water at a temperature of 95 °C was added into the funnel. The amount of time was recorded for each filtration, as shown in the table below. The coffee filter type, indicated by the pore size of the paper, is also indicated in the study.

Funnel brand	Time for filtration in seconds	Coffee filter type (pore size)
Q	150	20 microns
R	170	10 microns
S	180	11 microns
T	210	10 microns

Based on the information from the passage, which TWO choices below have the potential to be biased?
a. Funnel brand Q requires using its coffee filter type.
b. An instruction guide provides information on how to pour coffee into the funnel.
c. Funnel brand R is advertised to the person as a quick method for brewing coffee.
d. A coffee guide explains how to conduct pour-overs for different types of coffee funnels.

26. In one experiment, a researcher was studying how the gas pressure inside a closed container was affected by temperature and volume changes. In part A of the experiment, the researcher heated a cylindrical container containing a movable piston; the piston remained fixed, and the pressure was measured over time as the temperature varied. Approximately 10 data points were collected. In experiment B, the researcher kept the temperature fixed and moved the piston to different positions. For each unique position, the pressure was recorded until seven data points were obtained.

Select TWO variables from the choices below that the researcher was able to control in the study.
a. The pressure of the container
b. The volume inside the container
c. The temperature of the container
d. The amount of gas inside the container

27. Chlorofluorocarbons (CFCs) are nonflammable and nontoxic chemicals that are used as aerosol sprays and refrigerants, which were first produced in the late 1920s. The use of CFCs in the 1950s provided an alternative, less toxic, and inexpensive replacement for refrigerants used in home and building cooling systems.

In the late 1970s, it was discovered that CFCs are a main source of chlorine found in the stratosphere, which resulted in the destruction of ozone in the stratosphere. Since ozone is a gas that absorbs harmful radiation, its removal can result in harmful radiation hitting the Earth's surface. Consequently, skin cancer can become more prevalent, and damage to materials can occur; the effects on plants and marine ecosystems can also be damaging.

As of 2010, some countries banned the use of CFCs, and some countries limited the use of these chemicals. Check one box in the first column to identify the intended consequence of banning CFCs and check one box in the second column to identify the unintended consequence of limiting the use of CFCs.

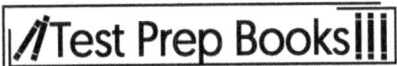

	Intended Consequence	Unintended Consequence
A. Synthetic polymers found in cars and buildings have a reduced lifetime usage.	☐	☐
B. The developmental impacts on fish are less severe.	☐	☐
C. Alternative refrigerants that are chosen may be ozone friendly but more toxic.	☐	☐
D. The ozone layer will become larger over the North and South Poles.	☐	☐

28. The use of hydrofluorocarbons (HFCs) has replaced CFCs as an ozone-friendly chemical. HFCs are produced each year for use in air conditioning and refrigeration. However, HFCs have been recognized as a greenhouse gas and can have a greater impact on climate change. Consequently, accelerated climate change can result in increased severe weather events such as wildfires, floods, and droughts. In regard to HFC usage, which of the following choices could most effectively mitigate the impact on the environment?
    a. Create a technology that uses natural, nonfluorinated refrigerants.
    b. Continue the use of CFCs to reduce climate change.
    c. Develop policies that will ensure cities have the resources to deal with floods.
    d. Create refrigerants that have the potential to stay in the Earth's atmosphere.

29. Renewable energy from wind turbines has continued to increase as technology costs have continued to go down. Several cities have considered the use of wind turbines for the generation of electricity. In one particular city, rich in wildlife, local officials have contracted with the government to build several wind turbines needed to provide electricity in more desolate and rural regions. Which of the following are an unintended consequence of the construction of wind turbines in a wildlife region? Select all that apply.
    a. Electricity will allow for video monitoring of wildlife.
    b. Wind turbines can result in increased fire hazards.
    c. Wind turbines require the use of oils for lubrication, which can contaminate groundwater.
    d. Rural economies will be boosted since energy revenue can be used to build roads and infrastructure.
    e. Noise pollution will result, causing specific species of wildlife to flee.
    f. Wind turbines can result in localized warming.

30. A company involved in the manufacturing of spacecraft was found to have released pollutants into nearby bodies of water. Hypergolic fluids have been used in the construction of missiles and rockets for decades but are toxic and will react spontaneously when not stored properly. While alternative fuels have been investigated, production of new fuel types will take years. Unintentional hypergolic fluid spills have occurred and have contaminated nearby bodies of water; this has been exacerbated when the spill sites are flushed out with bleach, which further contaminates the ground. Determine which choices complete the two provided statements shown below.
A method for effectively dealing with the risks of rocket and missile technology is:
    I. Avoiding the construction of rockets
    II. Providing procedures to ensure proper containment of hypergolic fuel

An example of a beneficial scientific solution is:
    III. Developing an alternative rocket fuel that is more eco-friendly
    IV. Moving the manufacturing site away from large bodies of water

    a. I and III
    b. I and IV

250

c. II and III
d. II and IV

31. A country was interested in the development of lightweight and durable materials for use in high-performance aircraft. A four-year contract was provided to a local university that allowed researchers to develop novel, lightweight, and durable materials. Which of the following choices describes the primary influencing factor for the described research?
   a. Social
   b. Political
   c. Public health
   d. Economic

32. Match each of the four perspectives shown below with the different situations that influence scientific research.

Perspectives			
Public health	Central dogma	Academic ethos	Political

Research descriptions corresponding to factors that influence scientific research	
An editor rejects a researcher's proposal since the editor believes there is not enough evidence to indicate that the proposal will have a positive impact.	
A government agency provides funding to researchers who have demonstrated a technology that can improve surveillance.	
Due to a world pandemic, governments around the world invest resources in the development of a vaccine.	
A scientist in the 1920s proposed a theory that continents moved slowly over the course of a million years. Despite the scientist's evidence, the idea of continental drift was rejected up until the 1960s.	

33. A university received millions of dollars from an oil company to focus on research related to the production of affordable, reliable, and clean energy technology. The gift to the university resulted in the construction of new buildings designated for undergraduate and graduate research in carbon and hydrogen management. Which of the following is the main factor influencing the research?
   a. Social
   b. Political
   c. Economic
   d. Collaboration

34. Which of the following is a man-made compound that is no longer approved for use due to its major detrimental effect on the ozone layer?
   a. Teflon
   b. Chlorofluorocarbons
   c. Carbon trioxide
   d. Fluorocarbon phosphates

35. "This flower is dead; someone must have forgotten to water it." This statement is an example of which of the following?
   a. A classification
   b. An observation
   c. An inference
   d. A collection

Social Studies

1. Which of the following is a government position held in the executive branch?
    a. Minister of National Defense
    b. Associate Chief Justice
    c. Member of Parliament
    d. Senator

2. Which of the following types of bill may NOT be proposed by a minister?
    a. Supply bill
    b. Government bill
    c. Private bill
    d. Private member's bill

3. What is an appellate court?
    a. A court that hears trials
    b. A court that hears appeals
    c. A court for military use
    d. A court with final authority over a case

The next two questions are based on the following passage.

> The government of Canada is split into three branches: the legislative branch, the executive branch, and the judicial branch. This separation of powers preserves democratic process by ensuring no one branch of the government will acquire too much authority. Likewise, preservation of democratic principles is why unelected members of the government—such as the Governor General—hold ceremonial authority but lack practical authority. Persons in such positions may, however, advise ministers or advocate for preferred policies without wielding practical authority.

4. Based on the passage above, the *Indian Act of 1876* is widely condemned because of which of the following? Select all that apply.
    a. It preserved democratic process in the First Nations, despite traditional customs.
    b. Indigenous persons held elections at the whim of the federal government.
    c. The act is archaic and has never been amended to modernize the law.
    d. First Nations governments were required to separate their powers as the federal government does.
    e. It was enacted by the House of Commons, not the Minister of Indigenous Services.
    f. Members of indigenous communities did not determine their own electoral procedure.

5. Which of the following best exemplifies a position with ceremonial authority in First Nations communities?
    a. Chief
    b. Councillor
    c. Elder
    d. Band

The next three questions are based on the following passage.

> Source 1: Municipal governments in Canada do not use the parliamentary system. Instead, a city or town's mayors and councillors are elected directly by the populace and govern the district's day-to-day life.

Consequently, the lack of a parliamentary system is justified because the electorate is still represented by their government.

Source 2: The direct election of a city's Privy Council equivalent is more efficient than operating a full parliamentary system for local governments. However, this also comes at a risk that the elected officials won't reflect the cultural plurality in Canadian society. For example, if a district's majority population is Anglophone, how likely is it that the Francophone minority will have meaningful representation on the city council? Thus, some cities may need a more representative government system.

6. Select the government structures from the parliamentary system to which local governments have an analogous structure.

Structure	Yes	No
House of Commons	☐	☐
Privy Council	☐	☐
Prime Minister	☐	☐
House of Lords	☐	☐

7. Based on the argument in Source 2, which of the following issues is MOST likely a topic of concern under the authority of a municipality?
   a. University education
   b. Indigenous self-government
   c. Roadways and signs
   d. Enforcement of law

8. Which of the following protected rights of an official language minority are being violated in the passages? Select all that apply.
   a. Right to receive public services in one's native language
   b. Right to education in one's native language, if the parents received education in it in the same location
   c. Right to speak one's native language in public
   d. Freedom from discrimination based upon one's native language
   e. Right to mandatory representation in government
   f. No rights are being violated in the passages.

The next two questions are based on the following passage.

News website headlines regarding a new law:

- *Timeline:* House Forces Change in Voting Districts
- *Day News:* Success—Minority Seats Guaranteed by Law
- *Canada Leads:* Stock Market Rises 3 Points After District Bill Passed
- *What Happened Today:* Equal Votes or Equal Representation?

9. Which of the following news websites published a headline advocating a specific political agenda? Select all that apply.
   a. *Timeline*
   b. *Day News*
   c. *Canada Leads*
   d. *What Happened Today*

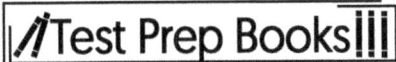

10. Based on these headlines, which of the following best describes the purpose of the new law?
    a. Facilitate increased immigration due to improved representation in the House of Commons.
    b. Provide for diversity of representation by establishing new districts for protected minorities.
    c. Improve the Canadian economy through reducing regulations on consumer goods.
    d. Protect the right of cultural identity among the First Nations, Métis, and Inuit.

The next two questions are based on the following passage.

List of Ministers:
- Minister of Finance
- Minister of Public Safety
- Minister of Democratic Institutions
- Minister of Foreign Affairs
- Minister of Small Business
- Minister of Indigenous Services
- Minister of Energy and Natural Resources

11. Which minister in this list is MOST likely to negotiate a trade agreement selling oil to the United States of America?
    a. Minister of Foreign Affairs
    b. Minister of Finance
    c. Minister of Energy and Natural Resources
    d. Minister of Small Business

12. Which ministers in this list frequently engage with the First Nations of Canada as part of their regular duties? Select all that apply.
    a. Minister of Finance
    b. Minister of Public Safety
    c. Minister of Democratic Institutions
    d. Minister of Foreign Affairs
    e. Minister of Small Business
    f. Minister of Indigenous Services
    g. Minister of Energy and Natural Resources

13. Which of the following features of Canada's economy demonstrates that it is a mixed economy?
    a. Nationalized healthcare system with private providers
    b. Municipal law enforcement in towns and cities
    c. International trade agreements with foreign nations
    d. Environmental protection regulations to reduce pollution

The next four questions are based on the following passage.

> The price of clothing going up has several causes. First, we have purchased fewer shipments of clothing this year from overseas manufacturers. Second, the CAD's value has gone down compared to other currencies (like the American dollar or the Japanese yen). We expect this to return to normal as we continue recovering from the pandemic's economic downturn. The increased spending required to avoid total economic collapse resulted in increased national debt, although revenues are beginning to turn around.

> In the meantime, recent studies show this is still impacting the quality of life in the lowest 20 percent of Canadian households. Increased clothing prices are making budgets tighter as families decide how to

CAEC Practice Test

prioritize their spending. While clothing is a material necessity, other necessities are often perceived as more urgent. Even if shipping returns to normal, it's likely budgets will remain difficult.

14. What are the MOST likely economic consequences of the decision-making by impoverished families described in the passage? Select one box in each row.

Economic Value	Increase	Decrease
Price of clothing	☐	☐
Price of food	☐	☐
Canadian dollar	☐	☐

15. This passage exemplifies the law of supply and demand because...
    a. When the availability of shipping went down, the price of clothing went up.
    b. When the availability of shipping went down, the price of food went up.
    c. When the availability of food went up, the price of food went up.
    d. When the Japanese yen went up, the Canadian dollar went down.

16. Sort each of the following economic terms into the correct category: Depression, Deflation, Income inequality, Inflation, Quality of life, Recession
    Box 1: Currency Change
    Box 2: State of Economy
    Box 3: Employment
    Box 4: Measuring Poverty

17. Which of the following may be evidence in the passage of an economic recession?

Fact	Yes	No
Reduced value of the Canadian dollar	☐	☐
Increasing interest rates from the federal bank	☐	☐
Reduced household budgets	☐	☐
Reduced purchase of overseas goods	☐	☐

The next two questions are based on the following passage.

> We don't live in a globalized nation. We live in a nation that participates in an *ongoing process* of globalization. The two most visible elements of globalization—trade and immigration—aren't a static event that happens once and is then completed by naturalization. In a global economy, immigration and emigration are never "finished." Compare immigration with trade—if we deliver a shipment to Mexico, does the Canadian economy become "complete," in some sense? Of course not.

18. Which of the following is true about trade in Canada's global economy?
    a. Most trade is domestic, but some trade takes place between independent nations.
    b. The Canadian economy became globalized once international trade became commonplace.
    c. Participating in a global economy means resources and labor constantly circulate.
    d. Canada is well suited for global trade because of its multicultural values.

255

19. Sort the following terms into the correct category: Emigration, Immigration, Multiculturalism, Naturalization, Overseas shipping, Trade agreement
   Box 1: Movement of People
   Box 2: Cultural Changes
   Box 3: Movement of Goods
   Box 4: Political Legislation

The next three questions are based on the following passage.

20. Based on this cartoon, which of the following best identifies the illustrator's political opinion?
    a. They prefer the opposition's policies to the government's policies.
    b. They believe the government is engaged in political oppression of the opposition.
    c. They generally support the government, but believe it has made an error.
    d. They claim the government's complaints about the opposition are unfounded.

21. Why could this cartoon be considered a secondary source?
    a. Because it depicts an eyewitness experience of a fight between politicians
    b. Because it uses research to determine political information about the past
    c. Because it portrays contemporary opinion, rather than actual events
    d. Because it represents the opinion of a majority of Canadians during its time

CAEC Practice Test

22. With which of the following statements might this cartoon's illustrator agree or disagree?

Statement	Agree	Disagree
The current government should be voted out of office during the next election.	☐	☐
We need laws preventing the opposition from allowing bills to pass the House of Commons.	☐	☐
It is ridiculous that members of the House of Commons are physically fighting while in session.	☐	☐
Criticism of the government is a necessary part of our democratic process—even in the House of Commons.	☐	☐

The next four questions are based on the following passage.

Source 1: The *Nunavut Land Claims Agreement Act of 1999* established Nunavut as a self-governing territory of Canada. It is governed democratically using a parliamentary system like Canada's other provinces. This process was established in the 1990s as this agreement was being negotiated. Nunavut has three official languages. In addition to English and French, the indigenous Inuktut languages are also recognized by the territory's government. Establishing this territory empowered the Inuit to preserve their cultural and linguistic identity. In 2016, over 60 percent of the people living in Nunavut Territory identified an Inuktut language as their native tongue. This is an exciting metric as reconciliation with Canada's indigenous peoples continues.

Source 2: Each year in June we celebrate National Indigenous Peoples Day to commemorate the collective contributions of the First Nations to Canadian society. Focusing on the traditions of these communities not only helps them preserve their cultural heritage, but it also helps Canadians throughout the country strengthen a sense of national identity. This goes beyond the awful injustices of the past—such as the illegal land claims made by European settlers—to recognizing how native attitudes toward community and the environment shape the way we regard one another.

23. Which of the following are sources of Inuit cultural identity? Select all that apply.
    a. Signing the *Nunavut Land Claims Agreement Act* to create Nunavut Territory
    b. Establishing the Inuktut languages as official languages in Nunavut
    c. Living off the land in the cold and often dangerous Arctic environment
    d. Inheriting an indigenous language from parents as one's first language
    e. Being an official language minority in Nunavut Territory
    f. Celebrating National Indigenous Peoples Day to commemorate all of the First Nations

24. Which of the following most likely describes how the Inuit felt about their ancestral lands prior to the creation of Nunavut Territory?
    a. No form of restitution could justify the forced relocation of the Inuit.
    b. Proud to be Canadian, but seeking greater agency in governing themselves.
    c. Illegal land claims were made in the past, so all Inuit lands ought to be returned.
    d. Theft of ancestral lands is a central element in Inuit cultural identity.

25. National Indigenous Peoples Day is important because it:
    a. Encourages sharing indigenous culture, and acknowledging Canada's unjust history
    b. Celebrates the reconciliation between European and indigenous Canadians
    c. Reminds Canadians of European heritage of the unpayable debt owed to the First Nations

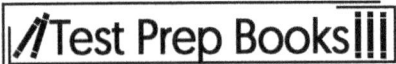

d. Commemorates the return of ancestral lands to the Inuit and other indigenous communities

26. How did Canada's recognition of the Inuit's right to self-government in Nunavut Territory have a cultural impact on European-heritage cultures?
    a. The federal government no longer had authority over natural resources in those lands.
    b. Other indigenous groups continued advocating for self-government in their ancestral territories.
    c. More Canadians became in favor of indigenous self-government of traditional territories.
    d. Recognition of Inuktut in Nunavut encouraged the languages' official use by other cultures.

The next two questions are based on the following passage.

The Arctic Archipelago is the furthest north geographical feature of Canada, as well as the northernmost extent of the continent of North America. It is covered mostly in tundra, with taiga on some southern islands. Europeans first arrived while searching for the Northwest Passage, while indigenous peoples have lived here for thousands of years. The Canadian islands are members of the Nunavut Territory and of the Northwest Territories. While Nunavut Territory is directly governed by its residents, the Northwest Territories is under the direct authority of the federal government. The border between the two territories runs along the 110° meridian through Victoria Island, Melville Island, and several smaller islands. The largest settlement in the archipelago is Iqaluit, on Baffin Island.

27. Sort the following geographic terms into the correct category: 110° meridian, Arctic Archipelago, Melville Island, Northwest Passage, Nunavut Territory, taiga
    Box 1: Physical Geography
    Box 2: Human Geography
    Box 3: Geographical Measurements
    Box 4: Environmental Geography

28. Based on the passage, Iqaluit is best described as a feature of:
    a. Human geography
    b. Physical geography
    c. Cultural geography
    d. Political geography

The next two questions are based on the following table.

Settlement	Population
Buffalo Lake	379
East Prairie	310
Elizabeth	594
Fishing Lake	414
Gift Lake	625
Kikino	978
Paddle Prairie	551
Peavine	387
Total Population of Métis Settlements in Alberta	4,238
Approximate Métis Population in Alberta	127,000
Approximate Population of the Province of Alberta	4,250,000

29. About _____ percent of Alberta's Métis population live in historically Métis settlements. Round to the nearest whole number.

30. The settlements listed in this table are all self-governing. Which of the following does this demographic information BEST imply about Métis culture in Alberta?
    a. Good jobs are more highly valued than traditional ways of living.
    b. Few Métis prioritize traditional expressions of culture.
    c. Self-government is not a major source of Métis cultural identity.
    d. These Métis value Canadian identity over indigenous identity.

The next three questions are based on the following passage.

Canada's most stalwart defenders of the environment historically come from the First Nations, Métis, and Inuit peoples. Not only are indigenous populations very knowledgeable about their ancestral lands, their cultures also highly value maintaining a relationship with those lands. This relationship extends to the flora and fauna of those environments, too. According to indigenous cultures, Canada's attitude toward environmental stewardship ought to be one of trust and respect toward nature, rather than seeing natural resources as objects to use.

31. Which of the following actions match the passage's description of the values of indigenous communities?

Action	Agree	Disagree
Visiting a local nature preserve to get some exercise by hiking.	☐	☐
Volunteer in environmental relief efforts after an industrial disaster.	☐	☐
Advocate for reduced use of non-renewable resources.	☐	☐

32. Why is the phrase *environmental stewardship* preferred over *environmental management* by indigenous communities?
    a. The first prioritizes community, while the second prioritizes ownership.
    b. The first prioritizes relationship, while the second prioritizes usefulness.

c. The first prioritizes ancestral claims, while the second prioritizes corporate claims.
d. The first prioritizes generating revenue, while the second prioritizes preserving territory.

33. Why do indigenous communities have strong feelings about the use of Canada's natural resources?
    a. Indigenous people lived in the land before European settlement and wish to preserve their home environment.
    b. As more land claims are negotiated, indigenous communities have increasing authority to exploit Canada's natural resources themselves.
    c. The First Nations of Canada feel a sense of ownership toward the land, since it was claimed unlawfully in many cases.
    d. Continuing to use Canada's natural resources feels akin to theft for many indigenous peoples, since their relationship to the land never ended.

The next two questions refer to the following map.

Map of Present-Day Canada

34. Which province is entirely landlocked?
    a. British Columbia
    b. Manitoba
    c. Nova Scotia
    d. Saskatchewan

35. Which province has the most Arctic tundra?
    a. Newfoundland and Labrador
    b. Northwest Territories
    c. Nunavut
    d. Quebec

36. Which term is best defined as a group of people joined by a common culture, language, heritage, history, and religion?
    a. State
    b. Nation
    c. Regime
    d. Government

37. The presidential and parliamentary systems differ in which of the following ways?
    a. The presidential system establishes a separation of powers.
    b. The legislature elects the chief executive in a presidential system.
    c. Voters directly elect the prime minister in a parliamentary system.
    d. The parliamentary system never includes a president.

38. Which of these choices BEST describes a participatory democracy?
    a. A system in which only the educated and wealthy members of society vote and decide upon the leaders of the country
    b. A system in which groups come together to advance certain select interests
    c. A system that emphasizes everyone contributing to the political system
    d. A system in which one group makes decisions for the population at large

39. Which of the following statements best describes international affairs between World War I and World War II?
    a. A lenient World War I peace treaty for Germany delayed the start of World War II.
    b. The policy of appeasement only encouraged further aggression by Hitler.
    c. A powerful League of Nations fostered increased cooperation and negotiation.
    d. Tensions grew between Germany and Japan.

40. Which one of the following best describes an economic benefit of free trade agreements?
    a. They increase international trade by reducing barriers to trade.
    b. They reduce the cost of reparations.
    c. They allow countries to protect domestic iron and steel production.
    d. They facilitate imperialism and the creation of lucrative empires.

Answer Explanations

Reading

1. 1-C; 2-A; 3-B: Choice *C* supports the idea that Coraline is credible in claiming a need for sponsorship because she is a dedicated athlete; Choice *A* seeks to provoke an emotional response from readers; and Choice *B* brings up practical concerns that lean on the reader's use of reason.

2. A, C: Both Choice *A* and Choice *C* accurately represent the issues with Coraline's tone. Coraline's phrasing does not suggest anger as in Choice *B* and is not formal in its use of language as Choice *D* suggests. The question of tone has nothing to do with the assertion of Choice *E* that she should be making statements instead of asking questions.

3. C: This is the only combination that preserves the use of present tense throughout. Choices *A* and *B* have mismatched verb tenses, and Choice *D* causes Paragraph 3 to be written in past tense while the rest of the post is written in present tense.

4. B, C, D: This sentence uses *are* as the verb for the singular noun *member*, uses *there* rather than *their*, and uses a semicolon where a comma should be used. There are no issues with verb tense agreement or uses of possessive signifiers.

5. B, D, E: All of these come up as reasons to do away with traditional lawns. Choice *A* is incorrect because gardens also require maintenance. Choice *C* is only a fact about herbs that does not elaborate on its reasoning.

6. A, C: These are the reasons given in the second paragraph, in which the author talks about why they made the switch. Choice *B* is something they discovered later, and the aesthetic of lawns, Choice *D*, only comes up at the very end of the passage.

7. A, C, E: These all come up as issues for the author. Choice *B* is true but not something that is mentioned in the passage. Choice *D* is an issue with lawns, not gardens.

8. 1-C; 2-A; 3-D; 4-B: The author provides a solution for each of the stated issues, providing persuasive reasons why the problems should not stand in the way of creating a full-yard garden.

9. Yes, Yes, No, Yes: Wages are increasing more slowly than inflation, but the other three options all contribute to young buyers no longer being able to afford homes.

10. A, B, E: These options are sensible conclusions to draw based on the fact that the change in the graphs shows the numbers becoming skewed much more in favor of older buyers. Choices *C* and *D* would require the change to move the numbers in the opposite direction.

11. B: Rising student debt would prevent someone from saving for a down payment. Difficulty selling a former home is not an issue faced by young buyers without homes to start with, and lending practices growing stricter does not specifically cause issues saving for down payments.

12. A-2; B-3; C-1; D-4: These answers reflect the changes shown by the graphs.

13. B, C: *Sammys* should be *Sammy's* in Choice *B* for the contraction of the words "Sammy is," and *been* should be *being* in Choice *C*. Choice *A* is incorrect because a complete sentence is not required before the colon. Choice *D* likewise claims that something grammatically correct is an error. Choice *E* wrongly calls *rooting* a misspelling of *routing*, but *routing* would not make sense in this sentence.

Answer Explanations

14. D: Sharon doesn't need to present herself as a formal authority to her family, and her casual, upbeat tone suggests that she is not concerned about not having her ideas viewed as important. She does, however, have reason to want to make this email easy to read so that she can get the most responses from her relatives that she possibly can.

15. 1-B; 2-D; 3-C; 4-A: Greg offered his projector for movie night, Sammy is highly in favor of movie night happening, Sharon sent the email about the activities, and Payton made the pie chart for his class.

16. A, B, E: Choice A would cut out superfluous words and aid clarity; Choice B would remove clunky phrasing with "said what we always do;" and Choice E removes the unnecessary pluralization of the word *categories*. Choices C and D make changes that introduce grammatical errors.

17. B: The speaker is referring to the current war, Choice B. The lines say: "I set and sew—my heart aches with desire— / That pageant terrible, that fiercely pouring fire / On wasted fields, and writhing grotesque things / Once men" (lines 8–11). Pageant is a metaphor for the battlefield in this poem. After she mentions the word "pageant," the speaker then goes on to describe the "pageant," or war, by describing the fire, fields, and dying men.

18. C: The speaker is referring to soldiers in these lines, so Choice C is correct. If we look at the surrounding context clues, the word "war" is mentioned before the description of these men. The word *tred* refers to a sort of weary marching.

19. D: The speaker effectively contrasts the idea between activeness and passiveness in the sense that the speaker views sewing as something passive and longs to do something active in order to help out in the war. Let's look at the poem for proof of this contrast. In the first stanza, the dull act of sewing is set in contrast with the horror that happens in her dreams. In the second stanza, the massacre in the war is contrasted by her, again "sitting and sewing" and yearning to help. Finally, in the third stanza, her "useless seam" is contrasted with the soldiers dying in the mud. The stark contrast of the comforts and ease of sewing to the pain and suffering of soldiers in active duty is a central theme in this poem.

20. C: Poetic lines that can be seen in this poem are rhyming couplets. Rhyming couplets are two pairs of lines that end with rhyming words. We see this all the way through, except for the last line in each stanza, which ends with the word *sew*. Here are some examples of the end rhymes of the rhyming couplets: *seems* and *dreams*, *things* and *flings*, *rain* and *slain*.

21. B: Readers should carefully focus their attention on the beginning of the passage to answer this series of questions. Even though the sentences may be worded a bit differently, all but one statement is true. It presents a false idea that descriptive details are not necessary until the climax of the story. Even if one does not read the passage, he or she probably knows that all good writing begins with descriptive details to develop the main theme the writer intends for the narrative.

22. C: This choice allows room for the fact that not all people who attempt to write a play will find it easy. If the writer follows the basic principles of narrative writing described in the passage, however, writing a play does not have to be an excruciating experience. None of the other options can be supported by points from the passage.

23. A: Choice A is true based on the sentence that reads, "Next, use dialogue to reveal the attitudes and personalities of each of the characters who have a key part in the unfolding story." Choice B is false because drama does not necessarily need to be predictable. Choice C is incorrect based on the information that claims an image is like using a thousand words. Choice D contradicts the point that the protagonist should experience self-discovery.

24. B: To suggest that a ten-minute play is accessible does not imply any timeline, nor does the passage mention how long a playwright spends with revisions and rewrites. So, Choice A is incorrect. Choice B is correct because of the opening statement that reads, "Learning how to write a ten-minute play may seem like a monumental task at

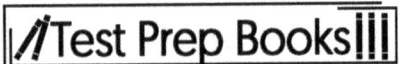

Answer Explanations

first; but, if you follow a simple creative writing strategy, similar to writing a narrative story, you will be able to write a successful drama." None of the remaining choices are supported by points in the passage.

25. A: Note that the only element not mentioned in the passage is the style feature that is part of a narrative writer's tool kit. It is not to say that ten-minute plays do not have style. The correct answer denotes only that the element of style was not illustrated in this particular passage.

26. C: The author contrasts two different viewpoints, then builds a case showing preference for one over the other. Choice A is incorrect because the introduction does not contain an impartial definition, but rather another's opinion. Choice B is incorrect. There is no puzzling phenomenon given, as the author doesn't mention any peculiar cause or effect that is in question regarding poetry. Choice D does contain another's viewpoint at the beginning of the passage; however, to say that the author has no stake in this argument is incorrect; the author uses personal experiences to build their case.

27. B: Choice B accurately describes the author's argument in the text—that poetry is not irrelevant. While the author does praise—and even value—Buddy Wakefield as a poet, he or she never heralds Wakefield as a genius. Eliminate Choice A, as it is an exaggeration. Not only is Choice C an exaggerated statement, but the author never mentions spoken word poetry in the text. Choice D is wrong because this statement contradicts the writer's argument.

28. D: *Exiguously* means not occurring often, or occurring rarely, so Choice D would LEAST change the meaning of the sentence. Choice A, *indolently*, means unhurriedly, or slow, and does not fit the context of the sentence. Choice B, *inaudibly*, means quietly or silently. Choice C, *interminably*, means endlessly, or all the time, and is the opposite of the word *exiguously*.

29. D: The author of the passage tries to insist that performance poetry is a subset of modern poetry, and therefore prove that modern poetry is not "dying," but thriving on social media for the masses. Choice A is incorrect, as the author is not refusing any kind of validation. Choice B is incorrect; the author's insistence is that poetry will *not* lose popularity. Choice C mimics the topic but compares two different genres, while the author makes no comparison in this passage.

30. B: The author's purpose is to disprove Gioia's article claiming that poetry is a dying art form that only survives in academic settings. In order to prove his argument, the author educates the reader about new developments in poetry, Choice A, and describes the brilliance of a specific modern poet, Choice C, but these are used to serve as examples of a growing poetry trend that counters Gioia's argument. Choice D is incorrect because it contradicts the author's argument.

31. C: Because the details in Choice A and Choice B are examples of how an emotionally intelligent leader operates, they are not the best choice for the definition of the term *emotional intelligence*. They are qualities observed in an EI leader. Choice C is true as noted in the second sentence of the passage: Emotional Intelligence (EI) includes developing the ability to know one's own emotions, to regulate impulses and emotions, and to use interpersonal communication skills with ease while dealing with other people. It makes sense that someone with well-developed emotional intelligence will have a good handle on understanding their emotions, be able to regulate impulses and emotions, and use interpersonal communication skills. Choice D is not a definition of EI.

32. C: Choice A can be eliminated because it does not reflect an accurate fact. Choices B and D do not support claims about how to be a successful leader.

33. D: The qualities of an unsuccessful leader possessing a transactional leadership style are listed in the passage. Choices A and B are incorrect because these options reflect the qualities of a successful leader. Choice C is definitely

Answer Explanations

not a characteristic of a successful leader; it is not presented in the passage and readers should do their best to ignore such options.

34. D: Even though some choices may be true of successful leaders, the best answer must be supported by sub-points in the passage. Therefore, Choices A and C are incorrect. Choice B is incorrect because uncompromising transactional leadership styles squelch success.

35. A: To support Choice A, the idea that a leader can develop emotional intelligence if desired, the passage says, "There are ways to develop emotional intelligence for the person who wants to improve their leadership style."

36. C: Choice C correctly uses *from* to describe the fact that dogs are related to wolves. The word *through* is incorrectly used here, so Choice A is incorrect. Choice B makes no sense. Choice D unnecessarily changes the verb tense in addition to incorrectly using *through*.

37. B: Choice B is correct because the Oxford comma is applied, clearly separating the specific terms. Choice A lacks this clarity. Choice C is correct but too wordy since commas can be easily applied. Choice D doesn't flow with the sentence's structure.

38. D: Choice D correctly uses the question mark, fixing the sentence's main issue. Thus, Choice A is incorrect because questions do not end with periods. Choice B, although correctly written, changes the meaning of the original sentence. Choice C is incorrect because it completely changes the direction of the sentence, disrupts the flow of the paragraph, and lacks the crucial question mark.

39. A: Choice A is correct since there are no errors in the sentence. Choices B and C both have extraneous commas, disrupting the flow of the sentence. Choice D unnecessarily rearranges the sentence.

40. D: Choice D is correct because the commas serve to distinguish that *artificial selection* is just another term for *selective breeding* before the sentence continues. The structure is preserved, and the sentence can flow with more clarity. Choice A is incorrect because the sentence needs commas to avoid being a run-on. Choice B is close but still lacks the required comma after *selection*, so this is incorrect. Choice C is incorrect because the comma to set off the aside should be placed after *breeding* instead of *called*.

41. B: Choice B is correct because the sentence is talking about a continuing process. Therefore, the best modification is to add the word *to* in front of *increase*. Choice A is incorrect because this modifier is missing. Choice C is incorrect because with the additional comma, the present tense of *increase* is inappropriate. Choice D makes more sense, but the tense is still not the best to use.

42. A: The sentence has no errors, so Choice A is correct. Choice B is incorrect because it adds an unnecessary comma. Choice C is incorrect because *advantage* should not be plural in this sentence without the removal of the singular *an*. Choice D is very tempting. While this would make the sentence more concise, this would ultimately alter the context of the sentence, which would be incorrect.

43. C: Choice C correctly uses *on to*, describing the way genes are passed generationally. The use of *into* is inappropriate for this context, which makes Choice A incorrect. Choice B is close, but *onto* refers to something being placed on a surface. Choice D doesn't make logical sense.

44. D: Choice D is correct, since only proper names should be capitalized. Because the name of a dog breed is not a proper name, Choice A is incorrect. In terms of punctuation, only one comma after *example* is needed, so Choices B and C are incorrect.

45. C: Choice C is correct because it fixes the core issue with this sentence: the singular *has* should not describe the plural *scientists*. Thus, Choice A is incorrect. Choices B and D add unnecessary commas.

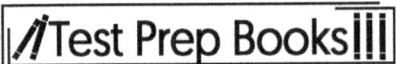

46. A: Choice A is correct, as the sentence does not require modification. Choices B and C implement extra punctuation unnecessarily, disrupting the flow of the sentence. Choice D incorrectly adds a comma in an awkward location.

47. B: Choice B is the strongest revision, as adding *to explore* is very effective in both shortening the sentence and maintaining, even enhancing, the point of the writer. To explore is to seek understanding in order to gain knowledge and insight, which coincides with the focus of the overall sentence. Choice A is not technically incorrect, but it is overcomplicated. Choice C is a decent revision, but the sentence could still be more condensed and sharpened. Choice D fails to make the sentence more concise and inserts unnecessary commas.

48. B: Choice B not only fixes the homophone issue from *its*, which is possessive, to *it's*, which is a contraction of *it is*, but also streamlines the sentence by adding a comma and eliminating *and*. Choice A is incorrect because of these errors. Choices C and D only fix the homophone issue.

49. A: Choice A is correct, as the sentence is fine the way it is. Choices B and C add unnecessary commas, while Choice D uses the possessive *its* instead of the contraction *it's*.

50. C: Choice C is correct because the phrase *even likely* is flanked by commas, creating a kind of aside, which allows the reader to see this separate thought while acknowledging it as part of the overall sentence and subject at hand. Choice A is incorrect because it seems to ramble after *even* due to a missing comma after *likely*. Choice B is better but inserting a comma after *that* warps the flow of the writing. Choice D is incorrect because there must be a comma after *plausible*.

Math Part I: No Calculator

1. D: This problem can be solved using basic arithmetic. Xavier starts with 20 apples, then gives his sister half, so 20 divided by 2.

$$\frac{20}{2} = 10$$

He then gives his neighbor 6, so 6 is subtracted from 10.

$$10 - 6 = 4$$

Lastly, he uses $\frac{3}{4}$ of his apples to make an apple pie, so to find remaining apples, the first step is to subtract $\frac{3}{4}$ from one and then multiply the difference by 4.

$$\left(1 - \frac{3}{4}\right) \times 4 = ?$$

$$\left(\frac{4}{4} - \frac{3}{4}\right) \times 4 = ?$$

$$\left(\frac{1}{4}\right) \times 4 = 1$$

2. C: The product of two irrational numbers can be rational or irrational. Sometimes, the irrational parts of the two numbers cancel each other out, leaving a rational number. For example, $\sqrt{2} \times \sqrt{2} = 2$ because the roots cancel each other out. Technically, the product of two irrational numbers can be complex because complex numbers can have either the real or imaginary part (in this case, the imaginary part) equal zero and still be considered a complex

Answer Explanations

number. However, Choice *D* is incorrect because the product of two irrational numbers is not an imaginary number so saying the product is complex *and* imaginary is incorrect.

3. B: The car is traveling at a speed of five meters per second. On the interval from one to three seconds, the position changes by ten meters. By making this change in position over time into a rate, the speed becomes ten meters in two seconds or five meters in one second.

4. C: The number negative four is classified as a real number because it exists and is not imaginary. It is rational because it does not have a decimal that never ends. It is an integer because it does not have a fractional component. The next classification would be whole numbers, for which negative four does not qualify because it is negative. Choice *D* is wrong because -4 is not considered an irrational number because it does not have a never-ending decimal component.

5. 380: To find the total driving time, the total distance of 350 miles can be divided by the constant speed of 60 miles per hour. This yields a time of 5.8333 hours, which is then rounded. Once the driving time is computed, the break times need to be found. If Gary takes a break for 10 minutes every 100 miles, he will take 3 breaks on his trip. This will yield a total of 30 minutes of break time. Since the answer is needed in minutes, 5.8333 can be converted to minutes by multiplying by 60, giving a driving time of 350 minutes. Adding the break time of 30 minutes to the driving time of 350 minutes gives a total travel time of 380 minutes.

6. D: A given number divides evenly by each of its factors to produce an integer (no decimals). The number 5, 7, 8, 9, 10, 11 (and their opposites) do not divide evenly into 12. Therefore, these numbers are not factors.

7. B: The formula can be manipulated by dividing both the length, *l*, and the width, *w*, on both sides. The length and width will cancel on the right, leaving height by itself.

8. D: Setting up a proportion is the easiest way to represent this situation. The proportion becomes $\frac{20}{x} = \frac{40}{100}$, where cross-multiplication can be used to solve for x. The answer can also be found by observing the two fractions as equivalent, knowing that twenty is half of forty, and fifty is half of one hundred.

9. C: Division with scientific notation can be solved by grouping the first terms together and grouping the tens together. The first terms can be divided, and the tens terms can be simplified using the rules for exponents. The initial expression becomes 0.4×10^4. This is not in scientific notation because the first number is not between 1 and 10. Shifting the decimal and subtracting one from the exponent yields 4.0×10^3.

10. 18: If Ray will be 25 in three years, then he is currently 22. The problem states that Lisa is 13 years younger than Ray, so she must be 9. Sam's age is twice that, which means that the correct answer is 18.

11. A: To find the fraction of the bill that the first three people pay, the fractions need to be added, which means finding the common denominator. The common denominator will be 60:

$$\frac{1}{5} + \frac{1}{4} + \frac{1}{3} = \frac{12}{60} + \frac{15}{60} + \frac{20}{60} = \frac{47}{60}$$

The remainder of the bill is:

$$1 - \frac{47}{60} = \frac{60}{60} - \frac{47}{60} = \frac{13}{60}$$

12. D: To convert a decimal to a fraction, remember that any number to the left of the decimal point will be a whole number. Then, sense 0.3 goes to the tenths place, it can be placed over 10.

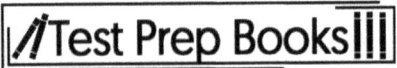

Math Part II: Calculator

1. B: Since $850 is the price *after* a 20% discount, $850 represents 80% of the original price. To determine the original price, set up a proportion with the ratio of the sale price (850) to original price (unknown) equal to the ratio of sale percentage (where x represents the unknown original price):

$$\frac{850}{x} = \frac{80}{100}$$

To solve a proportion, cross multiply and set the products equal to each other:

$$(850)(100) = (80)(x)$$

Multiplying each side results in the equation:

$$85{,}000 = 80x$$

To solve for x, divide both sides by 80:

$$\frac{85{,}000}{80} = \frac{80x}{80}$$

$$x = 1{,}062.5$$

Remember that x represents the original price. Subtracting the sale price from the original price ($1,062.50 − $850) indicates that Frank saved $212.50.

2. 17: To get 85% of a number, multiply it by 0.85.

$$\frac{17}{20} \times \frac{20}{1} = 17$$

3. D: First, list the givens.

$$\text{Store coffee} = \$1.23/\text{lb}$$

$$\text{Local roaster coffee} = \$1.98/1.5 \text{ lb}$$

Calculate the cost for 5 pounds of store brand.

$$\frac{\$1.23}{1 \text{ lb}} \times 5 \text{ lb} = \$6.15$$

Calculate the cost for 5 pounds of the local roaster.

$$\frac{\$1.98}{1.5 \text{ lb}} \times 5 \text{ lb} = \$6.60$$

Subtract to find the difference in price for 5 pounds.

$$\begin{array}{r} \$6.60 \\ -\$6.15 \\ \hline \$0.45 \end{array}$$

Answer Explanations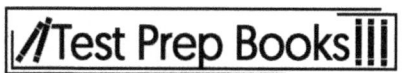

4. C: The first step in solving this problem is expressing the result in fraction form. Separate this problem first by solving the division operation of the last two fractions. When dividing one fraction by another, invert or flip the second fraction and then multiply the numerator and denominator.

$$\frac{7}{10} \times \frac{2}{1} = \frac{14}{10}$$

Next, multiply the first fraction with this value:

$$\frac{3}{5} \times \frac{14}{10} = \frac{42}{50}$$

In this instance, you can find the decimal form by converting the fraction into $\frac{x}{100}$, where x is the number from which the final decimal is found. Multiply both the numerator and denominator by 2 to get the fraction as an expression of $\frac{x}{100}$.

$$\frac{42}{50} \times \frac{2}{2} = \frac{84}{100}$$

In decimal form, this would be expressed as 0.84.

5. A: To find the average of a set of values, add the values together and then divide by the total number of values. In this case, include the unknown value of what Dwayne needs to score on his next test, in order to solve it.

$$\frac{78 + 92 + 83 + 97 + x}{5} = 90$$

Add the unknown value to the new average total, which is 5. Then multiply each side by 5 to simplify the equation, resulting in:

$$78 + 92 + 83 + 97 + x = 450$$

$$350 + x = 450$$

$$x = 100$$

Dwayne would need to get a perfect score of 100 in order to get an average of at least 90.

Test this answer by substituting back into the original formula:

$$\frac{78 + 92 + 83 + 97 + 100}{5} = 90$$

6. D: This system of equations involves one quadratic function and one linear function, as seen from the degree of each equation. One way to solve this is through substitution. Solving for y in the second equation yields $y = x + 2$. Plugging this equation in for the y of the quadratic equation yields:

$$x^2 - 2x + x + 2 = 8$$

Simplifying the equation, it becomes:

$$x^2 - x + 2 = 8$$

Setting this equal to zero and factoring, it becomes:

Answer Explanations

$$x^2 - x - 6 = 0 = (x-3)(x+2)$$

Solving these two factors for x gives the zeros $x = 3, -2$. To find the y-value for the point, each number can be plugged in to either original equation. Solving each one for y yields the points $(3, 5)$ and $(-2, 0)$.

7. 66: If the sixth graders bought 45% of the cookies, the number they bought is found by multiplying 0.45 by 500. They bought 225 cookies. The number of cookies left is:

$$500 - 225 = 275$$

During the second lunch, the seventh graders bought 40% of the cookies, which is found by multiplying 0.40 by the remaining 275 cookies. The seventh graders bought 110 cookies. This leaves 165 cookies to sell to the eighth graders. If they bought 60% of the remaining cookies, then they bought 99 cookies. Subtracting 99 from 165 cookies leaves Kelly with 66 cookies remaining after the three lunches.

8. 20: Because these are 2 parallel lines cut by a transversal, the angle with a measure of 45 degrees is equal to the measure of angle 6. Angle 6 and the angle labeled $5x + 35$ are supplementary to one another. The sum of these angles should be 180, so the following equation can be generated:

$$5x + 35 + 45 = 180$$

Solving for x, the sum of 35 and 45 is 80, which is then subtracted from 180 to yield 100. Dividing 100 by 5 gives the value of x, which is 20.

9. D: The expression is simplified by collecting like terms. Terms with the same variable and exponent are like terms, and their coefficients can be added.

10. A: Finding the product means distributing one polynomial onto the other. Each term in the first must be multiplied by each term in the second. Then, like terms can be collected. Multiplying the factors yields the expression:

$$20x^3 + 4x^2 + 24x - 40x^2 - 8x - 48$$

Collecting like terms means adding the x^2 terms and adding the x terms. The final answer after simplifying the expression is:

$$20x^3 - 36x^2 + 16x - 48$$

11. A: Using the given information of 1 nurse to 25 patients and 325 patients, set up an equation to solve for number of nurses (N):

$$\frac{N}{325} = \frac{1}{25}$$

Multiply both sides by 325 to get N by itself on one side.

$$\frac{N}{1} = \frac{325}{25} = 13 \text{ nurses}$$

12. C: The equation can be solved by factoring the numerator into $(x+6)(x-5)$.

Since that same factor exists on top and bottom, that factor $(x-5)$ cancels.

Answer Explanations

This leaves the equation $x + 6 = 11$.

Solving the equation gives the answer $x = 5$. When this value is plugged into the equation, it yields a zero in the denominator of the fraction. Since this is undefined, there is no solution.

13. D: This problem can be solved by using unit conversion. The initial units are miles per minute. The final units need to be feet per second. Converting miles to feet uses the equivalence statement 1 mile = 5,280 feet. Converting minutes to seconds uses the equivalence statement 1 minute = 60 seconds. Setting up the ratios to convert the units is shown in the following equation:

$$\frac{72 \text{ miles}}{90 \text{ minutes}} \times \frac{1 \text{ minute}}{60 \text{ seconds}} \times \frac{5280 \text{ feet}}{1 \text{ mile}} = 70.4 \text{ feet per second.}$$

The initial units cancel out, and the new units are left.

14. 10: 8 squared is 64, and 6 squared is 36. These should be added together to get:

$$64 + 36 = 100$$

Then, the last step is to find the square root of 100 which is 10.

15. D: This problem can be solved by setting up a proportion involving the given information and the unknown value. The proportion is:

$$\frac{21 \text{ pages}}{4 \text{ nights}} = \frac{140 \text{ pages}}{x \text{ nights}}$$

Solving the proportion by cross-multiplying, the equation becomes $21x = 4 \times 140$, where $x = 26.67$.

Since it is not an exact number of nights, the answer is rounded up to 27 nights. Twenty-six nights would not give Sarah enough time.

16. B: The slope from this equation is 50, and it is interpreted as the cost per gigabyte used. Since the g-value represents number of gigabytes and the equation is set equal to the cost in dollars, the slope relates these two values. For every gigabyte used on the phone, the bill goes up 50 dollars.

17. 50.7: The values for the missing sides must first be found before the perimeter can be calculated. The missing side that is the hypotenuse of the right triangle can be calculated using the Pythagorean Theorem as follows:

$$11^2 + 4^2 = x^2$$

$$121 + 16 = x^2$$

$$137 = x^2$$

$$x = 11.7$$

The other missing side is equal to the value of the length of the larger rectangle less than the value of the side of the square $12 - 4 = 8$. Then, all the sides can be added together to find the perimeter:

$$12 + 6 + 8 + 5 + 4 + 4 + 11.7 = 50.7$$

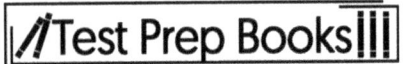

Answer Explanations

18. 15: Follow the *order of operations* in order to solve this problem. Solve the parentheses first, and then follow the remainder as usual.

$$(6 \times 4) - 9$$

This equals $24 - 9$, or 15.

19. C: Graphing the function $y = \cos(x)$ shows that the curve starts at $(0, 1)$, has an amplitude of 2, and a period of 2π. This same curve can be constructed using the sine graph, by shifting the graph to the left $\frac{\pi}{2}$ units. This equation is in the form:

$$y = \sin\left(x + \frac{\pi}{2}\right)$$

20. B: Start by squaring both sides to get $1 + x = 16$. Then subtract 1 from both sides to get $x = 15$.

21. C: A die has an equal chance for each outcome. Since it has six sides, each outcome has a probability of $\frac{1}{6}$. The chance of a 1 or a 2 is therefore $\frac{1}{6} + \frac{1}{6} = \frac{1}{3}$.

22. 87.5: For an even number of total values, the *median* is calculated by finding the *mean,* or average, of the two middle values once all values have been arranged in ascending order from least to greatest. In this case, $(92 + 83) \div 2$ would equal the median 87.5.

23. 6: The formula for the perimeter of a rectangle is $P = 2L + 2W$, where P is the perimeter, L is the length, and W is the width. The first step is to substitute all of the data into the formula:

$$36 = 2(12) + 2W$$

Simplify by multiplying 2×12:

$$36 = 24 + 2W$$

Simplifying this further by subtracting 24 on each side gives:

$$36 - 24 = 24 - 24 + 2W$$

$$12 = 2W$$

Divide by 2:

$$6 = W$$

The width is 6 cm. Remember to test this answer by substituting this value into the original formula:

$$36 = 2(12) + 2(6)$$

24. A: The slope is given by:

$$m = \frac{y_2 - y_1}{x_2 - x_1} = \frac{0 - 4}{0 - (-3)} = -\frac{4}{3}$$

Answer Explanations

25. C: The formula for continually compounded interest is:

$$A = Pe^{rt}$$

Plugging in the given values to find the total amount in the account yields the equation:

$$A = 2000e^{0.05 \times 8} = 2983.65$$

Choice A is incorrect because it uses annually compounded interest instead of continuous,

$$A = 2000 \times 1.05^8 = 2954.91$$

Choice B is incorrect because it fails to apply the formula for continuously compounded interest. Choice D is incorrect because it simply adds 40% (or eight times 5%) to the original investment rather than compounding annually.

26. D: The sample space is made up of $8 + 7 + 6 + 5 = 26$ balls. The probability of pulling each individual ball is $1/26$. Since there are 7 yellow balls, the probability of pulling a yellow ball is $7/26$.

27. B: For the first card drawn, the probability of a king being pulled is $\frac{4}{52}$. Since this card isn't replaced, if a king is drawn first, the probability of a king being drawn second is $\frac{3}{51}$. The probability of a king being drawn in both the first and second draw is the product of the two probabilities:

$$\frac{4}{52} \times \frac{3}{51} = \frac{12}{2,652}$$

This fraction, when divided by $\frac{12}{12}$, equals $\frac{1}{221}$.

28. A: Divide the total amount by the number of days: $\frac{150}{4} = 37.5$. She needs to save an average of $37.50 per day.

29. 4: The number of days can be found by taking the total amount Bernard needs to make and dividing it by the amount he earns per day:

$$\frac{300}{80} = \frac{30}{8} = \frac{15}{4} = 3.75$$

But Bernard is only working full days, so he will need to work 4 days, since 3 days is not enough time.

30. A: Convert the mixed fractions to improper fractions: $\frac{11}{3} - \frac{9}{5}$. Subtract using 15 as a common denominator and rewrite to get rid of the improper fraction:

$$\frac{11}{3} - \frac{9}{5} = \frac{55}{15} - \frac{27}{15} = \frac{28}{15} = 1\frac{13}{15}$$

Science

1. B, E, G, H: The scientific method requires questioning by making an educated guess or hypothesis. It involves observation of the physical world. It also involves the testing of predictions, with experiments performed to determine the accuracy of a prediction. Lastly, the scientific method involves the drawing of conclusions, where simple rules are formulated to create a hypothesis, predict the effects of the experiment, and generalize the experimental findings.

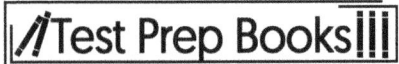

Answer Explanations

The scientific method can be carried out in many ways and generally involves observation, questioning, prediction, testing predictions, and drawing conclusions.

2. D: Choice *D* represents a question that can't be investigated through scientific inquiry since it is an aesthetic question. Whether unsweetened iced tea is more delicious than sweetened iced tea is a subjective question. Choice *A* is testable, and science has shown that drinking tea can lower levels of cortisone, the hormone responsible for stress. Choice *B* is a testable question since an experiment can be performed to confirm if teas contain sugar; teas generally do not contain sugar. Choice *C* is testable since a person's blood glucose levels can be monitored with a blood glucose monitor after consumption of the sugary beverage.

3. C: An inference is a conclusion that is based on knowledge of scientific principles, past observations, and experiences with the phenomenon. Choice *A* is incorrect since inferences are conclusions based on observation, while hypotheses are predictions about a particular event that has not occurred. Choice *B* is incorrect; the student's observations include recording the temperature and pressure data. Choice *D* is incorrect since inferences can lead to a hypothesis or educated guess.

4. B: In a double-blind study, the physician and participant are not provided any information on the nature of the vaccine. If the physician were to know which vaccine is a placebo, there is a possibility that they may accidentally reveal the information to the participants, which could influence their behavior and results. Choice *A* is incorrect; a random study or assignment involves the placement of participants from a sample into different groups based on random selection. Choice *C* is incorrect and generally refers to factors in research that lead to bias, such as selection or sampling bias. Choice *D* is incorrect; observer bias occurs when a researcher's opinions influence what they record in a study, which can affect the outcome of the study.

5. B, C, E: Choice *B* is an example of cherry-picking data or selective presentation of data. Choice *C* is an example of objective observer bias, where a person's opinion or prejudice influences how they record data. Choice *E* is an example of undercover bias since the researchers did not reach out to individuals who did not have email addresses, which could include an older population that does not use email. Choice *A*, called convenience sampling, is a method for avoiding sampling bias. Choice *D*, called random or stratified sampling, allows a researcher to get a representative sample in a study. Choice *F* is an example of a large sample size, which is selected to avoid sampling bias.

6. A: A reliable experiment requires repeated experiments with the same initial conditions. If a coffee roaster wanted to ensure that they get a consistent mass or roast profile for each roasting session, it would be ideal if they focused on roasting one bean with the same initial mass. For example, if the roaster picked an Ethiopian coffee bean with an initial mass of 113.0 milligrams, they should repeat the experiment more than once to ensure they obtain a consistent mass of 96.0 milligrams after roasting for 15 minutes at a specific temperature. If the mass is consistently the same after each roast, this ensures that the experiment is reliable because the mass does not change drastically. Such an experiment is important, especially if the roaster is trying to reproduce results to obtain a specific coffee profile and flavor. For example, if another roaster was trying to replicate the same coffee profile and mass, they would need to know the coffee origin type, time, and temperature. If the same method is applied again, the second roaster should get the same mass and results.

7. A: Precision refers to a measure of consistency and reproducibility in an experiment. Since the density has similar values and is reproducible, it is precise. However, since the values are not relatively close to the true value of 1.35 g/cm^3, the measurements are inaccurate. Inaccuracy can be due to several factors, such as systematic errors in measurement. Density can be calculated by finding the mass of the liquid using an analytical balance and by reading the total volume of liquid in a graduated cylinder. Dividing the mass by the volume gives the density. If the volume read on a graduated cylinder was read a few milliliters above the actual value, it would consistently result in a density that is slightly smaller.

Answer Explanations

8. Increases bias, reduces bias, increases bias, increases bias. When Company A provides several instruments to a researcher to help them perform their experiments, the researchers' bias will increase. A company that provides instrumentation to the researchers provides an incentive for the researchers to favor that company and would be an example of funding of research by interest groups. The researcher will see the company in a more favorable manner.

In a blind experiment, the researchers are not told which samples originated from which company; this will reduce bias. If the researchers are given carbon fiber samples but are not told about the source of the material, the researchers will not have a bias when testing these samples because they simply do not know where the sample came from.

If the researchers tested samples of different sizes, it could increase bias in favor of the company that had more samples. The greater sample size for Company A creates more bias since the results of testing for Company A will have better representation of a sample set.

In the last row, the researchers selectively picked data (high mechanical strength) and reported it without disclosing the possibility that other samples could have had low mechanical strengths; the selective reporting of data can misrepresent the data from the actual experiment. A researcher who publishes data selectively, such as only data on high mechanical strength materials, is biased toward data that shows information that the researcher is interested in showing.

9. B: Publication bias occurs when an article is published based on the strength of results with positive significance. Nonsignificant data can remain unpublished, and consequently, understanding of the subject matter may be skewed and not well represented in the literature. Selective reporting bias occurs when positive data is highlighted in an article while downplaying or not emphasizing the negative results. For example, suppose a researcher conducted an experiment that discussed the mechanical strength of carbon fibers. The researcher concluded that three out of the five tests showed high mechanical strength, while the other two results were relatively low. If the researcher published only the high mechanical strength data, then that would be an example of selective reporting bias.

10. D: A hypothesis is a statement that helps make a prediction and provides a reason that helps explain an event or phenomenon. A hypothesis must be testable. Choice *D* is a testable question. Water hardness, which measures the amount of metals in water, can be determined by an acid-base titration. To determine if the spring water has fewer metals, the experiment must be carried out for each investigation to confirm the stated hypothesis. Choice *A* is incorrect since it only provides a suggestion or action of what school officials should do. Choice *B* is not testable since the taste of water is subjective and is an aesthetic question related to pleasantness. Choice *C* is an opinion that states what the city should do in order to reduce costs.

11. Ruler, Beaker, Thermometer, Graduated Cylinder: A ruler can be used to measure the length or thickness of an object in centimeters or millimeters. A large beaker can be used as an ice bath; adding ice into the beaker and then nesting the test tube into the bath will help cool the salt mixture. A thermometer can provide a quantitative measurement, in Celsius or Fahrenheit, to accurately determine the freezing point. A graduated cylinder is a precise piece of equipment that can measure the volume of a liquid.

12. 15: The percentage strain at which the maximum stress occurs for both fibers is 15 percent. The maximum stress for each fiber is different. For the carbon fiber material, the maximum stress occurs at about 120 megapascals at 15 percent strain. For the chemically treated fiber, the maximum stress occurs at about 40 megapascals with 15 percent strain.

13. A, D: Choice *A* is classified as a category 1 hazard that relates to skin corrosion and irritation; eye irritation and damage can occur if exposed. Sulfuric acid can cause severe eye damage and skin burns. Choice *D* is a category 2 hazard and relates to acute toxicity if inhaled. Sulfuric acid is corrosive to the respiratory tract and is fatal if inhaled.

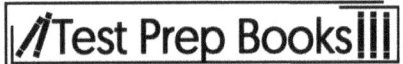

Answer Explanations

Choice B is incorrect; it refers to an oxidizing hazard. Choice C is incorrect; it refers to a hazard for gases under pressure in a container.

14. D: A chemical that has corrosive properties requires safety precautions that include eye, skin, and respiratory protection. Eye protection includes the use of safety goggles (chemical splash protection) and a face shield. Skin protection includes the use of aprons, boots, protective clothing, and suitable materials such as natural rubber. Respiratory protection includes the use of an air or chemical cartridge respirator. Proper storage of sulfuric acid or chemicals with similar hazards includes storing the container in a cool, dry area away from sun exposure. The container should not be near heat or ignition sources and must be kept separate from incompatible materials. Bulk storage should be avoided, and signs of leakage or crystallization should be inspected. When handling the acid, the generation of mists should be avoided, and cold water should not be added to a corrosive; instead, the corrosive should be added slowly into the water.

15. B: The independent variable is the type of coolant added since an independent variable is a parameter that the driver can pick or choose. The independent variable can be manipulated and is represented on the x-axis of a graph. The dependent variable is the temperature of the coolant, which will depend on the type of coolant used. The temperature is measured and will generally be labeled on the y-axis. Pure water would represent a control variable since water coolants generally contain both water and specific chemicals added to pure water.

16. C: The total amount of base transferred to the beaker is 50.0 milliliters. In Figure 1A, the total amount of base in the graduated cylinder is 200.0 milliliters. In Figure 1B, after the addition of the base into the beaker, the total amount of base reduces to 150.0 milliliters. The total amount of base is:

$$\Delta Volume = Volume_{initial} - Volume_{final} = 200.0\ mL - 150.0\ mL = 50.0\ mL$$

17. D: The atomic number of an element represents the number of protons. Hydrogen (H) has an atomic number of 1 and has the least number of protons of any other element in the periodic table. Radon (Rn), Choice A, has 86 protons. Boron (B), Choice B, has 5 protons. Nitrogen (N), Choice C, has 7 protons.

18. B: The mass of the ethanol sample in grams will have a measured value that has the decimal placed three places to the right, which will equal 39.45 grams. When converting from grams to kilograms, the unit type conversion is 1000 grams = 1 kilogram.

$$0.03945\ \text{kilograms} \times \frac{1000\ \text{grams}}{1\ \text{kilogram}} = 39.45\ \text{grams}$$

19. D: A protractor can be used to measure a bond angle in the provided example. The base of the protractor must be aligned with the center of the red atom (oxygen), with the right corner aligned with the bottom white atom (hydrogen). Molecules A and D are close to one another, so a protractor is needed to determine the approximate angle.

20. B: It is likely that the measured mass of caffeine in coffee tree III is incorrect since the mass is unusually high, but the amount of sugar is normal. If the mass of caffeine is generally between 5 and 10 milligrams, then a mass near 30.0 milligrams is questionable. Choice A is incorrect; if the mass is an indicator of a pricey coffee, then the statement is contradictory since coffee tree I has the greatest amount of sugar. Choice D is incorrect since the mass of sugar is greater than the mass of caffeine. The mass of caffeine is reported in milligrams and the mass of sugar in grams. For example, coffee tree II has a sugar mass of 90 milligrams, which is greater than the 6.7 milligrams of caffeine.

21. C: The manufacturer should add a label that will tell the consumer not to place the clothing near a heat source since it will make copper react with the polymer to create a toxic byproduct. It can also be inferred that the reaction will not occur if the material is not placed near hot surfaces. Adding a label indicating that copper was added to the

Answer Explanations

clothing does not warn the customer. If the consumer is aware that heat sources can be an issue, then they will hesitate to be near heat sources such as a kitchen stove or campfire. In the second part, future research and development should consider looking for an alternative odor-fighting material that will not react with the polymer. Adding less copper will not decrease its reactivity with the polymer near heat sources; it will only lessen the level of toxicity.

22. D: Using a temperature probe would provide more precision and reliability since it would allow the roaster to determine the appropriate temperature to stop the roast. While the passage provides a temperature range at which the experiment is stopped, using a temperature probe to stop the roast at a specific temperature as opposed to listening for a popping sound would provide more consistency. Using a temperature probe provides a quantitative measurement, while listening provides a qualitative measurement of when to stop. Choice *A* would be difficult to quantify since taste can be subjective; chemical analysis of sugar content could provide a more accurate measurement. Choice *B* is incorrect. Using a different coffee roast would not yield the same roast since choosing different beans can result in inconsistent results due to the differing composition density of beans. Choice *C* is incorrect since different roasters will not heat the beans in the same manner, which will make it difficult to quantify a stopping point in the experiment.

23. D, E: What constitutes ethical may be subjective depending on the person conducting the analysis. For example, the criteria for what constitutes ethical may only include ethical practices, such as those relating to ethical labor practices. For others, ethics may involve both ethical practices and eco-friendly materials that are recyclable. A smell can also be subjective depending on the person carrying out the analysis. It is difficult to quantify "what smells better," and therefore, this cannot be tested by scientific inquiry.

24. B: The hypothesis states the grass will grow taller since the weeds are eliminated. However, removal of the weeds with herbicide may not actually alter the grass height. The researcher would need to have a patch of grass to confirm their hypothesis; adding herbicide to pure grass would act as the control. Choice *A* would not be a good experimental design since the addition of the herbicide in the second part of the experiment is removed and replaced with water. Choice *C* is incorrect since herbicide is not added to the lawn containing weeds. Choice *D* is incorrect since the first part of the experiment only adds herbicide to weeds.

25. A, C: Choice *A* introduces bias since the company requires the use of its own paper. A closer analysis of the micron size of the paper indicates that it has the largest porosity. In general, a larger filter paper porosity will result in faster water filtering. The experiments should have all been done with the same type of filter paper. Choice *C* introduces bias by indicating it is a quick method for brewing. Based on the results of the study, the company selling funnel brand R can easily claim that its product is one of the fastest methods for brewing coffee. Choices *B* and *D* are both incorrect and unbiased since these statements are informational and provide methods or techniques for brewing coffee.

26. B, C: In part A of the experiment, the researcher was able to control the temperature of the container. The temperature is a control or independent variable that the researcher can change. Choice *A* is incorrect since the pressure is the dependent variable that will change based on the provided temperature. In part B of the experiment, the piston allows the researcher to change the volume inside the chamber. Volume is the independent variable that will change the pressure inside the container. Choice *D* is incorrect since the researcher did not indicate that the amount of gas can be controlled.

27. B-Intended consequence; C-Unintended consequence: An intended consequence of banning or limiting the use of CFCs is mitigating the harmful effects on wildlife such as fish. If CFCs are banned, then the ozone layer will have less depletion, which can result in less harmful ultraviolet radiation damaging marine and plant life. However, an unintended consequence of banning the use of CFCs is that countries will seek more available alternative refrigerants, which may pose a toxicity risk to people and possibly the environment to a lesser extent. HFCs were

Answer Explanations

introduced as an ozone-friendly alternative to CFCs. However, these substances are also greenhouse gases that are less damaging.

28. A: Research into refrigerant substitutes and new cooling technologies has been of interest since it would eliminate the use of HFCs and CFCs. Choice *B* is incorrect since using CFCs will still present an environmental risk and will result in ozone depletion, which will lead to environmental damage. Choice *C* is incorrect since the policies that provide resources will only provide a short-term solution. Choice *D* is incorrect since refrigerants in the atmosphere can have negative impacts on the ozone layer and climate change.

29. B, C, E, F: Fire hazards from wind turbines are not common but can be detrimental to wildlife once they occur. Proper positioning of the wind turbines in a wildlife region is generally considered. Wind turbines may have around 1400 liters of oil, which functions in lubrication and hydraulics. Over time, if the turbines are not maintained, damage such as cracking and breakage can lead to leaks. Meanwhile, noise pollution may affect the quality of life for local residents. Birds and bats are generally impacted by wind turbines since the drops in air pressure produced by the turbine-induced wind vortex can cause lung collapse. Finally, a wind turbine can create localized warming due to the mixing of warm air from above and can increase temperatures on the ground by up to 1°F.

30. C: Providing proper procedures for the containment of the fuel would provide an efficient short-term solution. A scientific solution that would benefit the environment would be the creation of rocket fuel that is less toxic to the environment. Avoiding the construction of rockets will not stop the risks associated with the use of hypergolic fuels since they are used in the construction of missiles and other rocket types. Moving the manufacturing site will not provide any benefit since contamination of the fuels can occur on the ground and possibly seep into underwater reservoirs.

31. B: The described research is an example of scientific research being influenced by political factors. The country or government's interest in the development of materials can influence scientific research since research scientists are funded through a government agency. If the agency providing the resources is not satisfied with the results or if the outcome of the research does not meet the objectives set by the agency, the researcher will not have the funding to continue their research.

32. Academic ethos, Political, Public health, Central dogma: Journal editors act as reviewers and may have personal biases when determining what constitutes a successful proposal. Political factors can influence the funding of research in academia. Governments interested in the development of surveillance technology can utilize taxpayer money to fund research projects conducted by governmental and academic institutions. Public health factors can result in governments providing money to companies, agencies, and academic institutions to develop novel vaccines. Due to central dogma or theories that have been well ingrained in academia, new and radical ideas are seen less favorably by other scientists. Researchers whose work supports less accepted ideas can be excluded by their peers and have their careers compromised.

33. C: The economy can influence companies to invest in research that will lead to company stability and increased profits in the future. Oil companies recognize that oil production may be limited in the future and must invest in new technology to ensure that the company continues to increase or stabilize its profits. During a strong economy, the oil company will have the funding to influence research; however, economic downturns can reduce funding. In addition, research is driven by market demand, and companies will fund research that will deliver products. Therefore, investment in research and development at universities will allow for technological innovation.

34. B: Chlorofluorocarbons (CFCs) were man-made compounds of chlorine, fluorine, and carbon used mainly in aerosol cans and refrigerants. Their use single-handedly caused significant depletion to the ozone layer, at a rate of about 20% globally and 70% over Antarctica. CFCs have mostly been banned from production, but it is unclear whether the ozone layer will ever reach pre-CFC usage levels. Teflon does not directly contribute to ozone layer depletion, and the other options listed are not real compounds.

Answer Explanations

35. C: An inference is a logical prediction of a why an event occurred based on previous experiences or education. The person in this example knows that plants need water to survive; therefore, the prediction that someone forgot to water the plant is a reasonable inference, hence Choice *C* is correct. A classification is the grouping of events or objects into categories, so Choice *A* is incorrect. An observation analyzes situations using human senses, so Choice *B* is incorrect. Choice *D* is incorrect because collecting is the act of gathering data for analysis.

Social Studies

1. A: Choice *A* is correct because *minister* is a title only held by persons appointed to the cabinet by the Prime Minister. Thus, ministers are officials of the executive branch. Choice *B* is incorrect because a justice is an official in the judicial branch. Choices *C* and *D* are incorrect because members of Parliament (MPs) and senators are both members of the legislative branch, serving in the legislative bodies themselves.

2. C: Choice *C* is correct because ministers may not introduce private bills; these bills are intended to confer benefits or legal exemptions on behalf of a person or group. Choices *A* and *B* are incorrect because government bills are typically introduced by ministers, and a supply bill is a type of government bill. Choice *D* is incorrect because a private member's bill *might* be a private bill, but it could also be a government bill proposed by an MP instead of a minister.

3. B: An appellate court is any court that hears appeals, typically when one side of a case believes legal procedure was not followed correctly. Thus, Choice *B* is correct. Choice *A* is incorrect because trials take place in a trial court. Choice *C* is incorrect because military cases are held in a military tribunal. Choice *D* is incorrect because a particular appellate court is the court of final authority—the Supreme Court of Canada. This answer is incorrect because it defines a *specific* court, rather than providing a *general* description of an appellate court.

4. B, F: Choices *B* and *F* are correct because the lack of participation in and lack of consent to the democratic process are both reasons why the *Indian Act* is deprecated. Choice *A* is incorrect because the *Indian Act* is not seen as having meaningfully encouraged democratic practices (for example, because the act's democratic elections were forced upon indigenous communities). Choice *C* is incorrect because the *Indian Act* has been amended numerous times since its enactment. Choice *D* is incorrect because separation of powers is generally regarded as a positive quality, not a negative one. Choice *E* is incorrect because an act ought to be enacted by the House of Commons—this answer describes appropriate parliamentary procedure.

5. C: Choice *C* is correct because an elder is typically a member of the community who is unelected, respected, and consulted for advice. Choices *A* and *B* are incorrect because chiefs and councillors are titles generally given to elected leaders and officials in indigenous communities that hold elections following the *Indian Act* or the *First Nations Elections Act*. Choice *D* is incorrect because *band* refers to a whole indigenous community, not an individual.

6. No, Yes, Yes, No: Local governments are run by a city council (analogous to the Privy Council), and led by a mayor (analogous to the Prime Minister or a provincial premier). They do not have an analogue to the House of Commons, since districts run by a local government do not appoint members who *then* select the city council; instead the electorate votes for the city council directly. The House of Lords is a structure of British government, not Canadian government.

7. D: The speaker in Source 2 uses an official language minority as an example in the passage. It's likely that they're concerned with accessibility for members of that minority in the district. Thus, Choice *C* is correct. Choice *D* is incorrect because, while police are under the authority of local governments, Source 2 does not provide evidence supporting this claim. Thus, *based on Source 2*, Choice *C* is a better answer. Choice *A* is incorrect because university education is under the authority of the provincial government, not the local government. Choice *B* is incorrect because the federal government negotiates with the First Nations regarding treaties and self-government, not the local government.

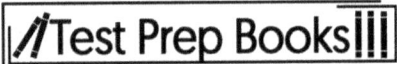

Answer Explanations

8. F: Source 2 raises *concerns* about minority representation, but does not claim that the rights of an official language minority are actually being violated. Thus, Choice *F* is correct. Choices *A*, *B*, *C*, and *D* are incorrect because the passages do not state that these rights are being violated. Choice *E* is incorrect because this is not a right of language minorities recognized in the *Charter*. Language minorities have the right to vote for members of their protected group, but are not guaranteed representation automatically.

9. A, B, D: *Canada Leads* is not selected because its headline is a neutral description of the economic impact of a new bill about voting districts. *Timeline* is selected because the headline suggests the site opposes the new law. *Day News* and *What Happened Today* are selected because each site's headline supports the new law through emphasizing minority representation is a good goal of legislation.

10. B: Choice *B* is correct because the headline of *Day News* specifies that minority seats will be guaranteed. This allows us to conclude that the law's changing of voting districts is designed to ensure minorities have additional seats in Parliament to represent their perspective. Choice *A* is incorrect because the headlines discuss minority groups, but do not discuss immigration. Choice *C* is incorrect because *Canada Leads* mentions the economic gains but attributes them to the voting law. Choice *D* is incorrect because the headlines indicate that the bill's goal is political representation, not the protection of rights.

11. C: Choice *C* is correct because oil is a natural resource. While provincial governments typically have authority over their own natural resources, it is the federal government's role to negotiate trade with foreign nations. In this case, the Minister of Energy and Natural Resources is the most likely answer because the Ministers of Foreign Affairs and of Finance have wider responsibilities, whereas such an agreement falls quite clearly into this minister's authority. Thus, Choices *A* and *B* are incorrect. Choice *D* is incorrect because oil companies are not reasonably considered small businesses.

12. C, F, G: The Ministers of Democratic Institutions, Indigenous Services, and Energy and Natural Resources are likely to engage with indigenous communities during the governmental processes of stewardship of Canada's natural resources, negotiating treaties reconciling unjust land claims, and facilitating transitions to self-government. Thus, Choices *C*, *F*, and *G* are correct, and Choices *A*, *B*, *D*, and *E* are incorrect.

13. A: A mixed economy is one that contains elements of both private and public enterprise in providing goods and services. Choice *A* is correct because Canada's universal healthcare demonstrates that this service is operated by the government, while the existence of private providers demonstrates that the economy remains mixed. Choice *B* is incorrect because law enforcement is not a feature of the economy. Choices *C* and *D* are incorrect because the existence of trade agreements or environmental regulations does not demonstrate that the economy contains both public and private elements.

14. Decrease, Increase, Increase: The price of clothing is likely to *decrease* because the households described are buying less of it, while the price of food is likely to *increase* because households are continuing to purchase it. This demonstrates how the decision-making of family groups on a large scale can impact the national economy. The passage does not support how this decision-making will impact the Canadian dollar's value; however, *increase* is the correct box to check because the passage does anticipate a "return to normal" after its value went down.

15. A: The law of supply and demand states that if supply is reduced while demand remains constant, the prices will increase. The first paragraph of the passage describes this situation in regard to clothing. Thus, Choice *A* is correct. Choices *B* and *C* are incorrect because the passage does not connect the availability of shipping or food to the price of food; further, if the supply of food goes up, then its price ought to go down. Choice *D* is incorrect because the passage does not describe how the value of currency changes, and therefore it cannot demonstrate the law of supply and demand.

Answer Explanations

16. Box 1: deflation, inflation. Box 2: depression, recession. Box 3: none. Box 4: income inequality, quality of life. Box 1 contains *deflation* and *inflation* because these terms describe the buying power of a currency going up or going down, respectively, when compared to the past or to other currencies. Box 2 contains *depression* and *recession* because these terms describe differing degrees of a worsening economy. Box 4 contains *income inequality* and *quality of life* because these metrics are used to study the frequency of poverty and its impact on citizens. Since all six words were used, Box 3 remains empty.

17. Yes, No, Yes, Yes: The first fact is evidence because inflation—reducing the currency's value—is a possible sign of economic recession. The second is not evidence because the passage does not mention interest rates. The third fact is evidence because a reduction in household budgets (and thereby spending) is potential evidence of recession, even if it is possible for the national economy to be growing while family spending recedes. The fourth fact is evidence because the passage does state that less clothing was purchased from overseas. This is evidence of reduced trade activity, which is a sign of economic recession.

18. C: Choice *C* is correct because the passage emphasizes that a global economy is never complete but rather is characterized by a constant flow of activity. Thus, Choice *B* is also incorrect. Choice *A* is incorrect because in a global economy international trade is a significant element of the economy. Choice *D* is incorrect because this statement does not describe *trade* itself. Instead, it describes why Canada is heavily involved in international trade.

19. Box 1: emigration, immigration. Box 2: multiculturalism, naturalization. Box 3: overseas shipping. Box 4: trade agreement. Box 1 contains *emigration* and *immigration* because these terms describe the movement of people out of their home nation, or into a foreign nation. Box 2 contains *multiculturalism* because the term describes a broad cultural change within a nation, and it contains *naturalization* because the process of becoming a citizen is a cultural change for that individual. Box 3 contains *overseas shipping* because this is the movement of goods from one nation to another. Box 4 contains *trade agreement* because this is the legislation required for such movement to be possible.

20. D: Choice *D* is correct because the cartoon satirizes the government by illustrating it restraining the opposition while telling the opposition's one free leg to "stop your kicking!" Choices *A* and *C* are incorrect because we can't infer preference from this cartoon—just that the opposition is being hindered or oppressed by the majority. Choice *B* is accurate, but is not the best answer because Choice *D* provides a more specific interpretation of this cartoon.

21. C: This political cartoon uses humor to satirize public figures, thereby expressing general sentiments of the illustrator or their audience. Thus, Choice *C* is correct. Choice *A* is incorrect because this would be true of *primary* sources, not secondary sources. Since the question specifies that the cartoon in question is being used as a secondary source, this answer cannot be correct. Choice *B* is incorrect because a cartoon generally does not make use of research and analysis. Choice *D* is incorrect because whether or not other people would agree with the cartoon's politics is irrelevant to its status as a secondary source.

22. Agree, Disagree, Disagree, Agree: The illustrator is likely to agree with the first and fourth statements because this cartoon criticizes the government. They are likely to disagree with the second statement because such a law contradicts the cartoon's satire. They are likely to disagree with the third statement because the illustration of kicking is humorous—we have no reason to believe it should be taken seriously.

23. C, D: Choices *C* and *D* are correct because the environment and one's first language are both significant sources of cultural identity that shape the Inuit's way of life. Choices *A* and *B* are incorrect because these political activities are the *result* of Inuit identity, not a *source* of it. Choice *E* is incorrect because Source 1 identifies the Inuktut languages as a majority, not a minority. Choice *F* is incorrect because a holiday that celebrates all First Nations is not a source of identity for a single indigenous community. Rather, it is a source of identity for indigenous citizens of Canada as a whole.

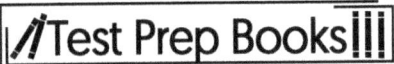

Answer Explanations

24. C: Choice C is correct because Source 2 notes that illegal land claims are commemorated during National Indigenous Peoples Day, and Source 1 describes the successful transition of authority from the federal government to the Inuit people. Choice A is incorrect because since the *Nunavut Land Claims Agreement* was signed, it's reasonable to infer that *some* form of restitution was possible—in this case, the return of the land. Choice B is incorrect because establishing Nunavut Territory supports the Inuit valuing their indigenous heritage over their Canadian heritage. Choice D is incorrect because the lands are central to indigenous cultures, but the trauma of land theft is not an element of the culture itself.

25. A: Choice A is correct because Source 2's description of the holiday emphasizes the positive, but also acknowledges the negative aspects of Canada's history with the First Nations, the Métis, and the Inuit. Choice B is incorrect because Source 1 describes reconciliation as an ongoing process, rather than as a largely complete event. Choice C is incorrect because Source 2 does not suggest that the holiday's purpose is to instill guilt into European Canadians. Choice D is incorrect because the holiday celebrates cultural heritage, without emphasizing land claims—or returns—in particular.

26. C: Choice C is correct because the successful establishment of Nunavut Territory had a cultural impact on the attitudes and beliefs of non-indigenous Canadians toward indigenous communities. Choice A is incorrect because this is not a cultural impact. Choice B is incorrect because indigenous groups are not of European heritage. Choice D is incorrect because the Inuktut languages are only officially recognized in Nunavut Territory, not throughout the whole nation.

27. Box 1: Arctic Archipelago, Melville Island. Box 2: Northwest Passage, Nunavut Territory. Box 3: 110° meridian. Box 4: taiga. Box 1 contains *Arctic Archipelago* and *Melville Island* because these are physical land masses of northern Canada. Box 2 contains *Northwest Passage* and *Nunavut Territory* because these are concepts humans use to shape and organize the physical territory (such as naming a certain extent of land "Nunavut"). Box 3 contains *110° meridian* because latitude and longitude lines are not geographical features—they're ways we measure the Earth. Box 4 contains *taiga* because this is a climate found in certain areas, and thus is part of the environment.

28. A: Choice A is correct because a settlement is a feature of human geography, not physical or cultural geography. Thus, Choices B and C are incorrect. Choice D is incorrect because political geography generally refers to the way politics shapes how we conceive of areas and landscapes, rather than describing a geographical feature built by humans (like a settlement).

29. 3: This demographic question is solved by dividing the number of Métis living in the listed settlements by the total Métis population. 4,238 divided by 127,000 gives us a result of 3.3 percent, which is rounded down to 3.

30. C: Choice C is correct because the Métis settlements listed in the table are self-governing, but the majority of Métis in Alberta live elsewhere. Thus, it is reasonable to conclude self-government is not major source of Métis cultural identity. Choice A is incorrect because the table does not provide information about *why* most Métis live in other communities. Choices B and C are incorrect because demography does not provide information about cultural choices made by the people studied in day-to-day life.

31. Disagree, Agree, Agree: The passage's description of indigenous culture disagrees with the first statement because visiting nature "to get some exercise" exemplifies seeing nature "as an object to use" rather than prioritizing a relationship with the environment. The second and third statements are in agreement because they reflect the mutually reliant perspective described in the passage.

32. B: Choice B is correct because the passage states that indigenous cultures are opposed to perspectives that see "natural resources as objects to use." Stewardship emphasizes relationship over utility. Choice A is incorrect because neither phrase emphasizes the idea of ownership. Choice C is incorrect because neither phrase implies the

Answer Explanations

validity of ancestral or modern claims to land or resources. Choice D is incorrect because stewardship does not prioritize revenue, and management does not prioritize preservation of territory.

33. A: Choice A is correct because it emphasizes the attitude of respect and mutual relationship with the land expressed by the First Nations, the Métis, and the Inuit. Choices B and C are incorrect because the concept of ownership expressed in these answers demonstrates a culture of using the land rather than maintaining a sustainable relationship with it. Choice D is incorrect because this answer also conceives of natural resources as an "object" to be stolen—the feeling of "loss" or "theft" expressed by indigenous peoples is typically regarding the land *itself*, not a loss of the land's natural resources.

34. D: Landlocked means being completely surrounded by land, so the correct answer is a province without a coastline. Saskatchewan borders the Northwest Territories, Alberta, Manitoba, and the United States. Thus, Choice D is the correct answer. British Columbia is bordered by the Pacific Ocean, so Choice A is incorrect. Manitoba borders Hudson Bay, so Choice B is incorrect. Nova Scotia borders the Atlantic Ocean, so Choice C is incorrect.

35. C: The northernmost region of Canada is mostly Arctic tundra due to its proximity to the Arctic Circle and frigid temperatures. Nunavut is the northernmost Canadian province, and it consists almost entirely of tundra. Thus, Choice C is the correct answer. The northern tip of Newfoundland and Labrador is covered in tundra, but the rest of the province is much more temperate. Therefore, Choice A is incorrect. The Northwest Territories have significant amounts of tundra; however, the Northwest Territories have a warmer climate than Nunavut, and some areas are covered in boreal forests. Therefore, Choice B is incorrect. Northern Quebec has tundra-like conditions, but the vast majority of Quebec isn't tundra. So Choice D is incorrect.

36. B: A nation is defined as a group of people who have common traits, such as heritage, history, language, culture, and religion. It has nothing to do with borders, sovereignty, power, people in office, or the rules by which a government operates (all of which are found in the other answer choices of state, government, and regime).

37. A: The presidential system establishes a separation of powers. In the presidential system, voters directly elect the chief executive, and the presidential system establishes a separation of powers between different branches of government. In contrast, in a parliamentary system, parliament elects the chief executive, and the increased collaboration and dependency creates a more responsive government. Choices B and C confuse how the executive is elected in each system. Choice D is incorrect because many parliamentary systems include a president, though the status of head of state is often purely ceremonial.

38. C: A participatory democracy in its truest form is a system in which everyone participates in the political system. Choice A describes an elite democracy. Choice B is a pluralist democracy—one where interest groups and advocacy for certain issues dominates the government. Choice D is the exact opposite of a democracy.

39. B: Eager to avoid another global conflict, European leaders tried to appease Hitler by letting him occupy Austria and Czechoslovakia. This policy failed because it only emboldened Hitler, and he invaded Poland in 1939. Rather than receiving leniency after World War I, Germany was forced to sign a humiliating peace treaty. Furthermore, the League of Nations failed to prevent conflict because it lacked any real power. This encouraged continued aggression from Italy, Germany, and Japan, which culminated in World War II.

40. A: Free trade agreements seek to increase international trade by limiting or eliminating tariffs and subsidies for domestic industries. Overall, international trade increased dramatically after the signing of the General Agreement on Tariffs and Trade (1947) and formation of the World Trade Organization (1995). Thus, Choice A is the correct answer. Although Keynes issued proposals to reduce German reparations and establish a Free Trade Union, they are separate proposals. Reparations aren't directly related to free trade agreements. As such, Choice B is incorrect. Choice C is incorrect because free trade agreements generally prohibit countries from subsidizing or protecting domestic industries. Free trade agreements don't facilitate imperialism, so Choice D is incorrect.

Dear CAEC Test Taker,

Thank you for purchasing this study guide for your CAEC exam. We hope that we exceeded your expectations.

Our goal in creating this study guide was to cover all of the topics that you will see on the test. We also strove to make our practice questions as similar as possible to what you will encounter on test day. With that being said, if you found something that you feel was not up to your standards, please send us an email and let us know.

We would also like to let you know about other books in our catalog that may interest you.

ACCUPLACER

This can be found on Amazon: amazon.com/dp/1637756356

ACT

amazon.com/dp/1637758596

SAT

amazon.com/dp/1637754051

We have study guides in a wide variety of fields. If the one you are looking for isn't listed above, then try searching for it on Amazon or send us an email.

Thanks Again and Happy Testing!
Product Development Team
support@testprepbooks.com

Online Resources & Audiobook

Included with your purchase are multiple online resources. This includes the practice tests in an interactive format and this book in audiobook format. There is also a convenient study timer to help you manage your time.

Scan the QR code or go to this link to access this content:

https://testprepbooks.com/online387/caec/

The first time you access the page, you will need to register as a "new user" and verify your email address.

If you have any issues, please email support@testprepbooks.com.

Thank you for letting us be a part of your studying journey!

www.ingramcontent.com/pod-product-compliance
Lightning Source LLC
Chambersburg PA
CBHW080332170426
43194CB00014B/2539